ABOUT THE ARTIST

Born in 1936, Kazuo Umezu is Japan's most respected and influential horror manga artist. Umezu began his artistic career at the age of 18, creating stories for both *shôjo* (girls) and *shonen* (boys) manga magazines, and working in an amazingly diverse range of genres. In Japan he is most famous for the gag manga *Makoto-chan* (1971), but his most ambitious works are horror and science fiction, including *The Drifting Classroom* (1972-1974), *My Name is Shingo* (1982-1986), *The Left Hand of God, the Right Hand of the Devil* (1986-1989) and *Fourteen* (1990-1995). His works have been adapted into anime and live-action films.

THE DRIFTING CLASSROOM
Vol. 8

STORY AND ART BY KAZUO UMEZU

Translation/Yuji Oniki
Touch-up Art & Lettering/Kelle Han
Design/Izumi Evers
Editor/Jason Thompson

Editor in Chief, Books/Alvin Lu
Editor in Chief, Magazines/Marc Weidenbaum
VP of Publishing Licensing/Rika Inouye
VP of Sales/Gonzalo Ferreyra
Sr. VP of Marketing/Liza Coppola
Publisher/Hyoe Narita

Printed in the U.S.A.

Published by VIZ Media, LLC
P.O. Box 77010
San Francisco, CA 94107

10 9 8 7 6 5 4 3 2 1
First printing, October 2007

www.viz.com
store.viz.com

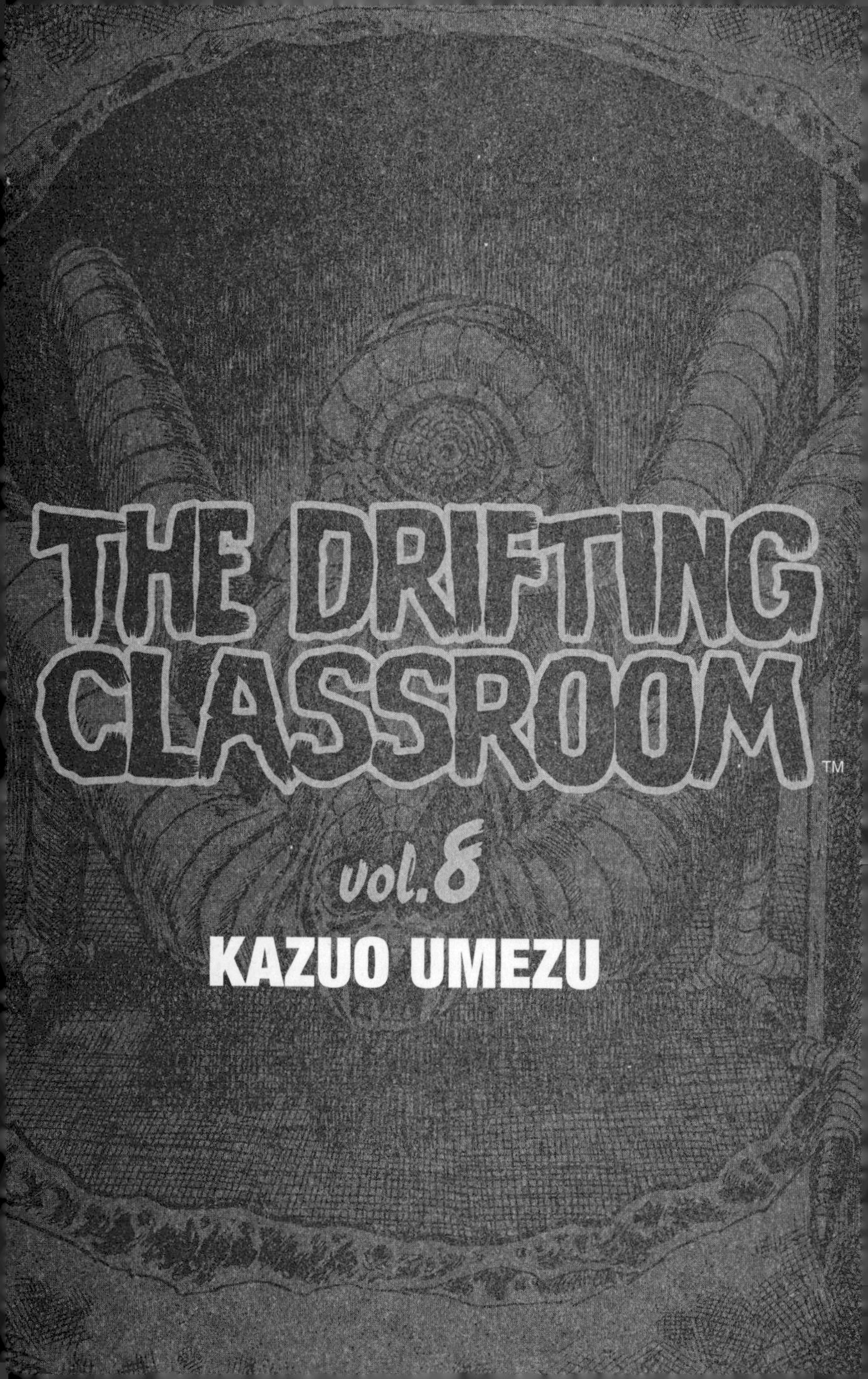

THE DRIFTING CLASSROOM™

vol. 8

KAZUO UMEZU

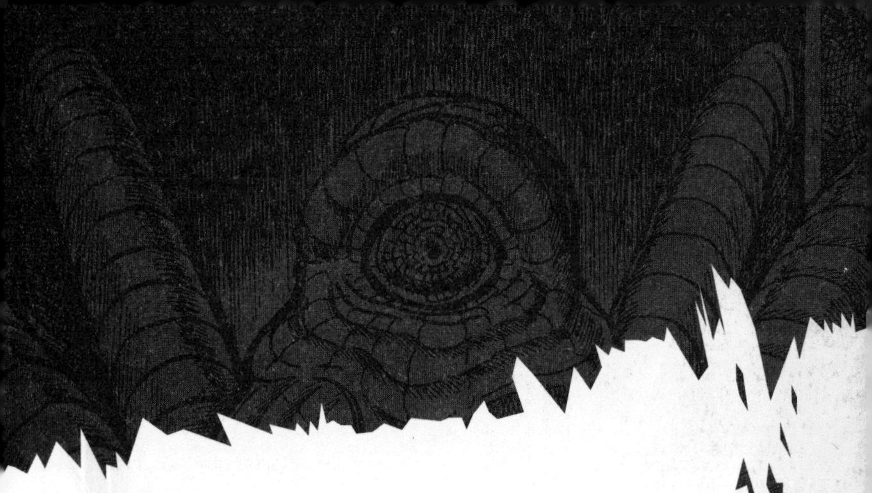

CONTENTS

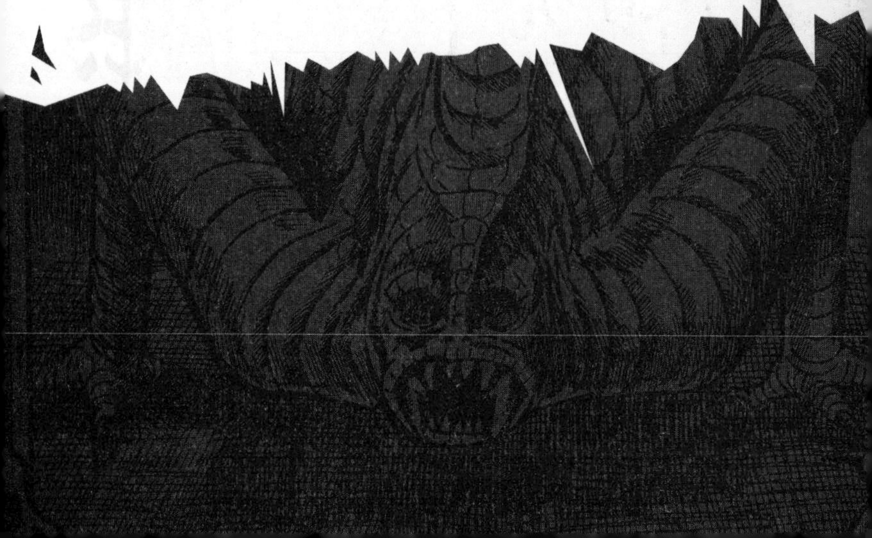

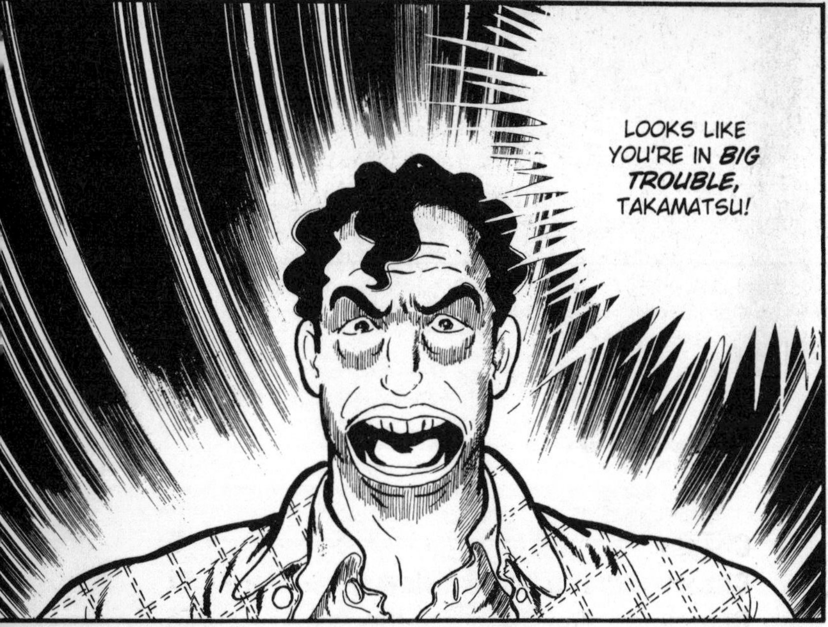
LOOKS LIKE YOU'RE IN *BIG TROUBLE,* TAKAMATSU!

CHAPTER 29: COLD STARES

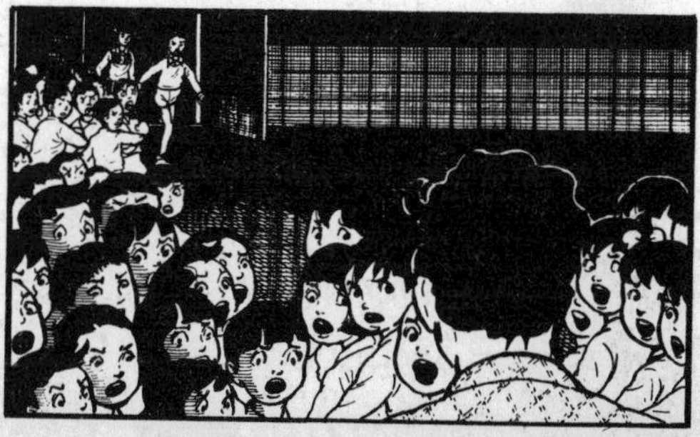

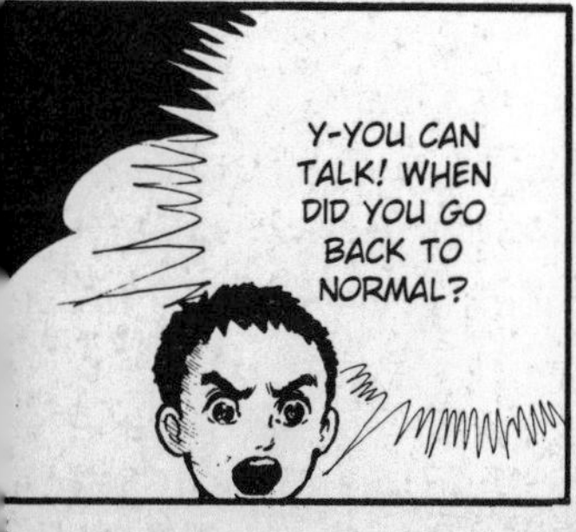
Y-YOU CAN TALK! WHEN DID YOU GO BACK TO NORMAL?

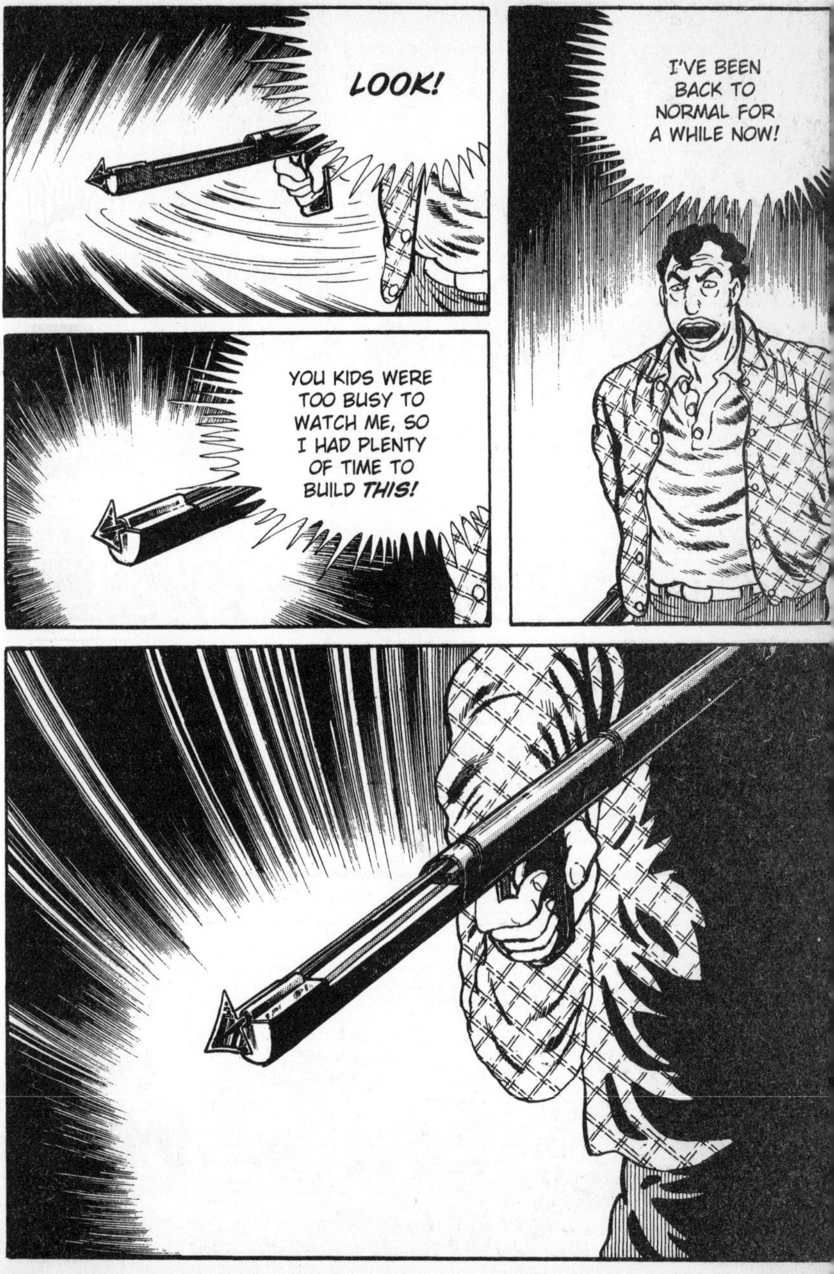
I'VE BEEN BACK TO NORMAL FOR A WHILE NOW!
LOOK!
YOU KIDS WERE TOO BUSY TO WATCH ME, SO I HAD PLENTY OF TIME TO BUILD *THIS!*

WATCH *THIS*.

GASP!

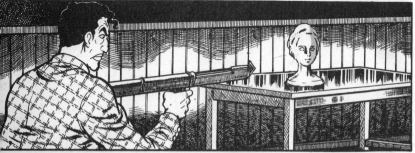

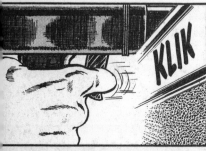

KLIK

NO! DON'T! THAT'S OUR *GOD*!

CHOOM

KRAKK

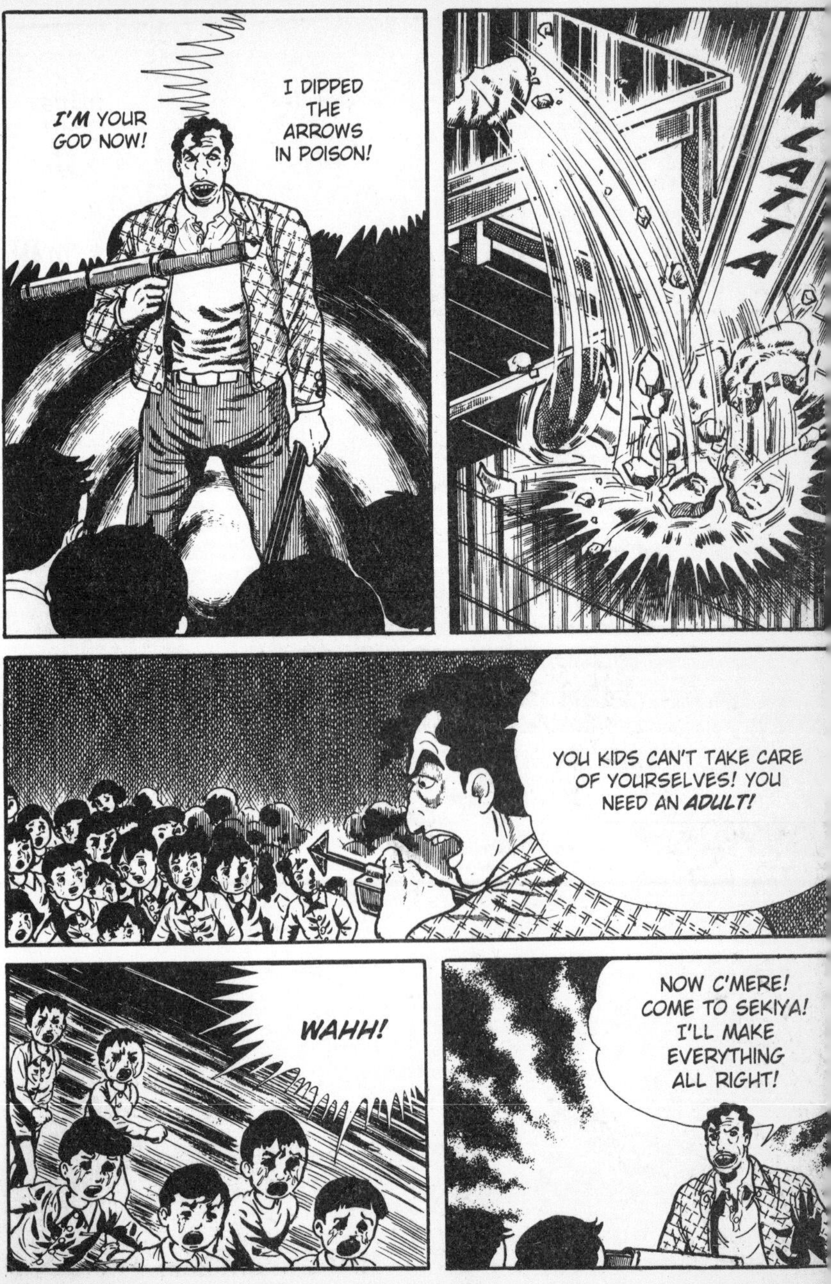
KLATTA
I DIPPED THE ARROWS IN POISON!
I'M YOUR GOD NOW!
YOU KIDS CAN'T TAKE CARE OF YOURSELVES! YOU NEED AN ADULT!
NOW C'MERE! COME TO SEKIYA! I'LL MAKE EVERYTHING ALL RIGHT!
WAHH!

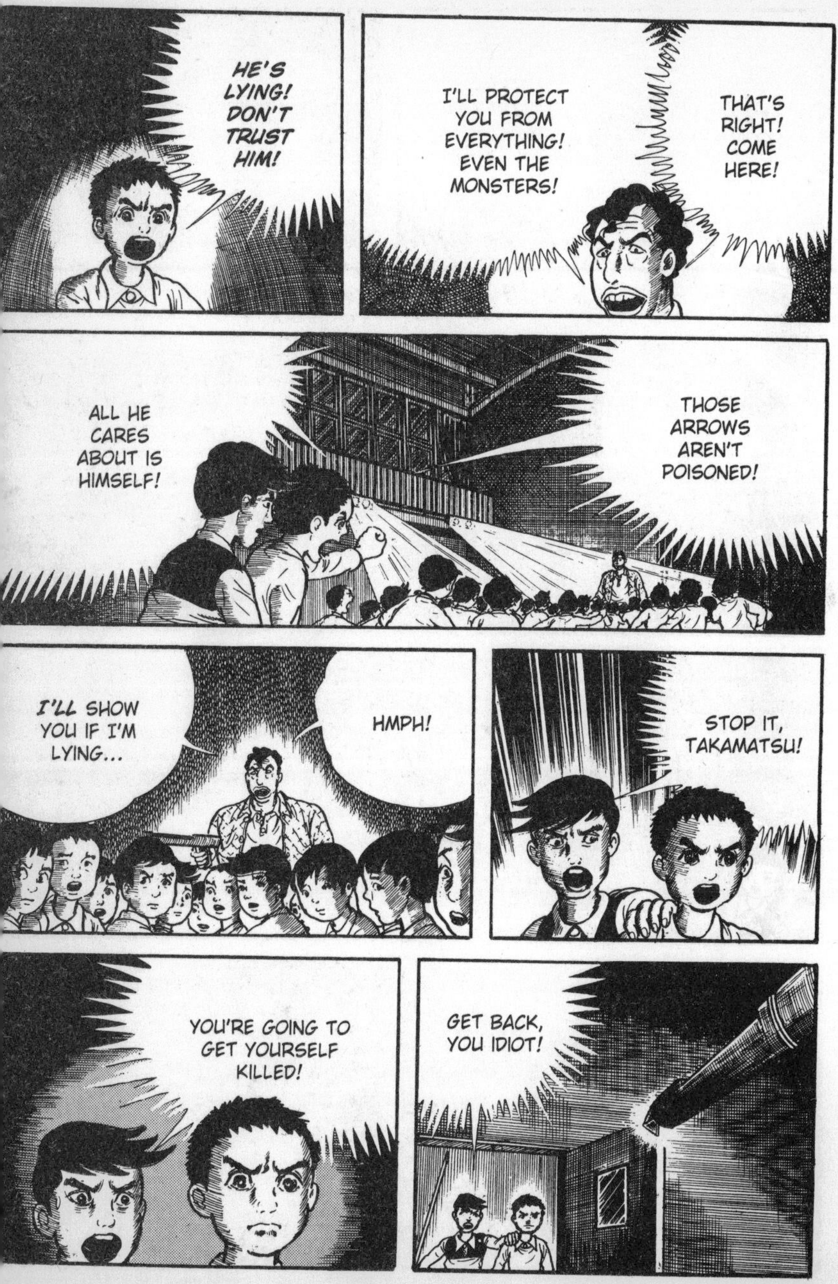
THAT'S RIGHT! COME HERE!
I'LL PROTECT YOU FROM EVERYTHING! EVEN THE MONSTERS!
HE'S LYING! DON'T TRUST HIM!
THOSE ARROWS AREN'T POISONED!
ALL HE CARES ABOUT IS HIMSELF!
STOP IT, TAKAMATSU!
HMPH!
I'LL SHOW YOU IF I'M LYING...
GET BACK, YOU IDIOT!
YOU'RE GOING TO GET YOURSELF KILLED!

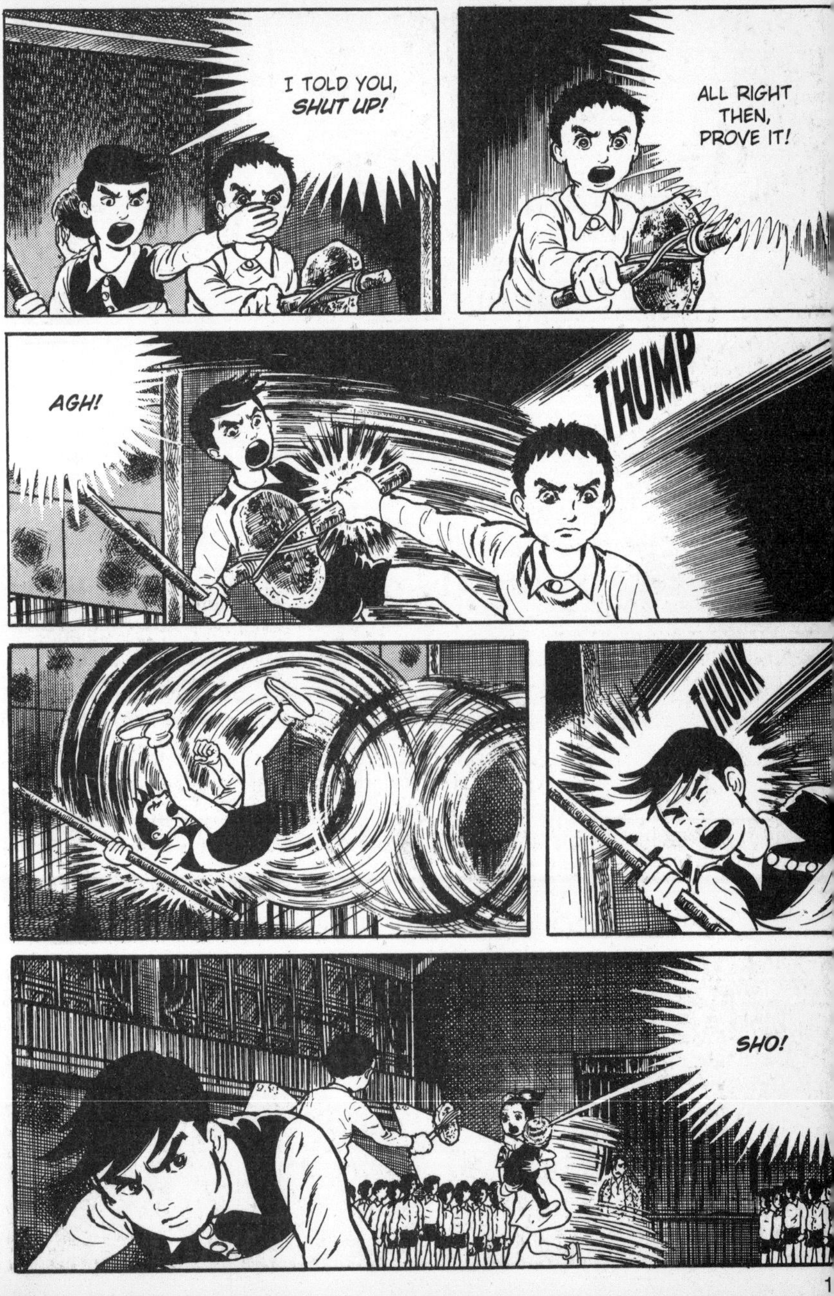
I TOLD YOU, SHUT UP!
ALL RIGHT THEN, PROVE IT!
AGH!
THUMP
THUNK
SHO!

I'LL LET YOU OFF *THIS* TIME.

HMPH!

AH!

GO AWAY!

WHO SAW IT?!

ALL RIGHT THEN! SOMEONE SAY WHAT TAKAMATSU DID!

YOU?

I-I DID...

I SAW HIM!

TELL EVERYBODY!

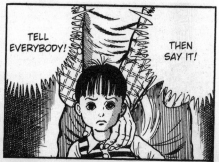

THEN SAY IT!

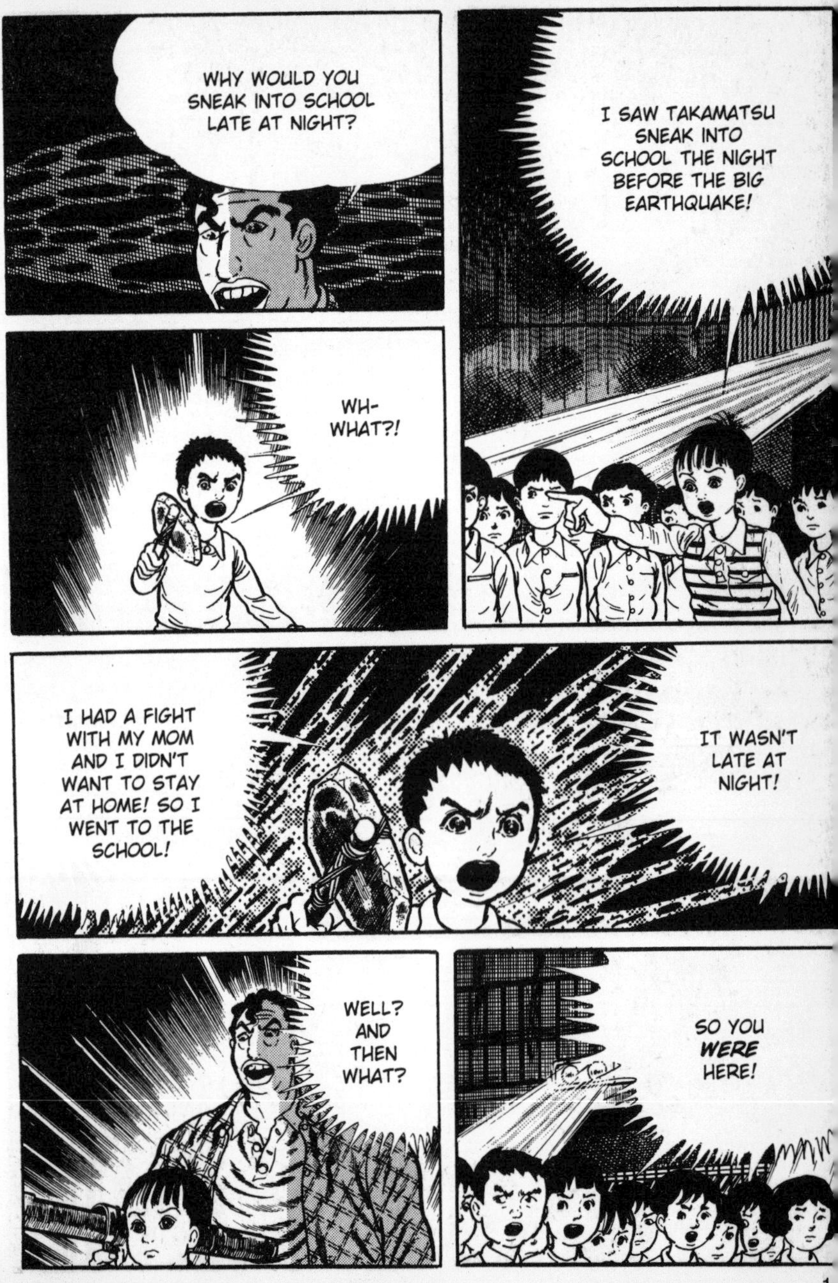
I SAW TAKAMATSU SNEAK INTO SCHOOL THE NIGHT BEFORE THE BIG EARTHQUAKE!
WHY WOULD YOU SNEAK INTO SCHOOL LATE AT NIGHT?
WH- WHAT?!
IT WASN'T LATE AT NIGHT!
I HAD A FIGHT WITH MY MOM AND I DIDN'T WANT TO STAY AT HOME! SO I WENT TO THE SCHOOL!
SO YOU *WERE* HERE!
WELL? AND THEN WHAT?

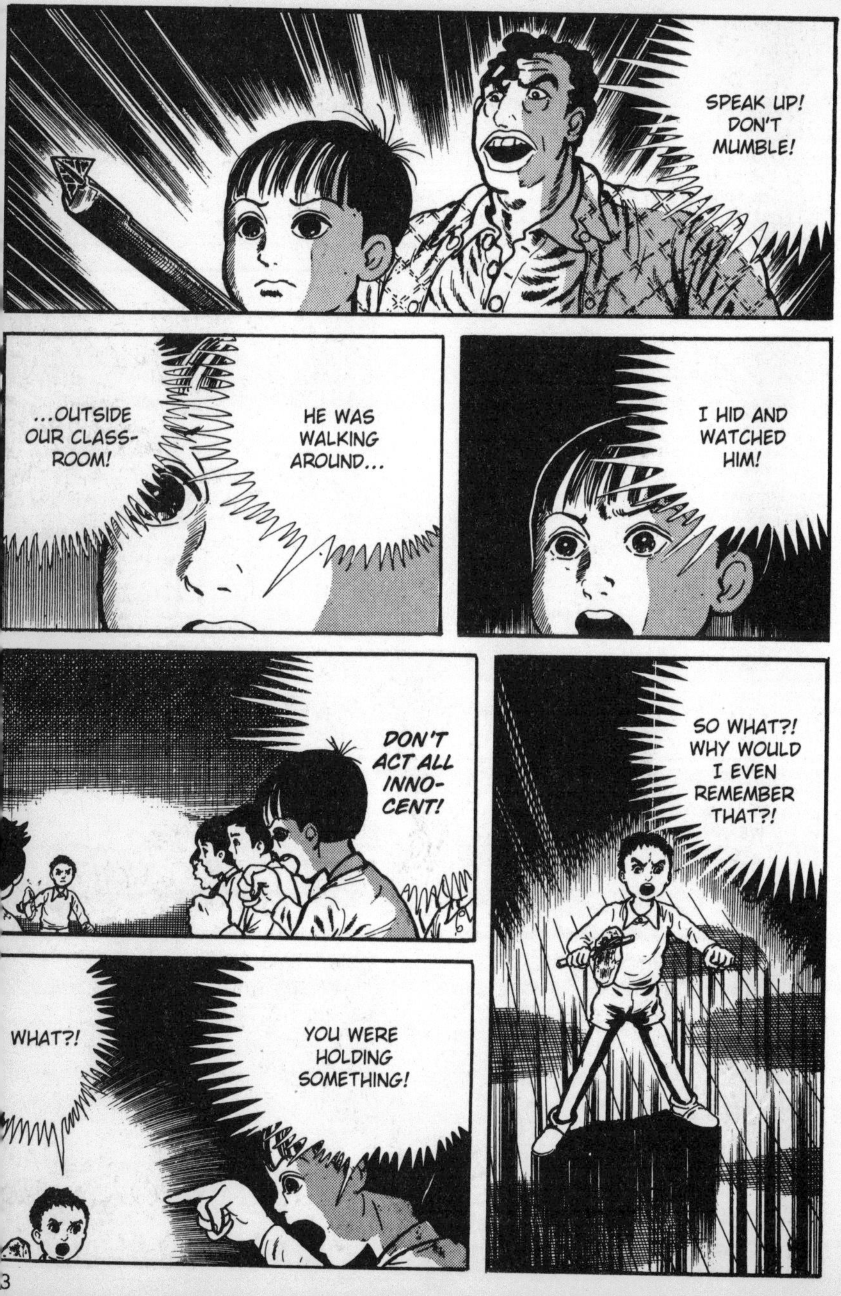
SPEAK UP! DON'T MUMBLE!
I HID AND WATCHED HIM!
HE WAS WALKING AROUND...
...OUTSIDE OUR CLASS-ROOM!
SO WHAT?! WHY WOULD I EVEN REMEMBER THAT?!
DON'T ACT ALL INNO-CENT!
YOU WERE HOLDING SOMETHING!
WHAT?!

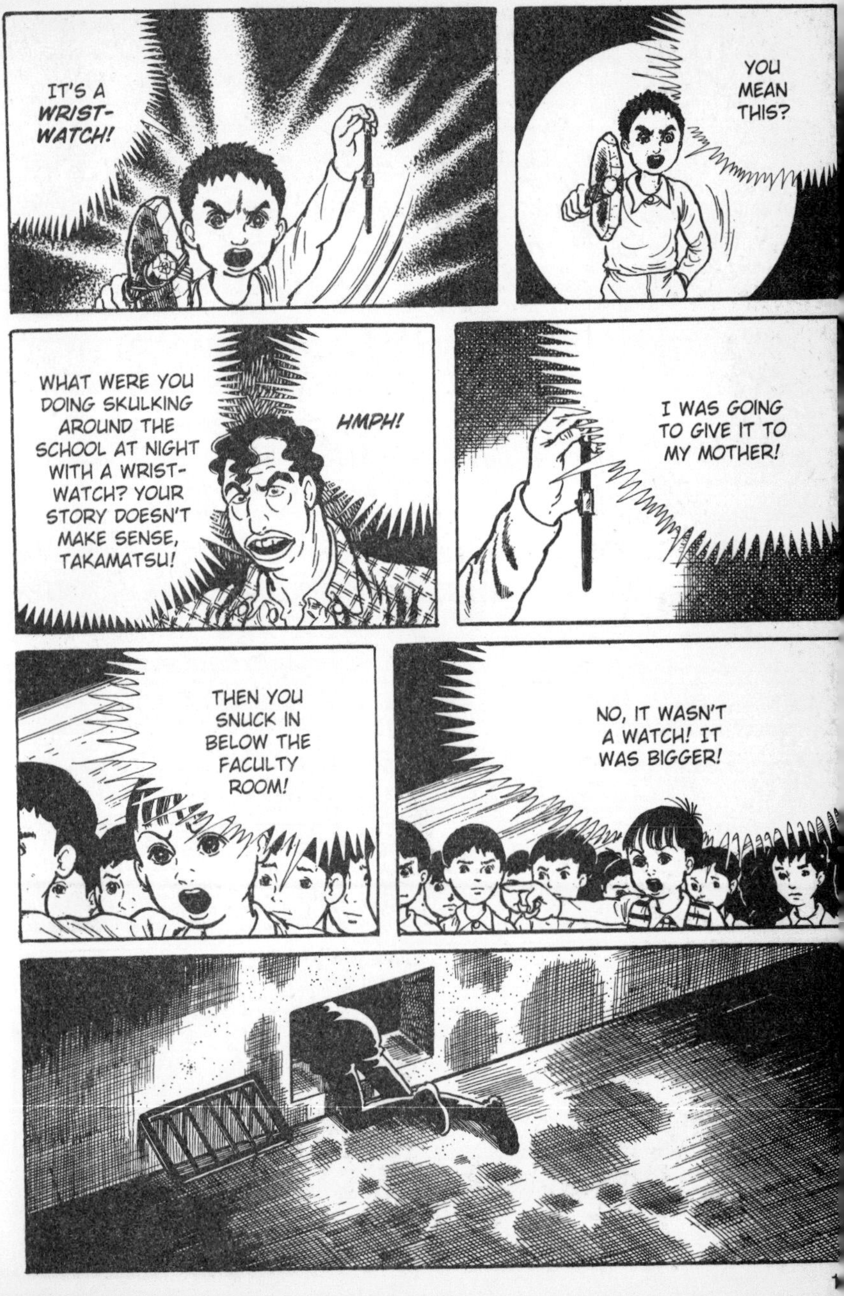
YOU MEAN THIS?
IT'S A *WRIST-WATCH!*
I WAS GOING TO GIVE IT TO MY MOTHER!
HMPH!
WHAT WERE YOU DOING SKULKING AROUND THE SCHOOL AT NIGHT WITH A WRIST-WATCH? YOUR STORY DOESN'T MAKE SENSE, TAKAMATSU!
NO, IT WASN'T A WATCH! IT WAS BIGGER!
THEN YOU SNUCK IN BELOW THE FACULTY ROOM!

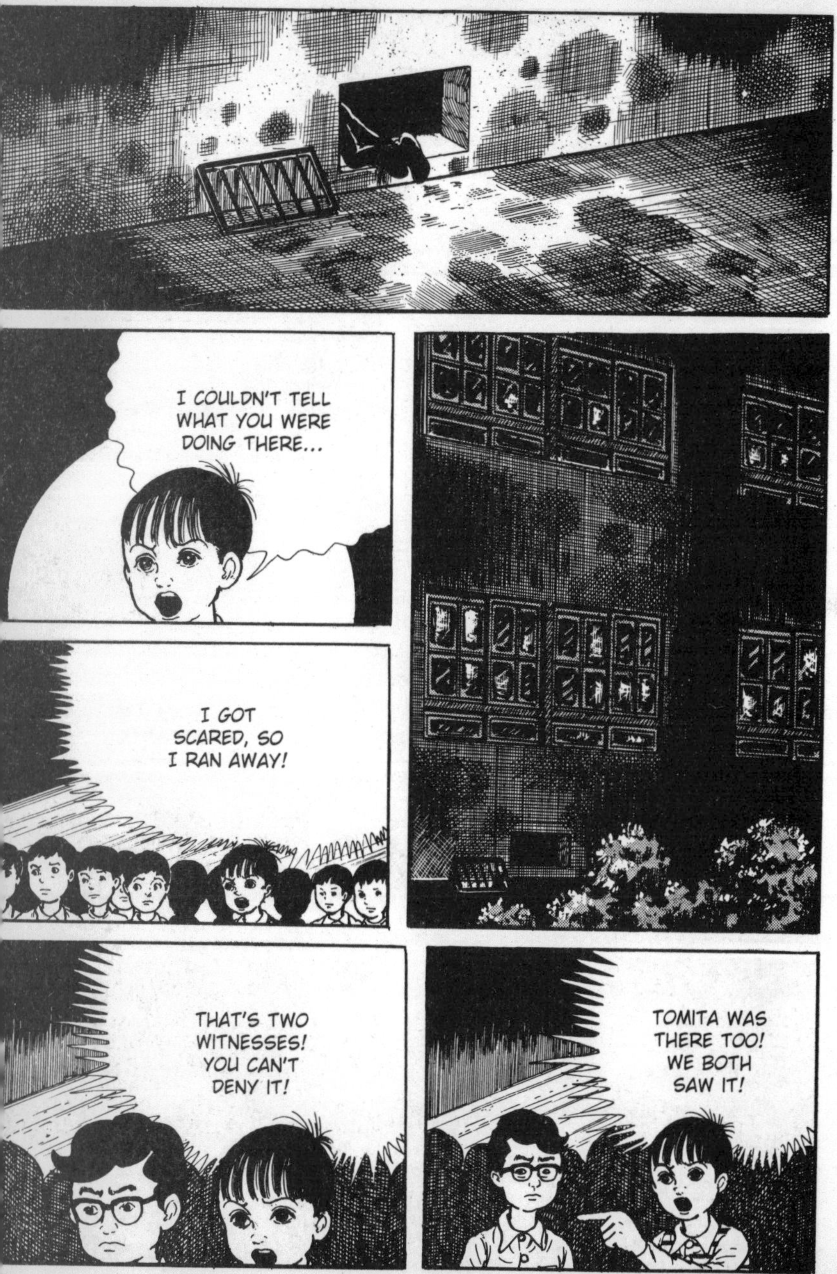
I COULDN'T TELL WHAT YOU WERE DOING THERE...
I GOT SCARED, SO I RAN AWAY!
TOMITA WAS THERE TOO! WE BOTH SAW IT!
THAT'S TWO WITNESSES! YOU CAN'T DENY IT!

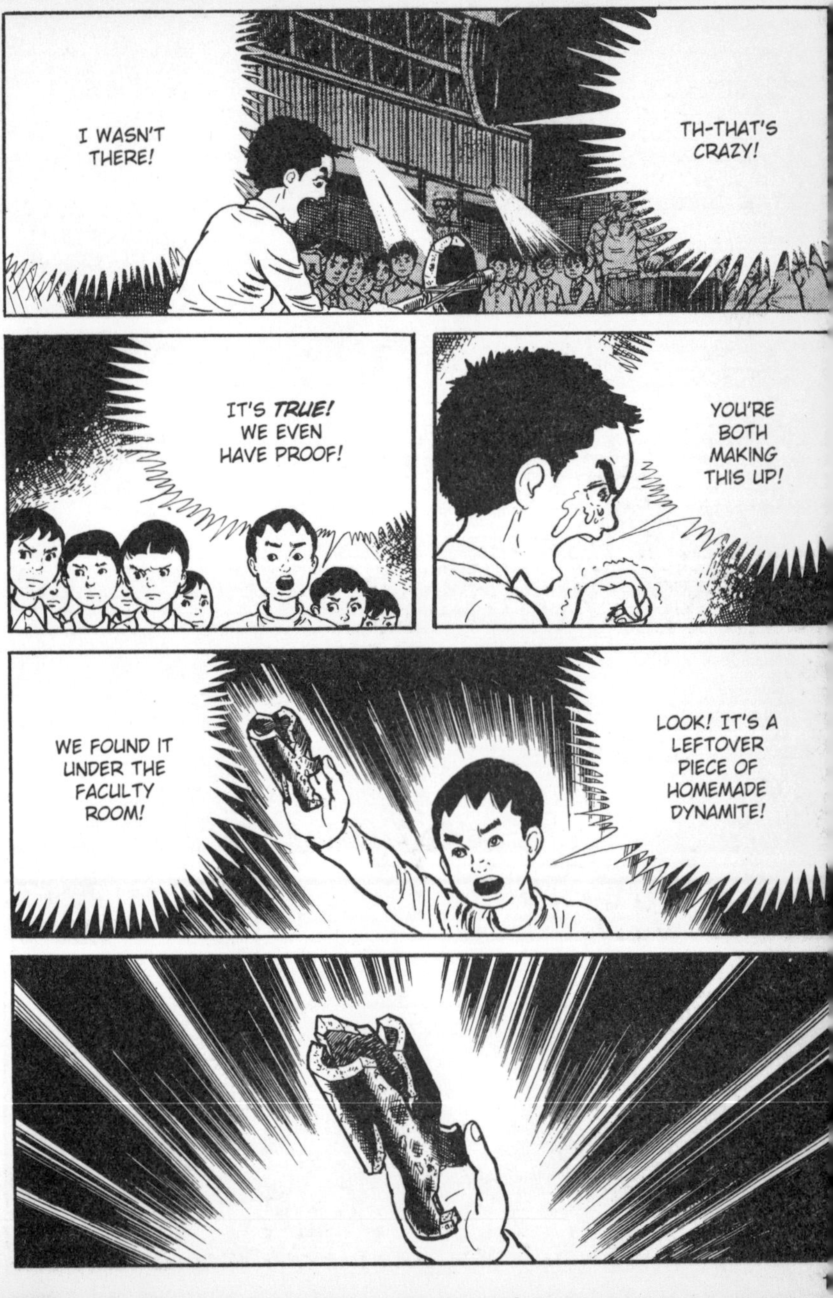
TH-THAT'S CRAZY!
I WASN'T THERE!
YOU'RE BOTH MAKING THIS UP!
IT'S *TRUE!* WE EVEN HAVE PROOF!
LOOK! IT'S A LEFTOVER PIECE OF HOMEMADE DYNAMITE!
WE FOUND IT UNDER THE FACULTY ROOM!

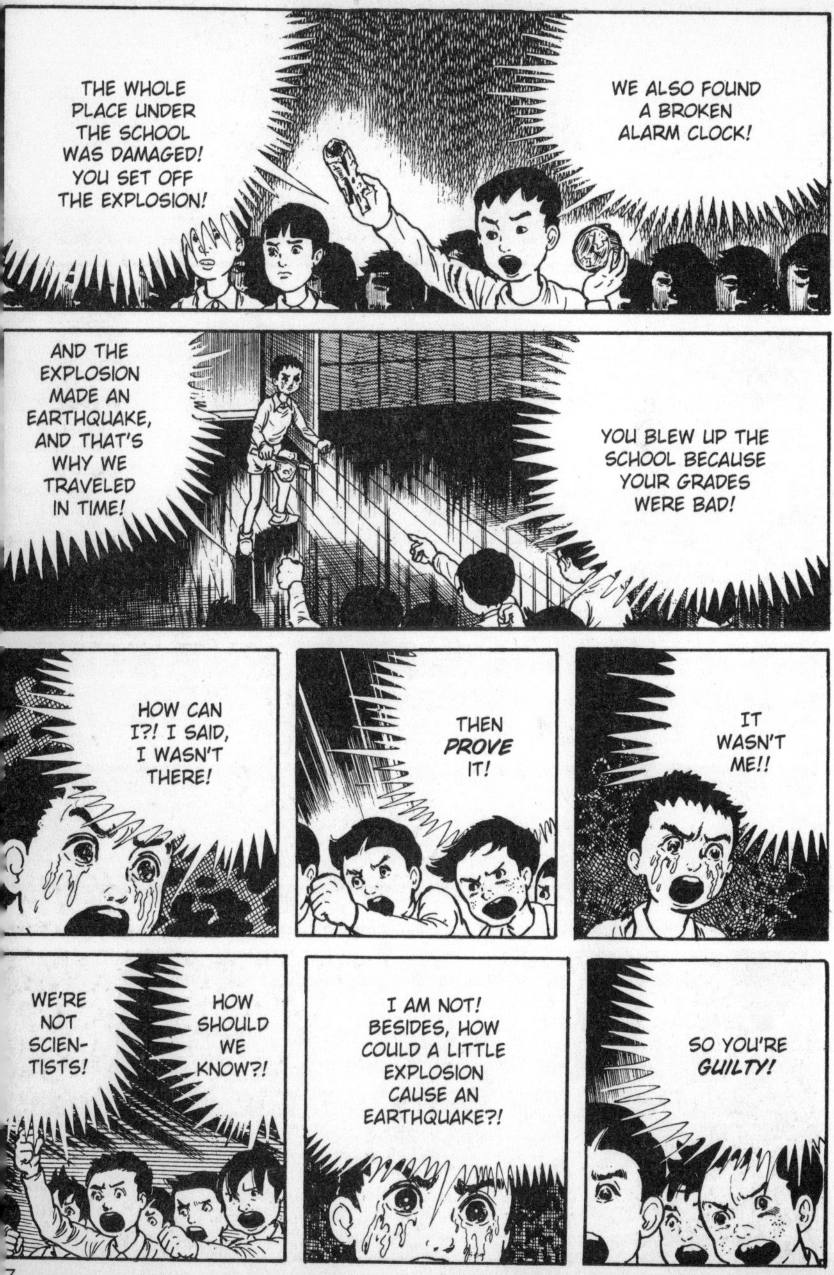
WE ALSO FOUND A BROKEN ALARM CLOCK!
THE WHOLE PLACE UNDER THE SCHOOL WAS DAMAGED! YOU SET OFF THE EXPLOSION!
YOU BLEW UP THE SCHOOL BECAUSE YOUR GRADES WERE BAD!
AND THE EXPLOSION MADE AN EARTHQUAKE, AND THAT'S WHY WE TRAVELED IN TIME!
IT WASN'T ME!!
THEN *PROVE* IT!
HOW CAN I?! I SAID, I WASN'T THERE!
SO YOU'RE *GUILTY!*
I AM NOT! BESIDES, HOW COULD A LITTLE EXPLOSION CAUSE AN EARTHQUAKE?!
HOW SHOULD WE KNOW?!
WE'RE NOT SCIEN-TISTS!

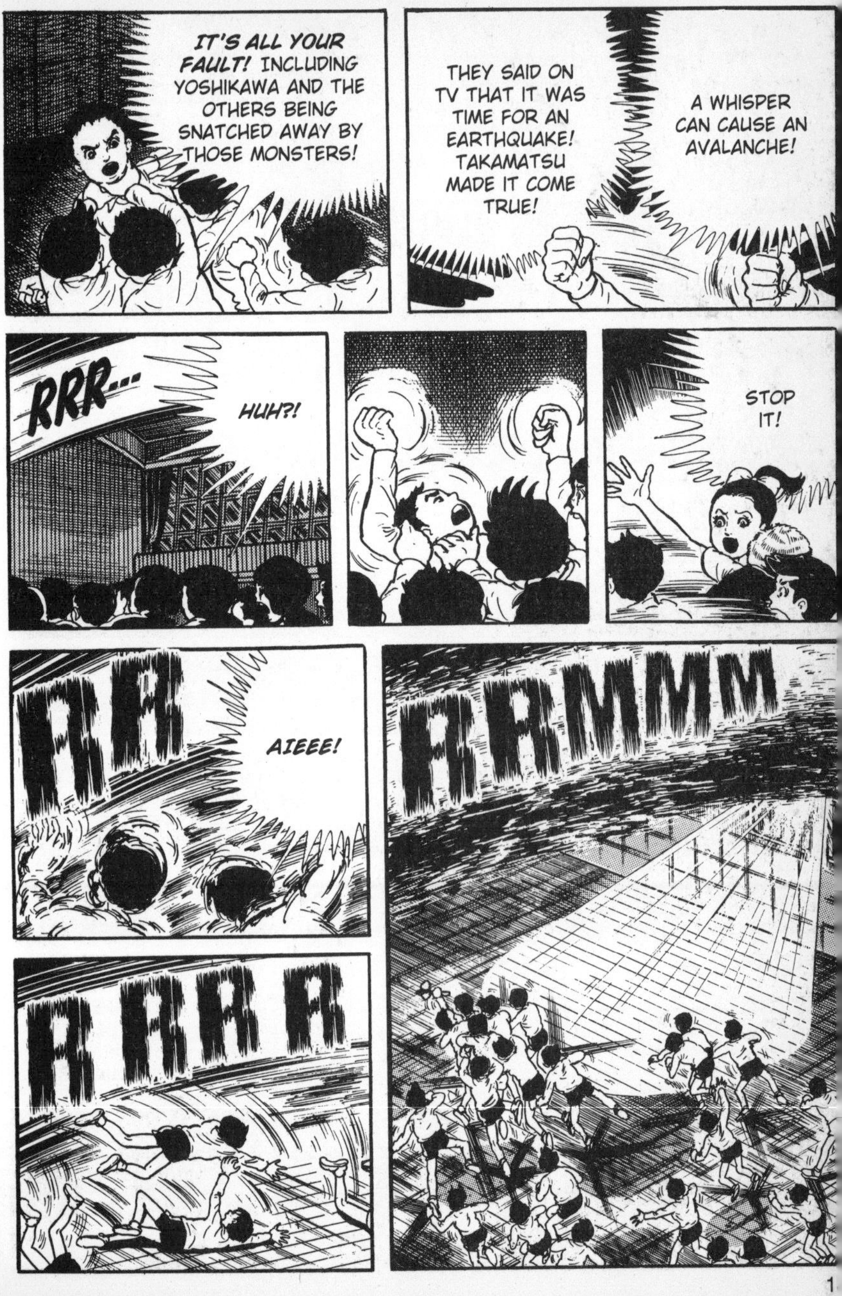
IT'S ALL YOUR FAULT! INCLUDING YOSHIKAWA AND THE OTHERS BEING SNATCHED AWAY BY THOSE MONSTERS!
THEY SAID ON TV THAT IT WAS TIME FOR AN EARTHQUAKE! TAKAMATSU MADE IT COME TRUE!
A WHISPER CAN CAUSE AN AVALANCHE!
RRR...
HUH?!
STOP IT!
RR
AIEEE!
RRRR
RRMMMM

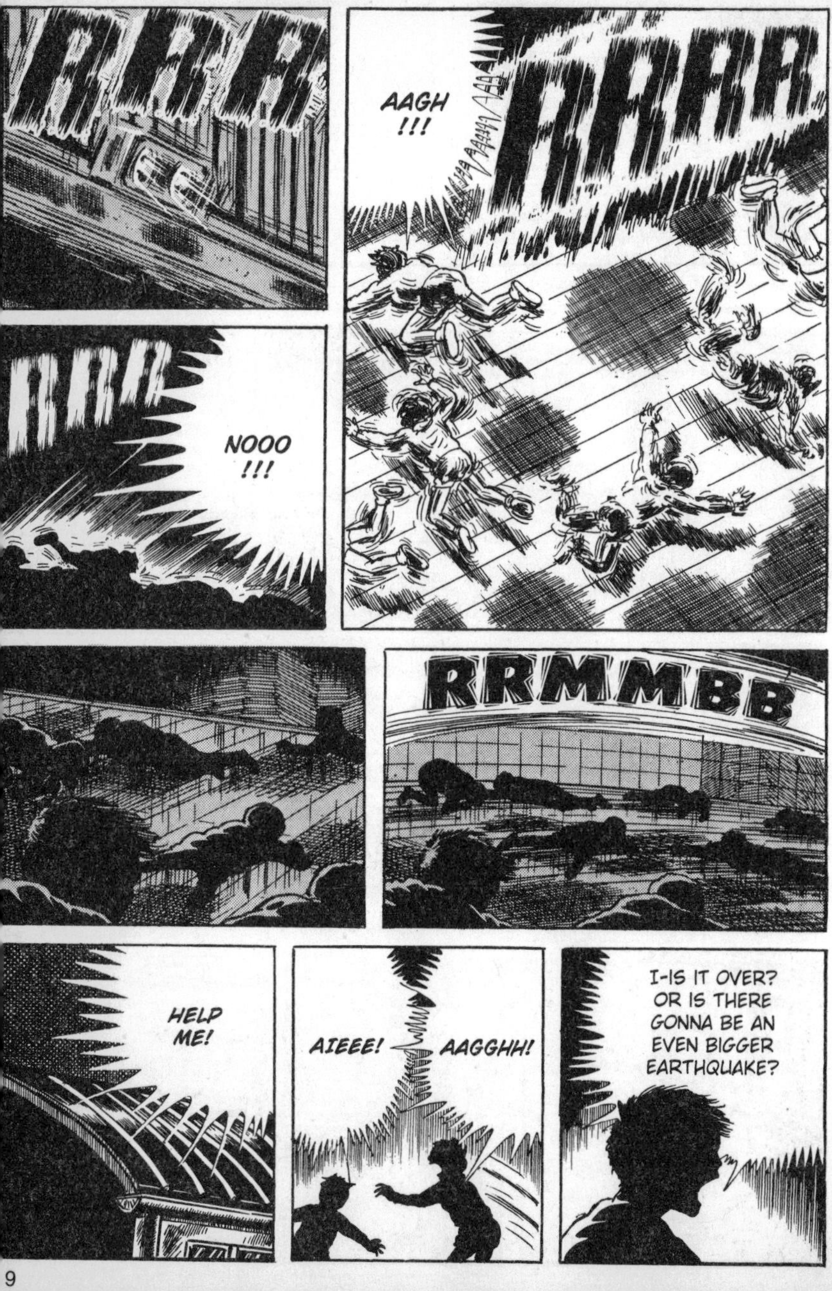
RRRR
AAGH !!!
NOOO !!!
RRMMBB
I-IS IT OVER? OR IS THERE GONNA BE AN EVEN BIGGER EARTHQUAKE?
AAGGHH!
AIEEE!
HELP ME!

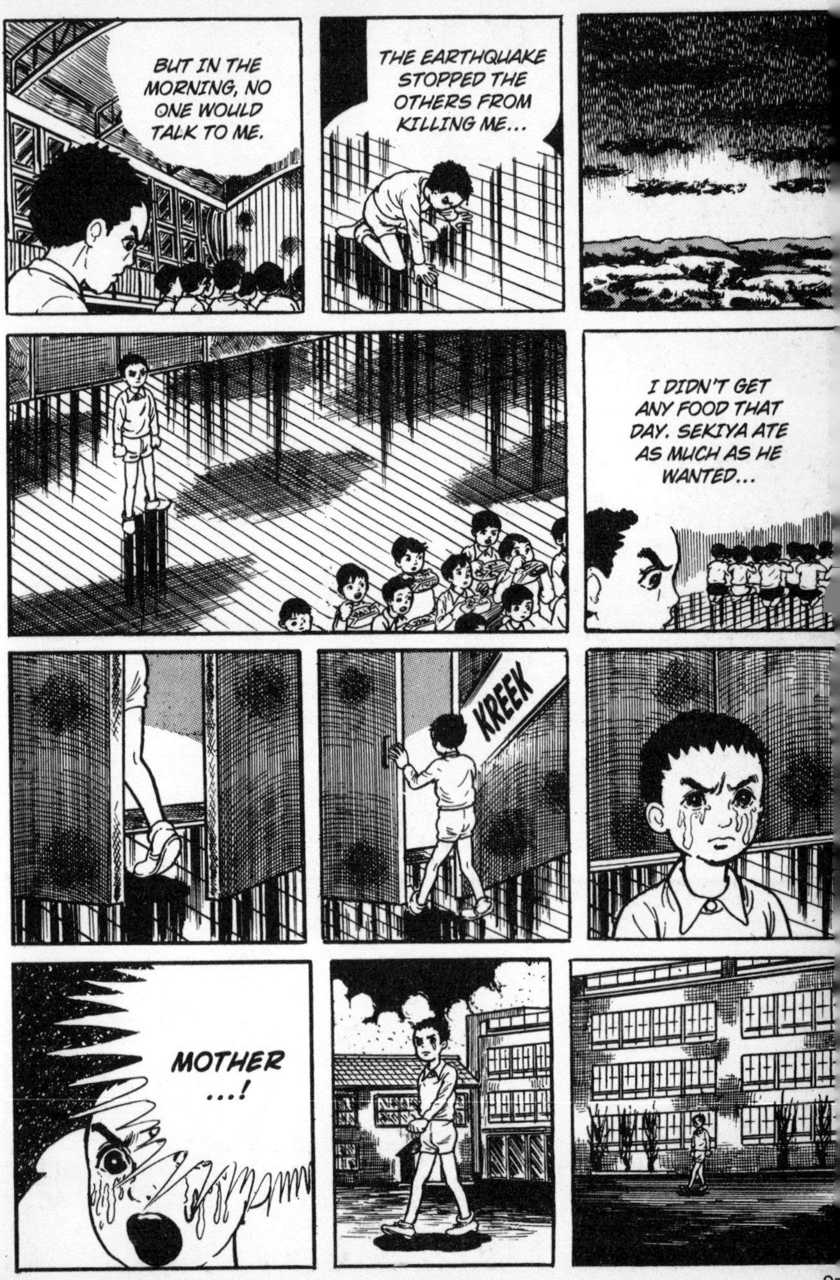
THE EARTHQUAKE STOPPED THE OTHERS FROM KILLING ME...
BUT IN THE MORNING, NO ONE WOULD TALK TO ME.
I DIDN'T GET ANY FOOD THAT DAY. SEKIYA ATE AS MUCH AS HE WANTED...
KREEK
MOTHER ...!

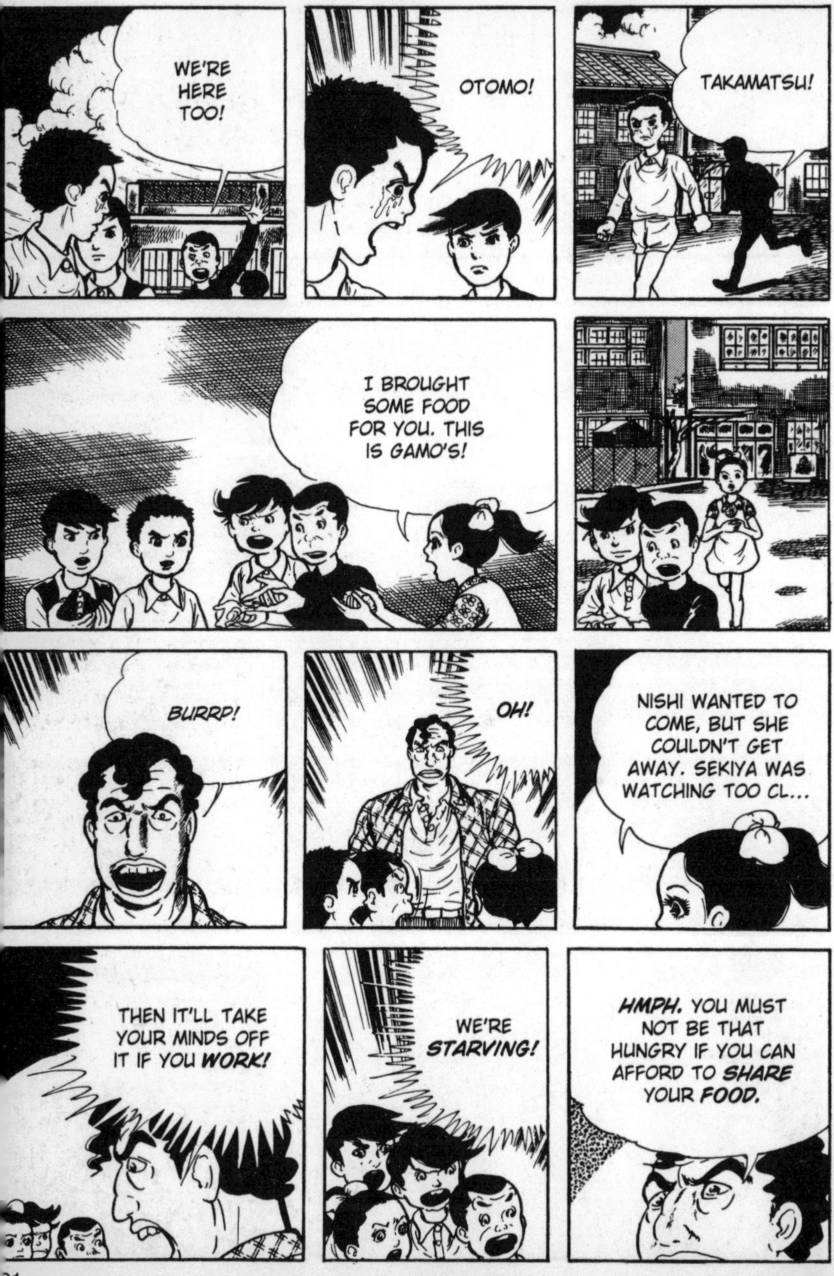
WE'RE HERE TOO!
OTOMO!
TAKAMATSU!
I BROUGHT SOME FOOD FOR YOU. THIS IS GAMO'S!
BURRP!
OH!
NISHI WANTED TO COME, BUT SHE COULDN'T GET AWAY. SEKIYA WAS WATCHING TOO CL...
THEN IT'LL TAKE YOUR MINDS OFF IT IF YOU WORK!
WE'RE STARVING!
HMPH. YOU MUST NOT BE THAT HUNGRY IF YOU CAN AFFORD TO SHARE YOUR FOOD.

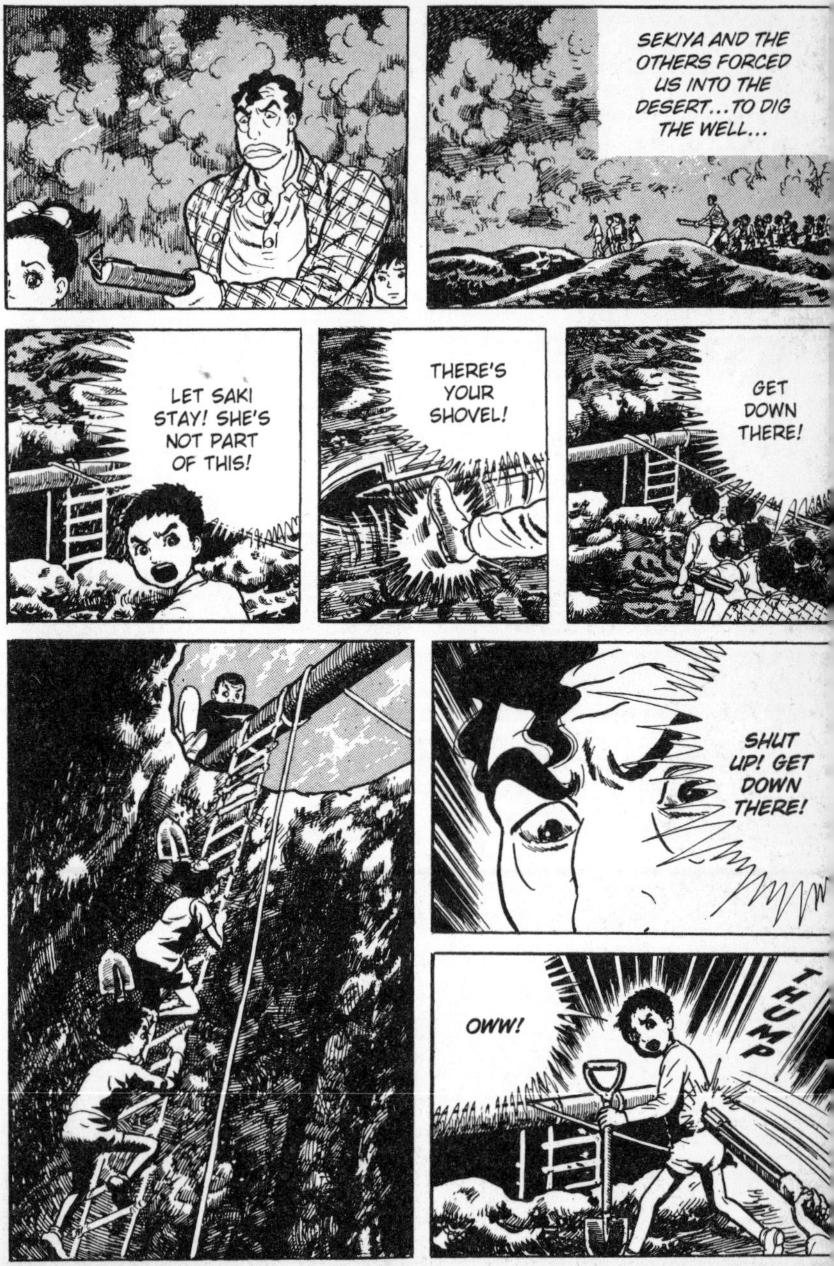
SEKIYA AND THE OTHERS FORCED US INTO THE DESERT...TO DIG THE WELL...
GET DOWN THERE!
THERE'S YOUR SHOVEL!
LET SAKI STAY! SHE'S NOT PART OF THIS!
SHUT UP! GET DOWN THERE!
THUMP
OWW!

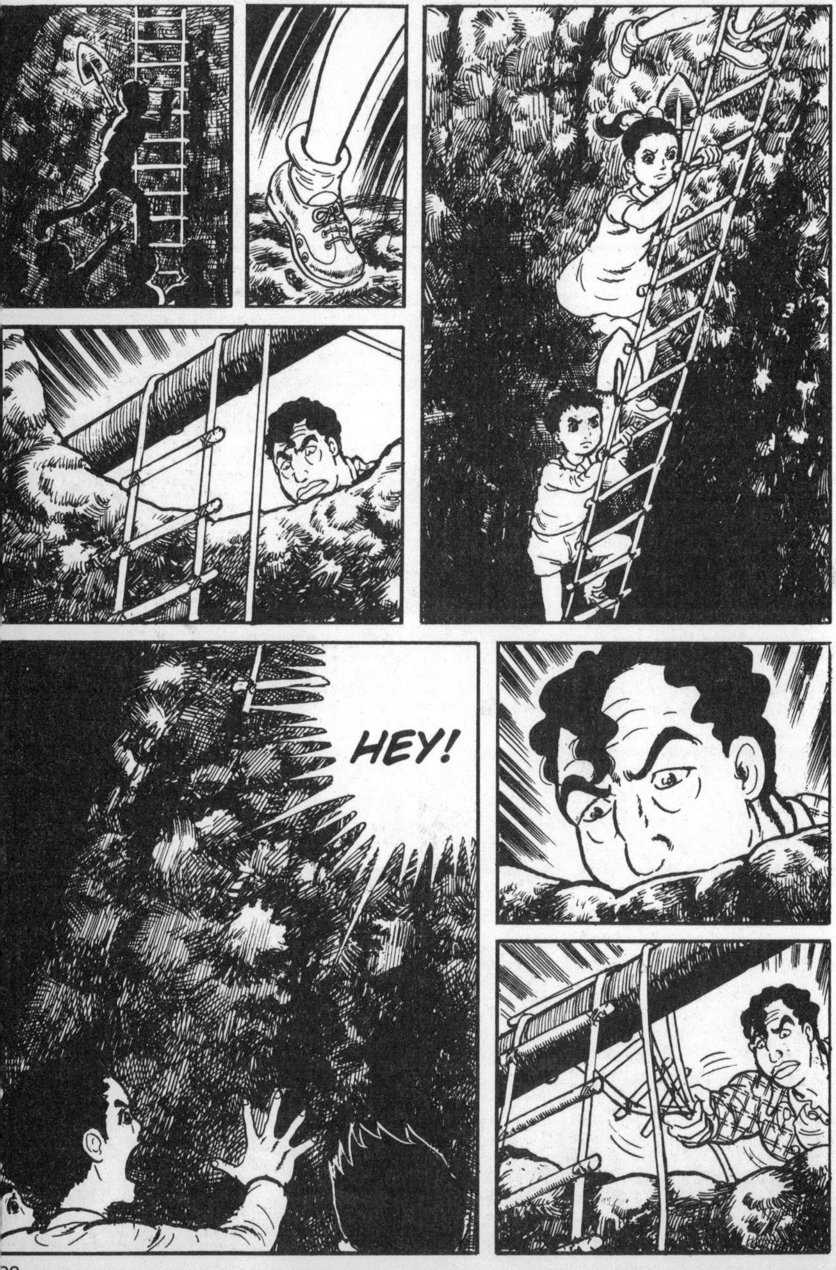
HEY!

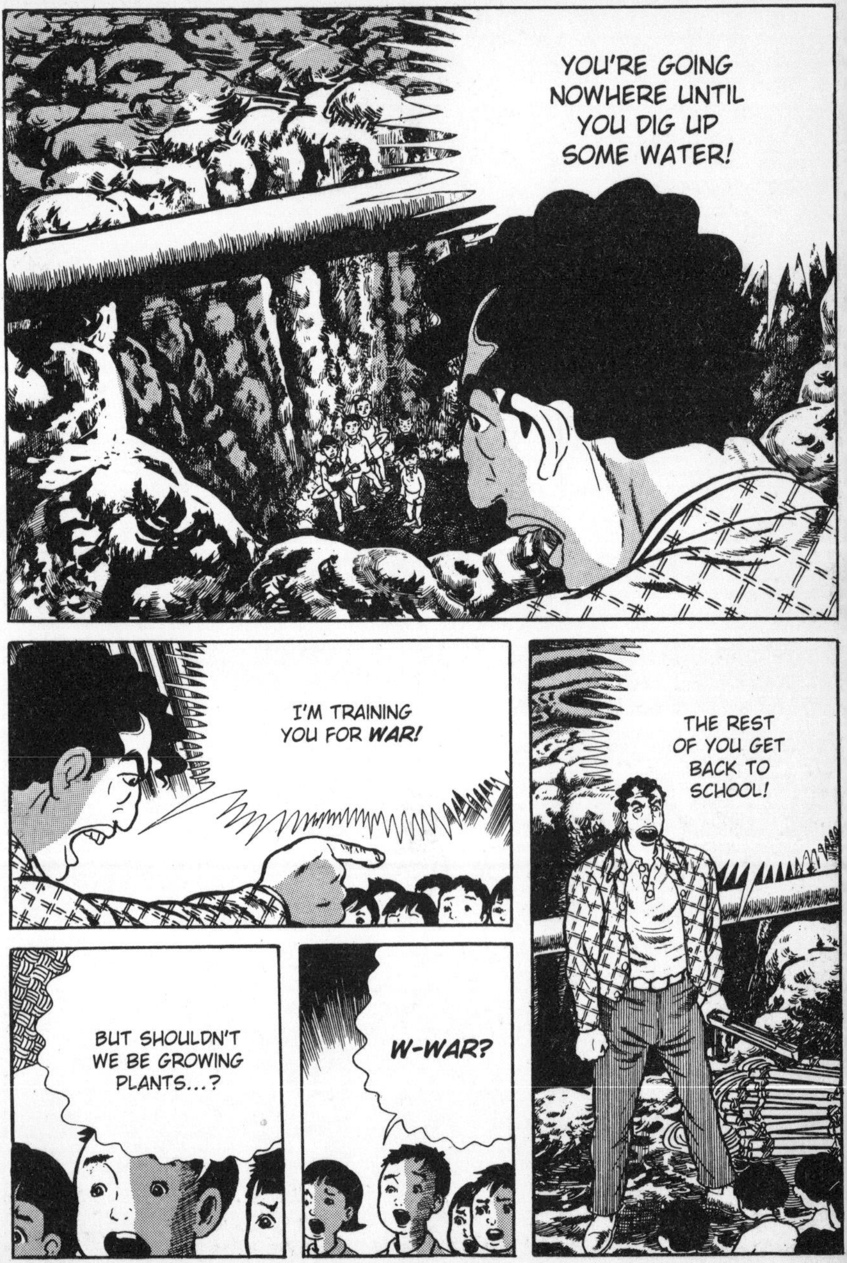
YOU'RE GOING NOWHERE UNTIL YOU DIG UP SOME WATER!
THE REST OF YOU GET BACK TO SCHOOL!
I'M TRAINING YOU FOR *WAR!*
W-WAR?
BUT SHOULDN'T WE BE GROWING PLANTS...?

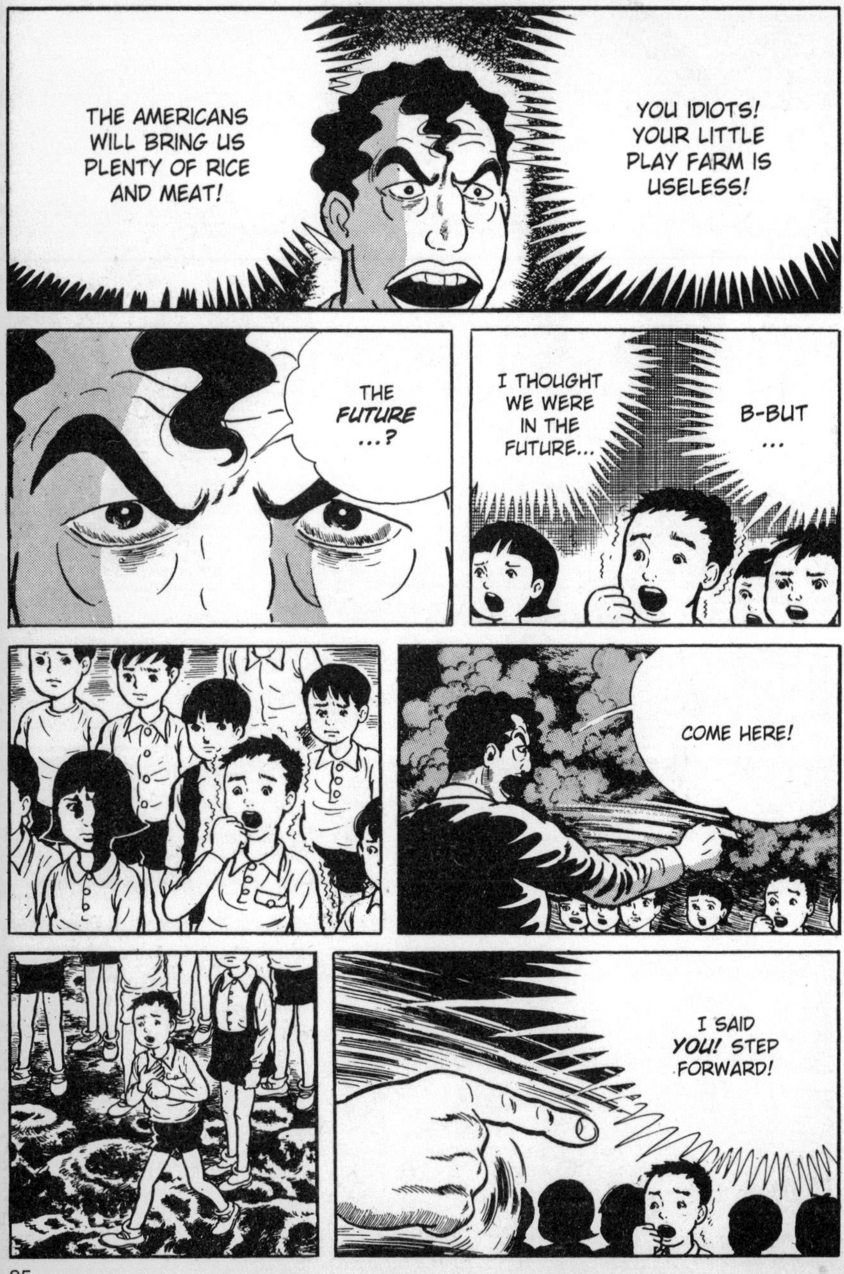
YOU IDIOTS! YOUR LITTLE PLAY FARM IS USELESS!
THE AMERICANS WILL BRING US PLENTY OF RICE AND MEAT!
B-BUT ...
I THOUGHT WE WERE IN THE FUTURE...
THE *FUTURE* ...?
COME HERE!
I SAID *YOU!* STEP FORWARD!

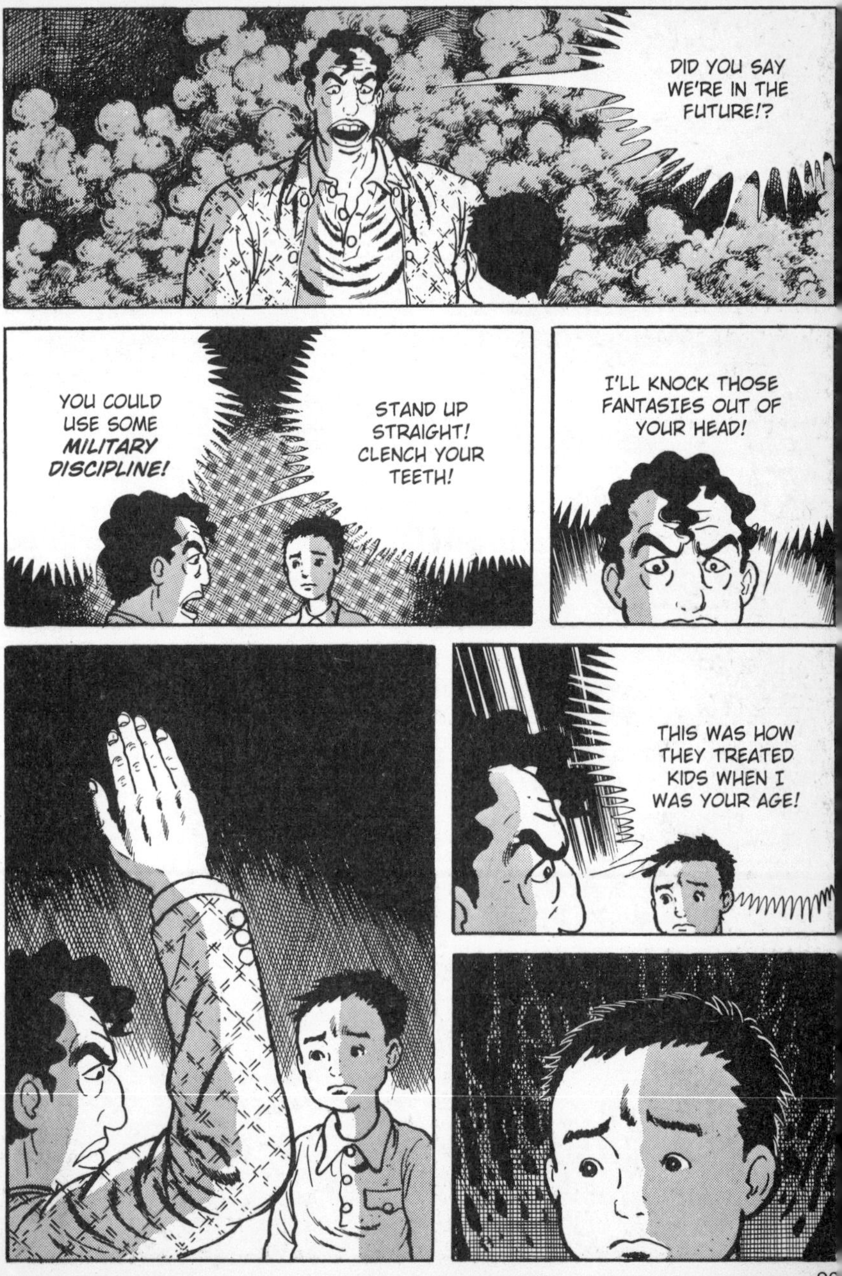
DID YOU SAY WE'RE IN THE FUTURE!?
I'LL KNOCK THOSE FANTASIES OUT OF YOUR HEAD!
STAND UP STRAIGHT! CLENCH YOUR TEETH!
YOU COULD USE SOME MILITARY DISCIPLINE!
THIS WAS HOW THEY TREATED KIDS WHEN I WAS YOUR AGE!

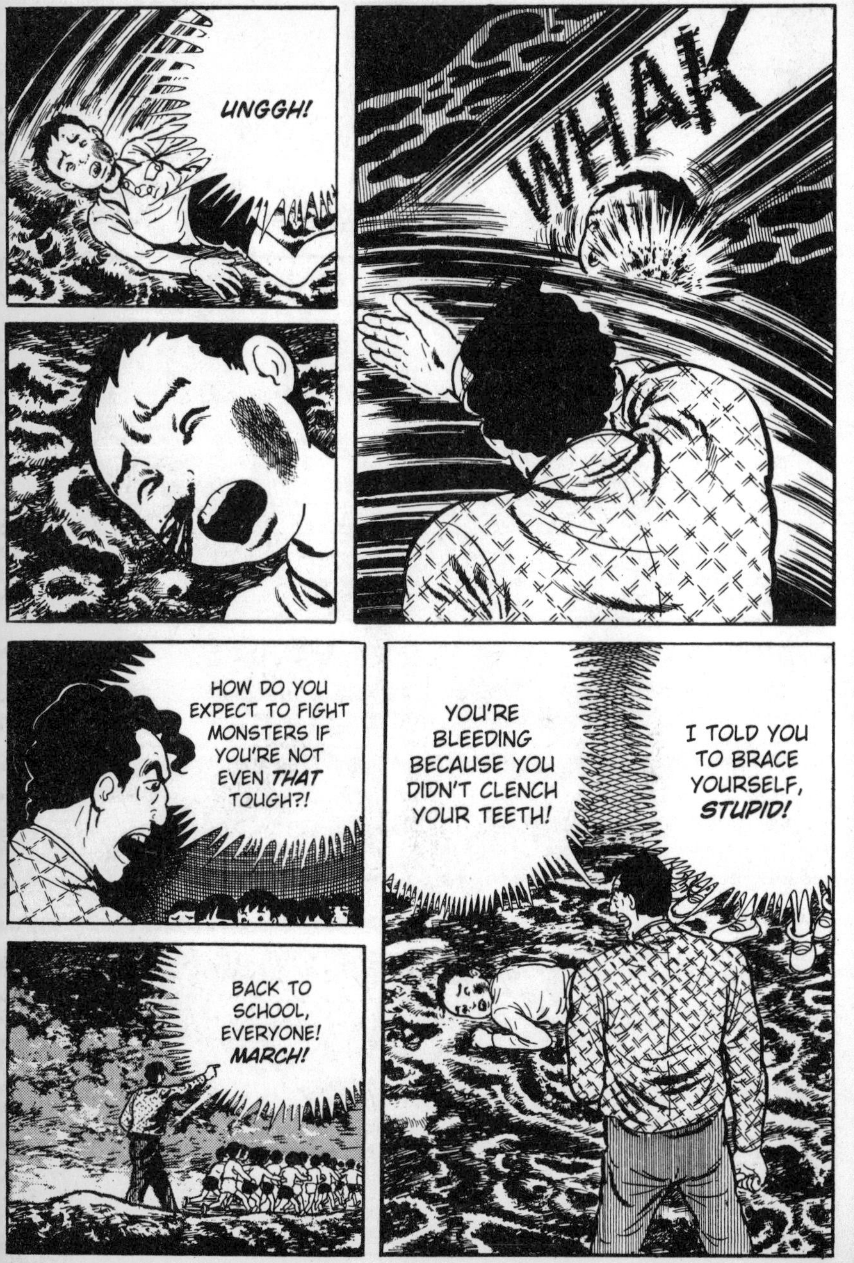
WHAK
UNGGH!
I TOLD YOU TO BRACE YOURSELF, STUPID!
YOU'RE BLEEDING BECAUSE YOU DIDN'T CLENCH YOUR TEETH!
HOW DO YOU EXPECT TO FIGHT MONSTERS IF YOU'RE NOT EVEN THAT TOUGH?!
BACK TO SCHOOL, EVERYONE! MARCH!

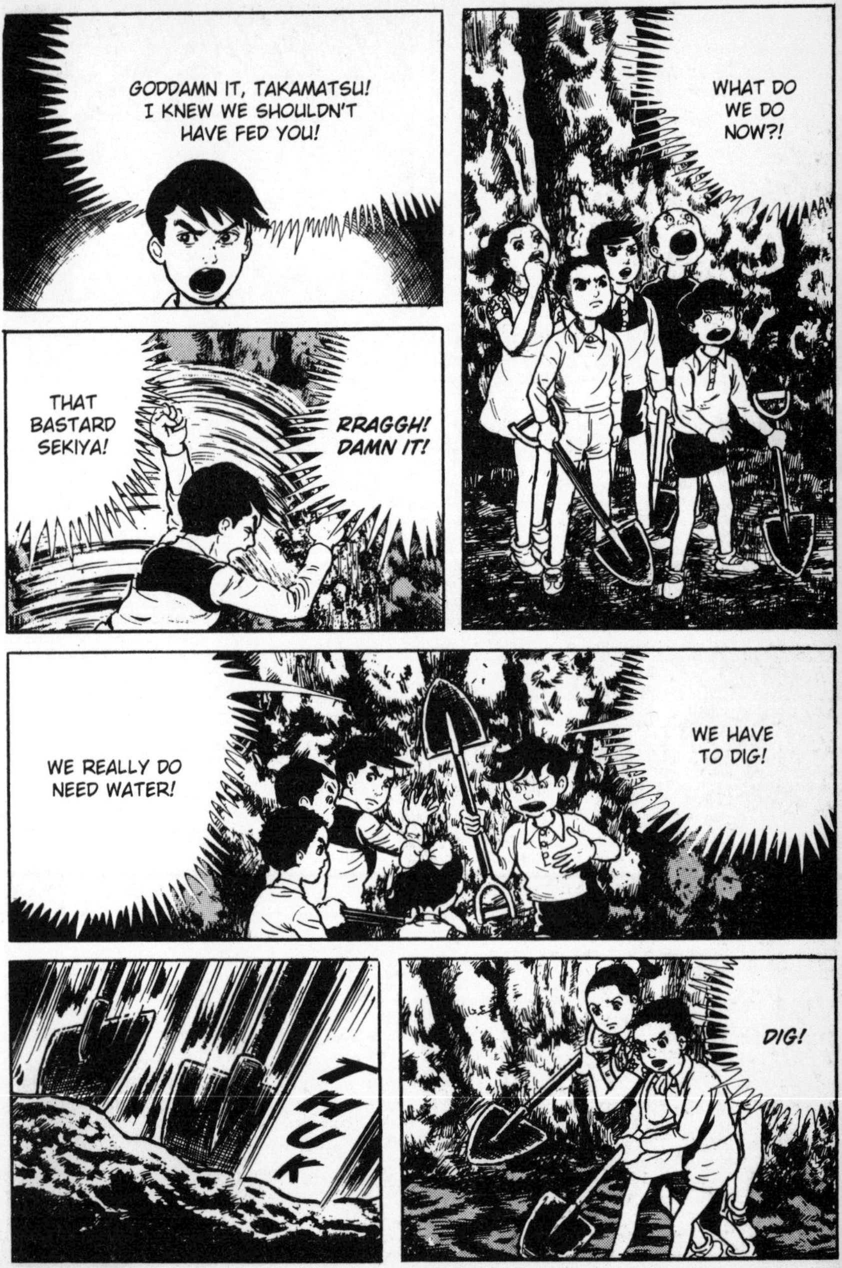
WHAT DO WE DO NOW?!
GODDAMN IT, TAKAMATSU! I KNEW WE SHOULDN'T HAVE FED YOU!
RRAGGH! DAMN IT!
THAT BASTARD SEKIYA!
WE HAVE TO DIG!
WE REALLY DO NEED WATER!
DIG!
THUK

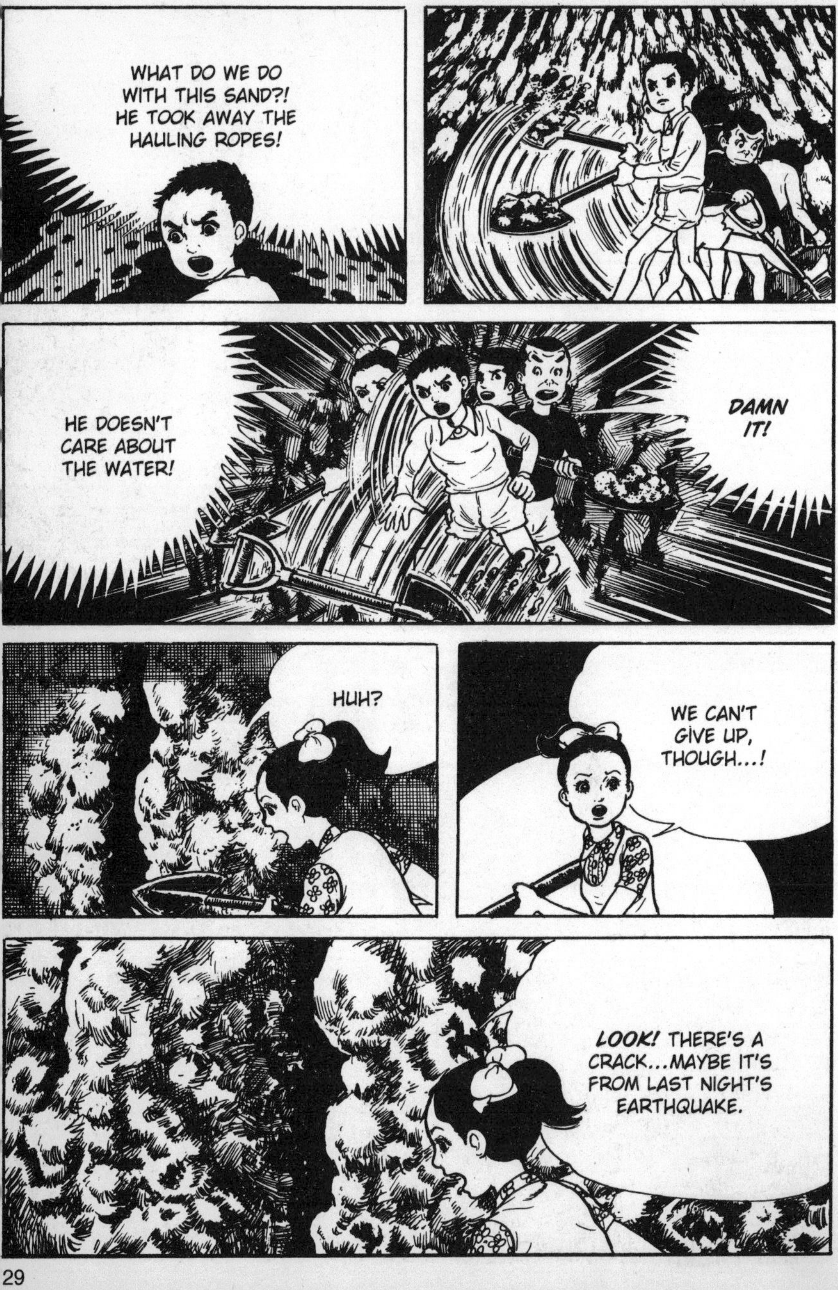
WHAT DO WE DO WITH THIS SAND?! HE TOOK AWAY THE HAULING ROPES!
DAMN IT!
HE DOESN'T CARE ABOUT THE WATER!
WE CAN'T GIVE UP, THOUGH...!
HUH?
LOOK! THERE'S A CRACK...MAYBE IT'S FROM LAST NIGHT'S EARTHQUAKE.

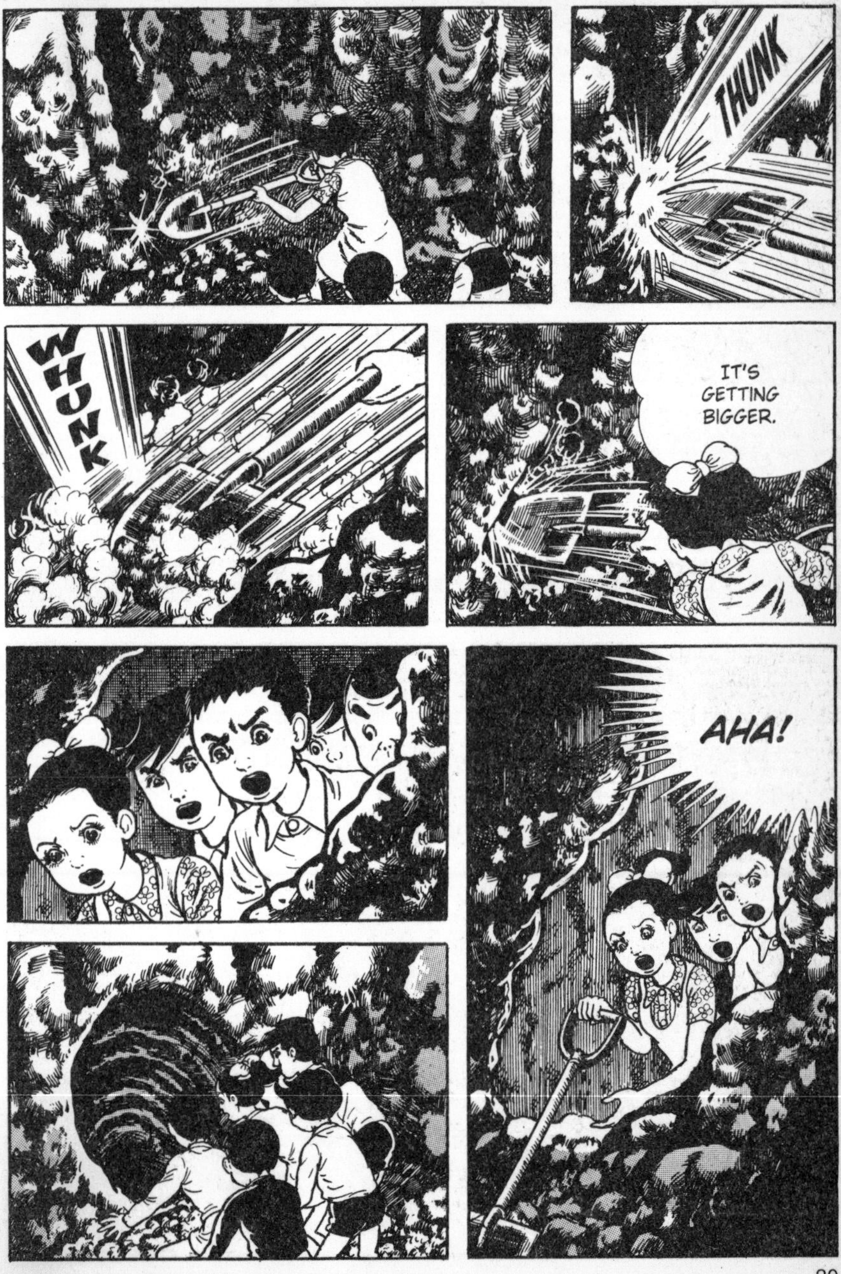
THUNK
IT'S GETTING BIGGER.
WHUNK
AHA!

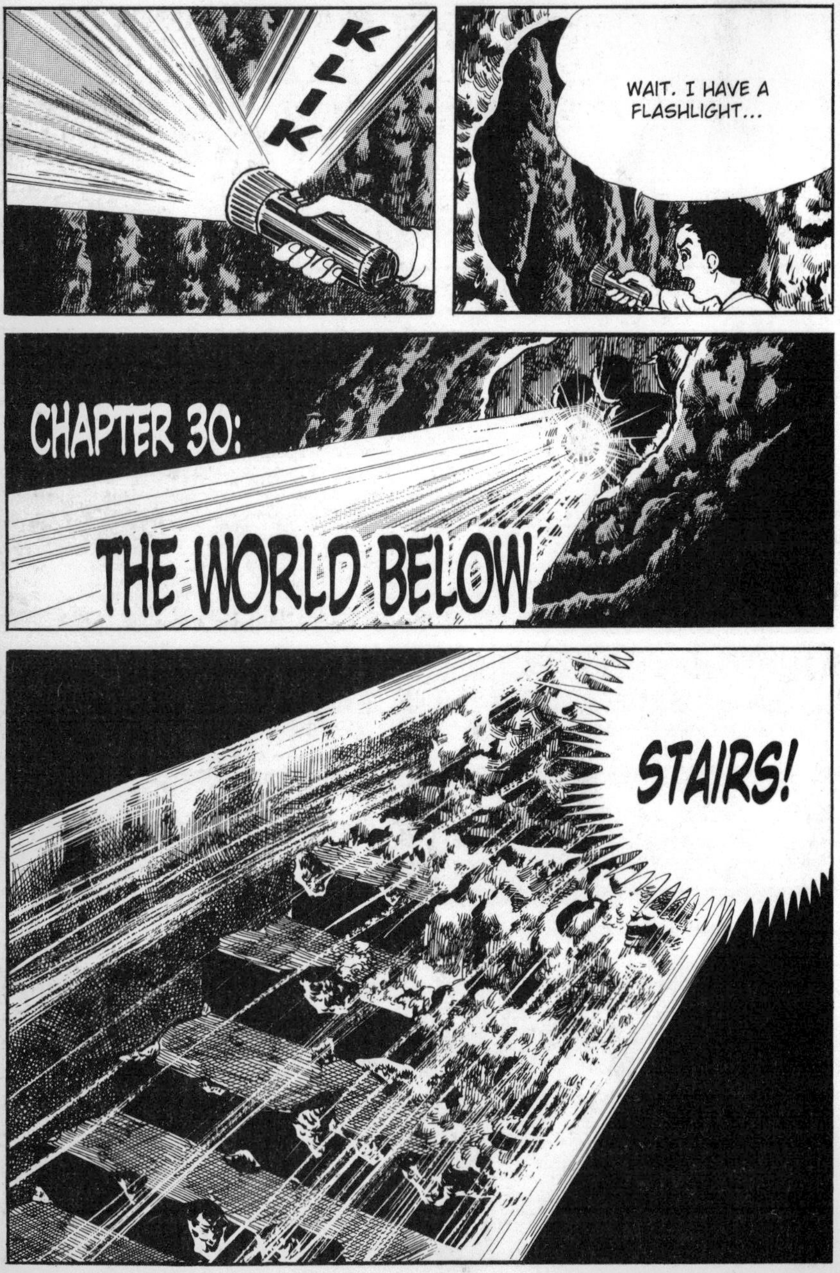
WAIT. I HAVE A FLASHLIGHT...
KLIK
CHAPTER 30:
THE WORLD BELOW
STAIRS!

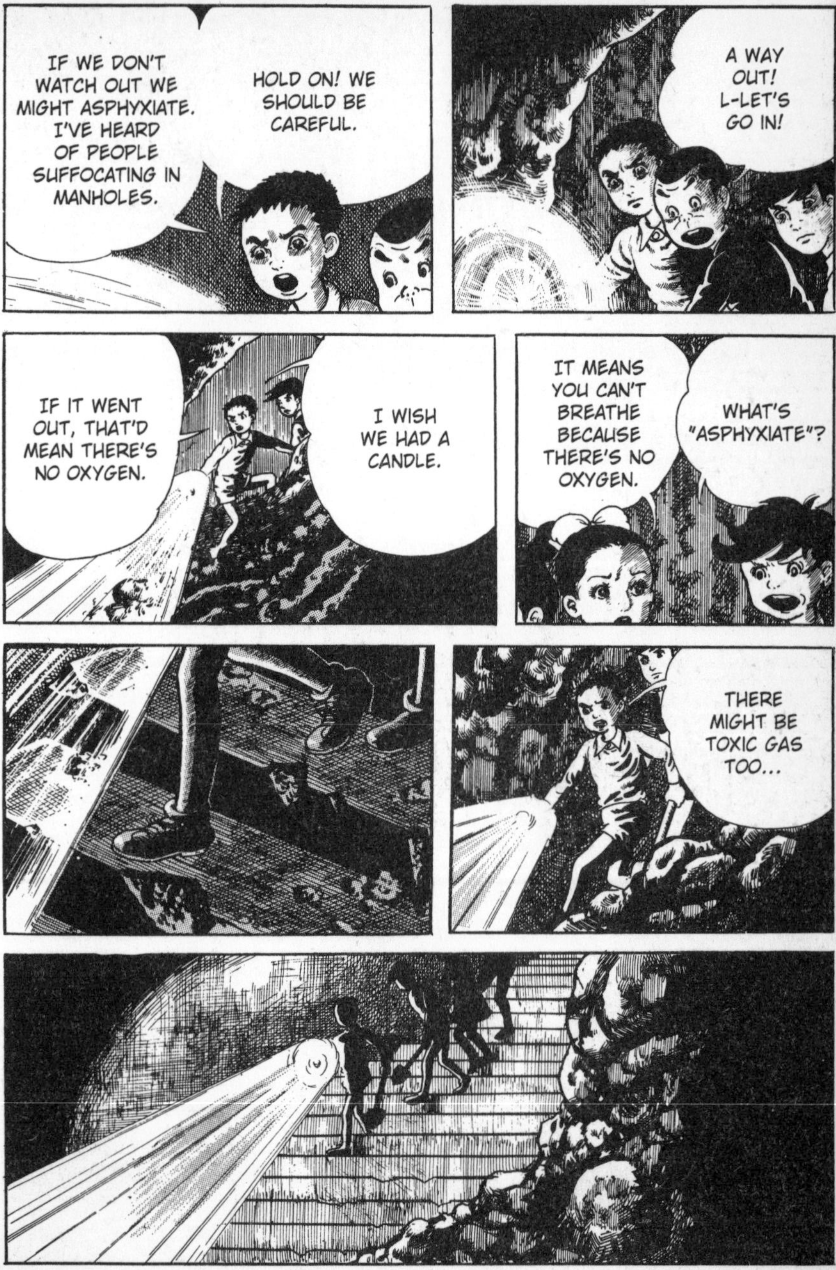
A WAY OUT! L-LET'S GO IN!
HOLD ON! WE SHOULD BE CAREFUL.
IF WE DON'T WATCH OUT WE MIGHT ASPHYXIATE. I'VE HEARD OF PEOPLE SUFFOCATING IN MANHOLES.
WHAT'S "ASPHYXIATE"?
IT MEANS YOU CAN'T BREATHE BECAUSE THERE'S NO OXYGEN.
I WISH WE HAD A CANDLE.
IF IT WENT OUT, THAT'D MEAN THERE'S NO OXYGEN.
THERE MIGHT BE TOXIC GAS TOO...

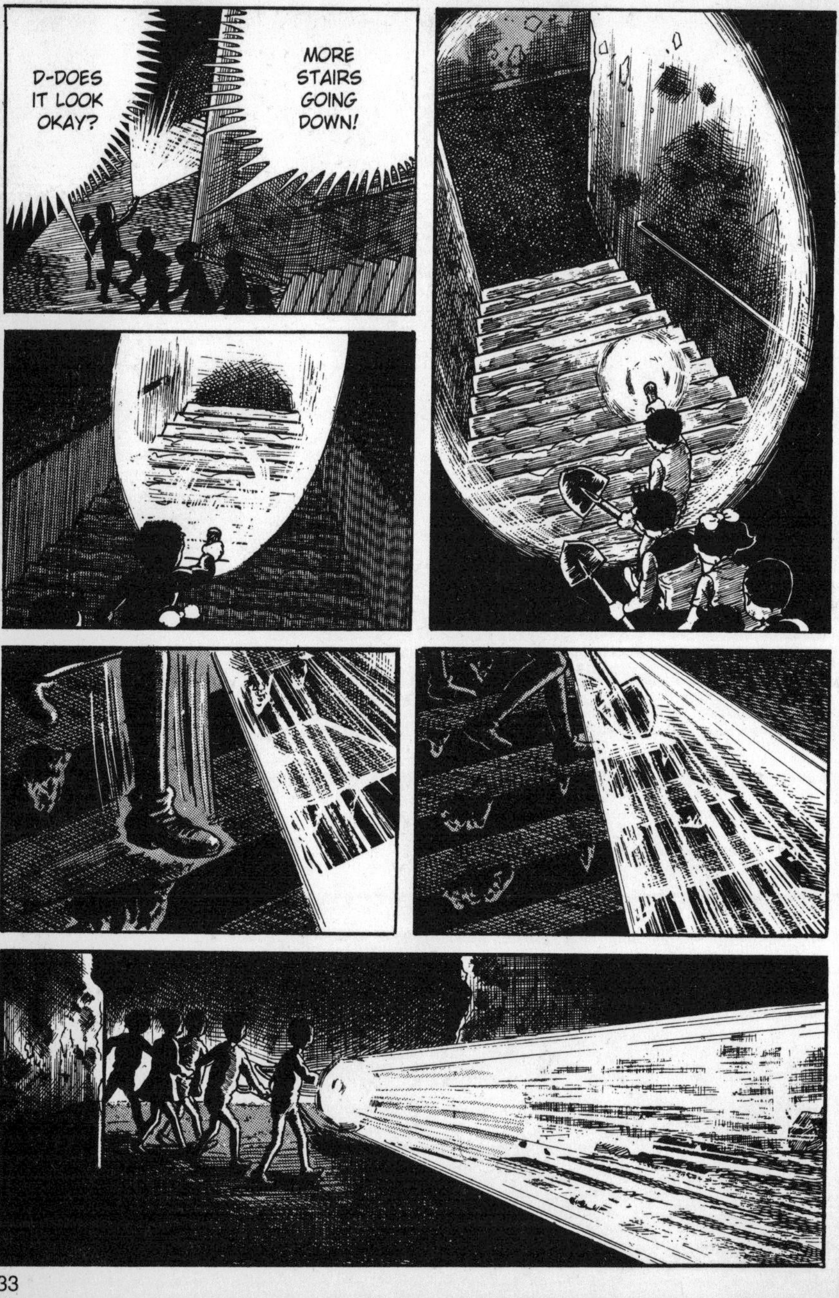
MORE STAIRS GOING DOWN!
D-DOES IT LOOK OKAY?

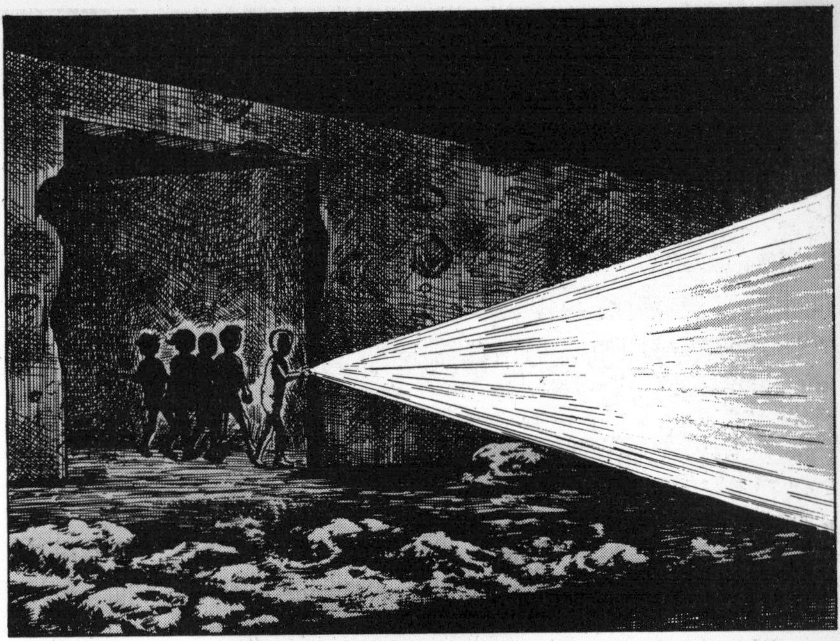

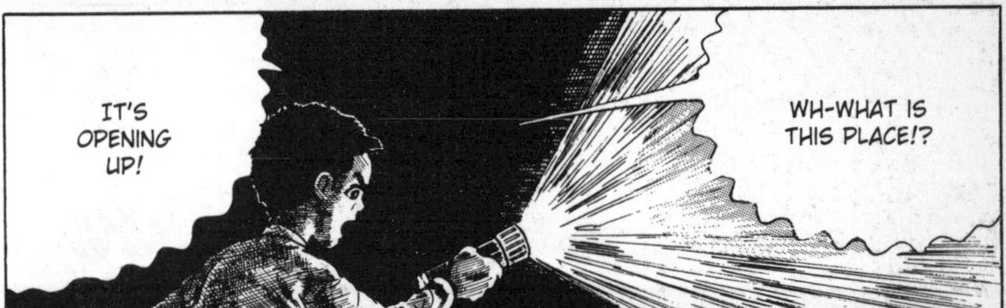
WH-WHAT IS THIS PLACE!?
IT'S OPENING UP!

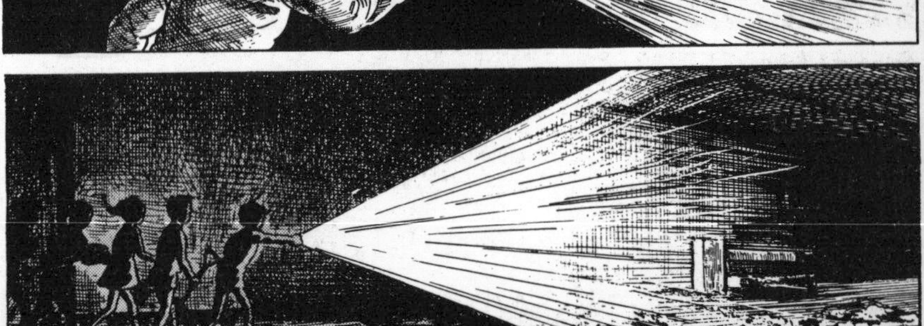

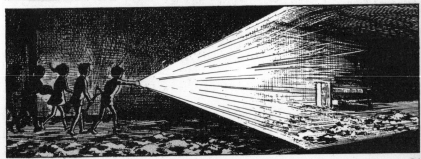

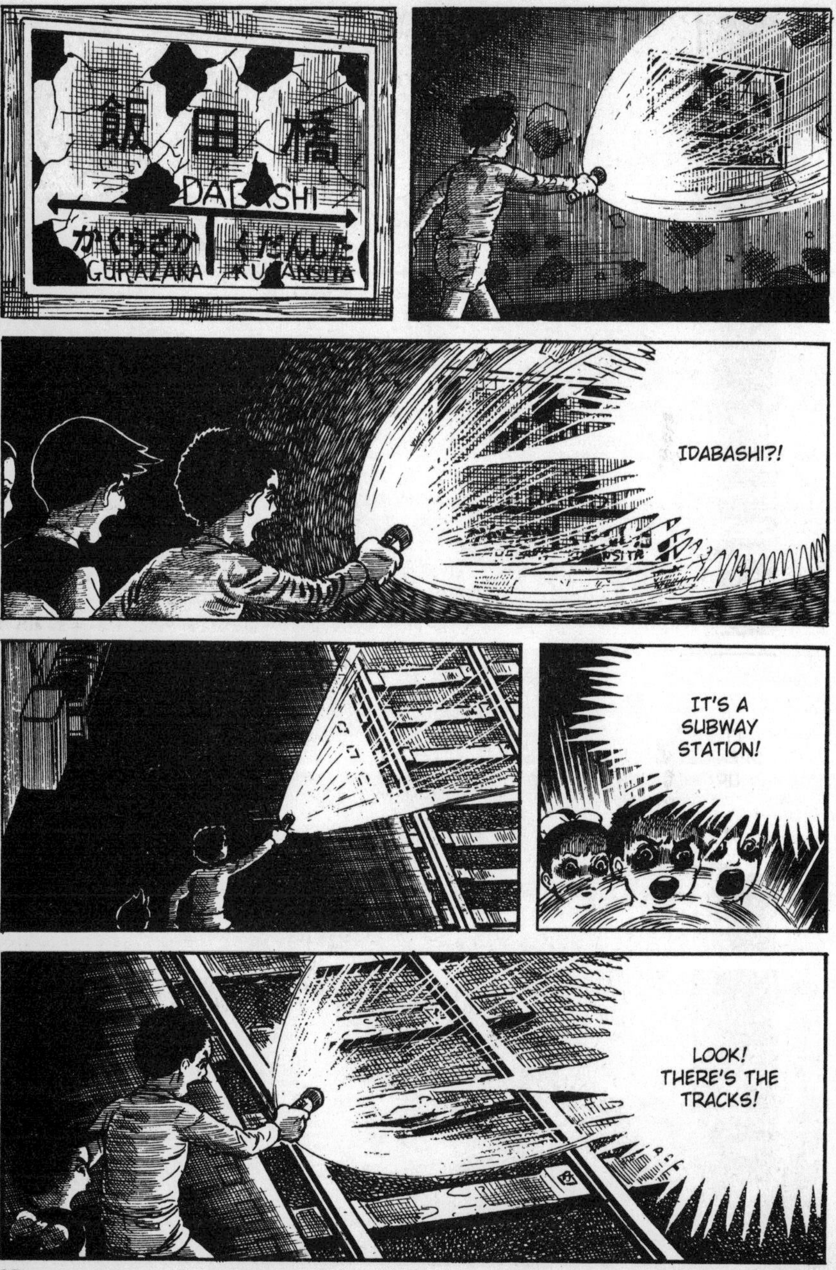
飯田橋
DABASHI
かぐらざか
GURAZAKA
くだんした
IDABASHI?!
IT'S A SUBWAY STATION!
LOOK! THERE'S THE TRACKS!

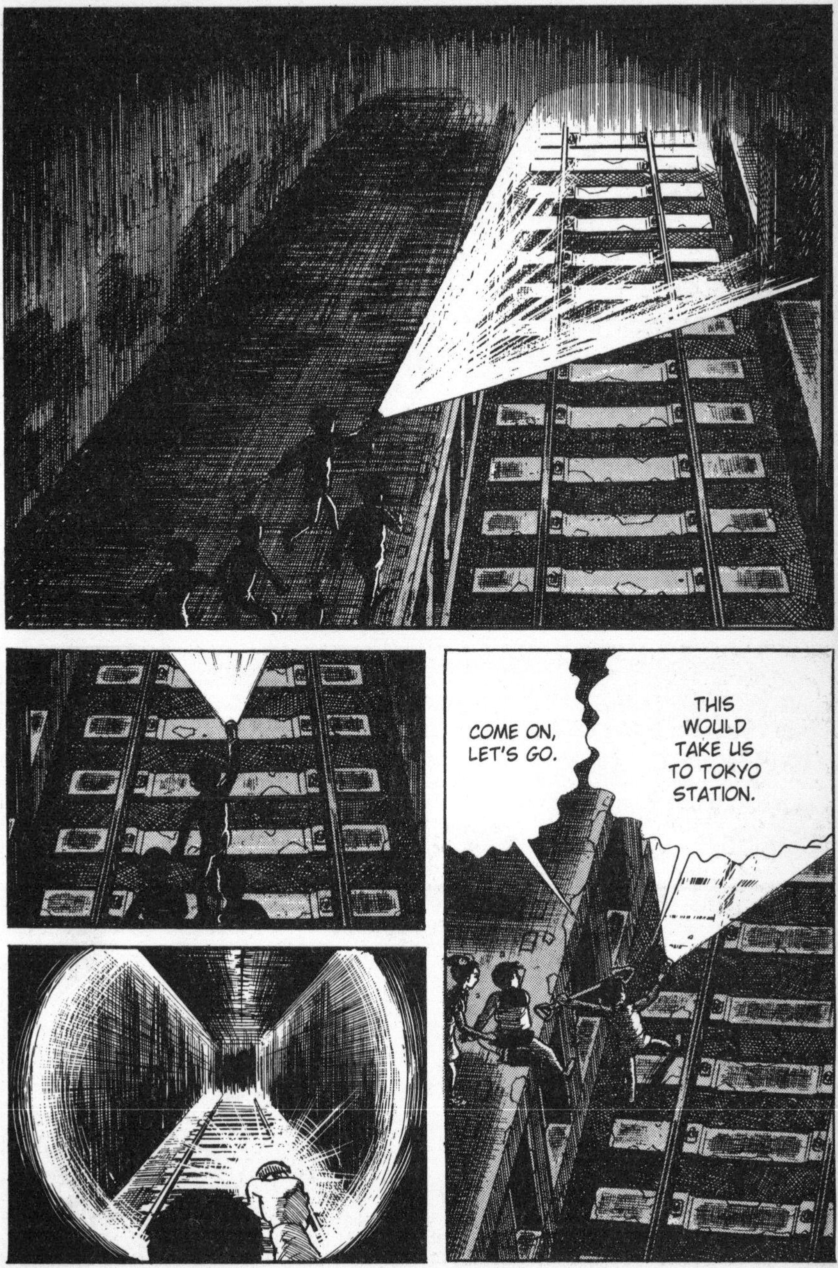
THIS WOULD TAKE US TO TOKYO STATION.
COME ON, LET'S GO.

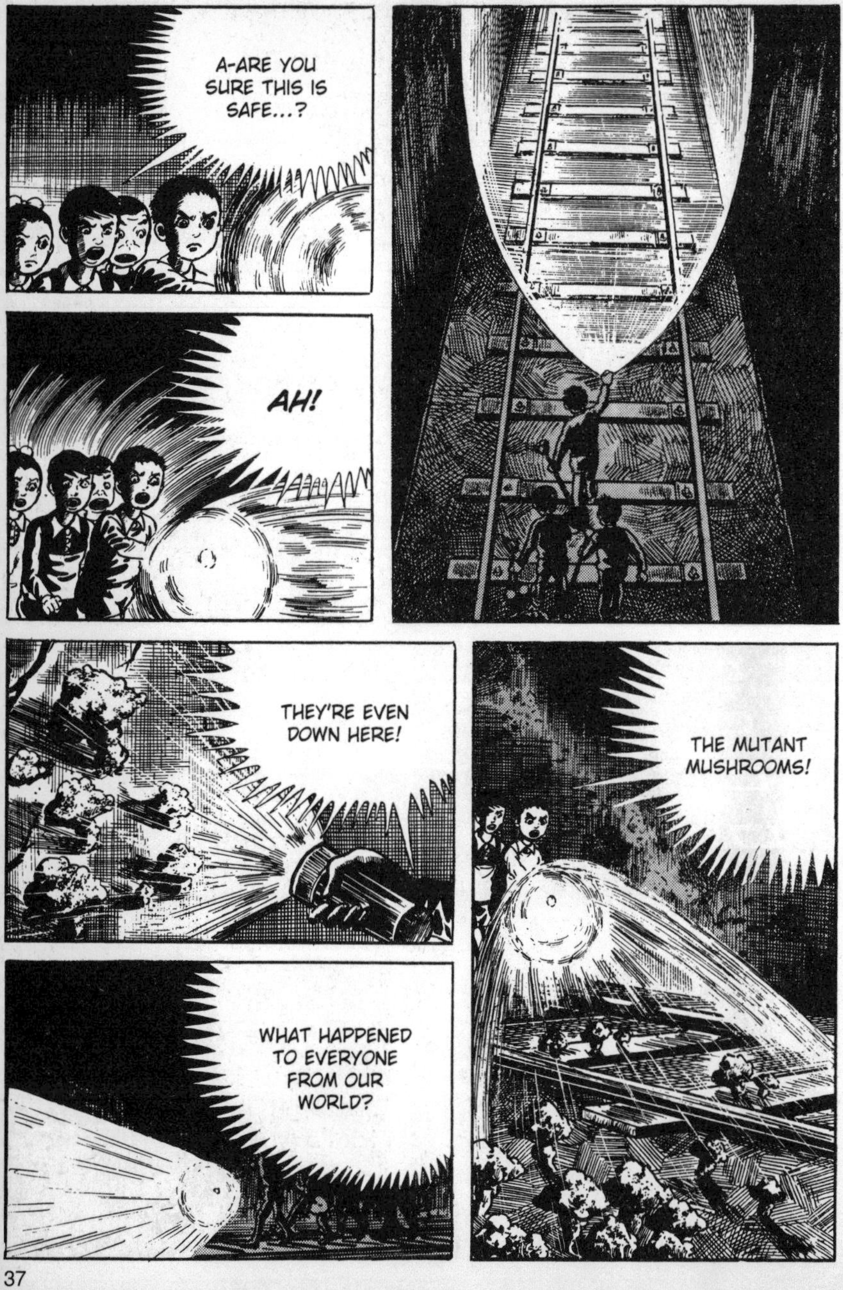
A-ARE YOU SURE THIS IS SAFE...?
AH!
THE MUTANT MUSHROOMS!
THEY'RE EVEN DOWN HERE!
WHAT HAPPENED TO EVERYONE FROM OUR WORLD?

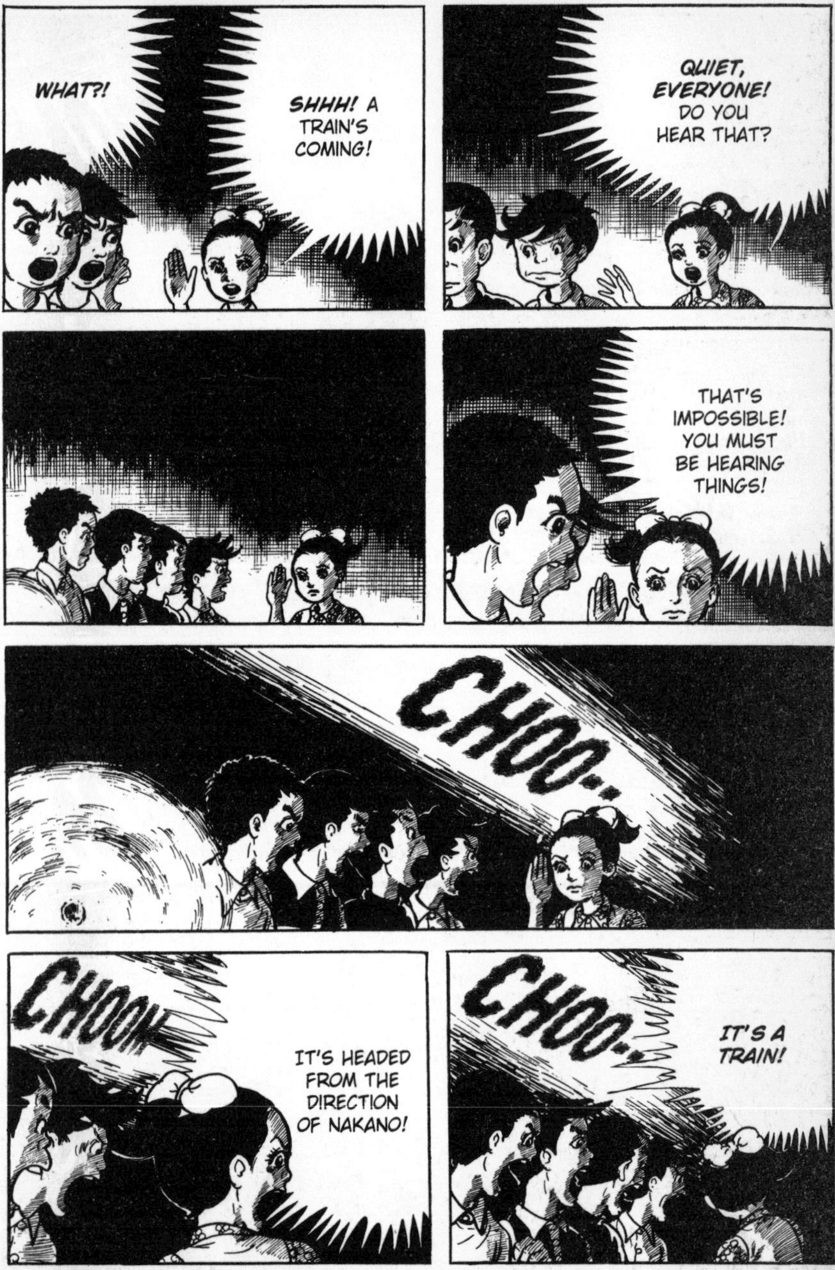
QUIET, EVERYONE! DO YOU HEAR THAT?
WHAT?!
SHHH! A TRAIN'S COMING!
THAT'S IMPOSSIBLE! YOU MUST BE HEARING THINGS!
CHOO...
CHOO...
IT'S A TRAIN!
CHOOH
IT'S HEADED FROM THE DIRECTION OF NAKANO!

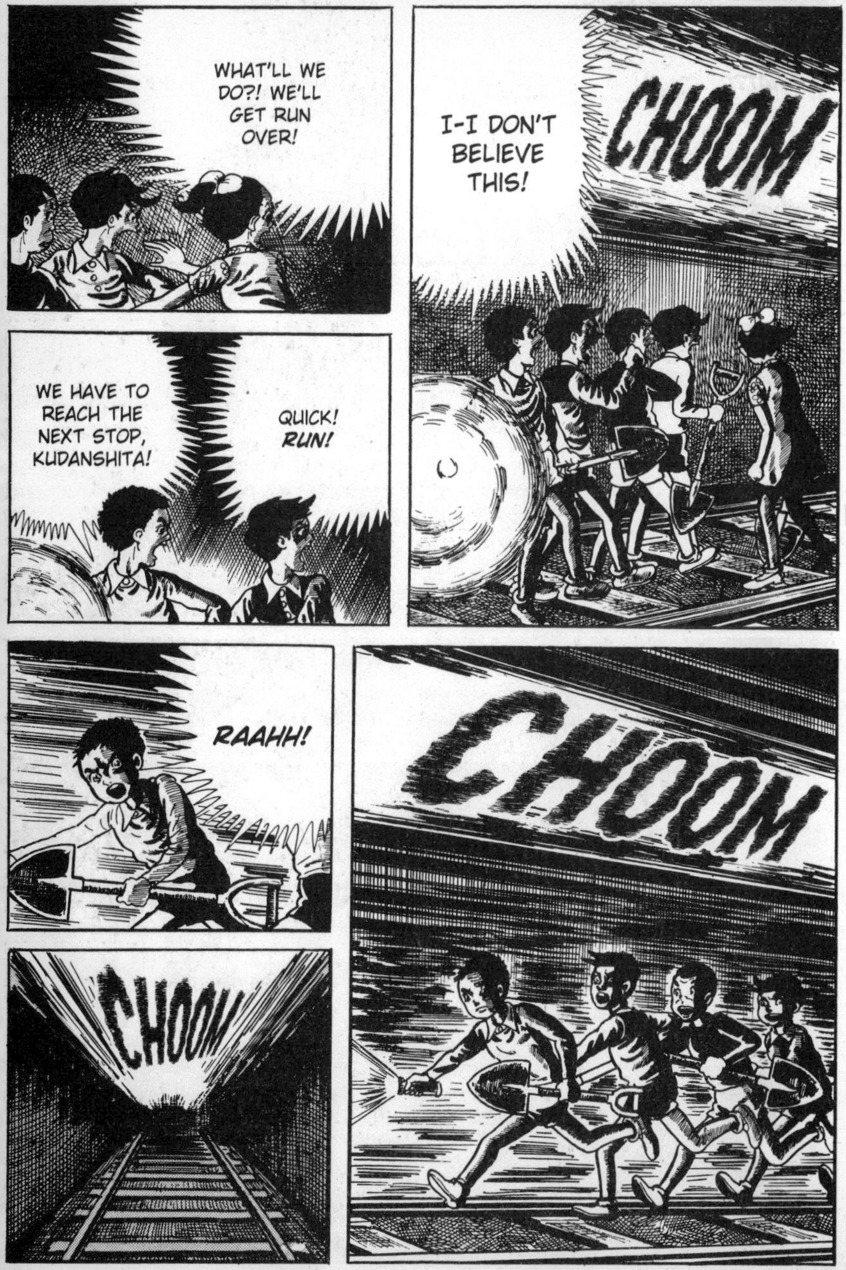
CHOOM
I-I DON'T BELIEVE THIS!
WHAT'LL WE DO?! WE'LL GET RUN OVER!
QUICK! *RUN!*
WE HAVE TO REACH THE NEXT STOP, KUDANSHITA!
CHOOM
RAAHH!
CHOOM

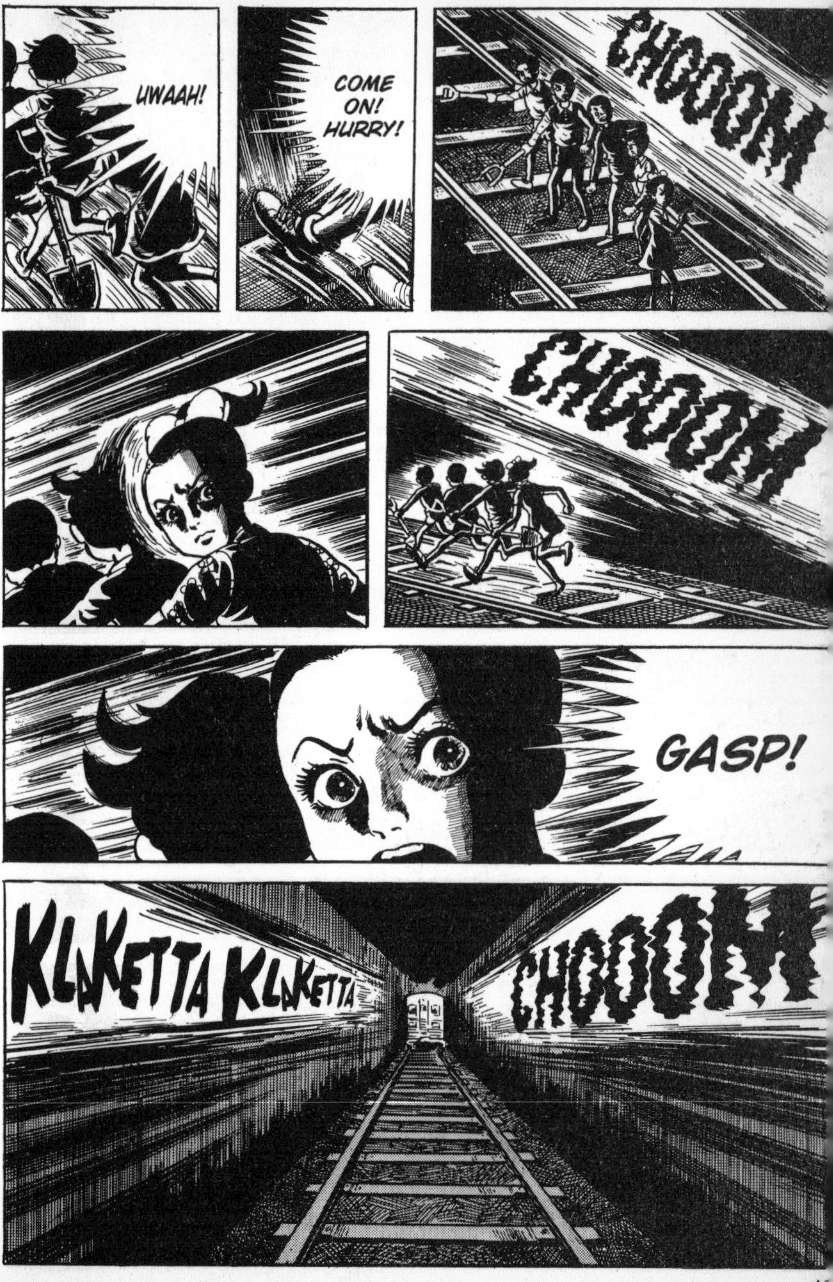
CHOOOM
COME ON! HURRY!
UWAAH!
CHOOOM
GASP!
CHOOOM
KLAKETTA KLAKETTA

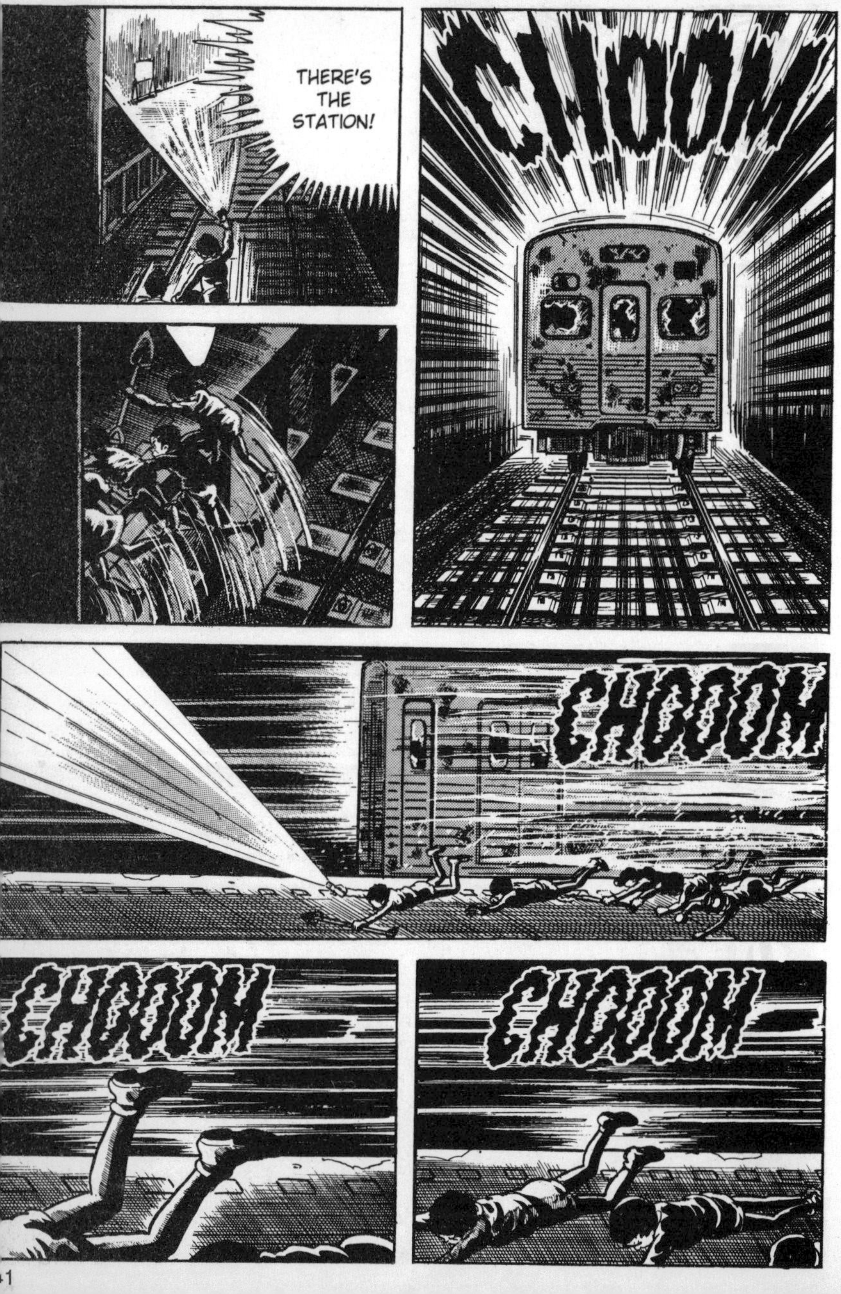
CHOOM
THERE'S THE STATION!
CHOOOM
CHOOOM
CHOOOM

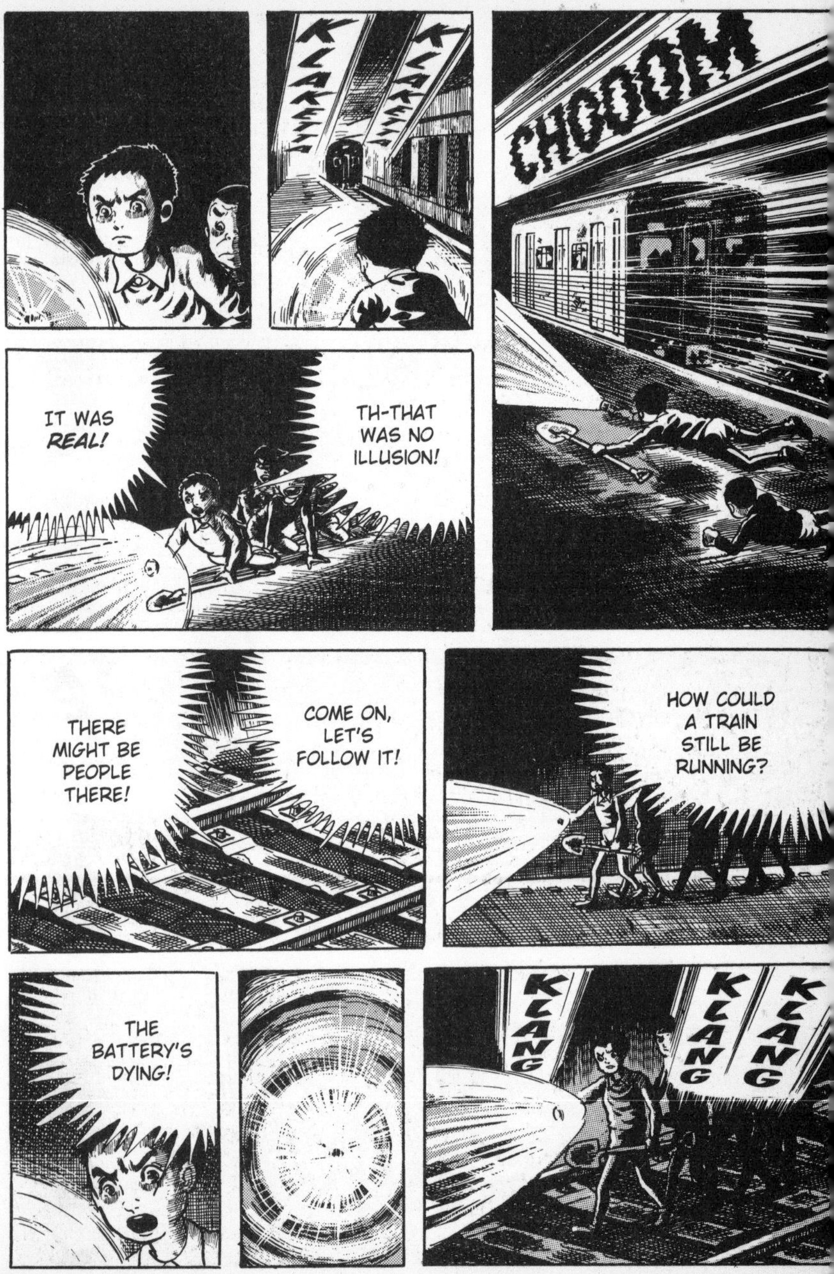
CHOOOM
KLAKETTA KLAKETTA
TH-THAT WAS NO ILLUSION!
IT WAS REAL!
HOW COULD A TRAIN STILL BE RUNNING?
COME ON, LET'S FOLLOW IT!
THERE MIGHT BE PEOPLE THERE!
KLANG KLANG KLANG
THE BATTERY'S DYING!

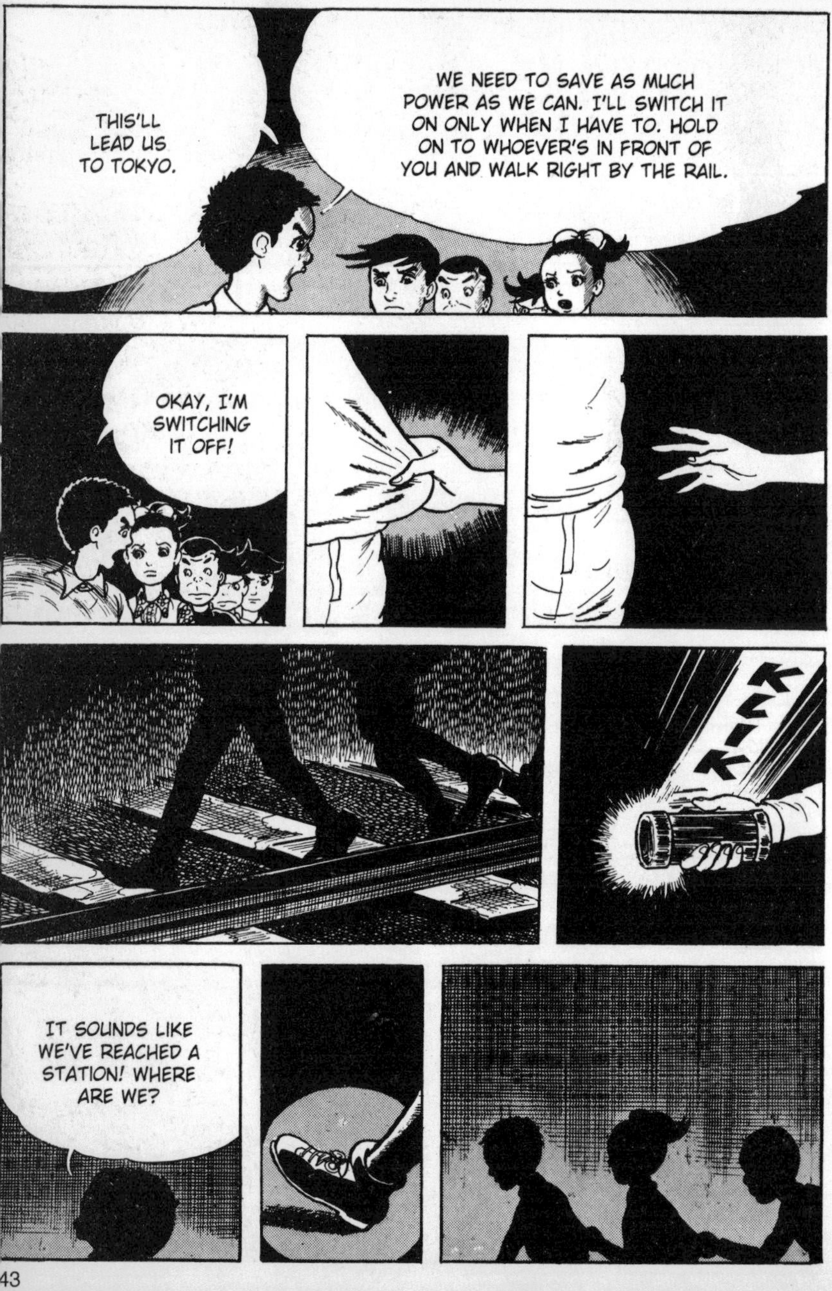
THIS'LL LEAD US TO TOKYO.
WE NEED TO SAVE AS MUCH POWER AS WE CAN. I'LL SWITCH IT ON ONLY WHEN I HAVE TO. HOLD ON TO WHOEVER'S IN FRONT OF YOU AND WALK RIGHT BY THE RAIL.
OKAY, I'M SWITCHING IT OFF!
KLIK
IT SOUNDS LIKE WE'VE REACHED A STATION! WHERE ARE WE?

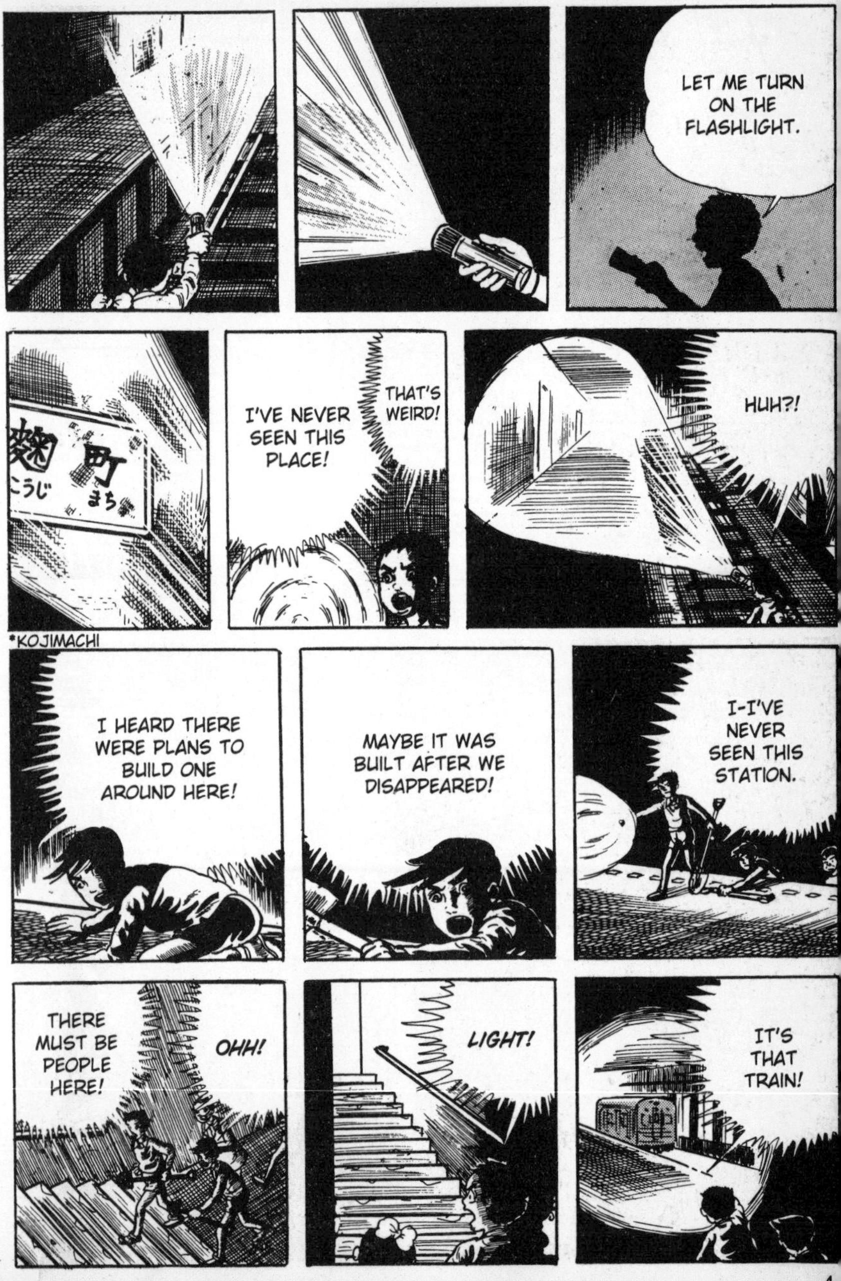
LET ME TURN ON THE FLASHLIGHT.
HUH?!
THAT'S WEIRD!
I'VE NEVER SEEN THIS PLACE!
麴町
こうじ まち
*KOJIMACHI
I-I'VE NEVER SEEN THIS STATION.
MAYBE IT WAS BUILT AFTER WE DISAPPEARED!
I HEARD THERE WERE PLANS TO BUILD ONE AROUND HERE!
IT'S THAT TRAIN!
LIGHT!
OHH!
THERE MUST BE PEOPLE HERE!

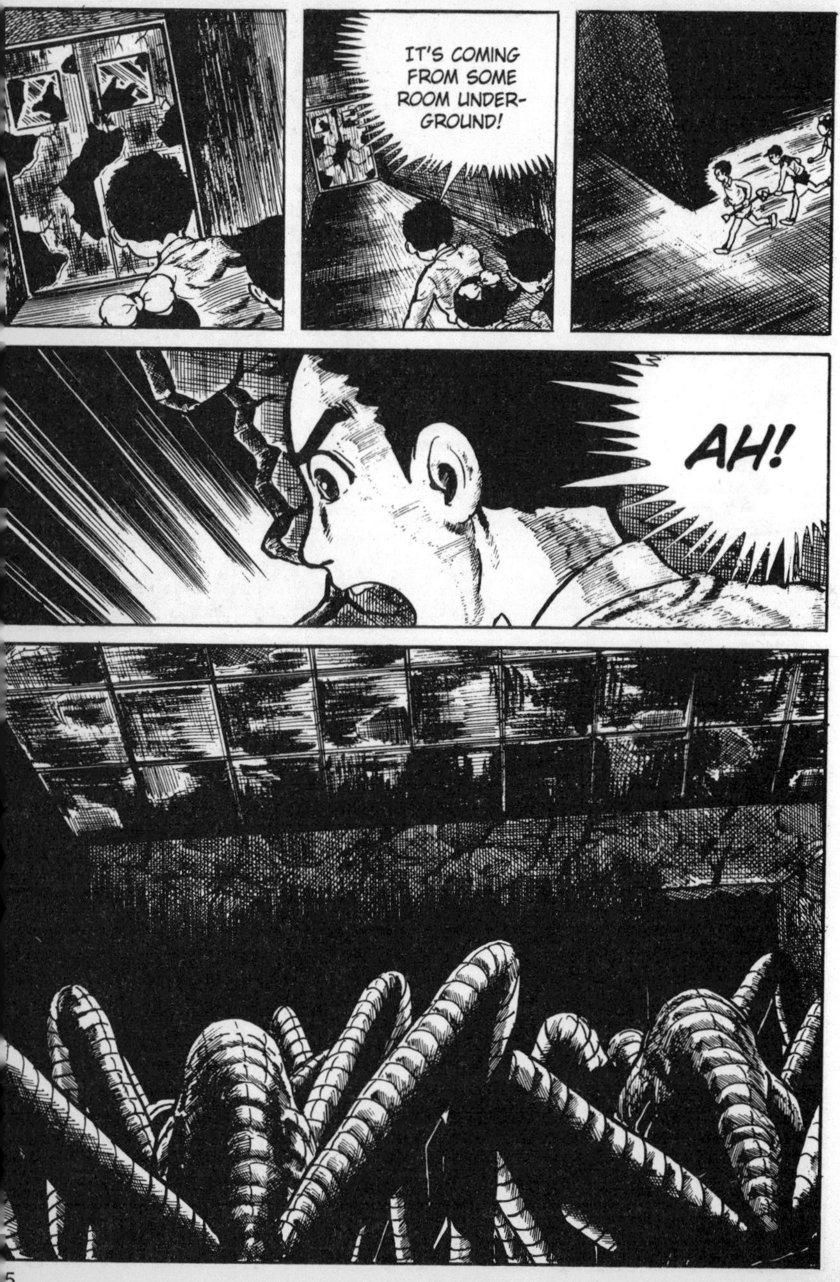
IT'S COMING FROM SOME ROOM UNDER-GROUND!
AH!

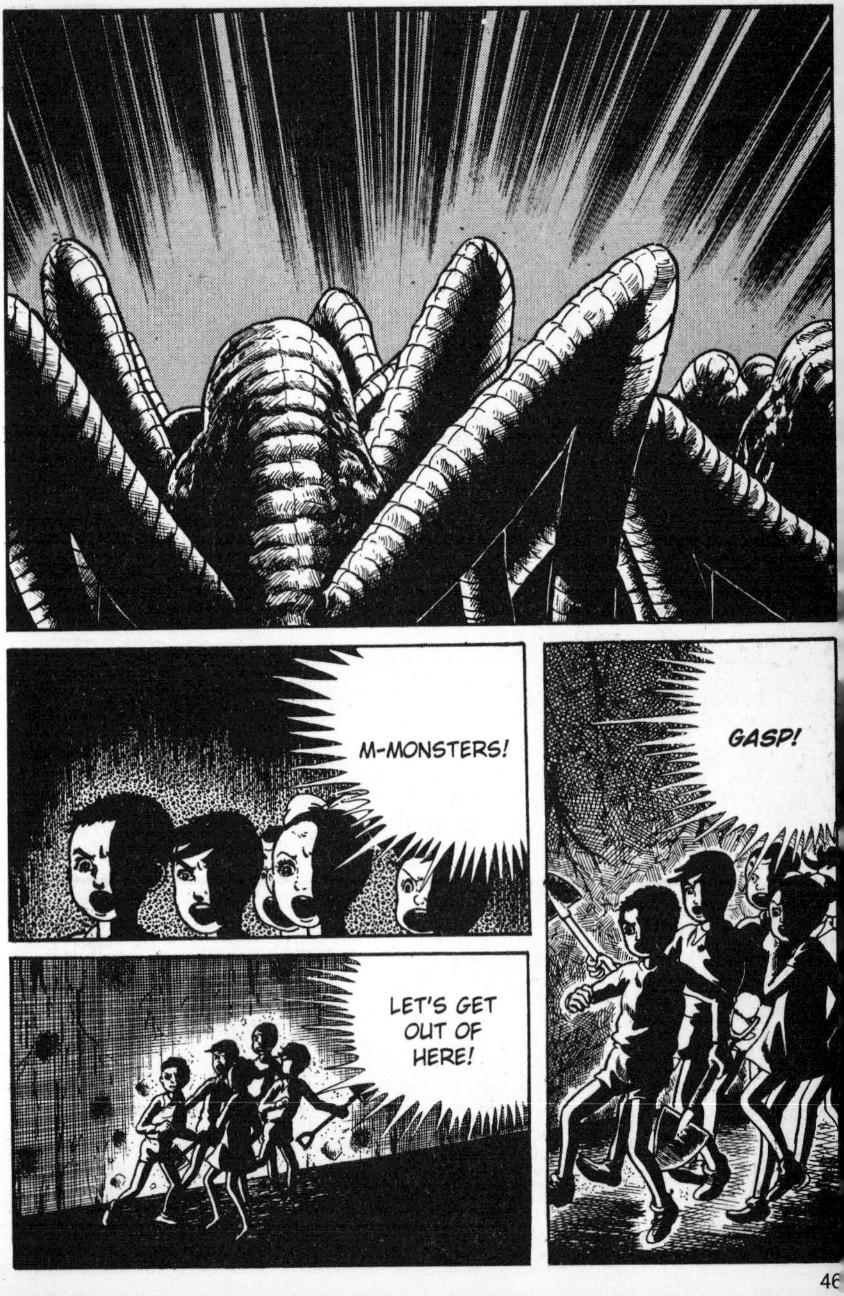
GASP!
M-MONSTERS!
LET'S GET OUT OF HERE!

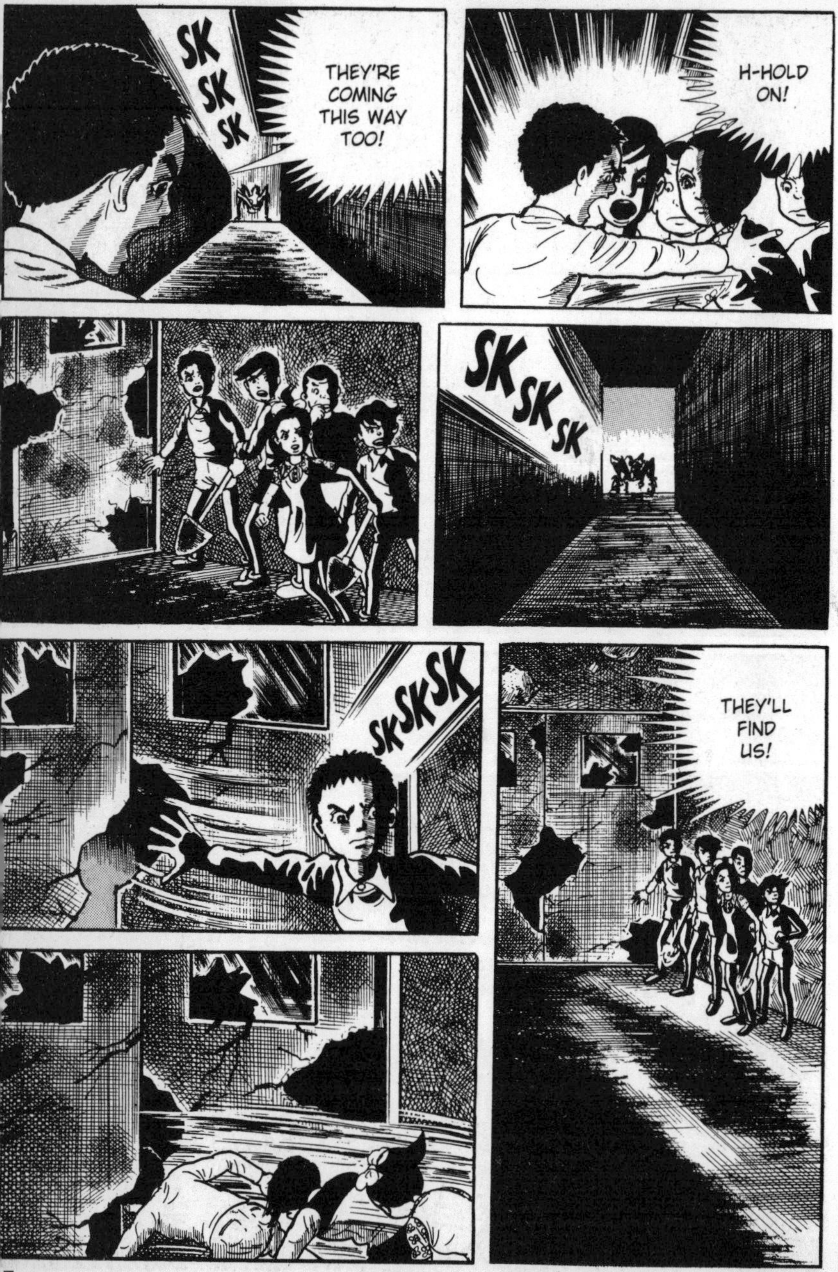
SK
SK
SK
THEY'RE COMING THIS WAY TOO!
H-HOLD ON!
SK SK SK
SKSKSK
THEY'LL FIND US!

4

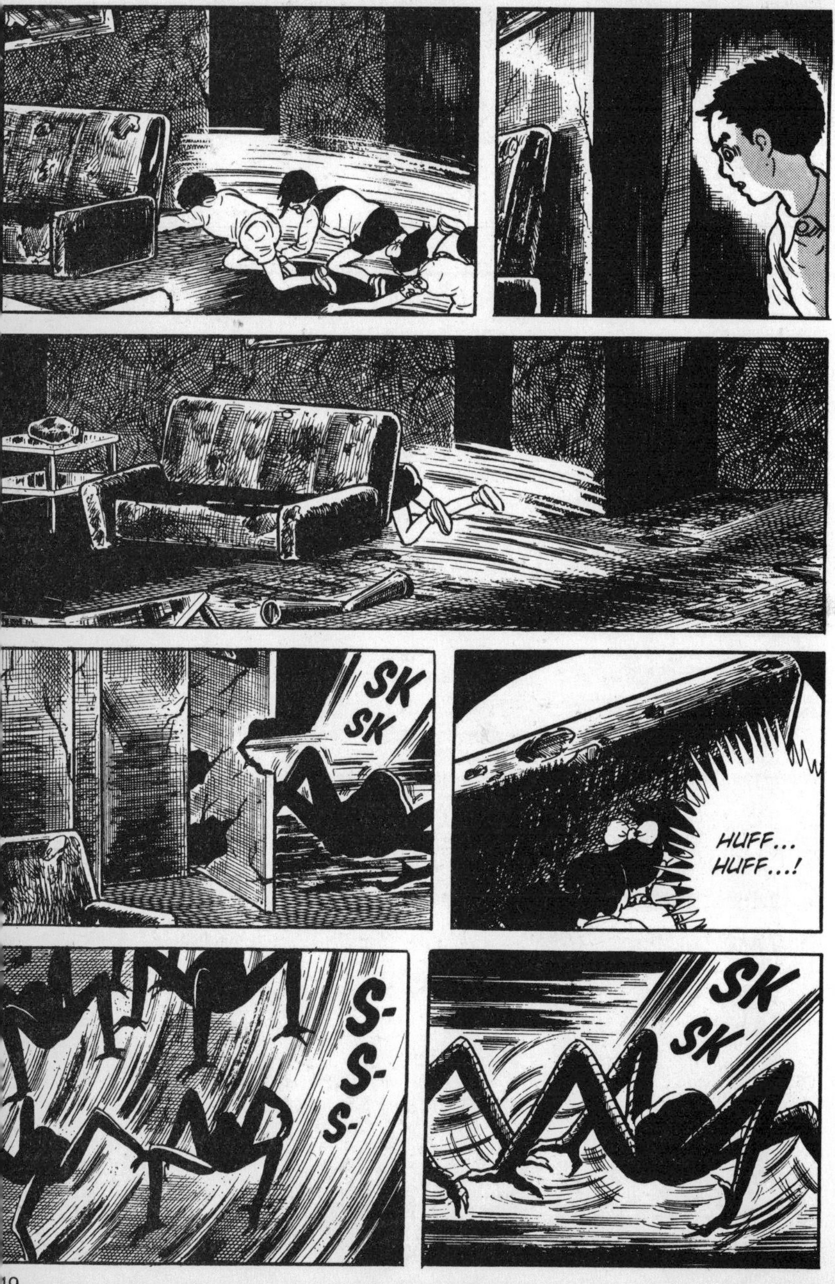
HUFF... HUFF...!
SK SK
SK SK
S-S-S-

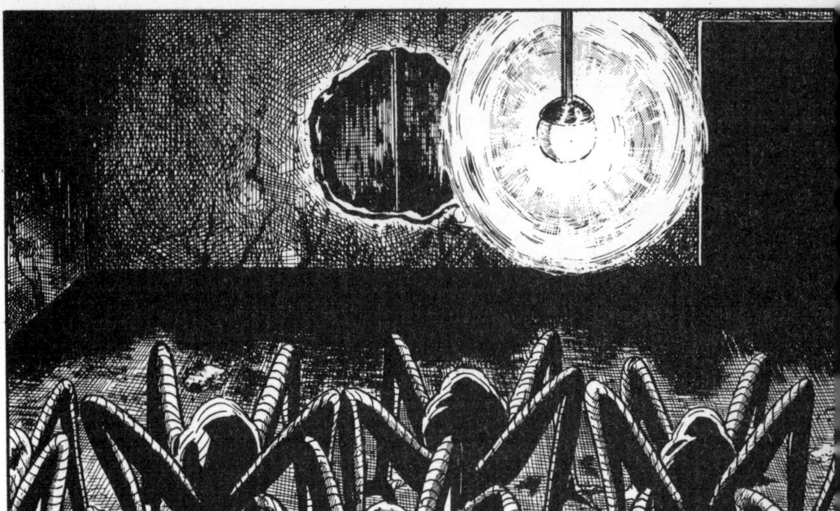

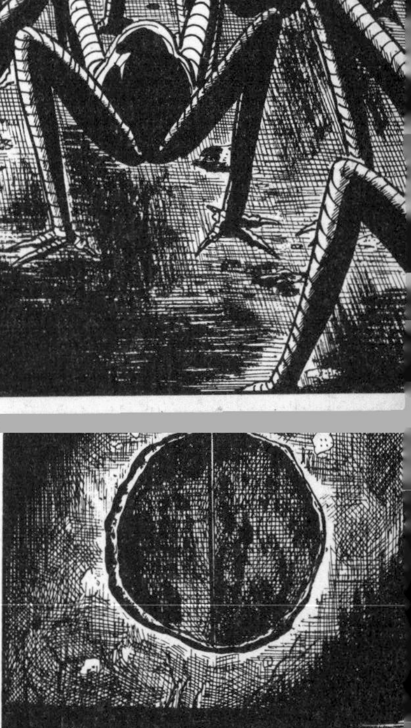

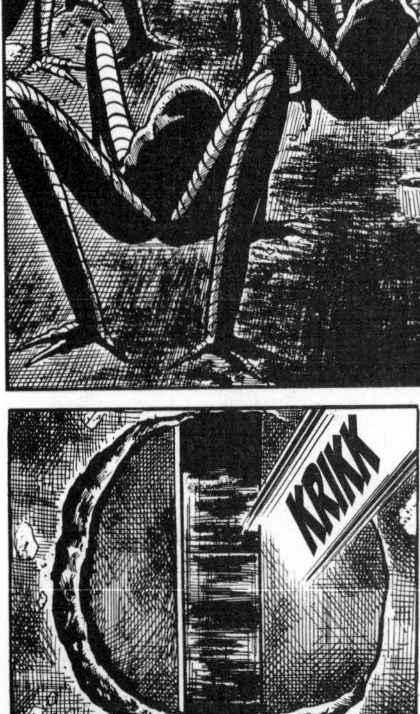
KRIKK

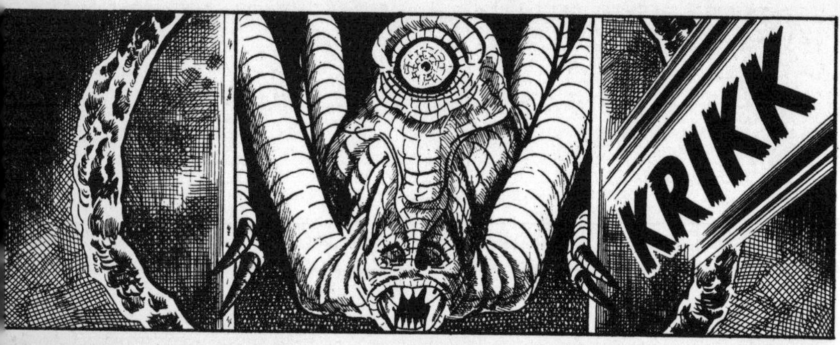
KRIKK

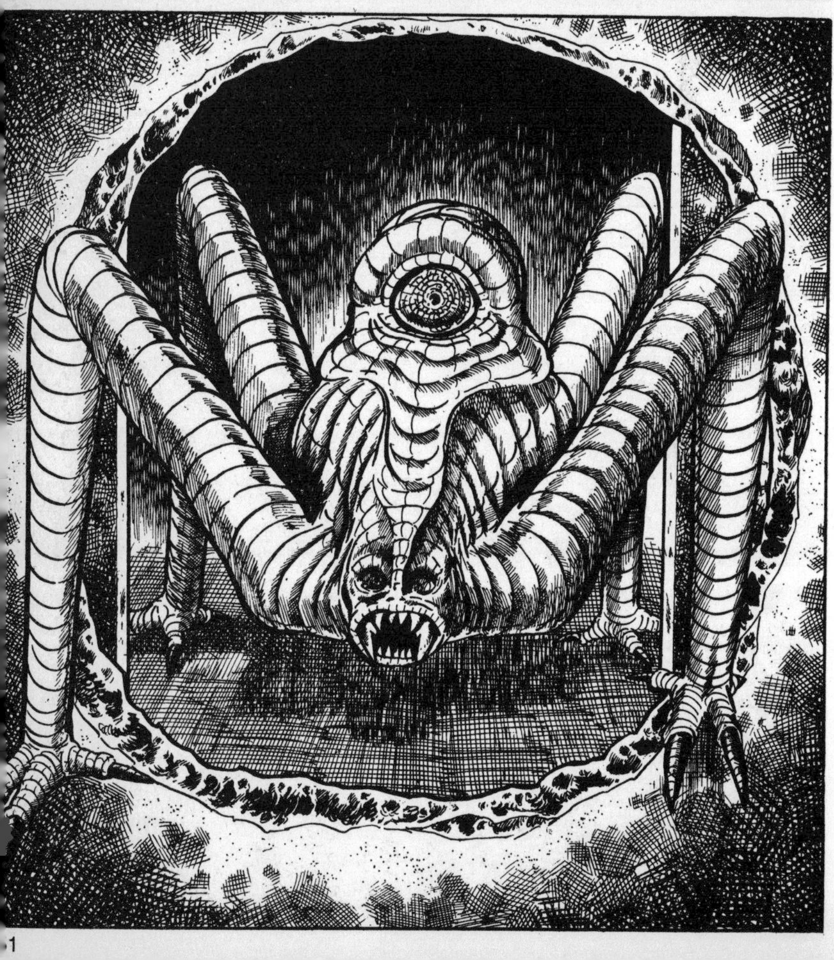

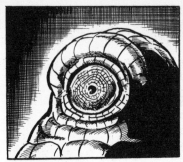

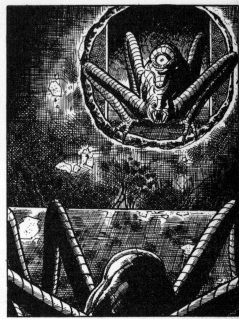

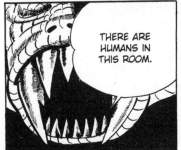

THERE ARE HUMANS IN THIS ROOM.
HUMANS?
THAT'S RIGHT!
I FEEL THEIR PRESENCE.
YOU MEAN THESE ONES.

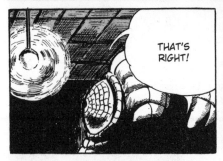

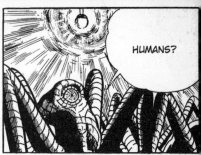

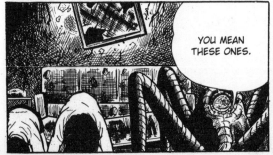

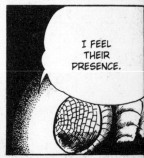

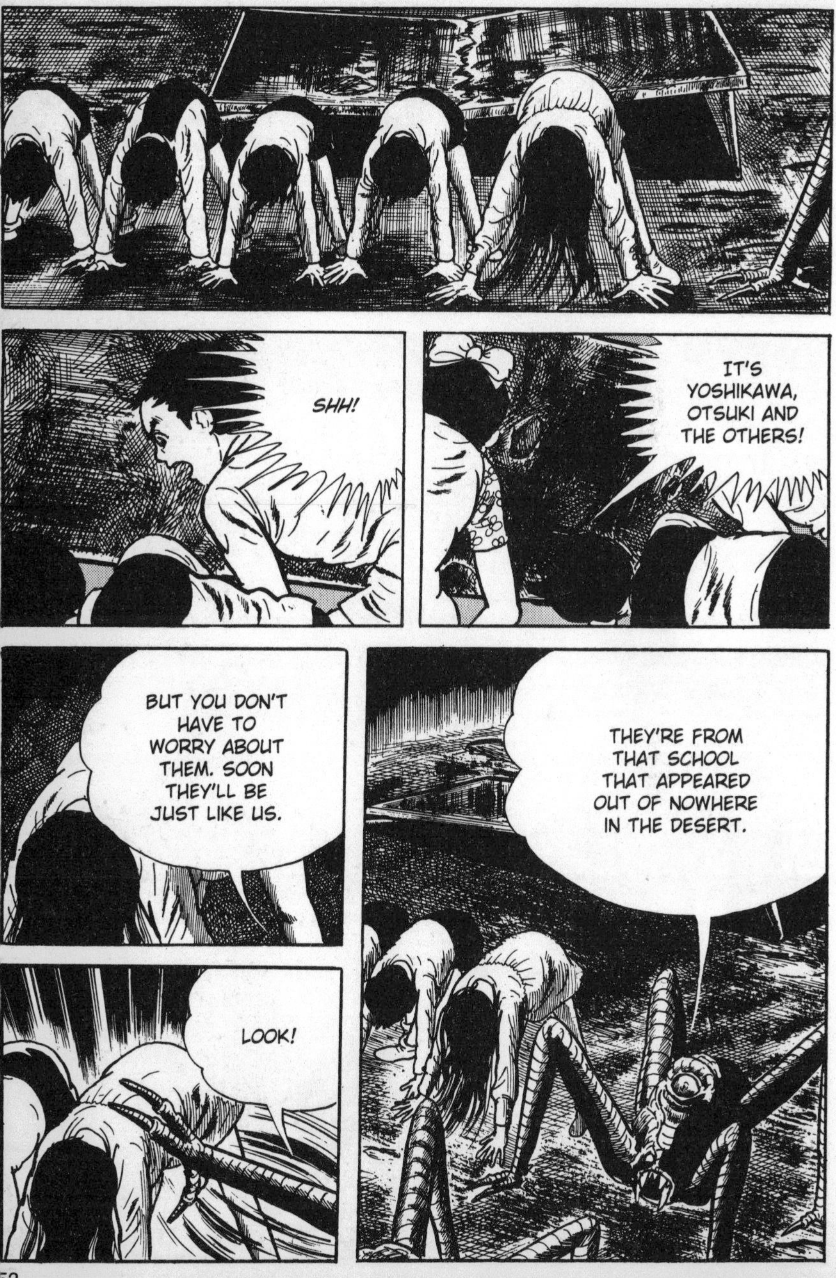
IT'S YOSHIKAWA, OTSUKI AND THE OTHERS!
SHH!
THEY'RE FROM THAT SCHOOL THAT APPEARED OUT OF NOWHERE IN THE DESERT.
BUT YOU DON'T HAVE TO WORRY ABOUT THEM. SOON THEY'LL BE JUST LIKE US.
LOOK!

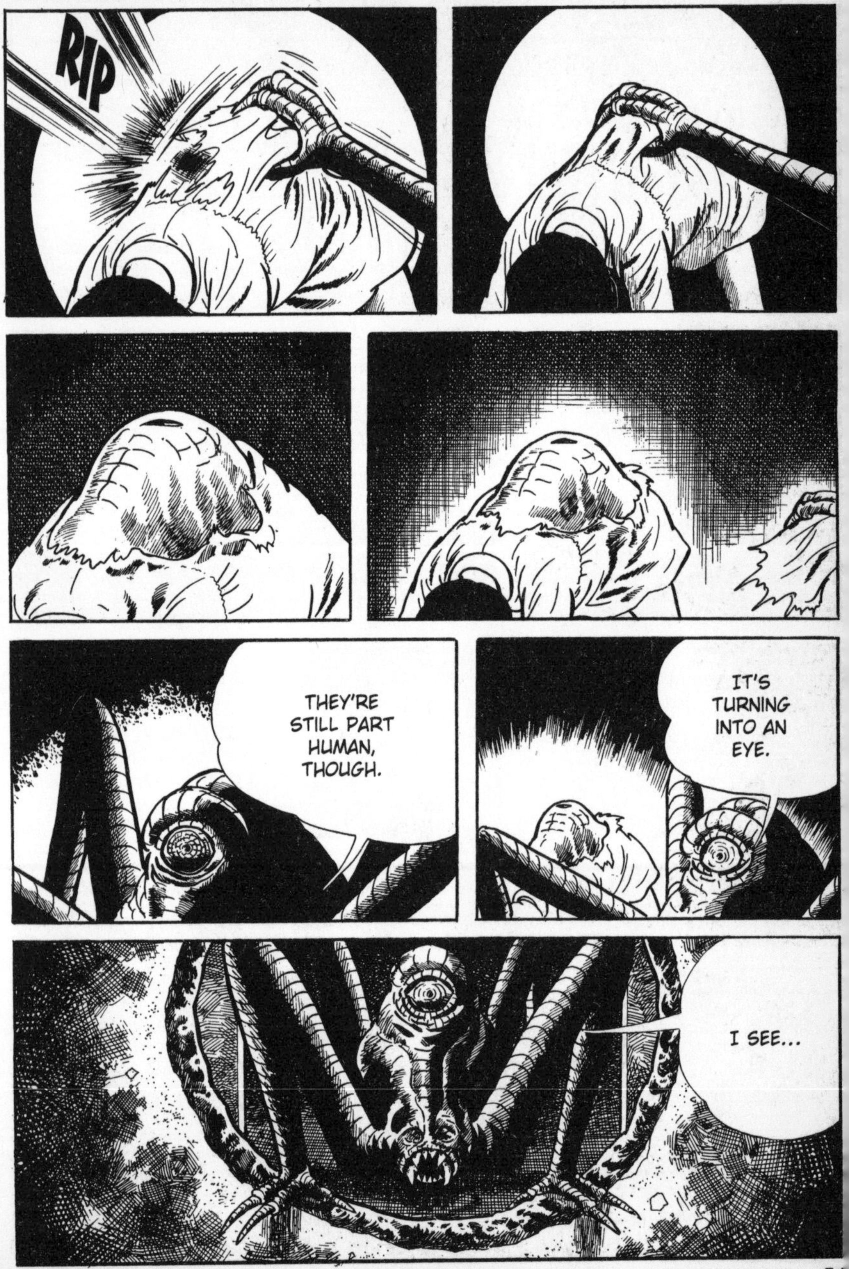
RIP
IT'S TURNING INTO AN EYE.
THEY'RE STILL PART HUMAN, THOUGH.
I SEE...

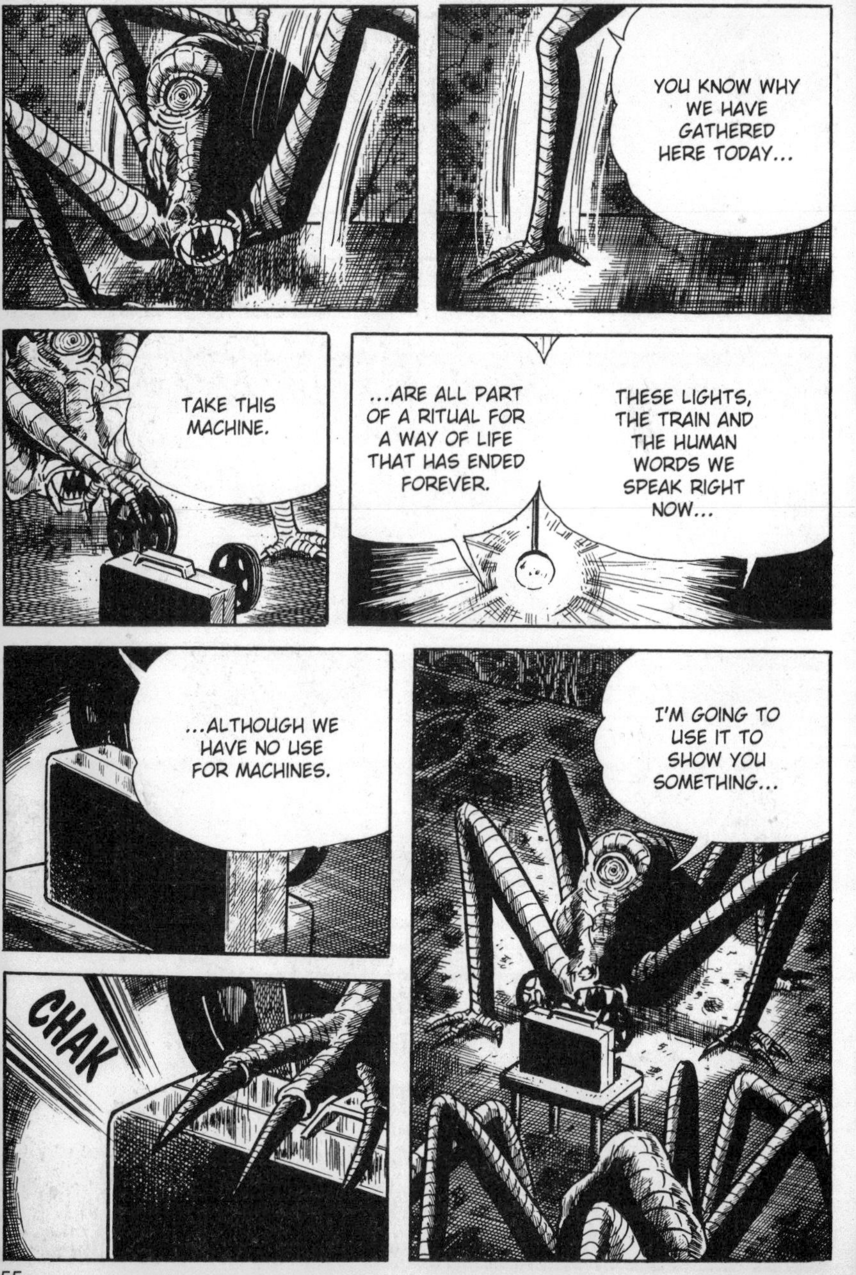
YOU KNOW WHY WE HAVE GATHERED HERE TODAY...
THESE LIGHTS, THE TRAIN AND THE HUMAN WORDS WE SPEAK RIGHT NOW...
...ARE ALL PART OF A RITUAL FOR A WAY OF LIFE THAT HAS ENDED FOREVER.
TAKE THIS MACHINE.
I'M GOING TO USE IT TO SHOW YOU SOMETHING...
...ALTHOUGH WE HAVE NO USE FOR MACHINES.
CHAK

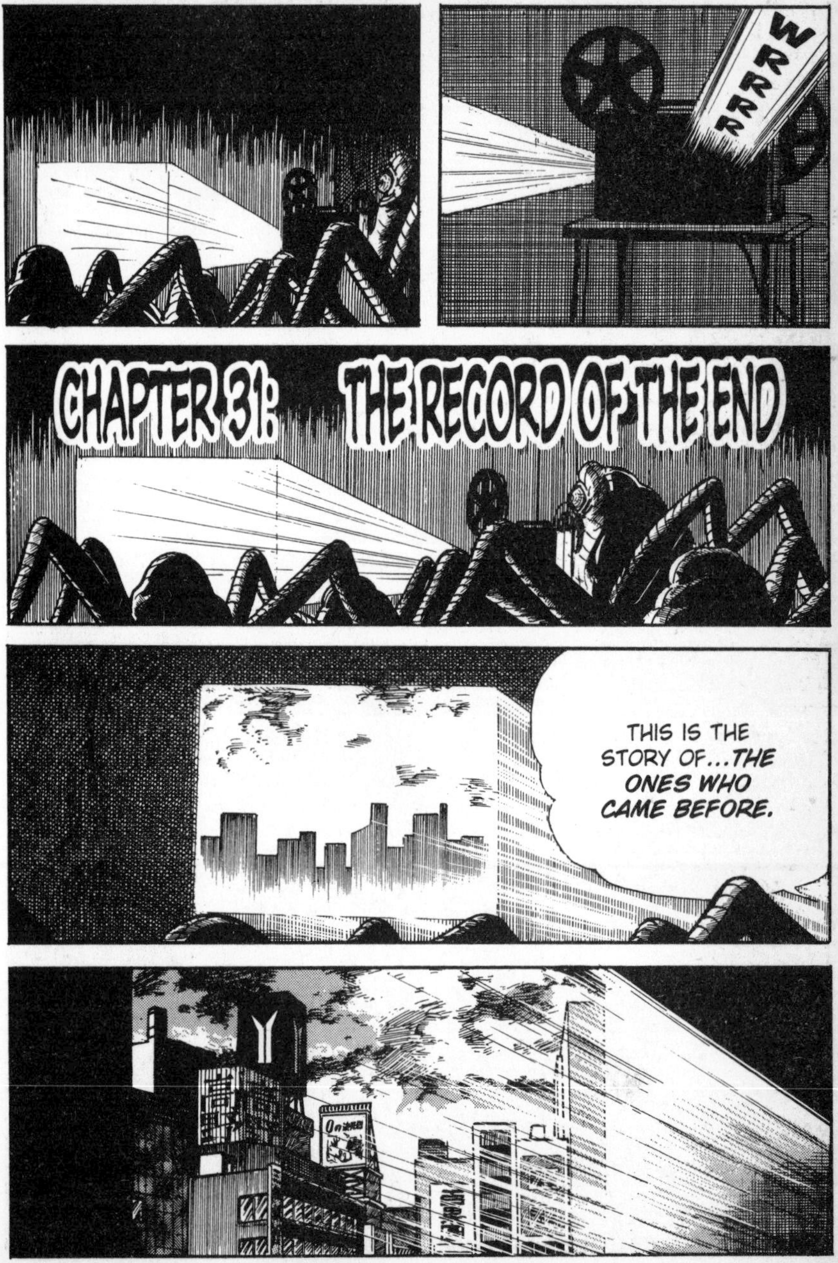
WRRRR
CHAPTER 31: THE RECORD OF THE END
THIS IS THE STORY OF...*THE ONES WHO CAME BEFORE.*

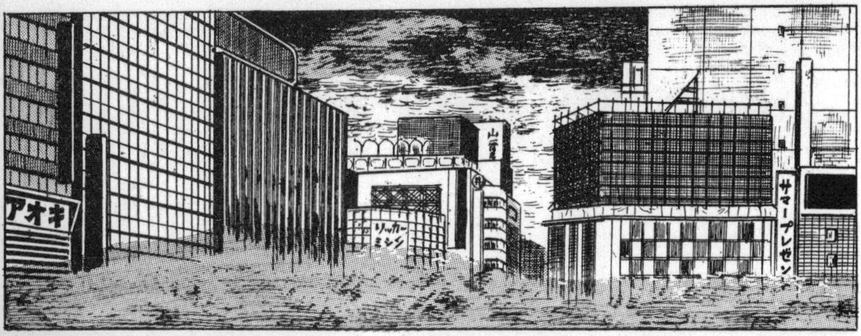
アオキ
リッカーミシン
サマープレゼン
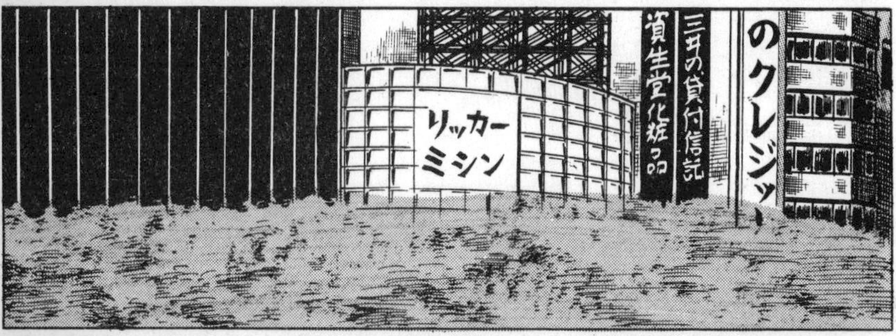
リッカーミシン
資生堂化粧品
三井の貸付信託
のクレジッ
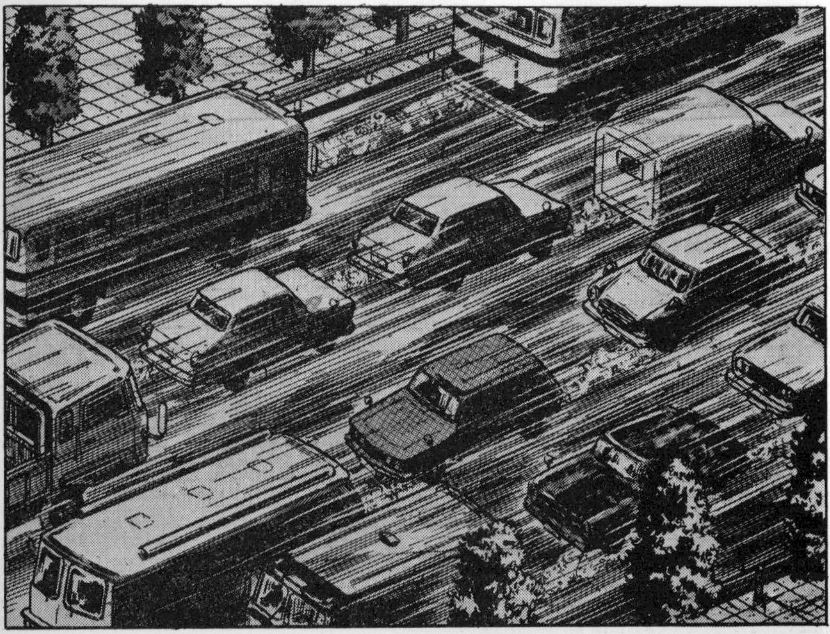

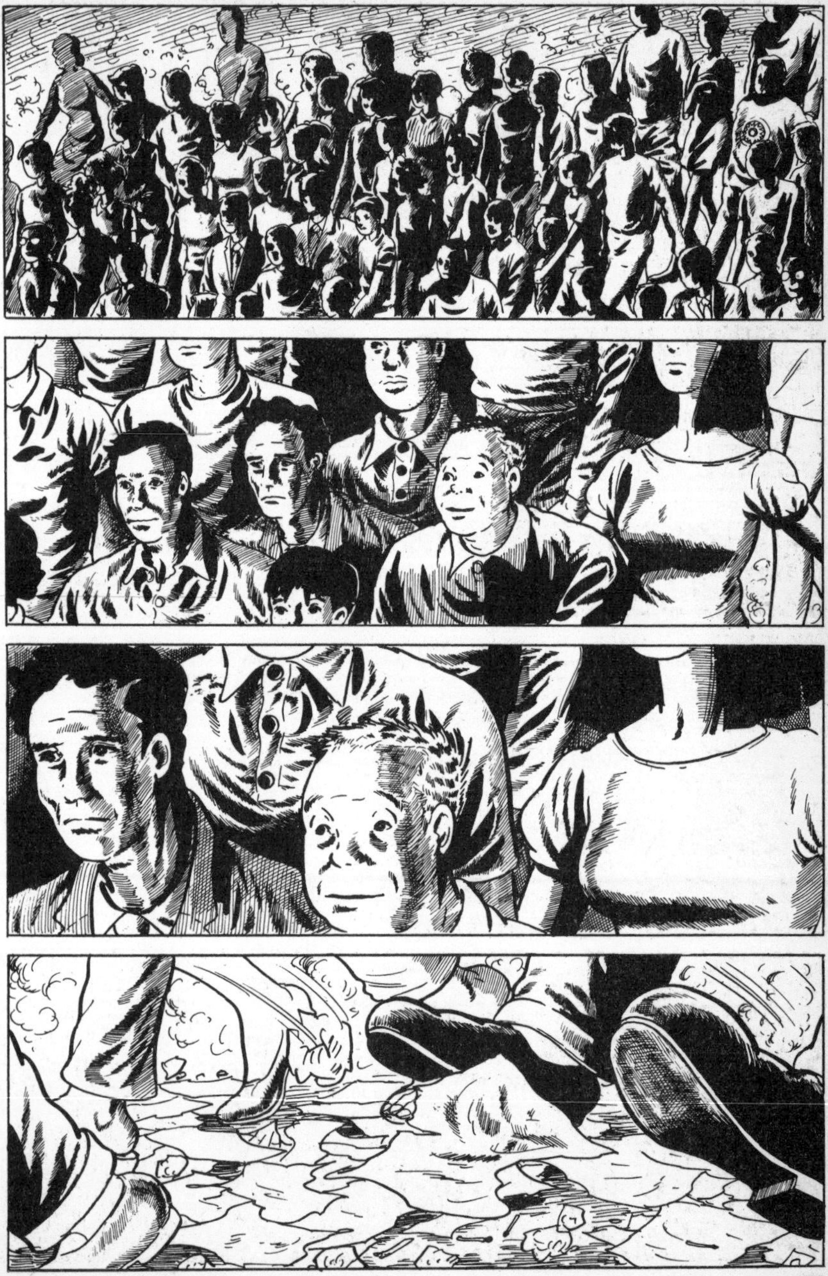

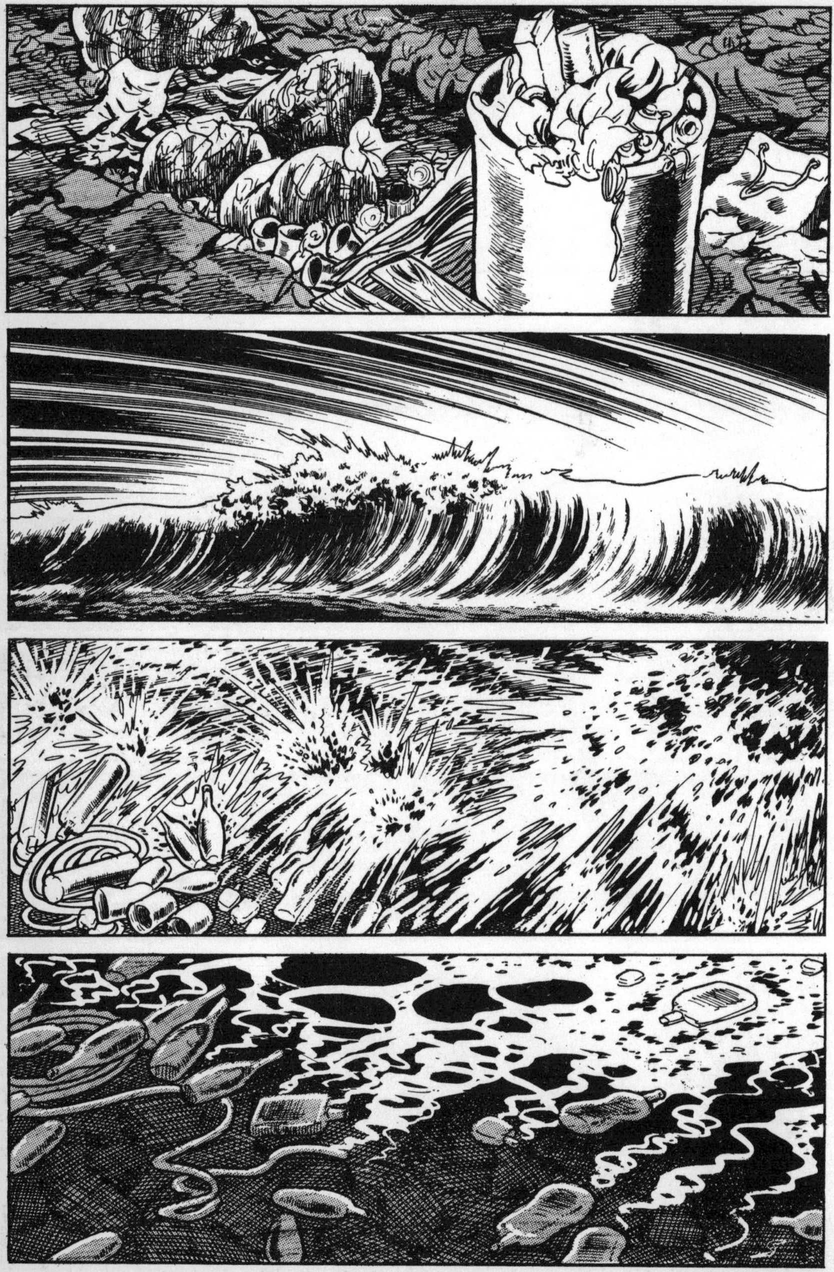

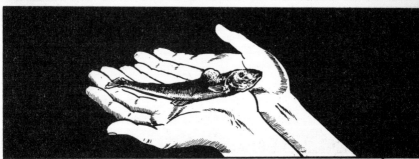

Daikyo News

Coral-
Eating
Starfish
Threaten
Reefs
Worldwide

Another
Mother
Murders
Her
Baby!

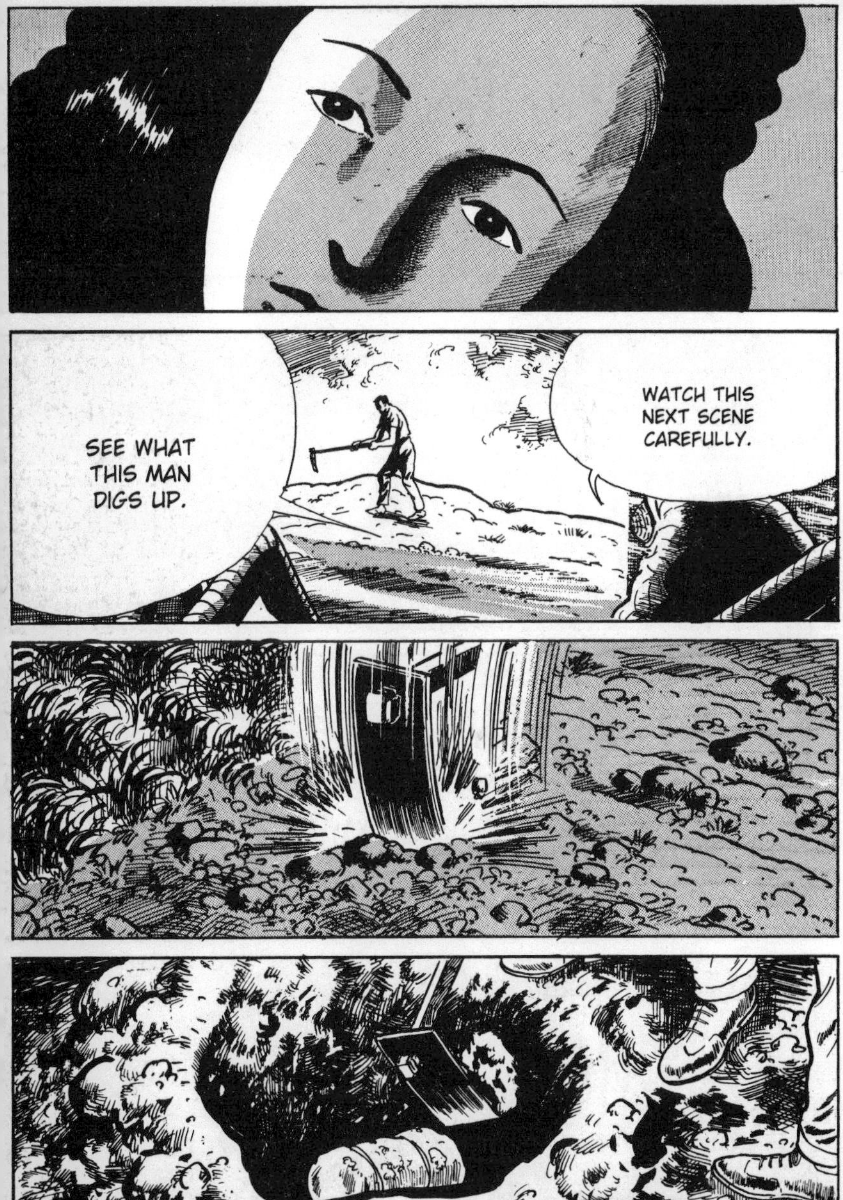
WATCH THIS NEXT SCENE CAREFULLY.
SEE WHAT THIS MAN DIGS UP.

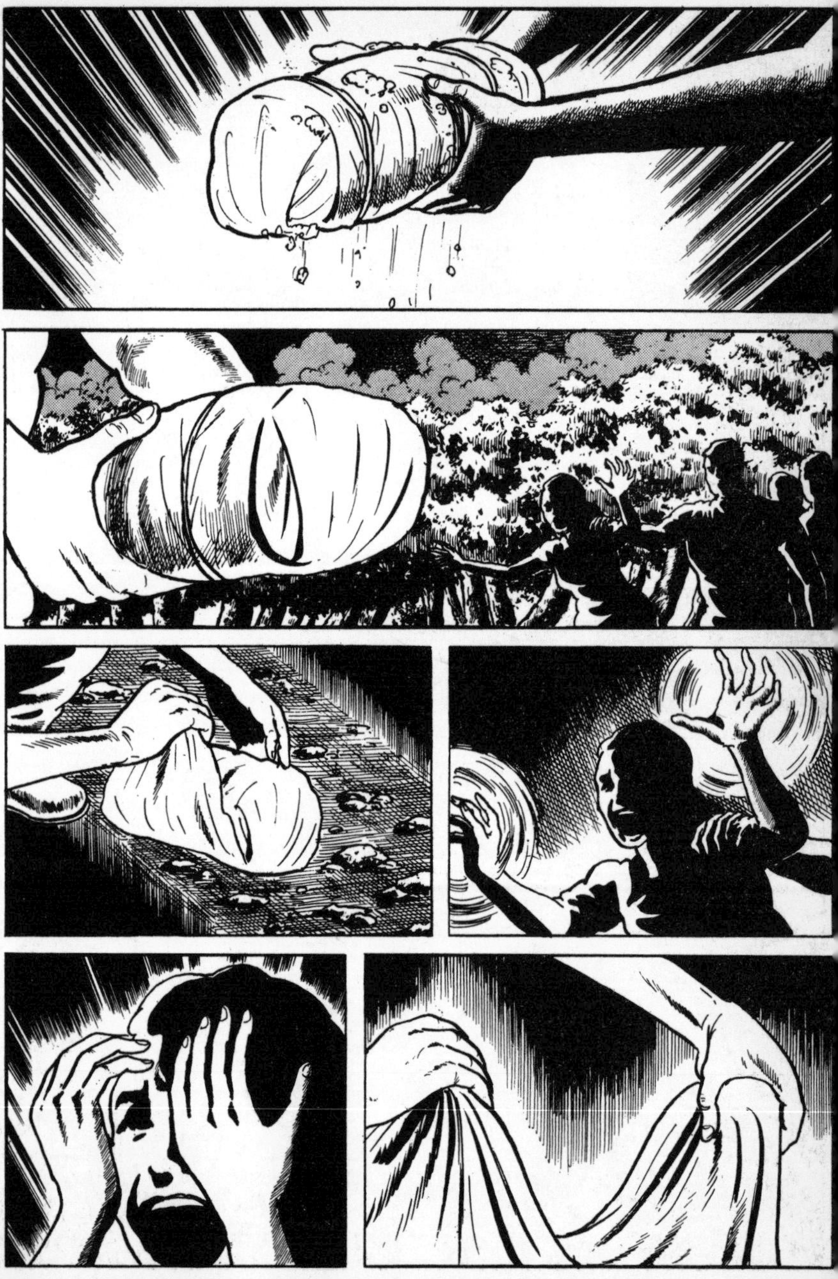

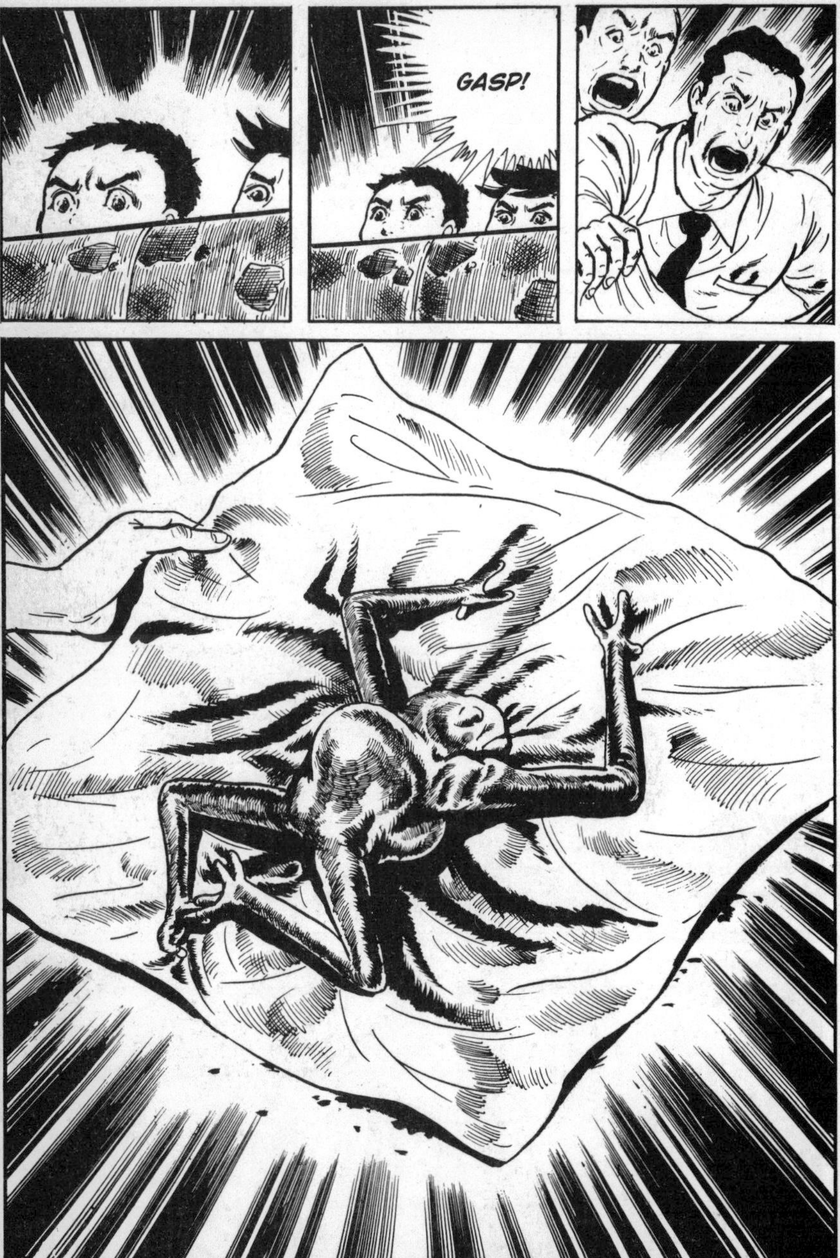
GASP!

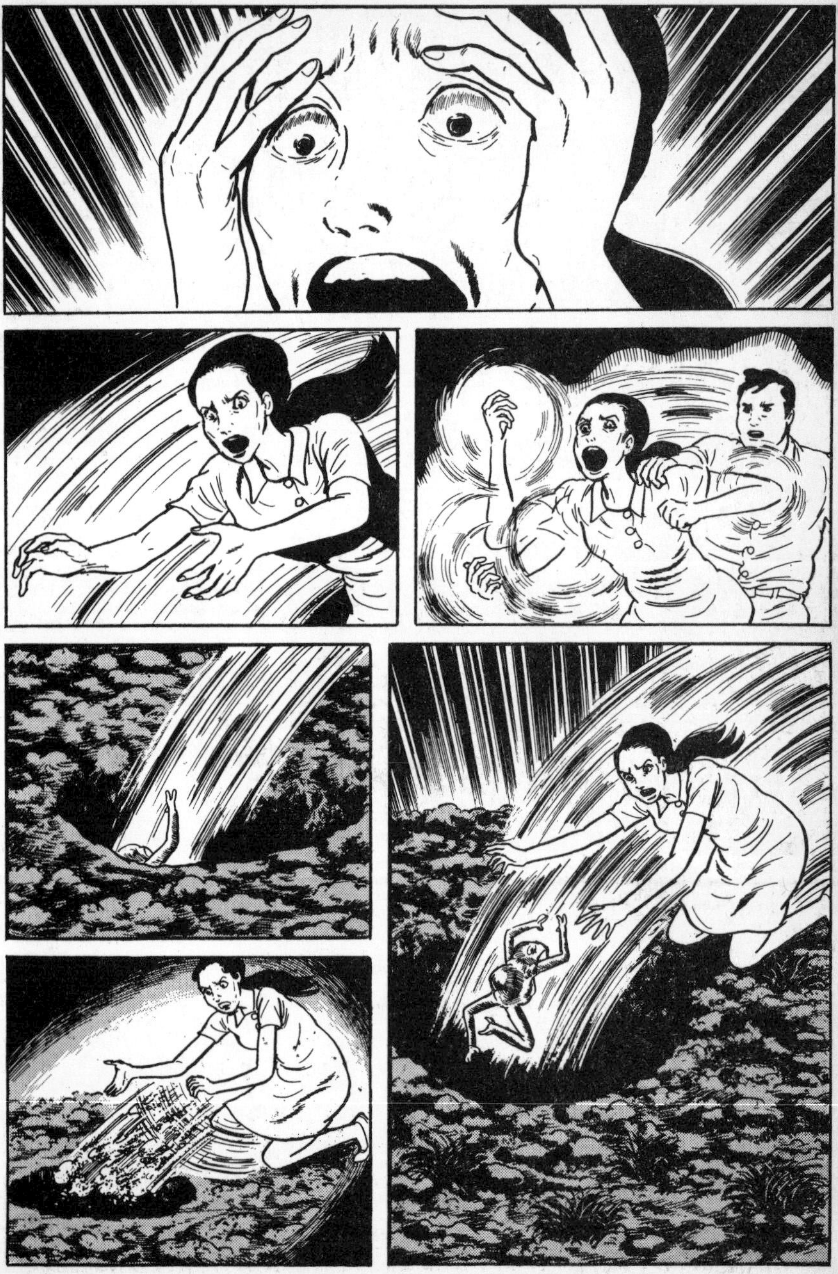

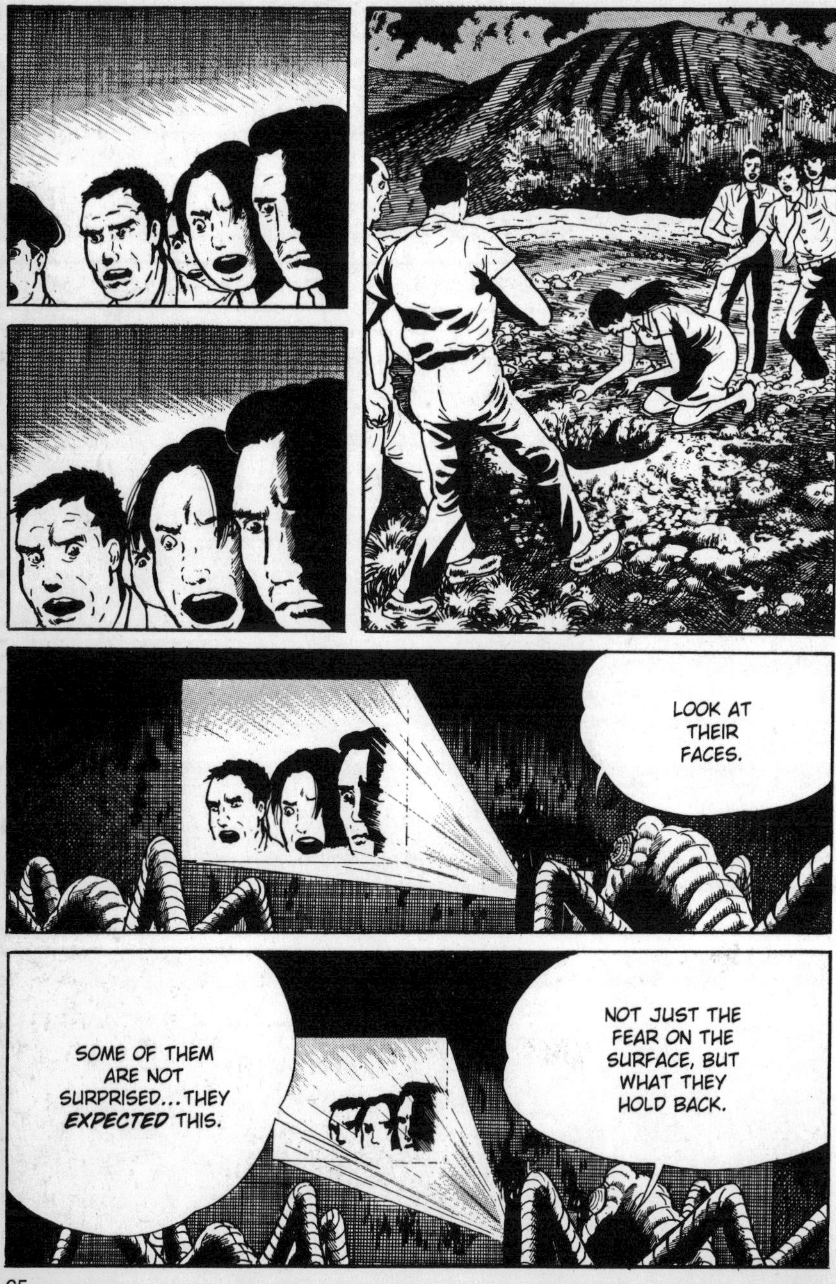
LOOK AT THEIR FACES.
NOT JUST THE FEAR ON THE SURFACE, BUT WHAT THEY HOLD BACK.
SOME OF THEM ARE NOT SURPRISED...THEY *EXPECTED* THIS.

THE NEXT IMAGES ARE ALL LANDSCAPES, THE SCENES THAT "WARMED THEIR HEARTS."

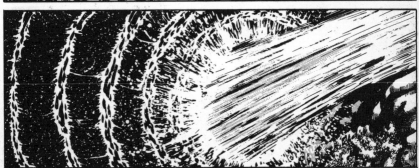

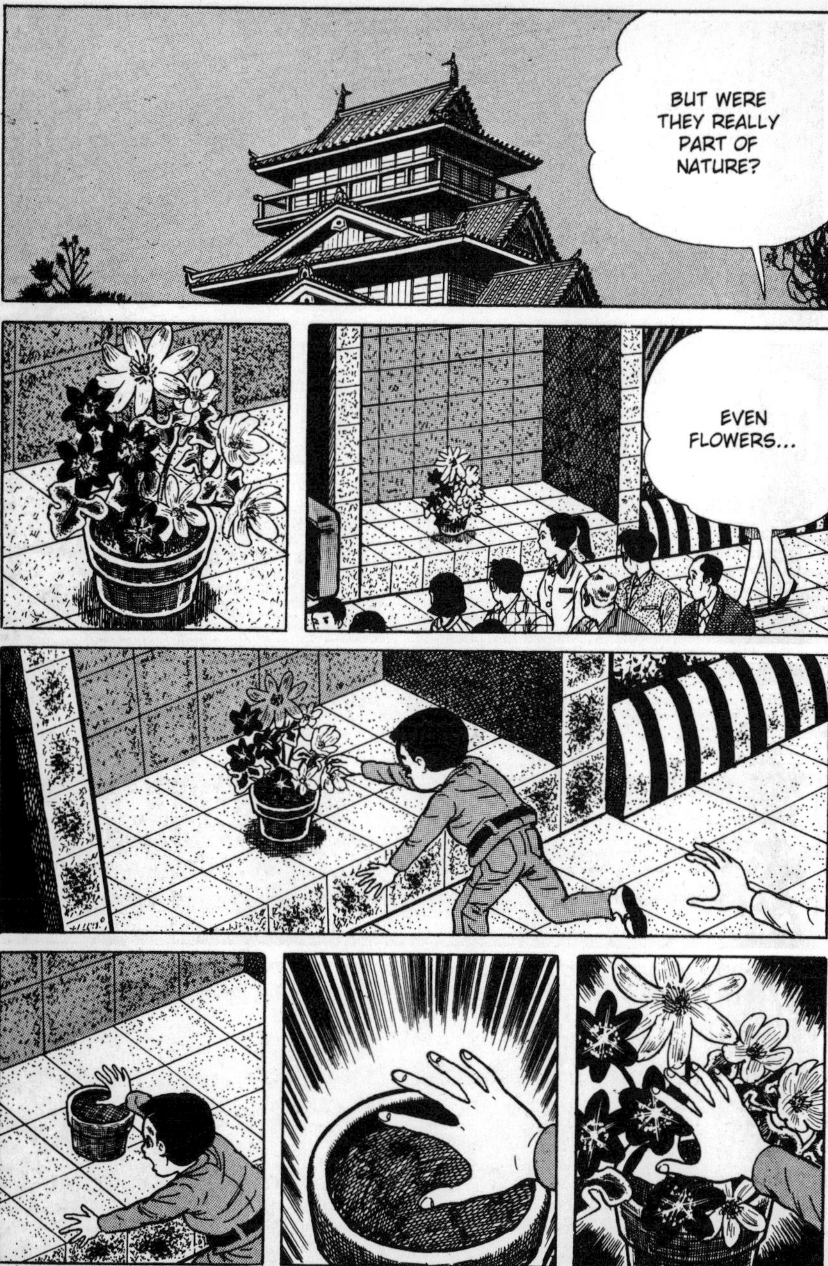
BUT WERE THEY REALLY PART OF NATURE?
EVEN FLOWERS...

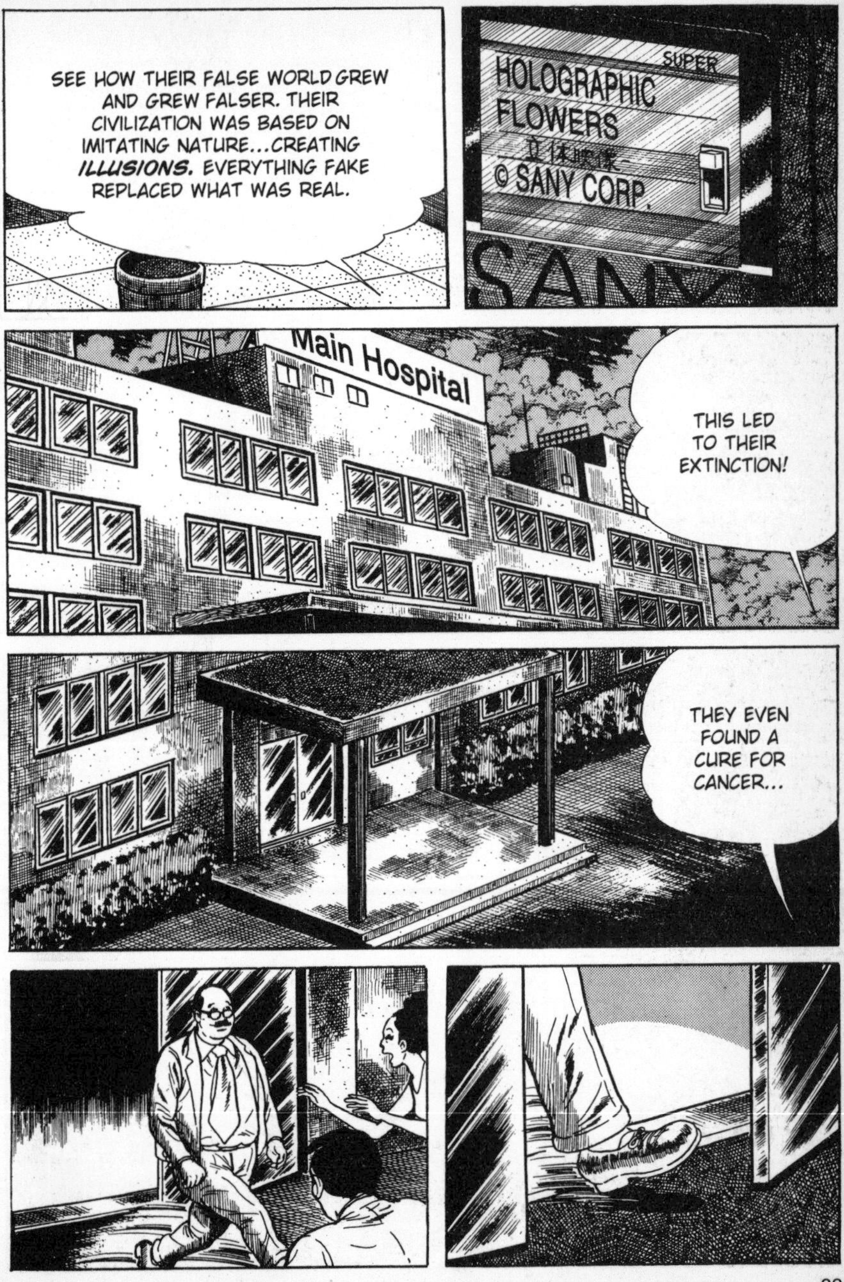
SEE HOW THEIR FALSE WORLD GREW AND GREW FALSER. THEIR CIVILIZATION WAS BASED ON IMITATING NATURE...CREATING *ILLUSIONS.* EVERYTHING FAKE REPLACED WHAT WAS REAL.
SUPER
HOLOGRAPHIC FLOWERS
立体映像
© SANY CORP.
SANY
Main Hospital
THIS LED TO THEIR EXTINCTION!
THEY EVEN FOUND A CURE FOR CANCER...

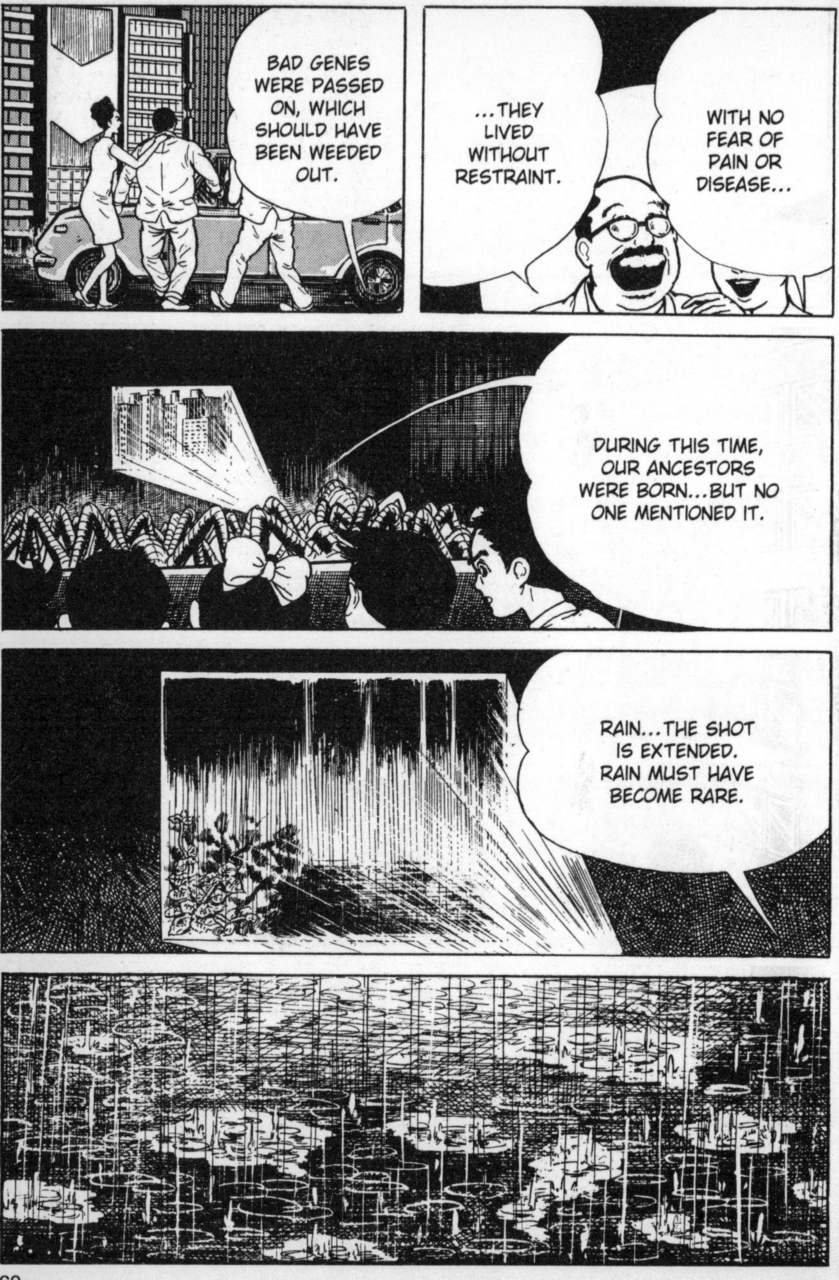
WITH NO FEAR OF PAIN OR DISEASE...
...THEY LIVED WITHOUT RESTRAINT.
BAD GENES WERE PASSED ON, WHICH SHOULD HAVE BEEN WEEDED OUT.
DURING THIS TIME, OUR ANCESTORS WERE BORN...BUT NO ONE MENTIONED IT.
RAIN...THE SHOT IS EXTENDED. RAIN MUST HAVE BECOME RARE.

BUT THIS, TOO, CAN TEACH US SOMETHING.

SEE THESE LITTLE PUDDLES FORMING? LOOK HOW THEY LINK UP TO FORM A LARGE ONE.

WHAT IS THE HUMAN RACE...? IT WILL ONLY KNOW THE MOMENT ITS PUDDLE BECOMES FULL.

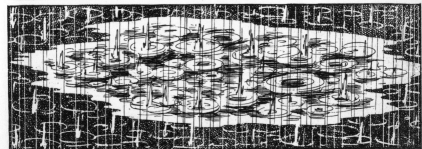

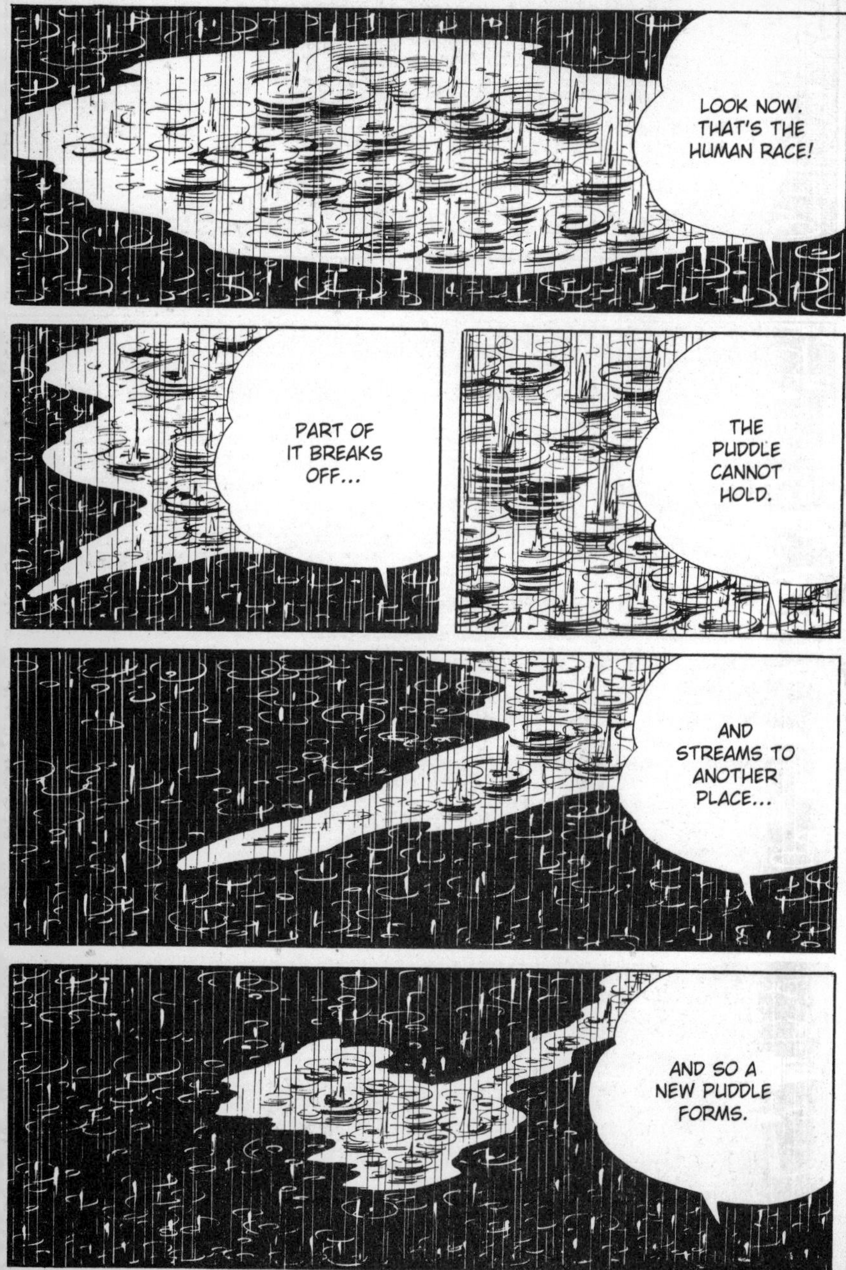
LOOK NOW. THAT'S THE HUMAN RACE!
THE PUDDLE CANNOT HOLD.
PART OF IT BREAKS OFF...
AND STREAMS TO ANOTHER PLACE...
AND SO A NEW PUDDLE FORMS.

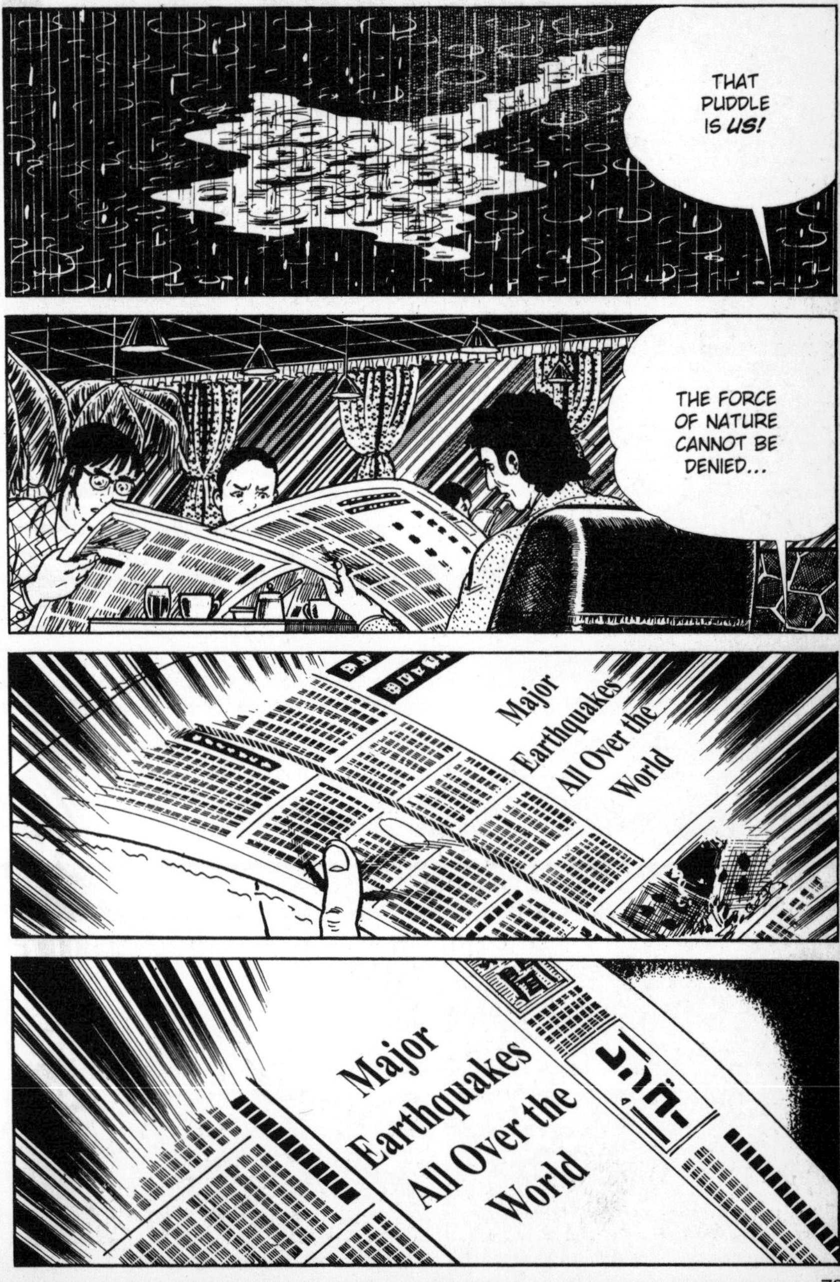
THAT PUDDLE IS US!
THE FORCE OF NATURE CANNOT BE DENIED...
Major Earthquakes All Over the World
Major Earthquakes All Over the World

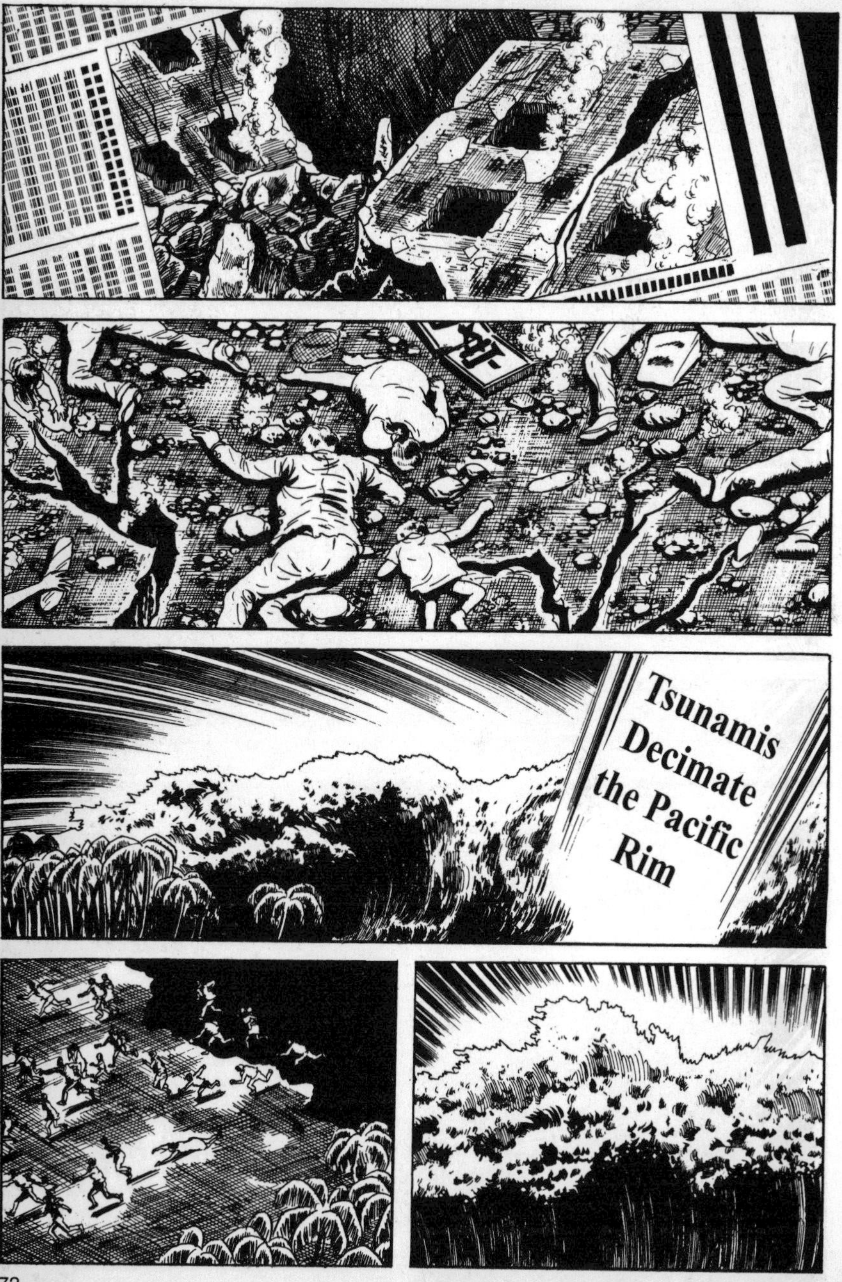
Tsunamis Decimate the Pacific Rim

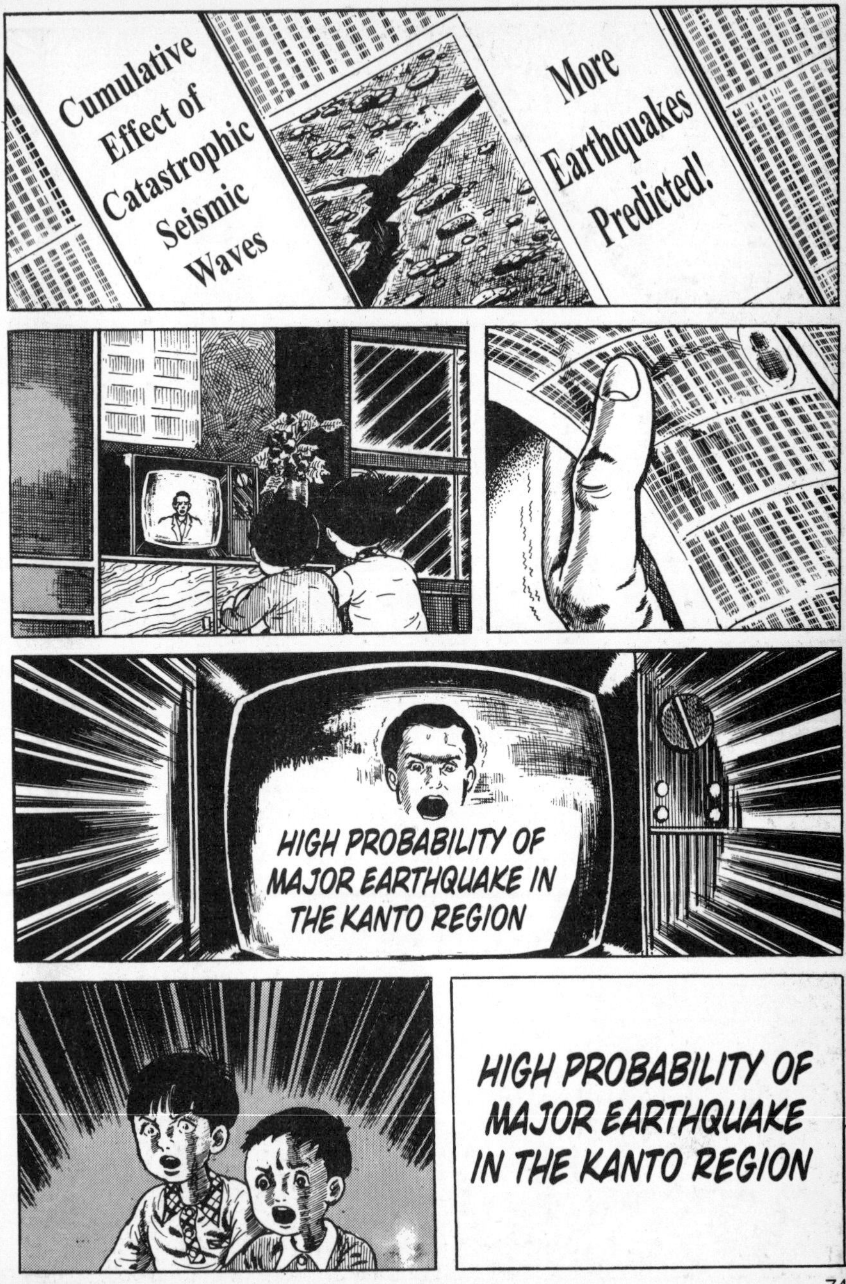
More Earthquakes Predicted!
Cumulative Effect of Catastrophic Seismic Waves
HIGH PROBABILITY OF MAJOR EARTHQUAKE IN THE KANTO REGION
HIGH PROBABILITY OF MAJOR EARTHQUAKE IN THE KANTO REGION

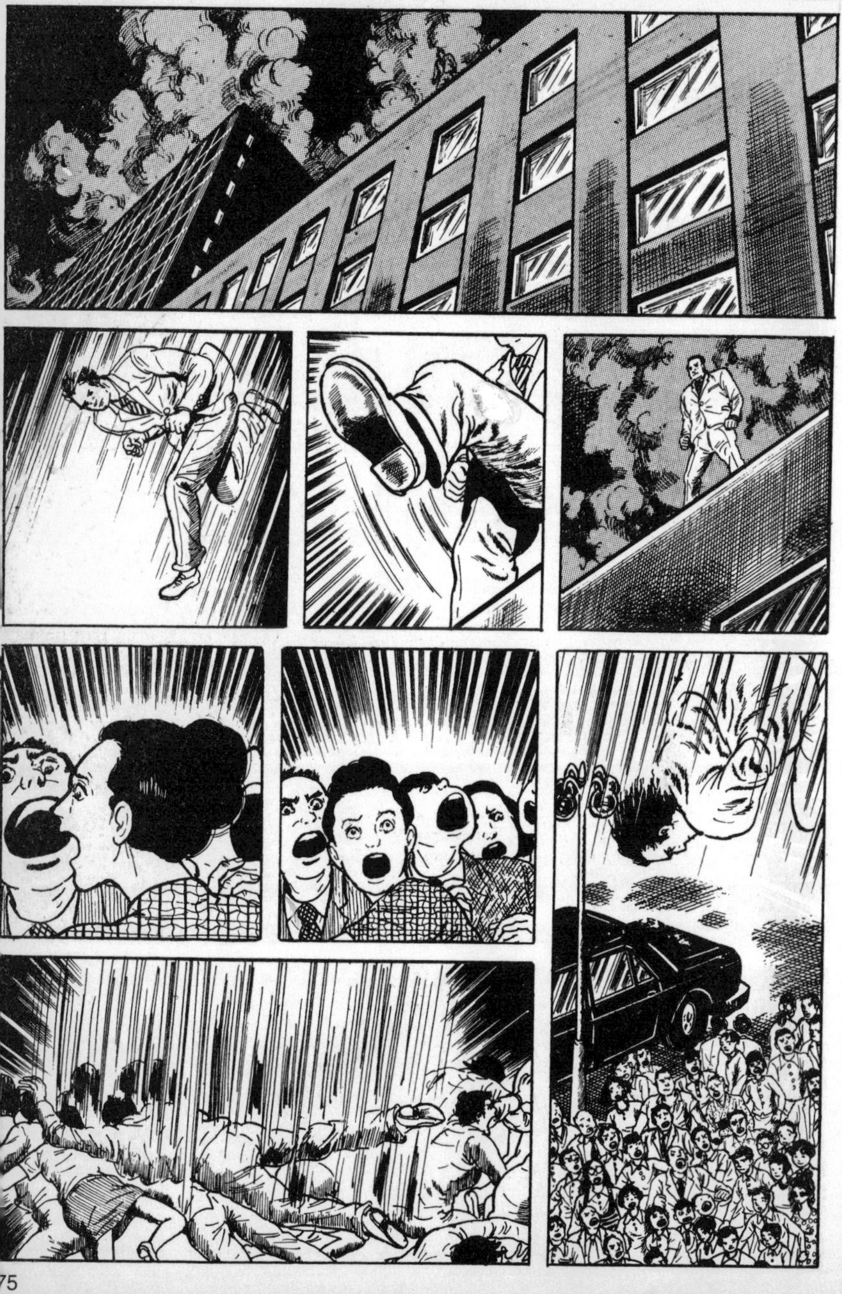

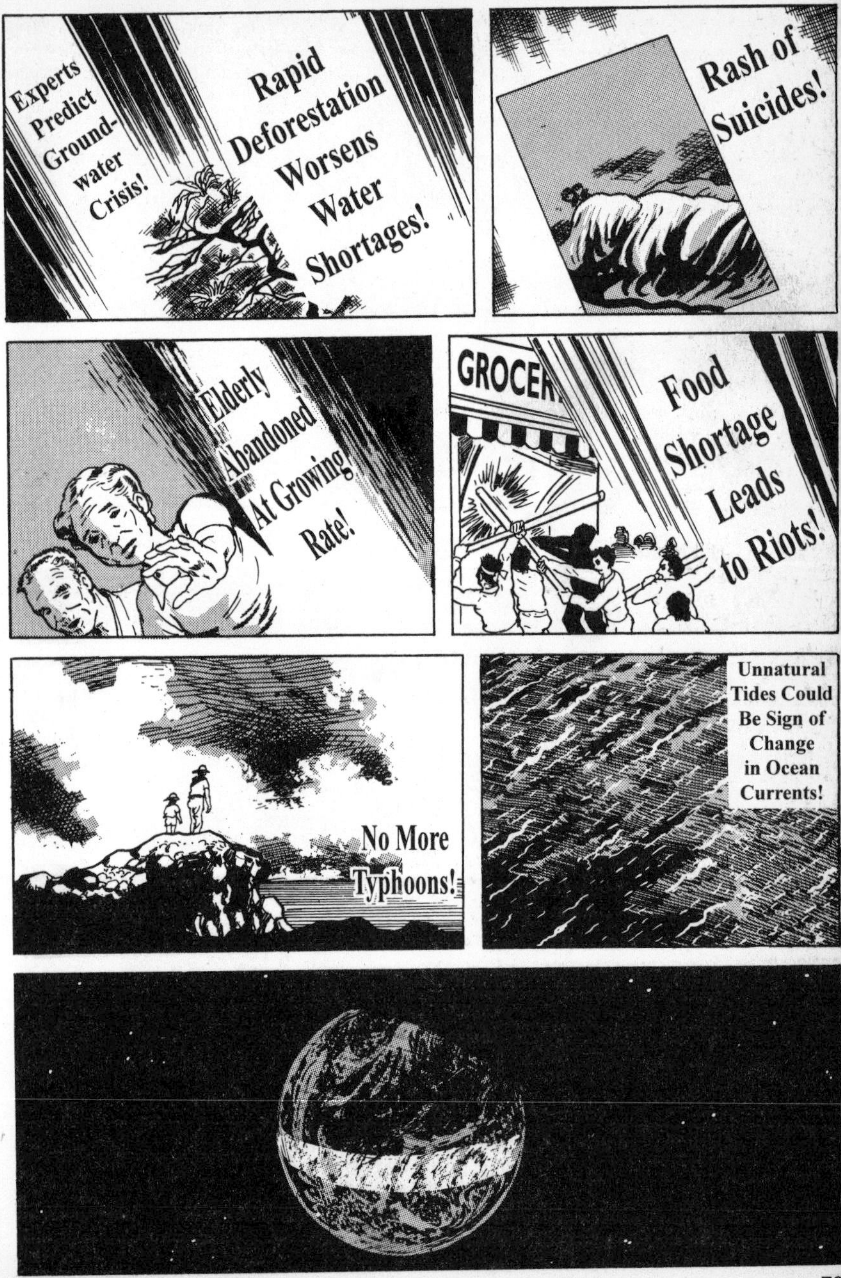
Rash of Suicides!
Rapid Deforestation Worsens Water Shortages!
Experts Predict Ground-water Crisis!
Food Shortage Leads to Riots!
GROCER
Elderly Abandoned At Growing Rate!
Unnatural Tides Could Be Sign of Change in Ocean Currents!
No More Typhoons!

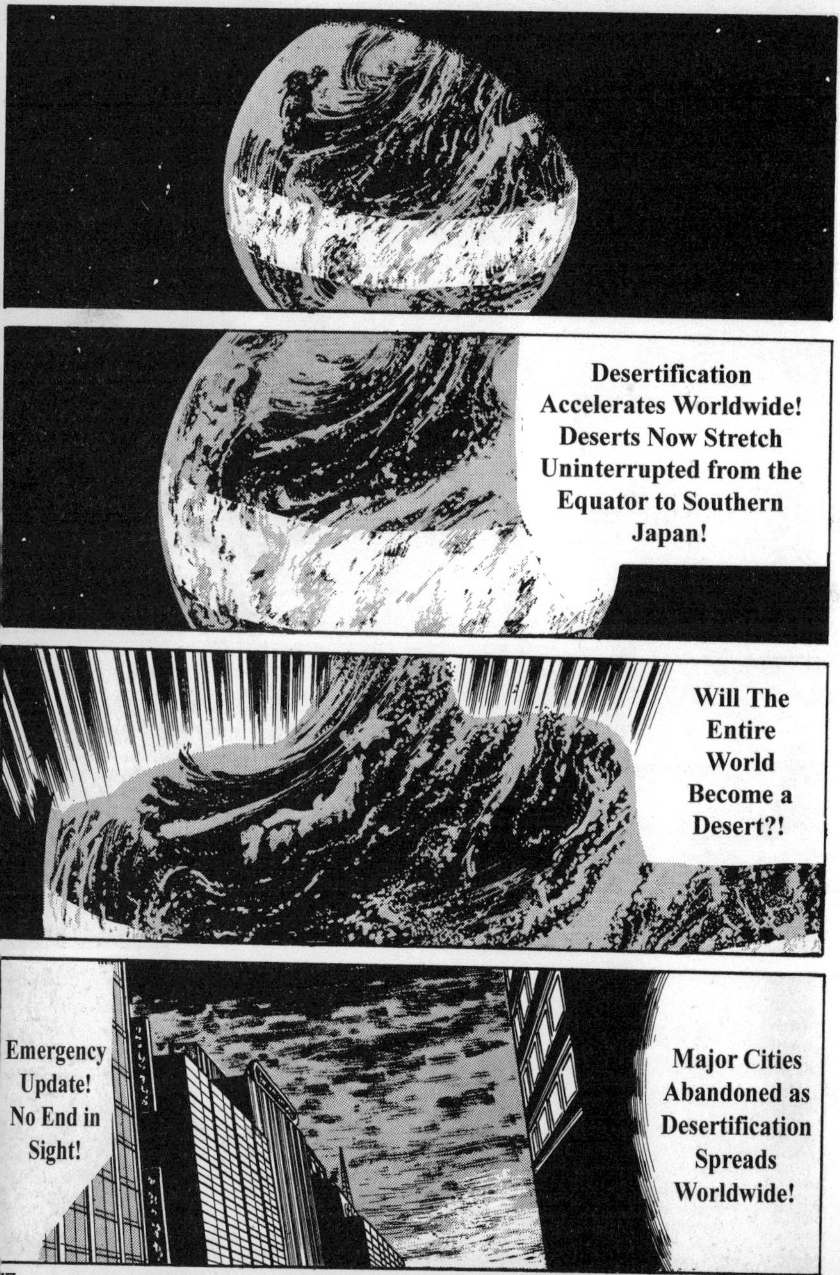
Desertification Accelerates Worldwide! Deserts Now Stretch Uninterrupted from the Equator to Southern Japan!
Will The Entire World Become a Desert?!
Major Cities Abandoned as Desertification Spreads Worldwide!
Emergency Update! No End in Sight!

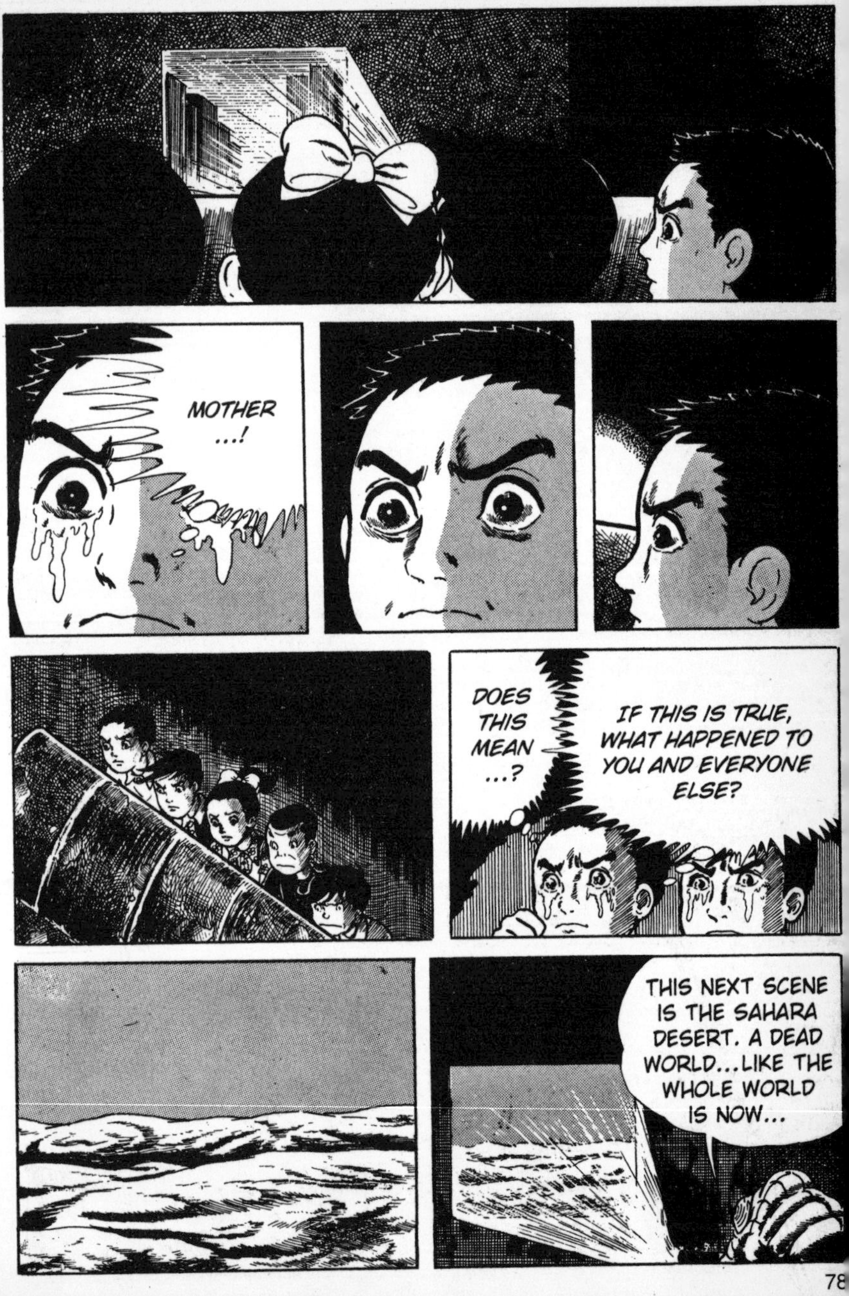
MOTHER ...!
IF THIS IS TRUE, WHAT HAPPENED TO YOU AND EVERYONE ELSE?
DOES THIS MEAN ...?
THIS NEXT SCENE IS THE SAHARA DESERT. A DEAD WORLD...LIKE THE WHOLE WORLD IS NOW...

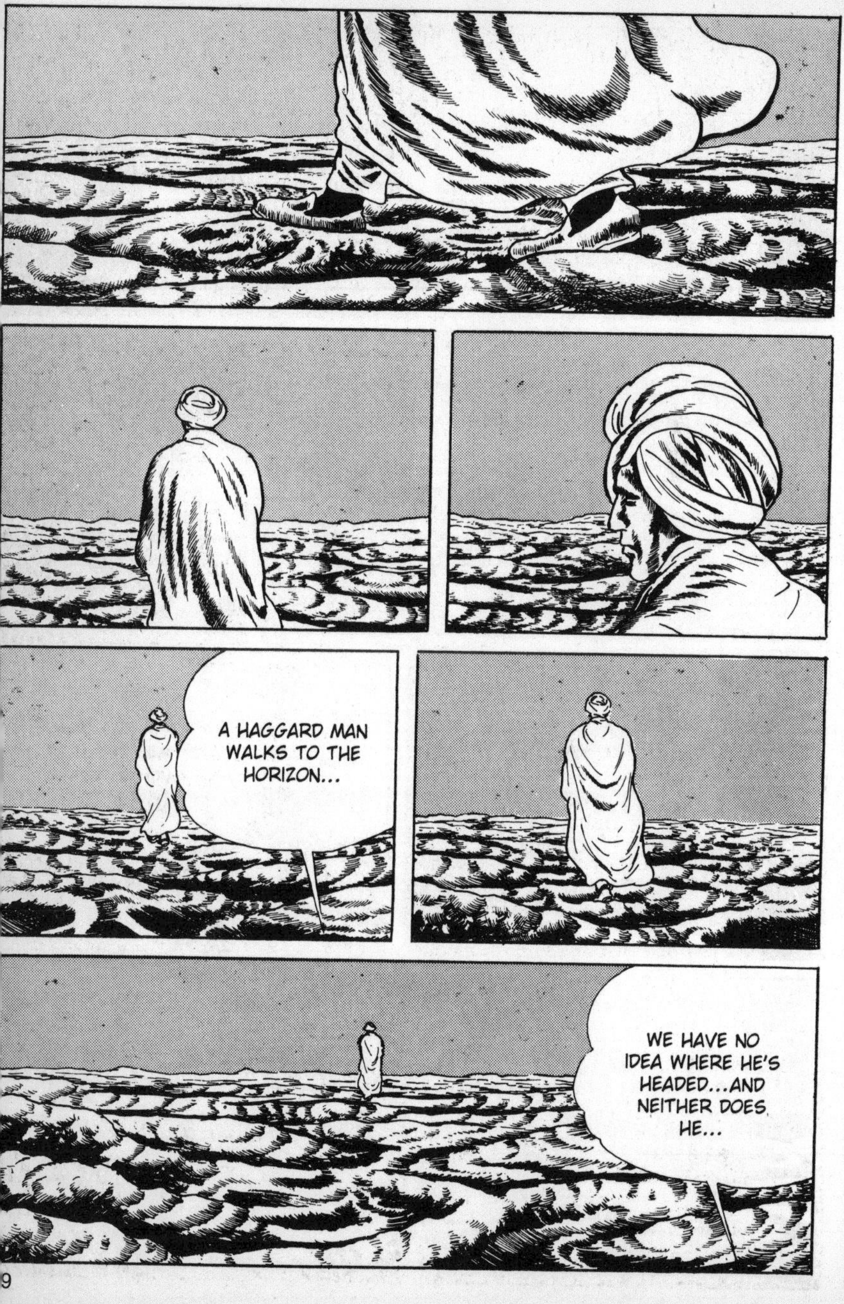
A HAGGARD MAN WALKS TO THE HORIZON...
WE HAVE NO IDEA WHERE HE'S HEADED...AND NEITHER DOES HE...

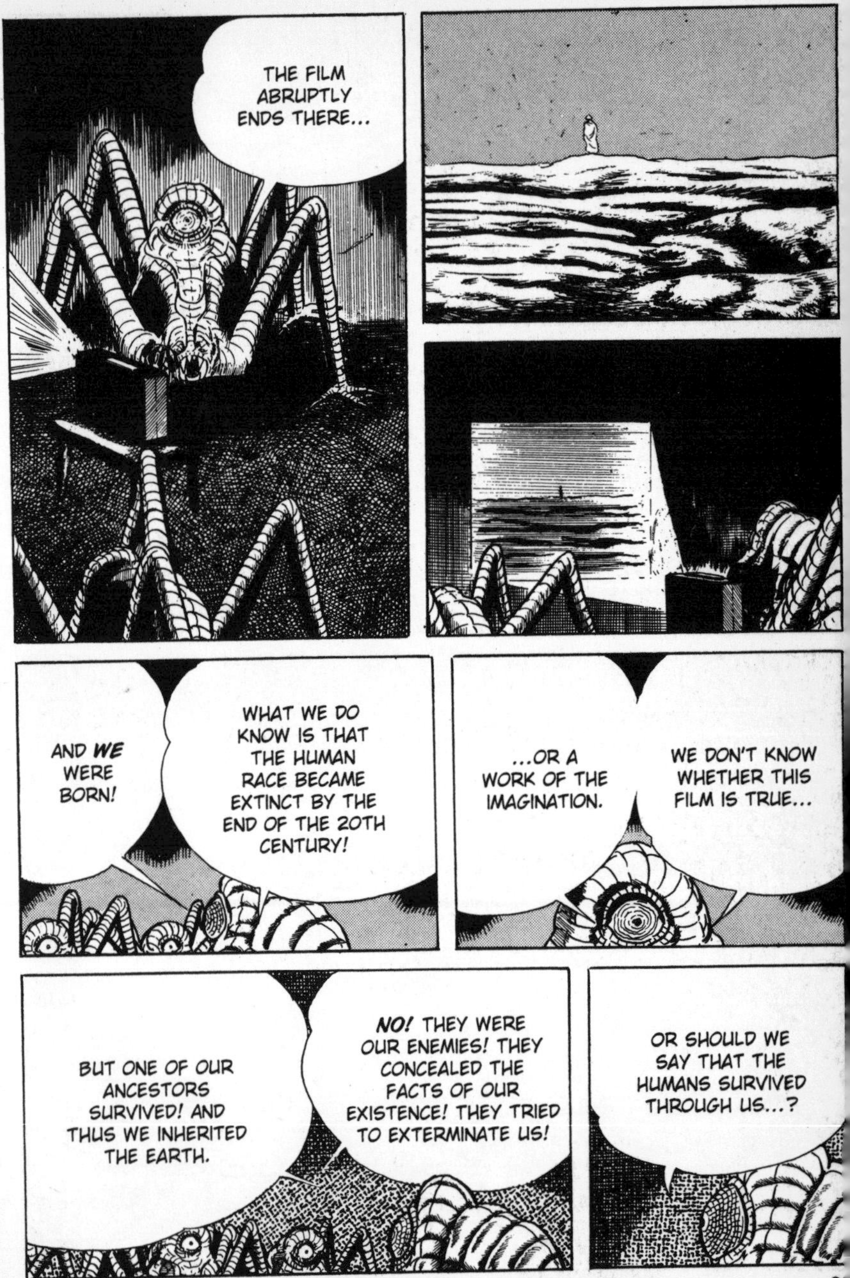
THE FILM ABRUPTLY ENDS THERE...
WE DON'T KNOW WHETHER THIS FILM IS TRUE...
...OR A WORK OF THE IMAGINATION.
WHAT WE DO KNOW IS THAT THE HUMAN RACE BECAME EXTINCT BY THE END OF THE 20TH CENTURY!
AND *WE* WERE BORN!
OR SHOULD WE SAY THAT THE HUMANS SURVIVED THROUGH US...?
NO! THEY WERE OUR ENEMIES! THEY CONCEALED THE FACTS OF OUR EXISTENCE! THEY TRIED TO EXTERMINATE US!
BUT ONE OF OUR ANCESTORS SURVIVED! AND THUS WE INHERITED THE EARTH.

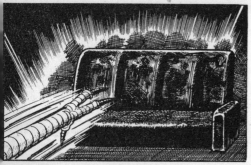

THAT IS OUR ANCESTOR!

BEHOLD!

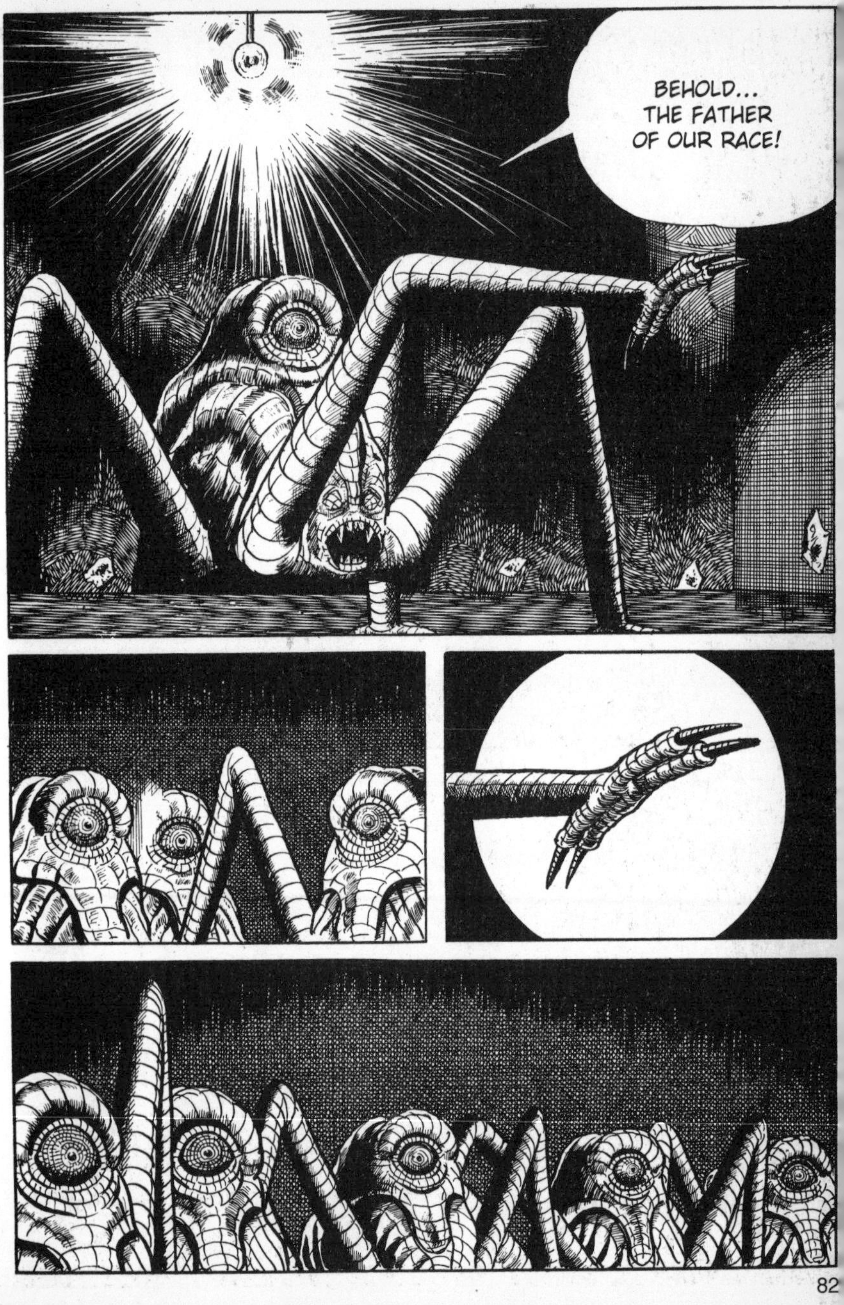
BEHOLD... THE FATHER OF OUR RACE!

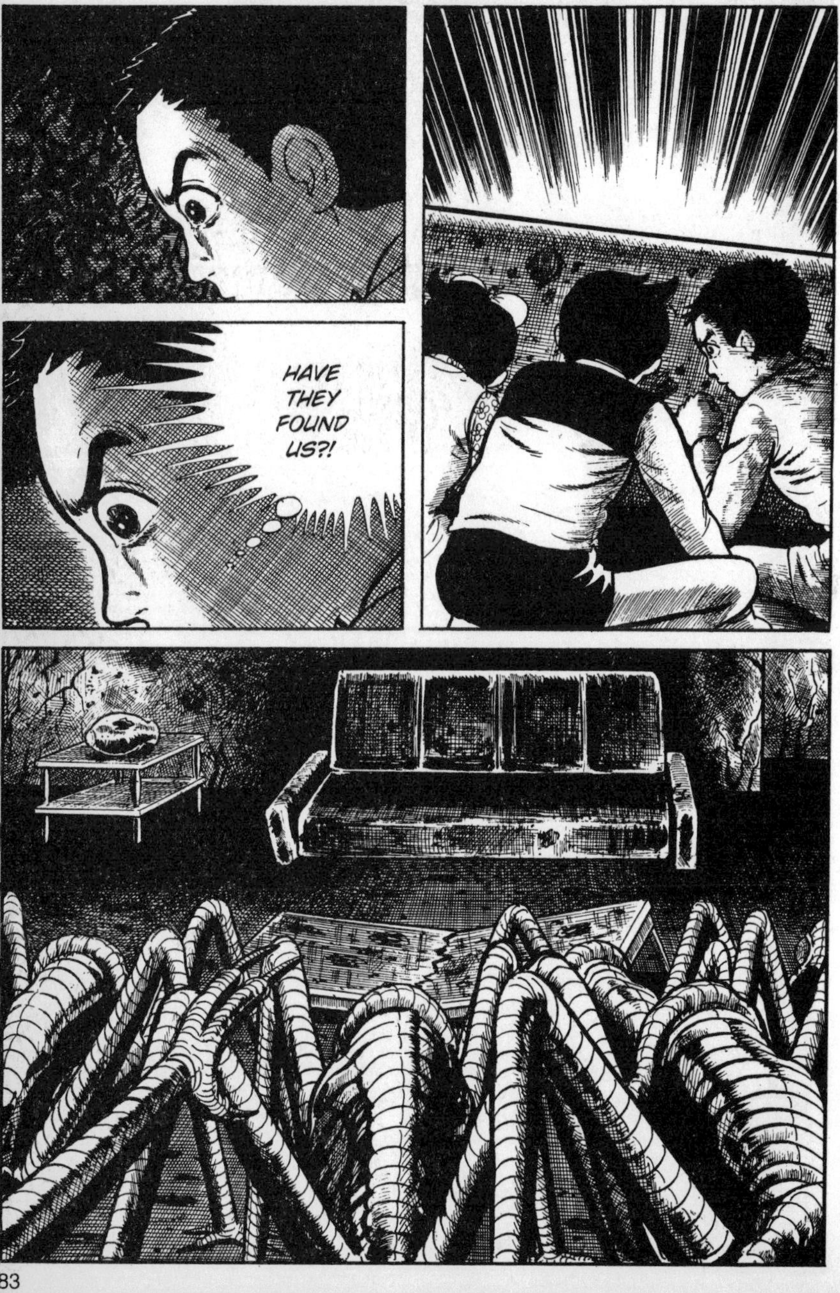
HAVE THEY FOUND US?!

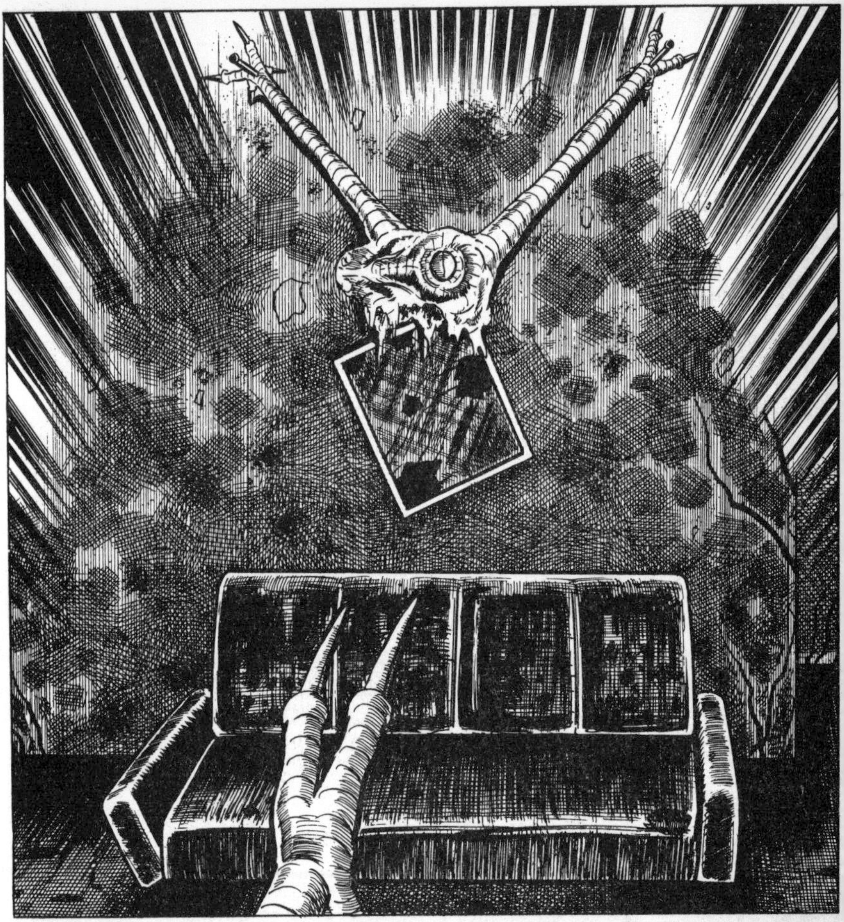

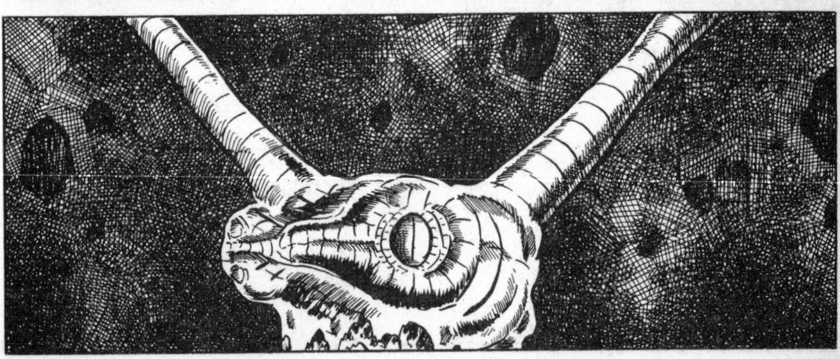

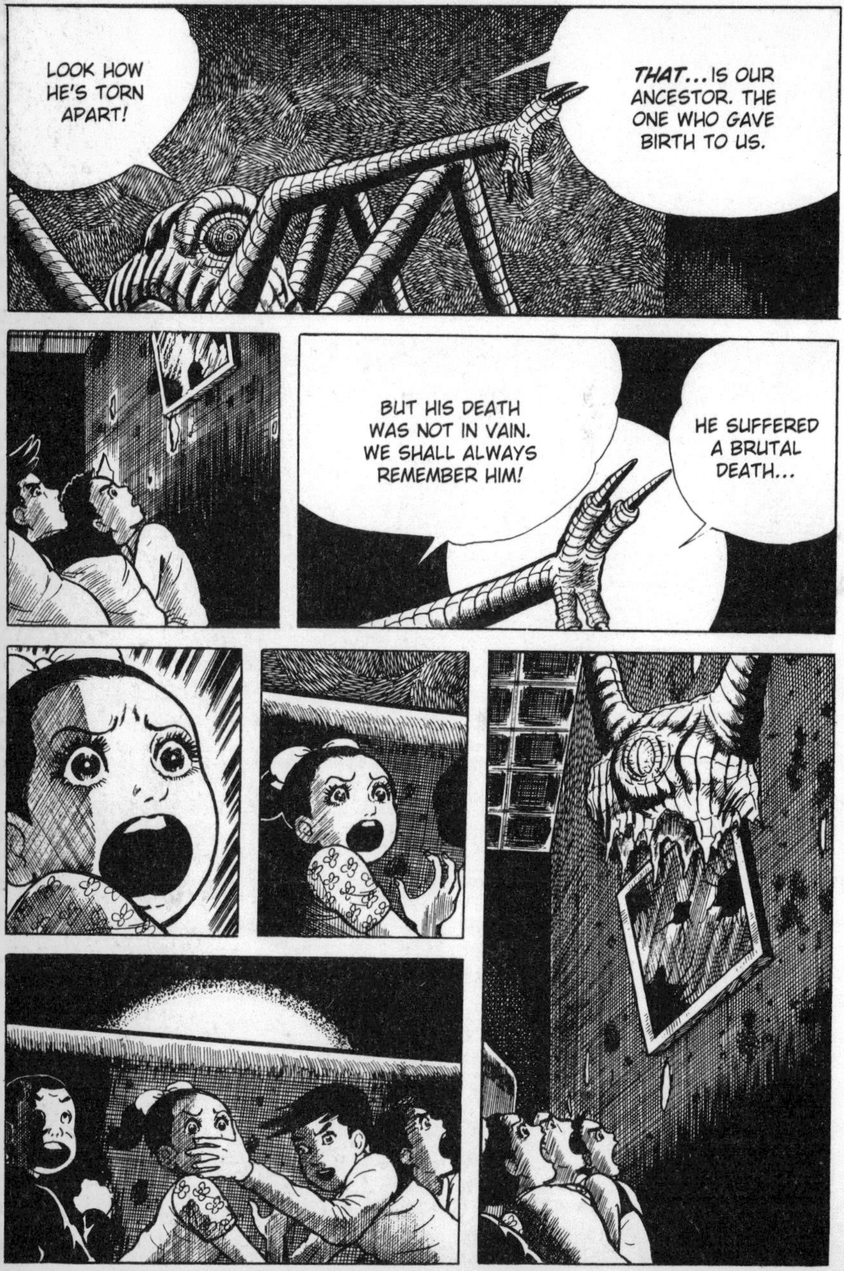
THAT... IS OUR ANCESTOR. THE ONE WHO GAVE BIRTH TO US.
LOOK HOW HE'S TORN APART!
HE SUFFERED A BRUTAL DEATH...
BUT HIS DEATH WAS NOT IN VAIN. WE SHALL ALWAYS REMEMBER HIM!

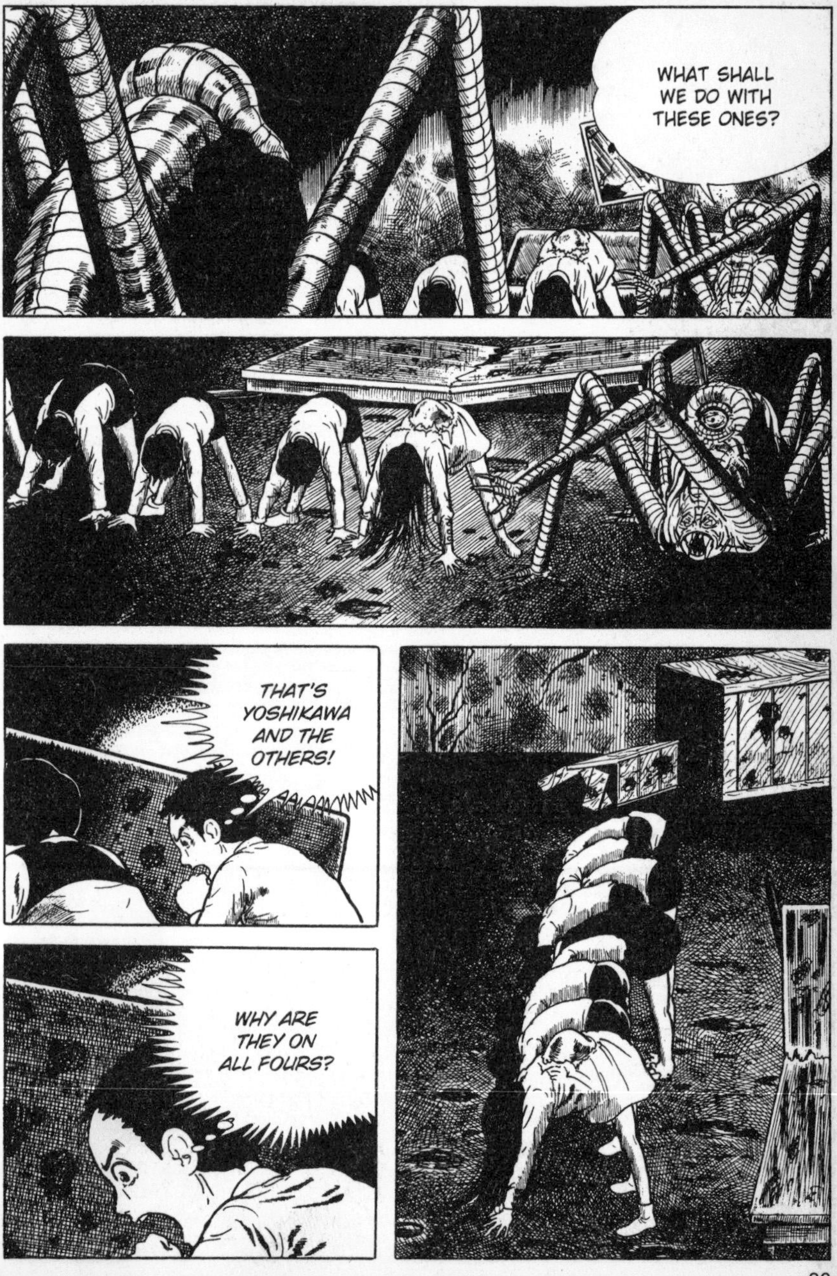
WHAT SHALL WE DO WITH THESE ONES?
THAT'S YOSHIKAWA AND THE OTHERS!
WHY ARE THEY ON ALL FOURS?

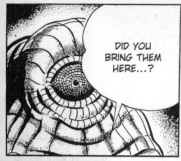

DID YOU BRING THEM HERE...?

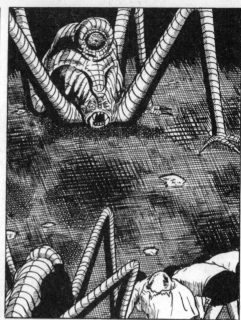

YES, SIR!

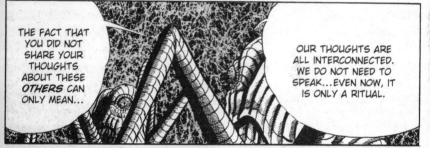

THE FACT THAT YOU DID NOT SHARE YOUR THOUGHTS ABOUT THESE *OTHERS* CAN ONLY MEAN...

OUR THOUGHTS ARE ALL INTERCONNECTED. WE DO NOT NEED TO SPEAK...EVEN NOW, IT IS ONLY A RITUAL.

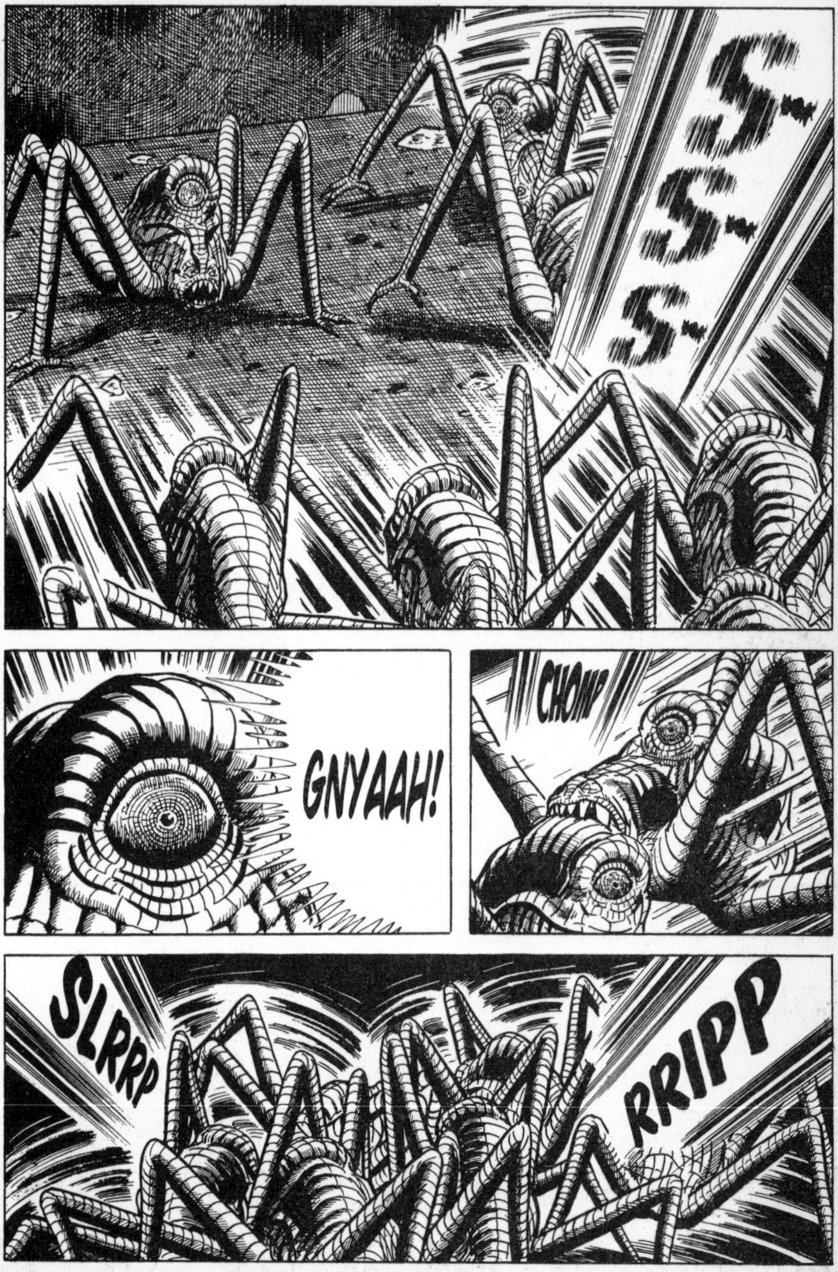
S- S- S-
CHOMP
GNYAAH!
RRIPP
SLRRP

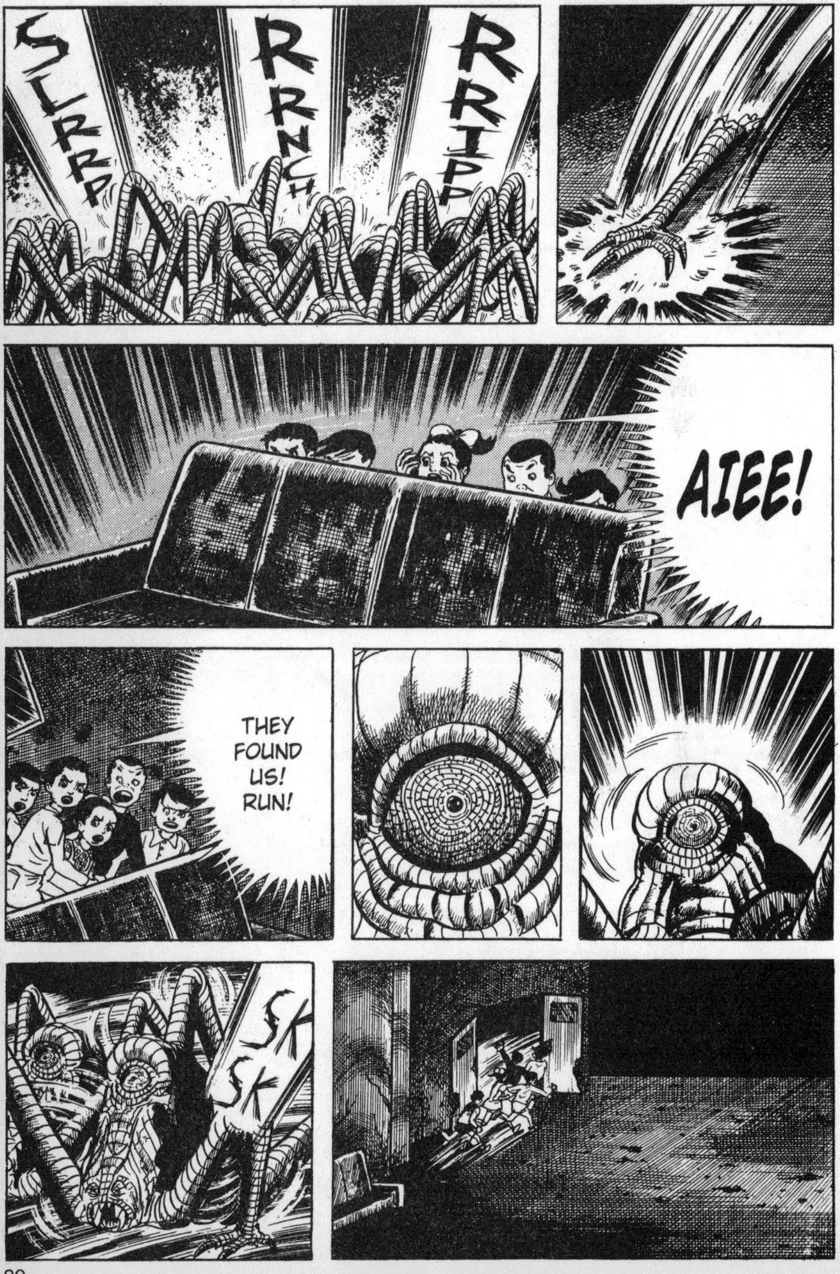
RRIPP
RRNCH
SLRRP
AIEE!
THEY FOUND US! RUN!
SK
SK

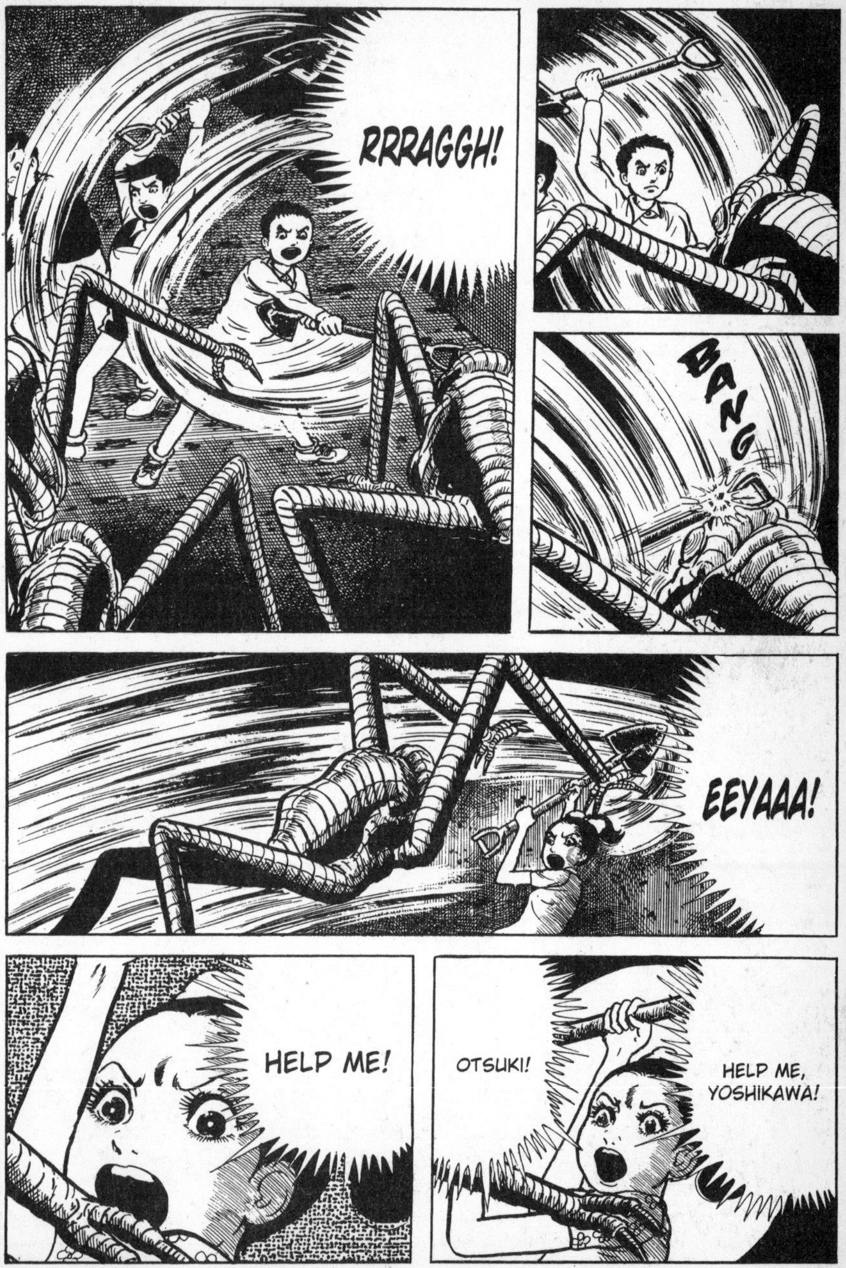
BANG
RRRAGGH!
EEYAAA!
HELP ME, YOSHIKAWA!
OTSUKI!
HELP ME!

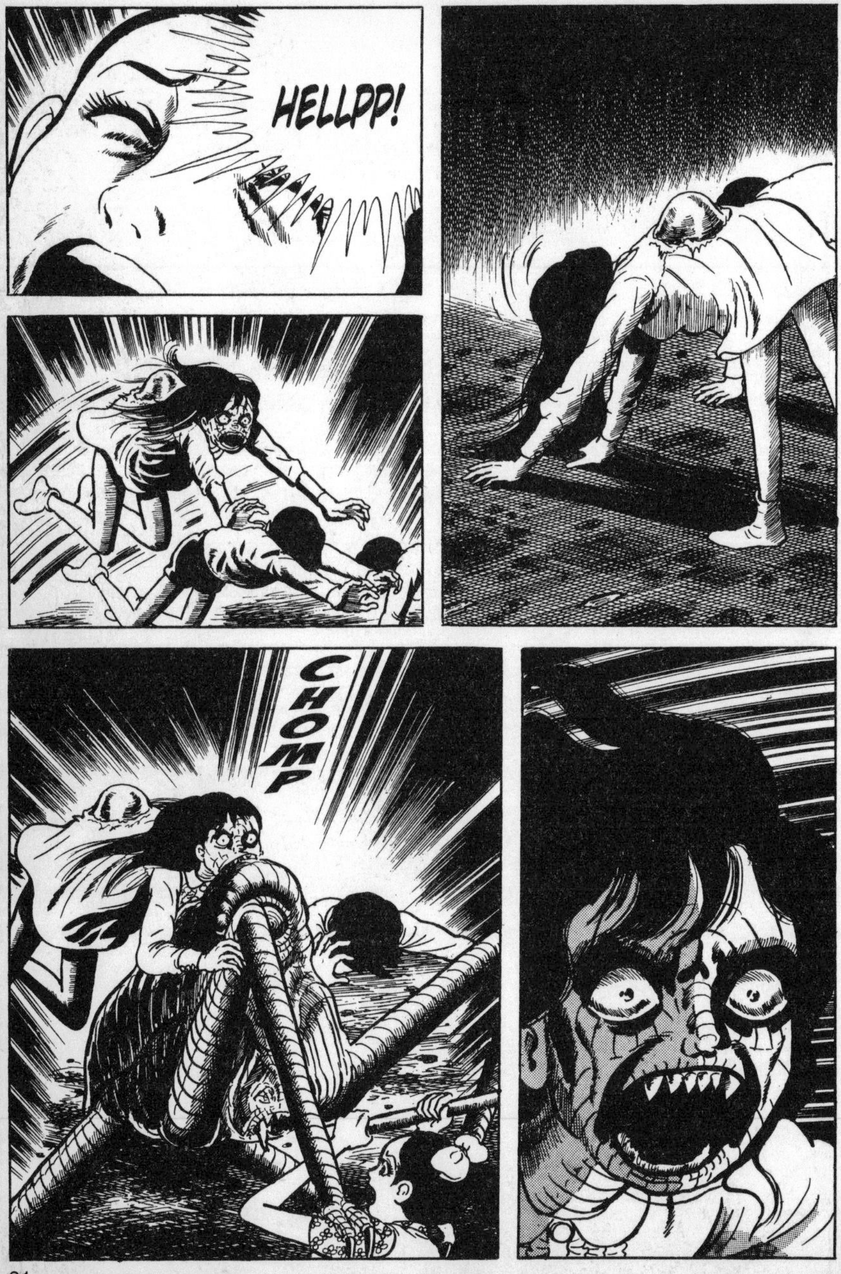
HELLPP!
CHOMP

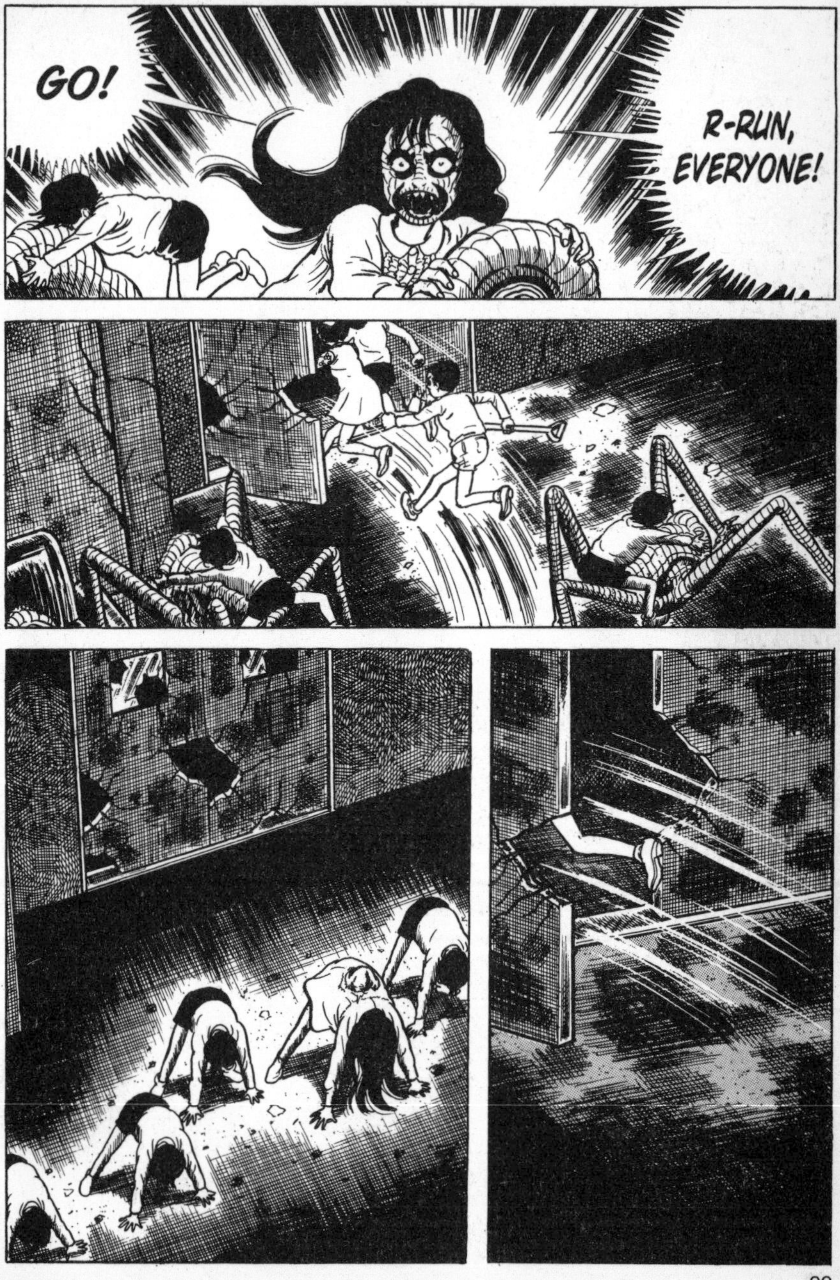
R-RUN, EVERYONE!
GO!

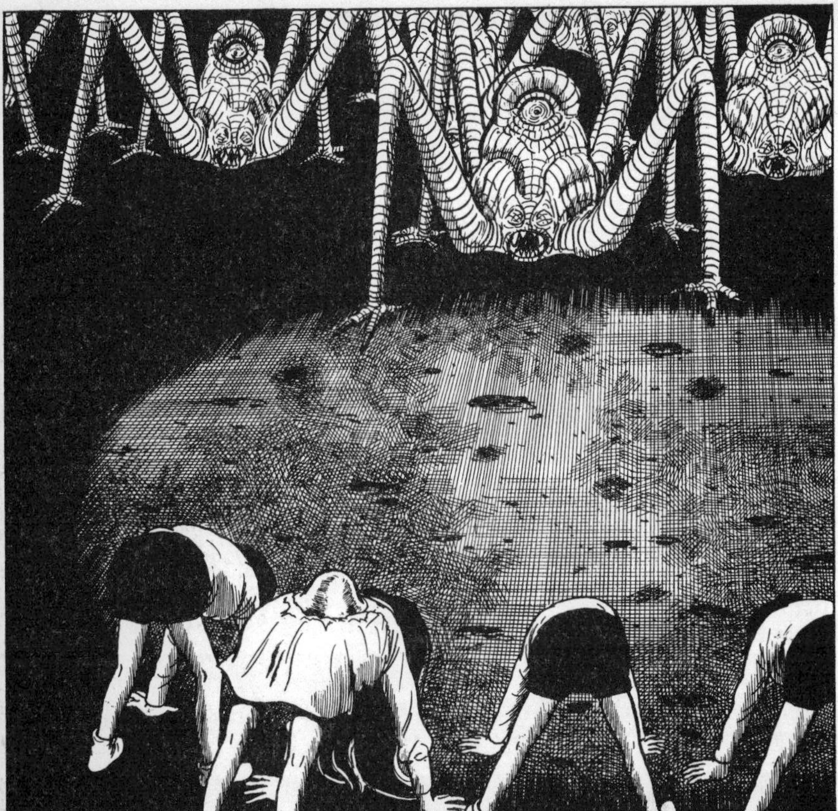
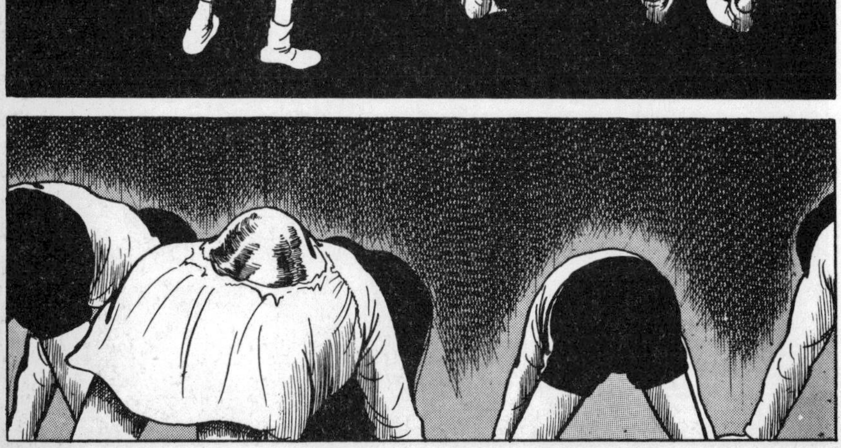

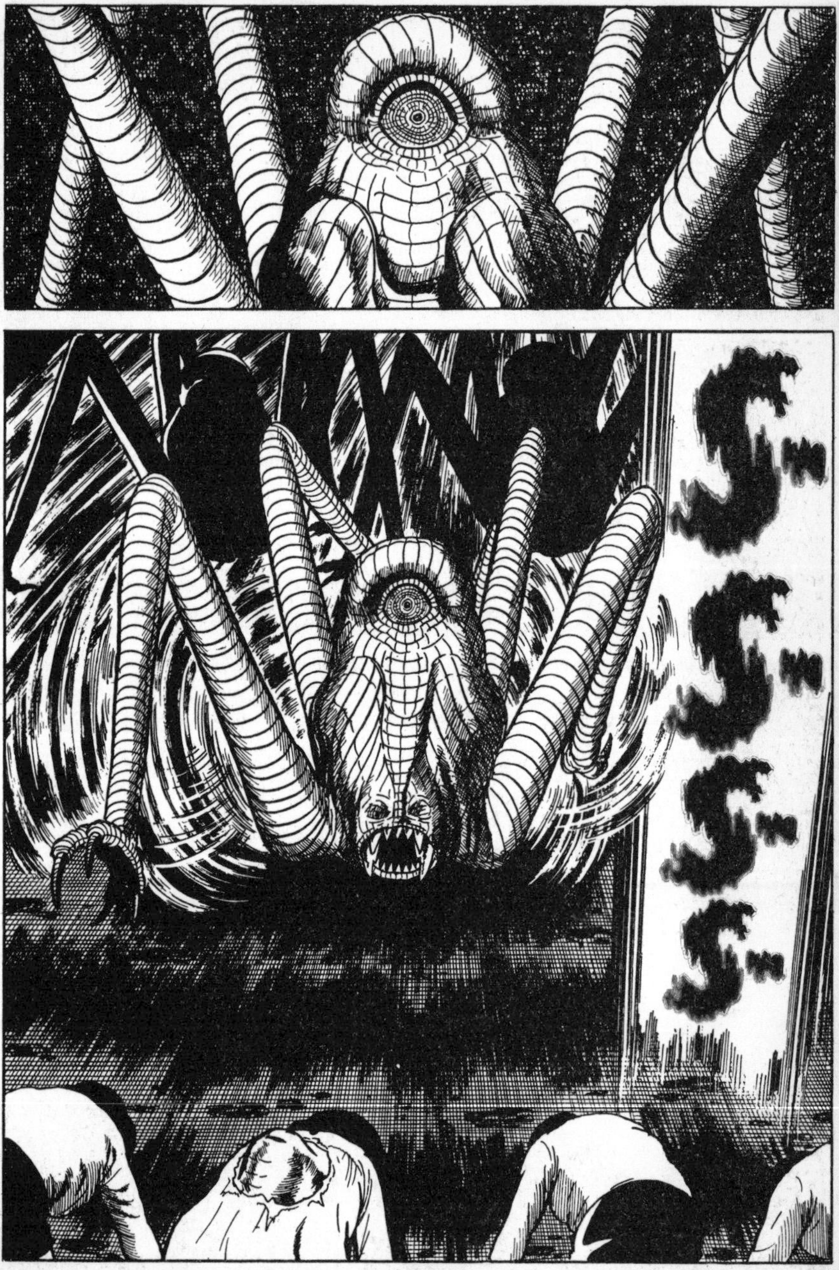
S
S
S
S

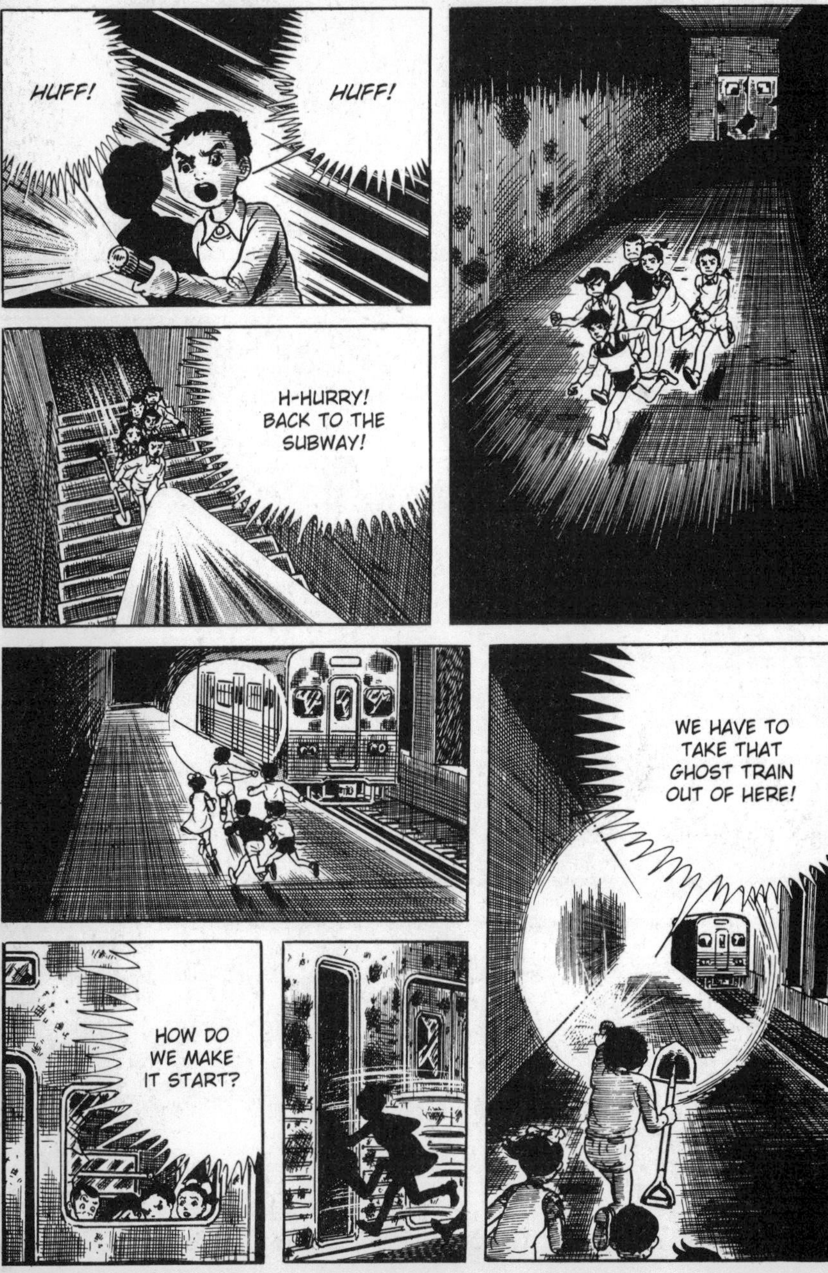
HUFF!
HUFF!
H-HURRY! BACK TO THE SUBWAY!
WE HAVE TO TAKE THAT GHOST TRAIN OUT OF HERE!
HOW DO WE MAKE IT START?

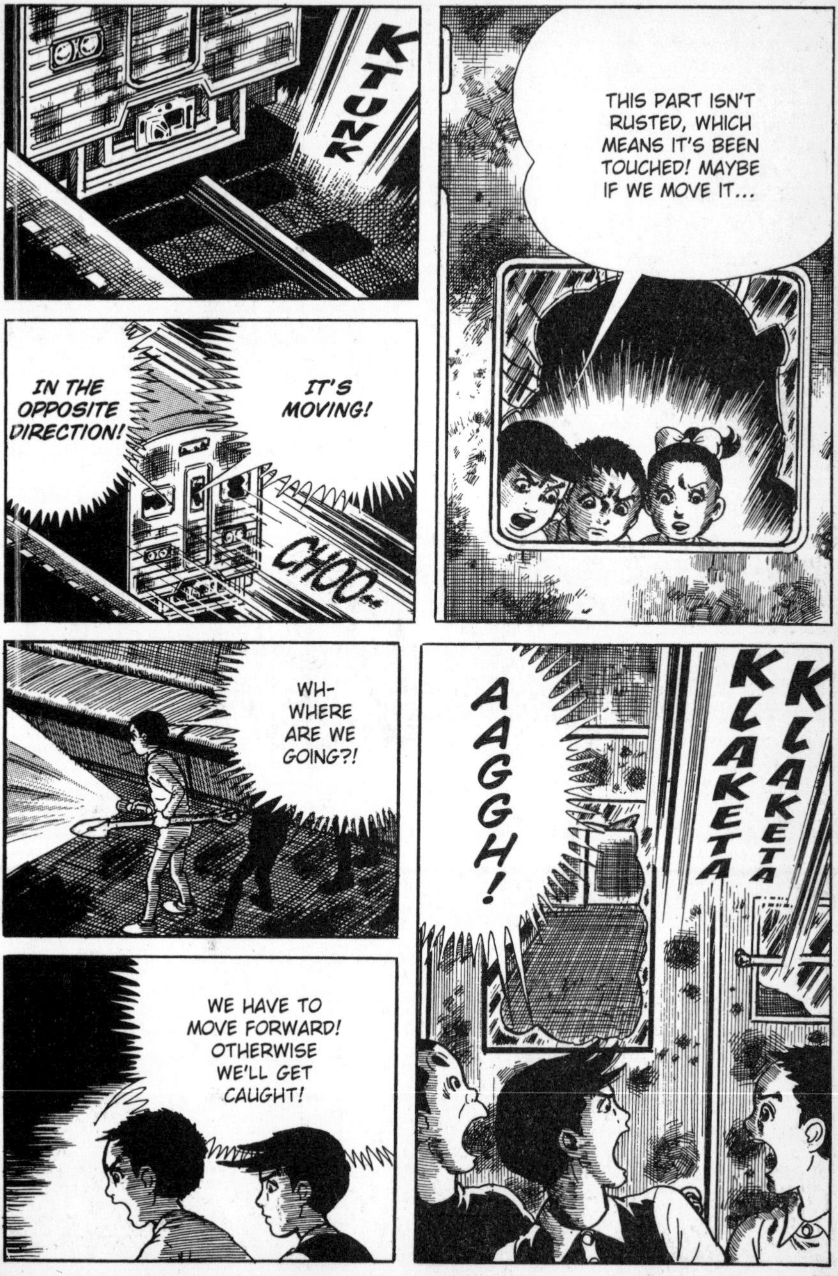
THIS PART ISN'T RUSTED, WHICH MEANS IT'S BEEN TOUCHED! MAYBE IF WE MOVE IT...
KTUNK
IT'S MOVING!
IN THE OPPOSITE DIRECTION!
CHOO-
KLAKETA
KLAKETA
AAGGH!
WH- WHERE ARE WE GOING?!
WE HAVE TO MOVE FORWARD! OTHERWISE WE'LL GET CAUGHT!

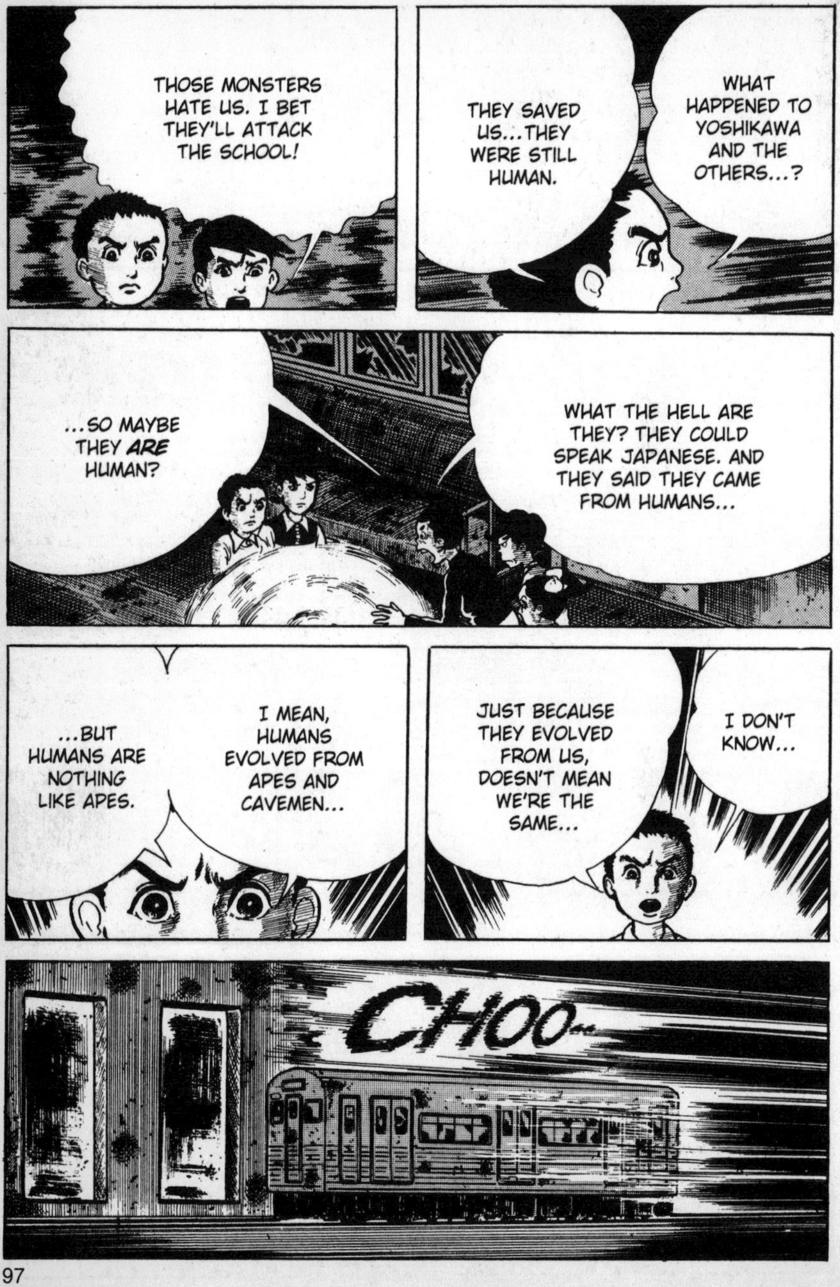
WHAT HAPPENED TO YOSHIKAWA AND THE OTHERS...?
THEY SAVED US...THEY WERE STILL HUMAN.
THOSE MONSTERS HATE US. I BET THEY'LL ATTACK THE SCHOOL!
WHAT THE HELL ARE THEY? THEY COULD SPEAK JAPANESE. AND THEY SAID THEY CAME FROM HUMANS...
...SO MAYBE THEY *ARE* HUMAN?
I DON'T KNOW...
JUST BECAUSE THEY EVOLVED FROM US, DOESN'T MEAN WE'RE THE SAME...
I MEAN, HUMANS EVOLVED FROM APES AND CAVEMEN...
...BUT HUMANS ARE NOTHING LIKE APES.
CHOO--

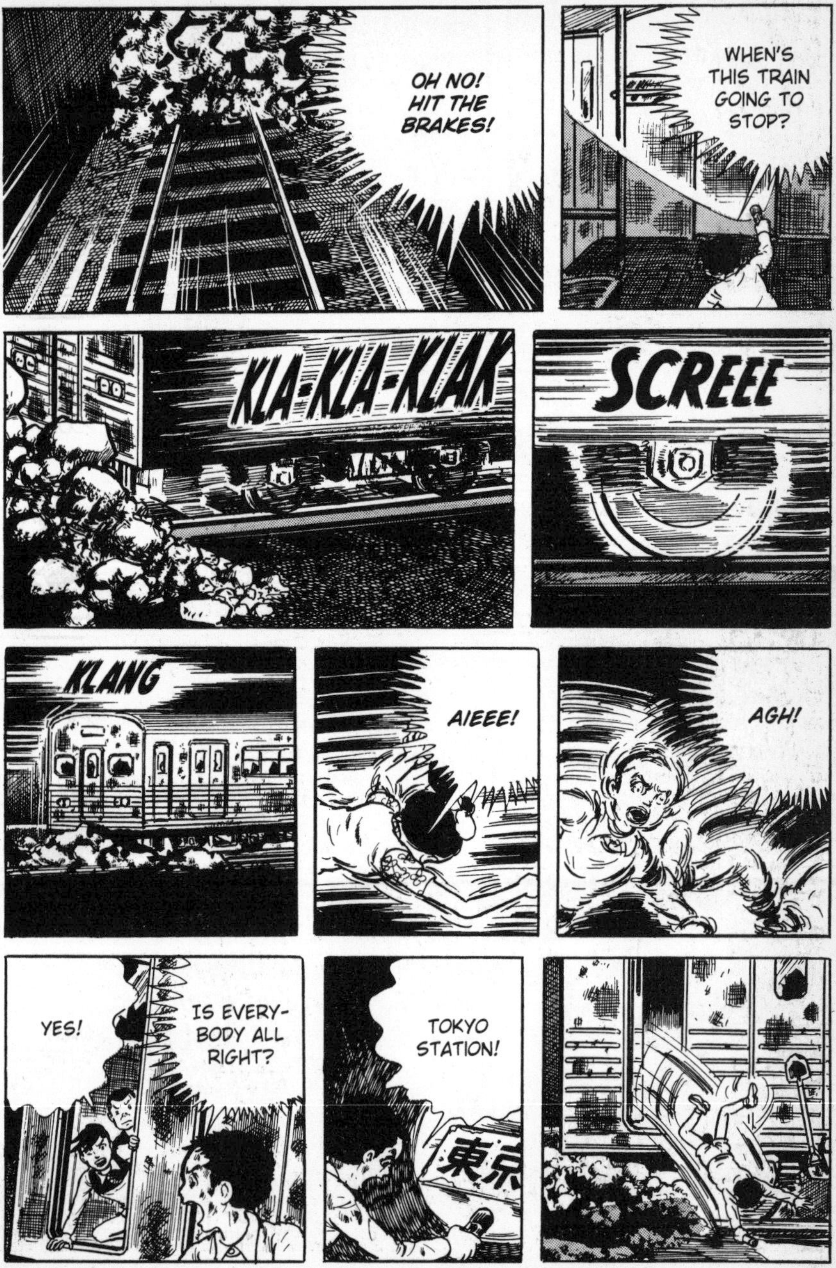
WHEN'S THIS TRAIN GOING TO STOP?
OH NO! HIT THE BRAKES!
SCREEE
KLA-KLA-KLAK
AGH!
AIEEE!
KLANG
TOKYO STATION!
東京
IS EVERY-BODY ALL RIGHT?
YES!

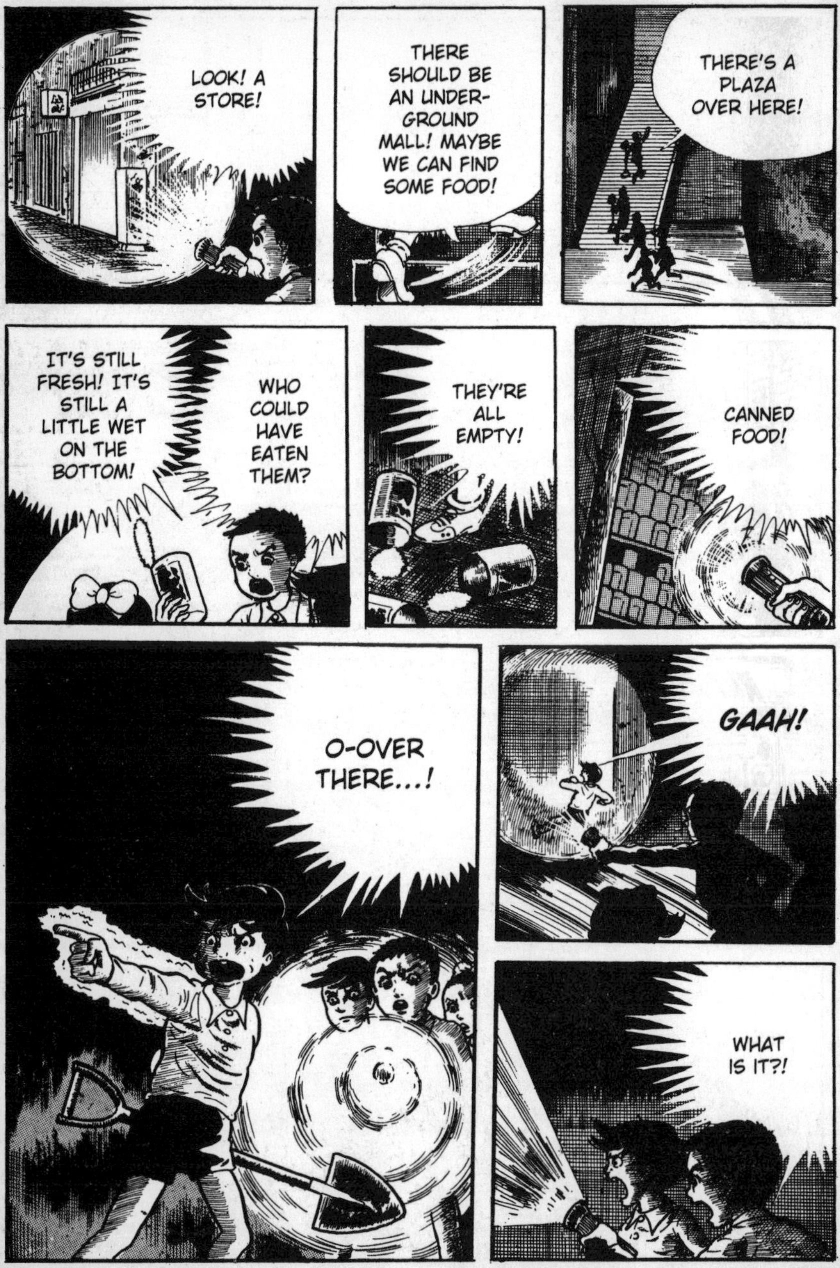
THERE'S A PLAZA OVER HERE!
THERE SHOULD BE AN UNDER-GROUND MALL! MAYBE WE CAN FIND SOME FOOD!
LOOK! A STORE!
CANNED FOOD!
THEY'RE ALL EMPTY!
WHO COULD HAVE EATEN THEM?
IT'S STILL FRESH! IT'S STILL A LITTLE WET ON THE BOTTOM!
GAAH!
WHAT IS IT?!
O-OVER THERE...!

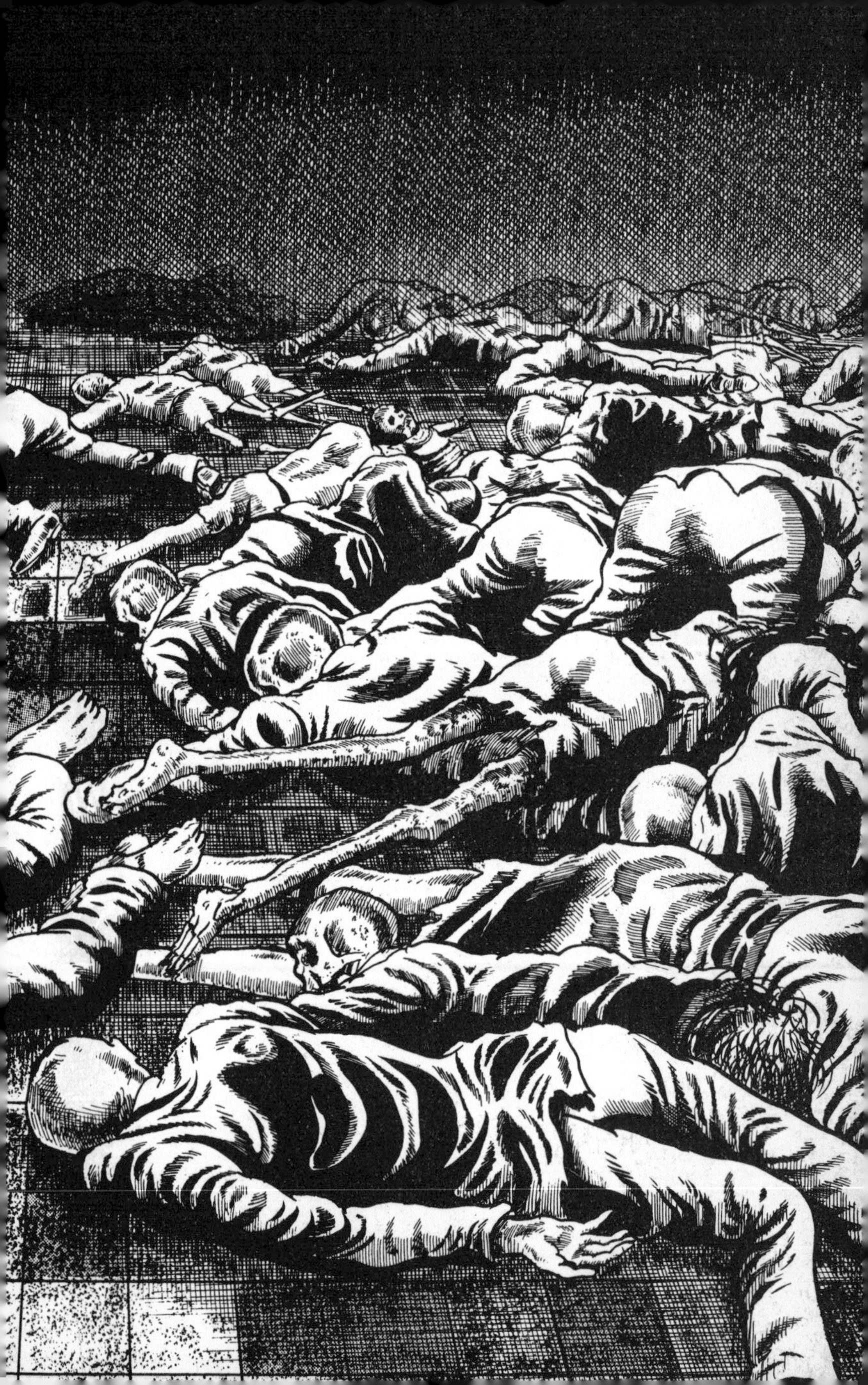

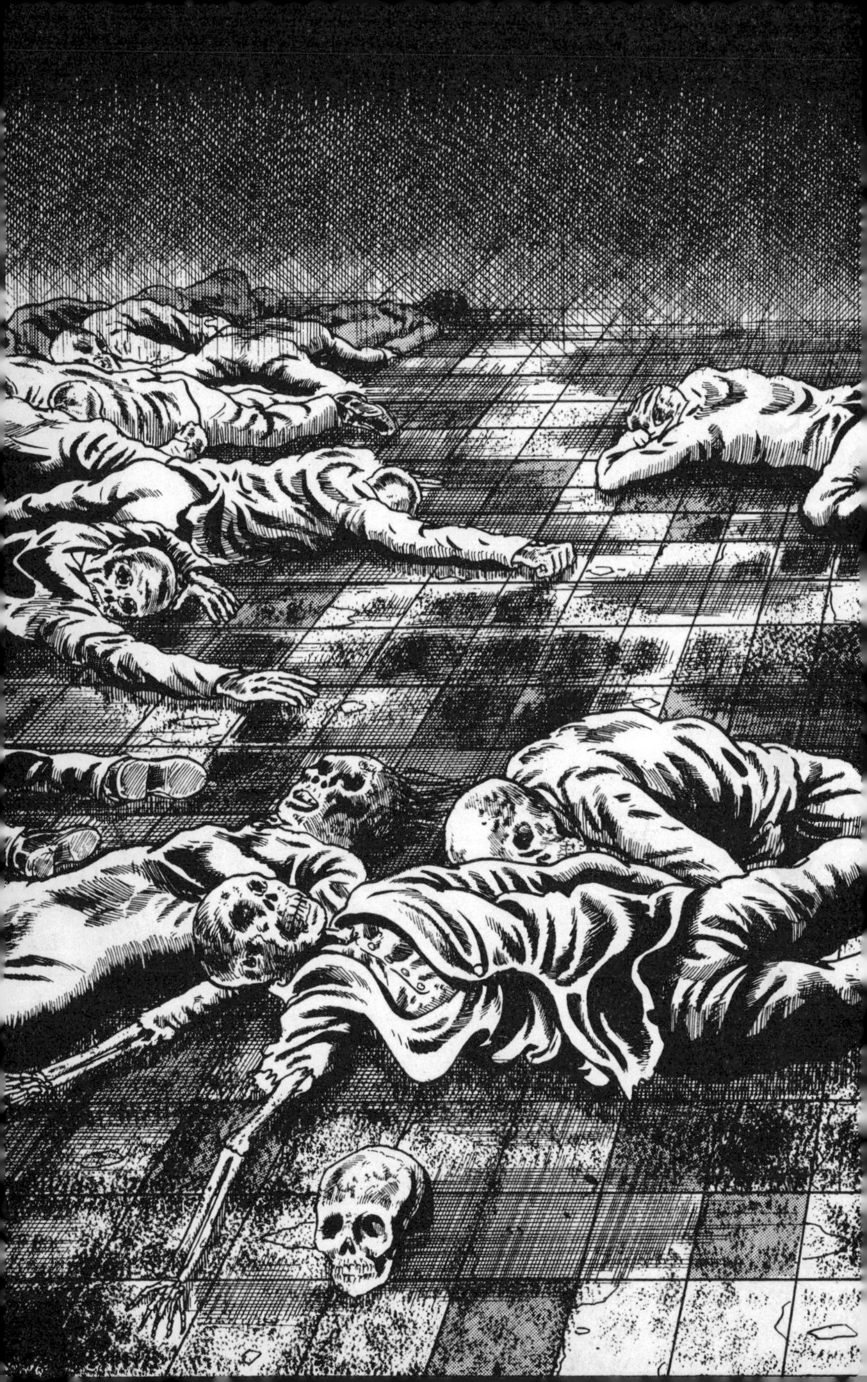

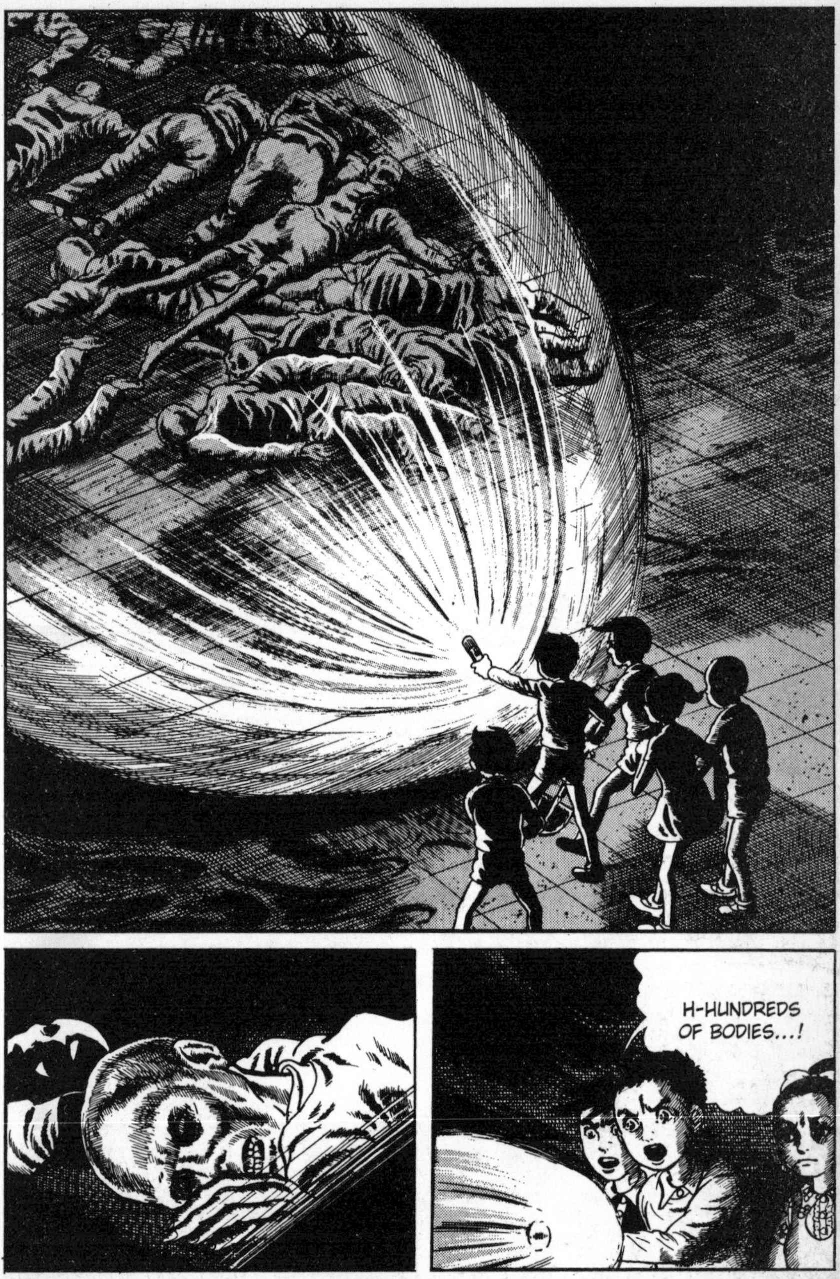
H-HUNDREDS
OF BODIES...!

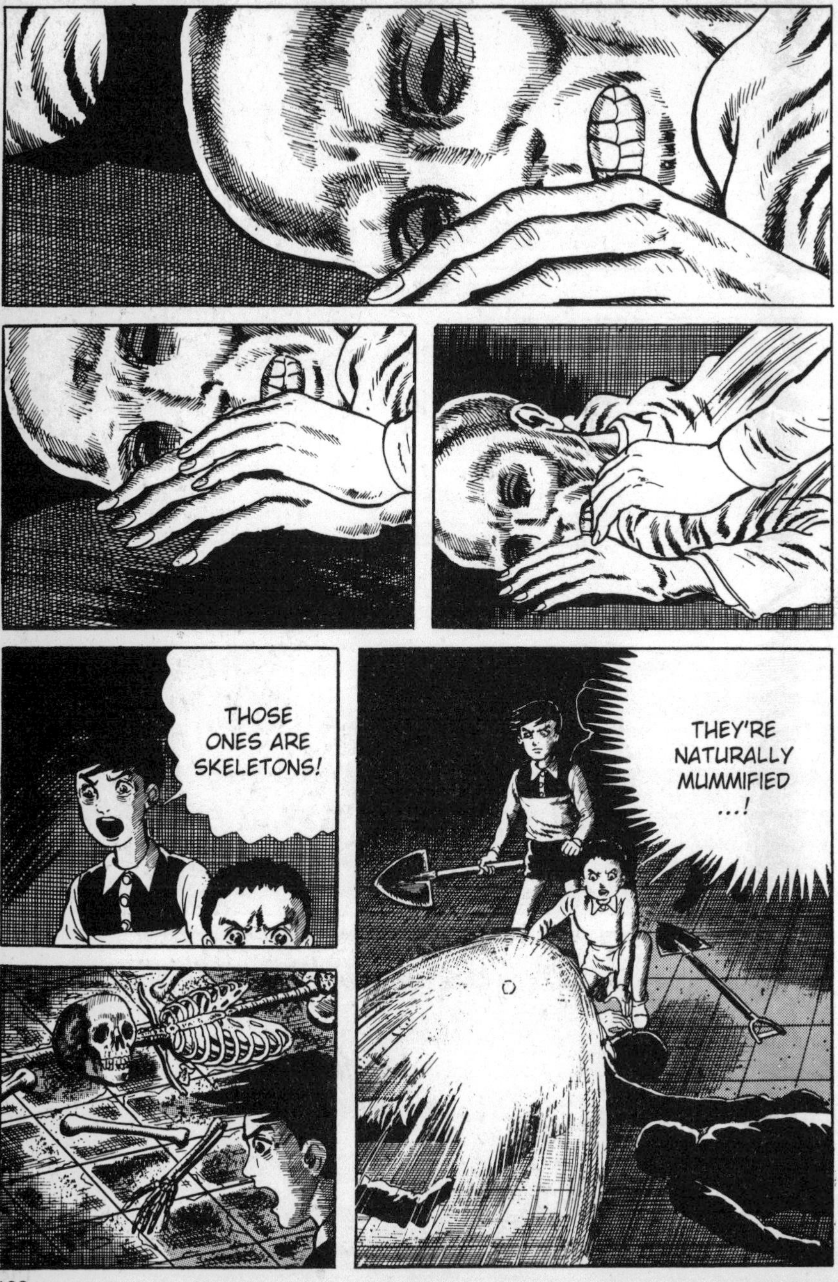
THEY'RE NATURALLY MUMMIFIED ...!
THOSE ONES ARE SKELETONS!

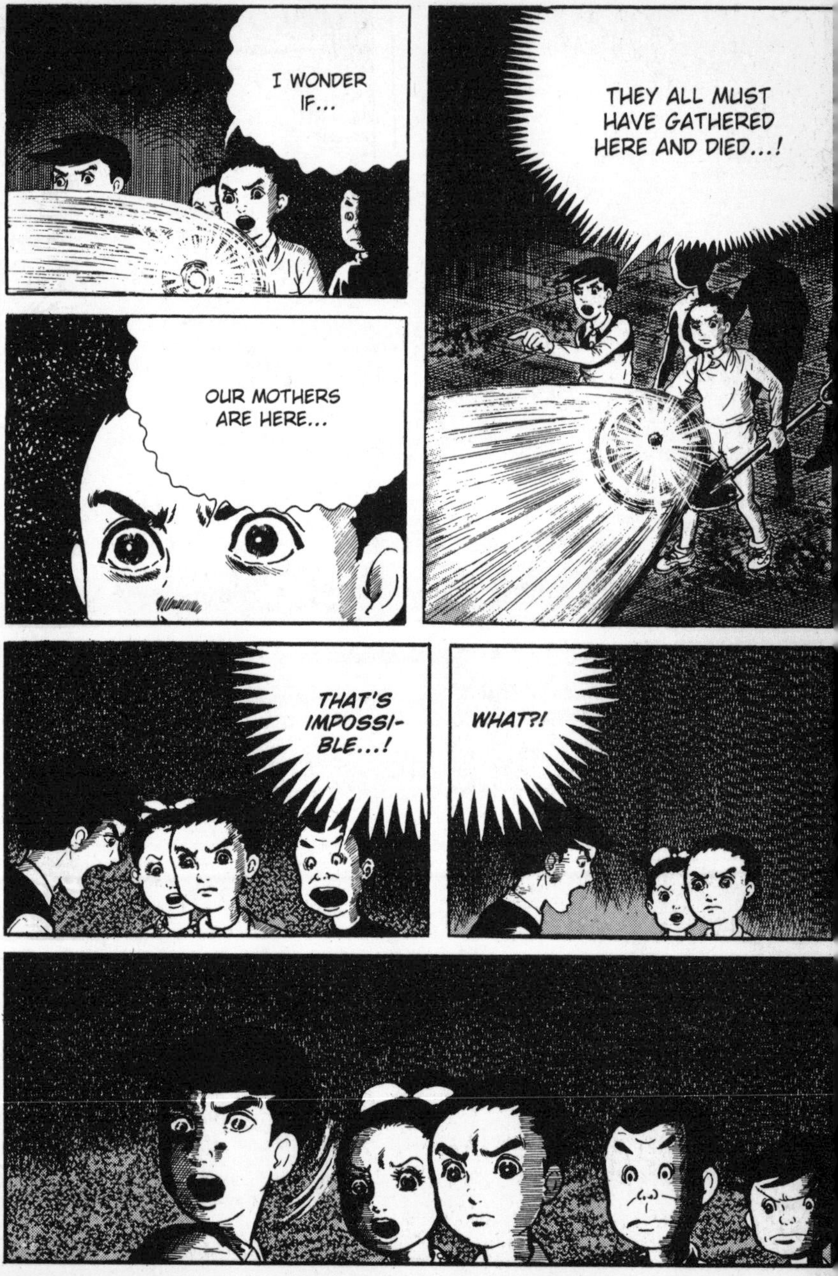
I WONDER IF...
OUR MOTHERS ARE HERE...
THEY ALL MUST HAVE GATHERED HERE AND DIED...!
THAT'S IMPOSSI-BLE...!
WHAT?!

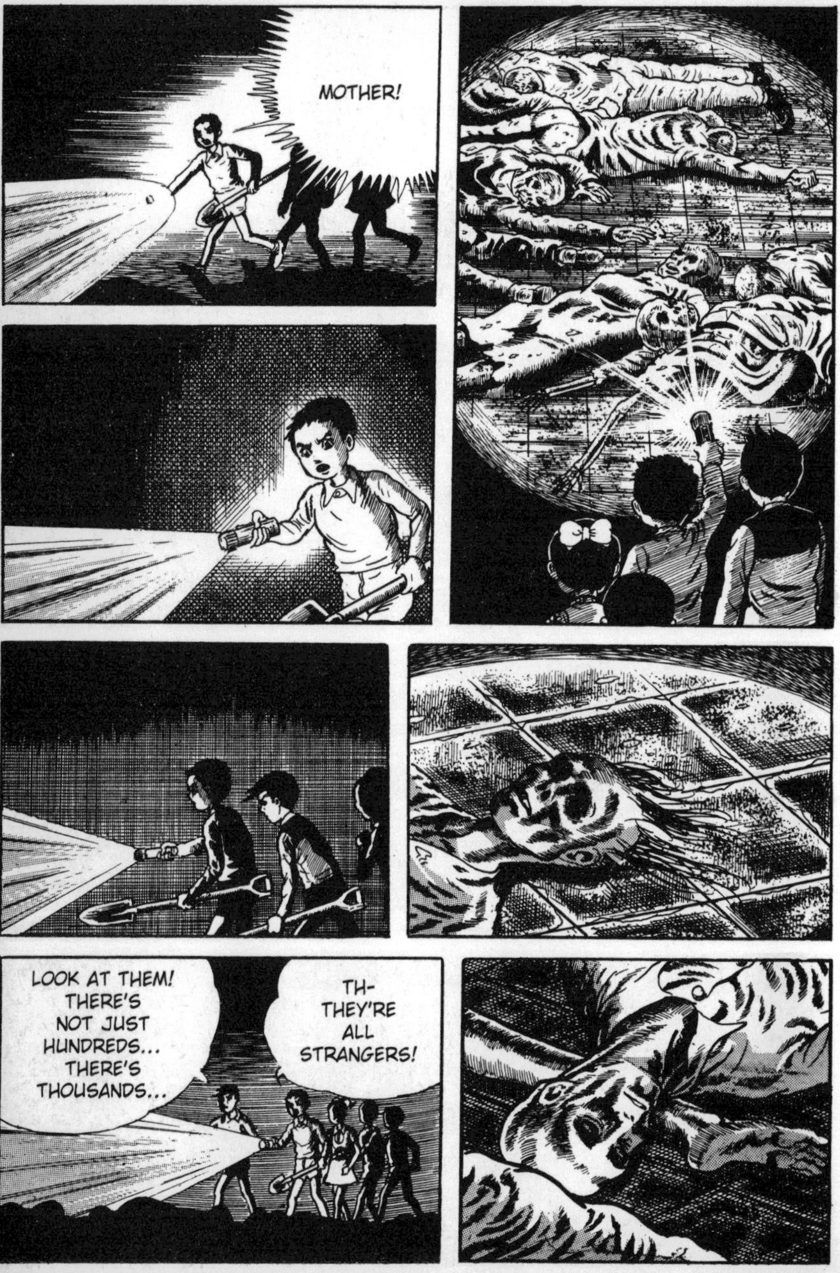
MOTHER!
TH- THEY'RE ALL STRANGERS!
LOOK AT THEM! THERE'S NOT JUST HUNDREDS... THERE'S THOUSANDS...

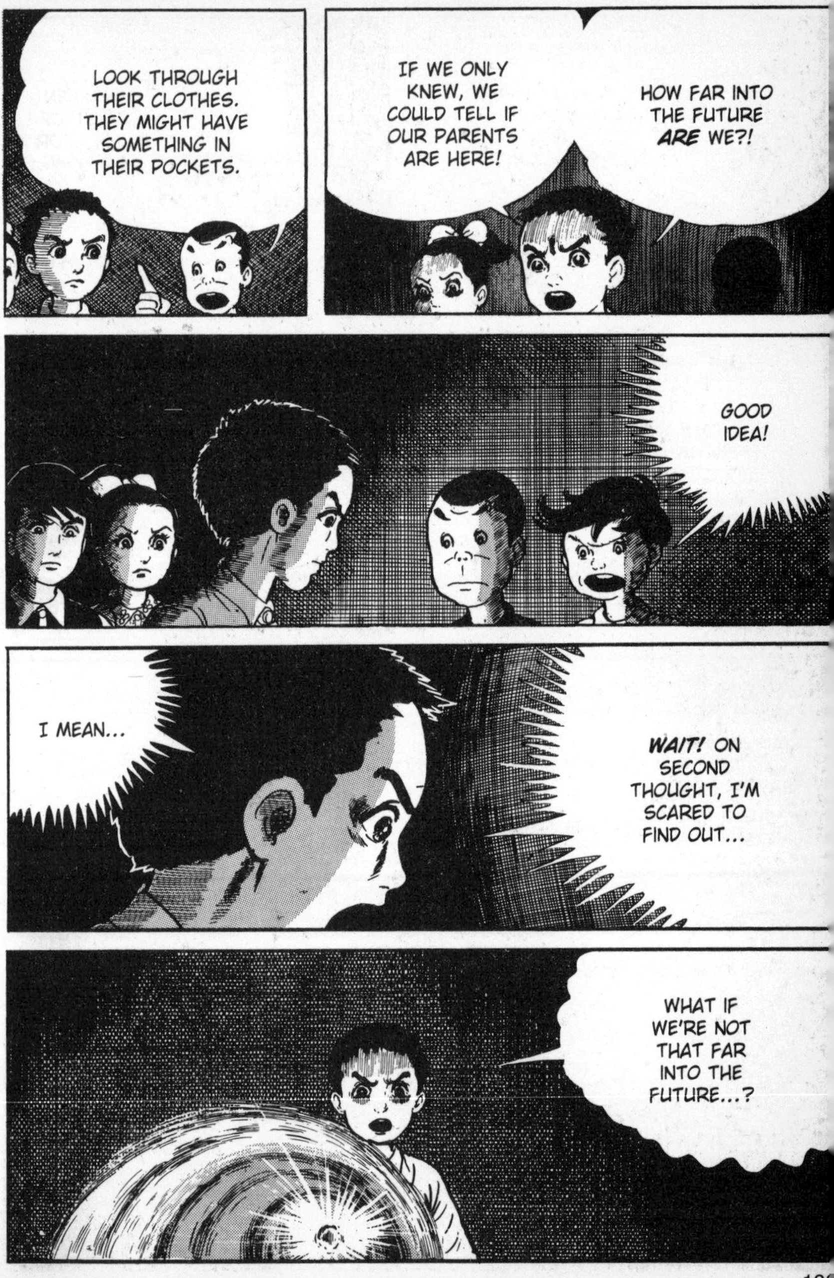
HOW FAR INTO THE FUTURE ***ARE*** WE?!
IF WE ONLY KNEW, WE COULD TELL IF OUR PARENTS ARE HERE!
LOOK THROUGH THEIR CLOTHES. THEY MIGHT HAVE SOMETHING IN THEIR POCKETS.
GOOD IDEA!
WAIT! ON SECOND THOUGHT, I'M SCARED TO FIND OUT...
I MEAN...
WHAT IF WE'RE NOT THAT FAR INTO THE FUTURE...?

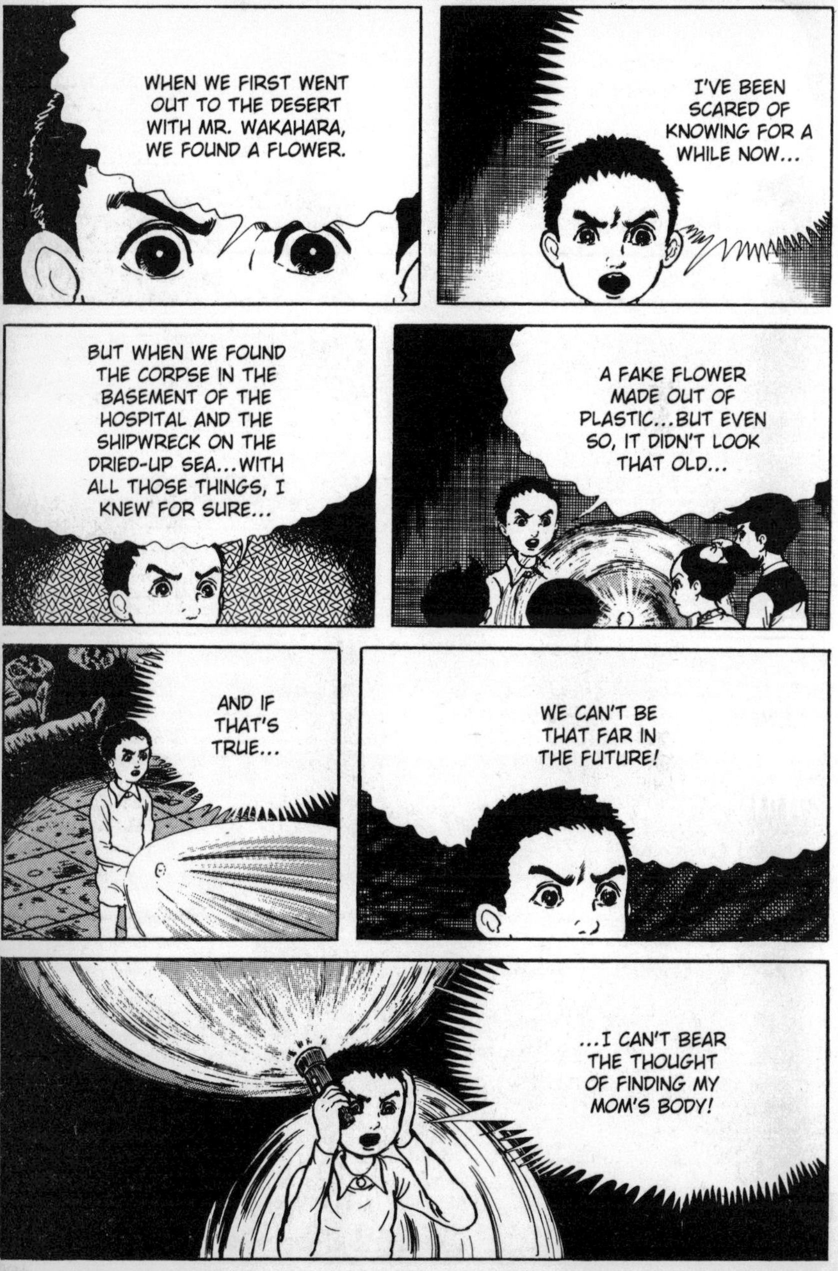
I'VE BEEN SCARED OF KNOWING FOR A WHILE NOW...
WHEN WE FIRST WENT OUT TO THE DESERT WITH MR. WAKAHARA, WE FOUND A FLOWER.
A FAKE FLOWER MADE OUT OF PLASTIC...BUT EVEN SO, IT DIDN'T LOOK THAT OLD...
BUT WHEN WE FOUND THE CORPSE IN THE BASEMENT OF THE HOSPITAL AND THE SHIPWRECK ON THE DRIED-UP SEA...WITH ALL THOSE THINGS, I KNEW FOR SURE...
WE CAN'T BE THAT FAR IN THE FUTURE!
AND IF THAT'S TRUE...
...I CAN'T BEAR THE THOUGHT OF FINDING MY MOM'S BODY!

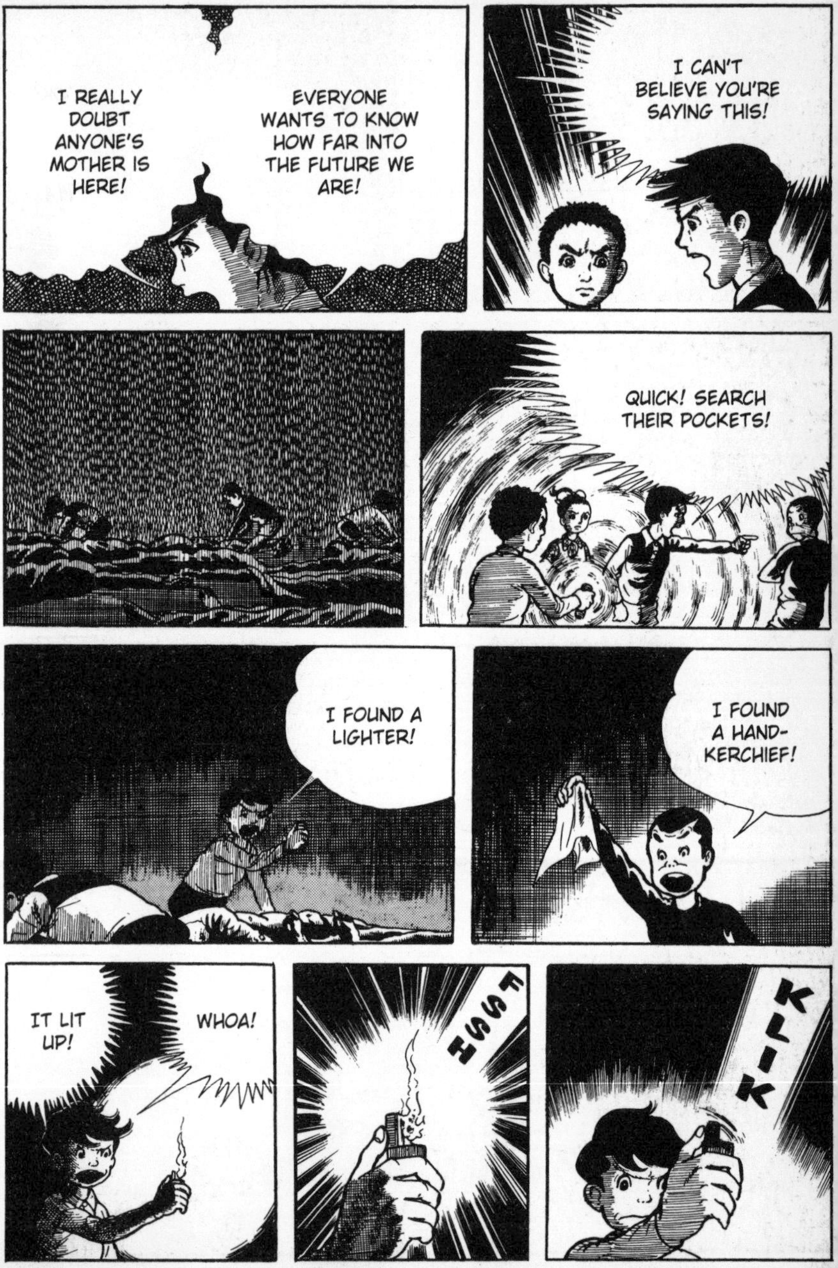
I CAN'T BELIEVE YOU'RE SAYING THIS!
EVERYONE WANTS TO KNOW HOW FAR INTO THE FUTURE WE ARE!
I REALLY DOUBT ANYONE'S MOTHER IS HERE!
QUICK! SEARCH THEIR POCKETS!
I FOUND A HAND-KERCHIEF!
I FOUND A LIGHTER!
KLIK
FSSH
WHOA!
IT LIT UP!

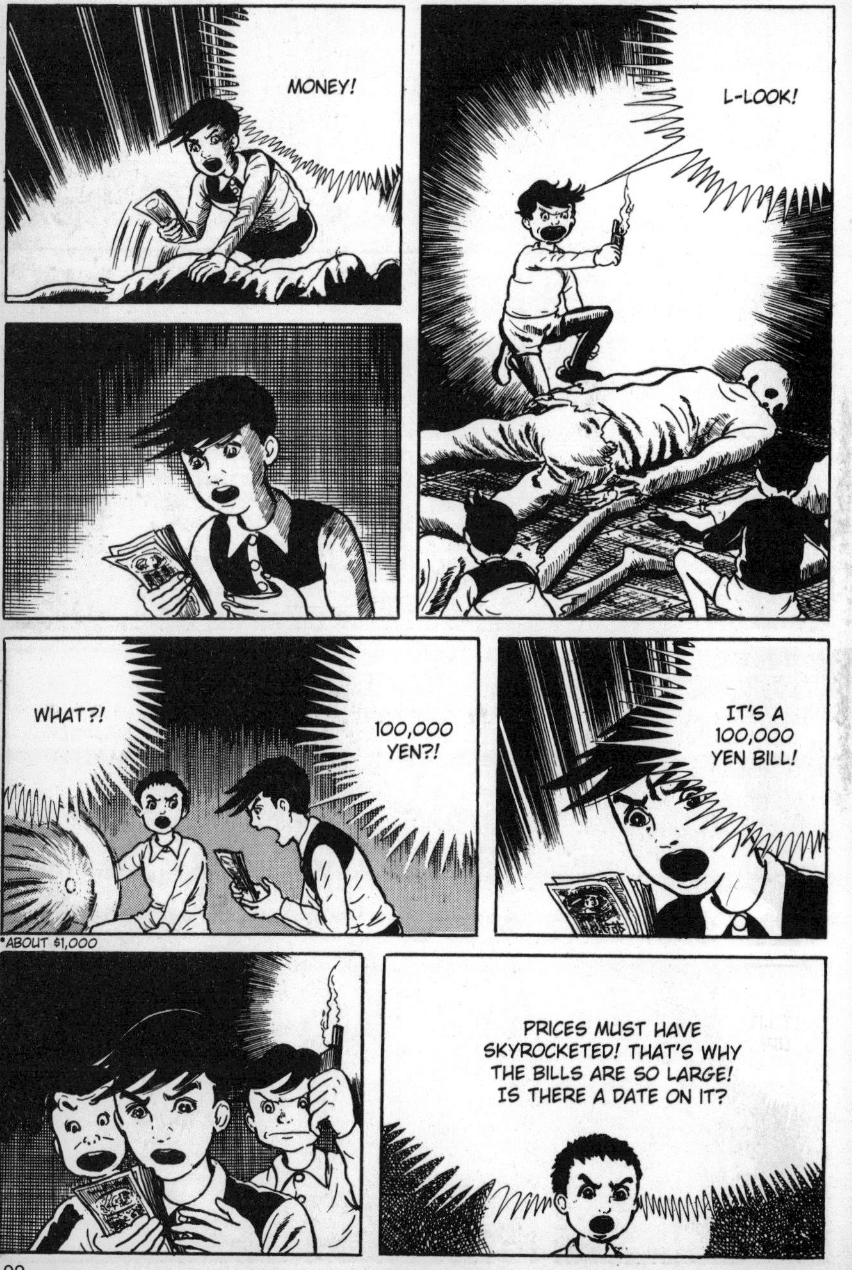
L-LOOK!
MONEY!
IT'S A 100,000 YEN BILL!
100,000 YEN?!
WHAT?!
PRICES MUST HAVE SKYROCKETED! THAT'S WHY THE BILLS ARE SO LARGE! IS THERE A DATE ON IT?
*ABOUT $1,000

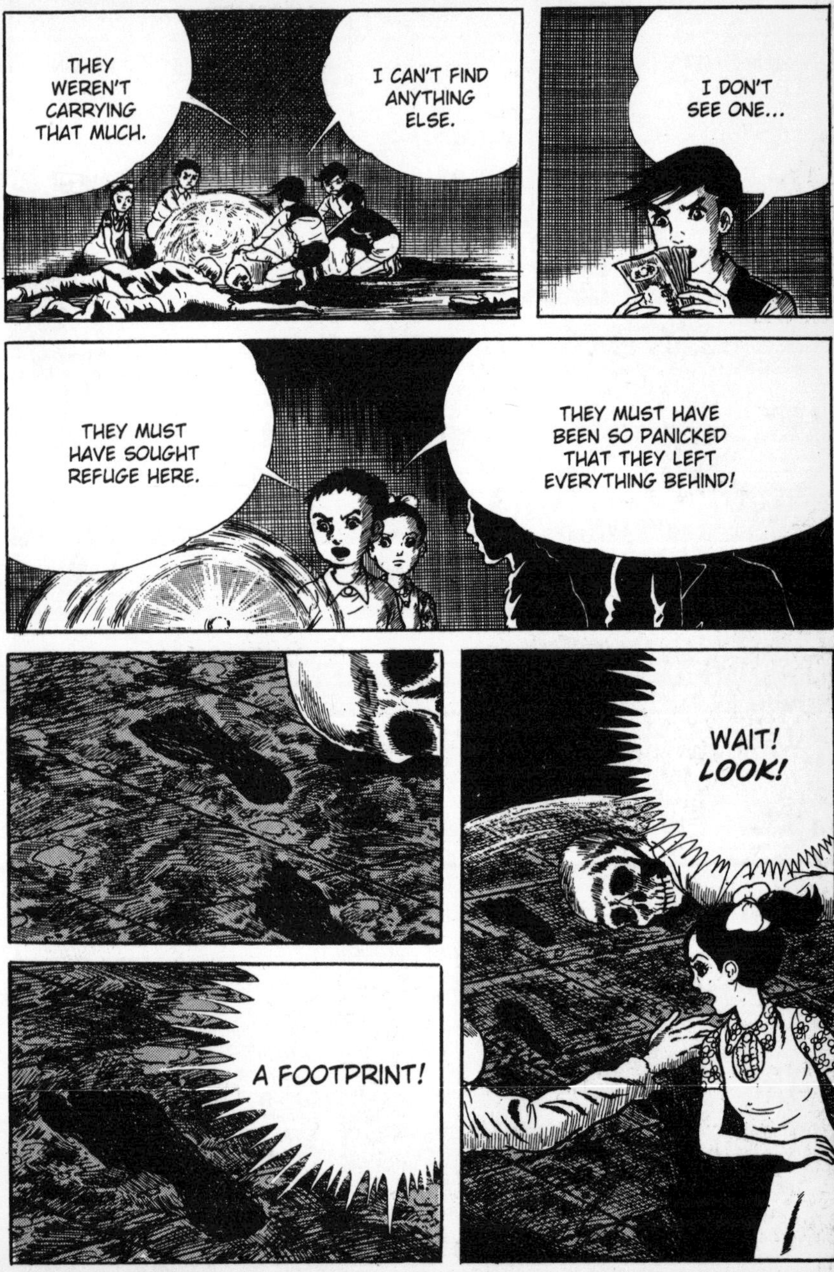
I DON'T SEE ONE...
I CAN'T FIND ANYTHING ELSE.
THEY WEREN'T CARRYING THAT MUCH.
THEY MUST HAVE BEEN SO PANICKED THAT THEY LEFT EVERYTHING BEHIND!
THEY MUST HAVE SOUGHT REFUGE HERE.
WAIT! LOOK!
A FOOTPRINT!

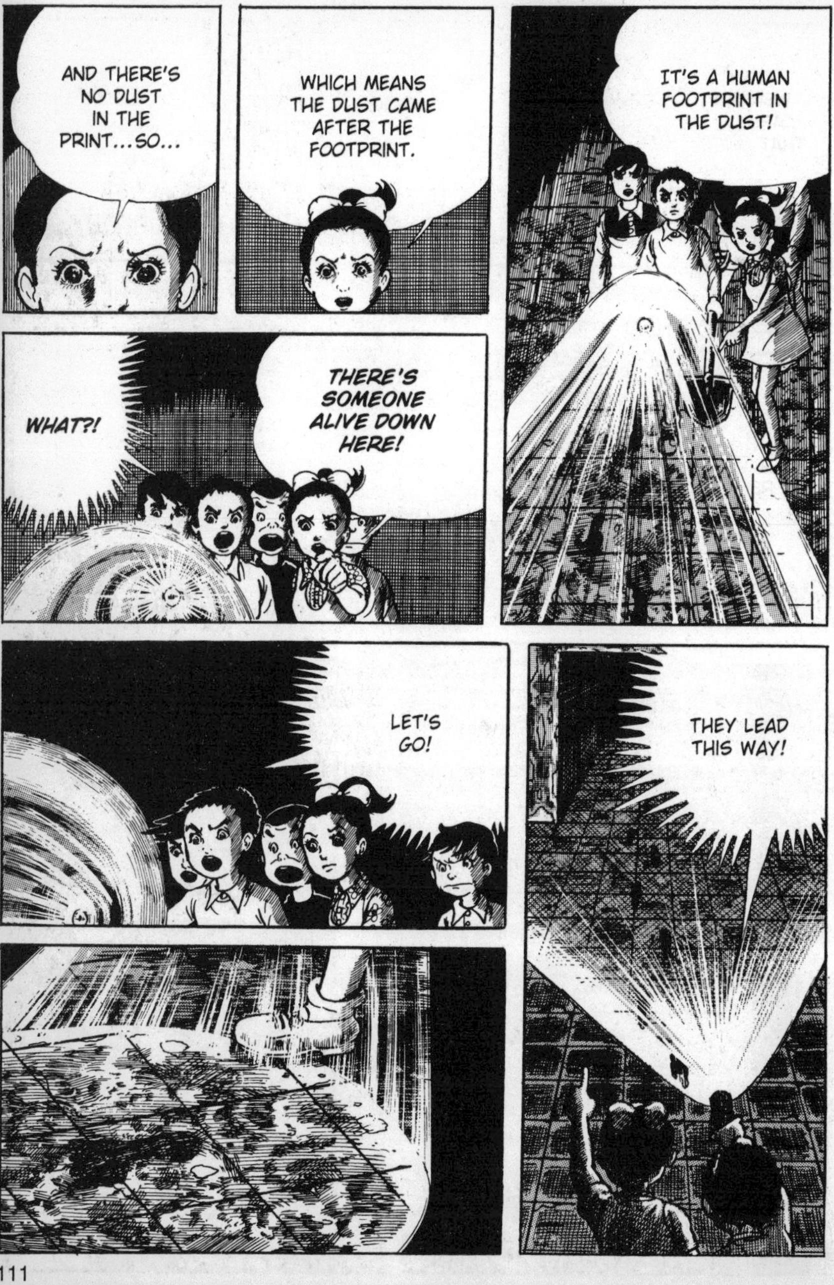
AND THERE'S NO DUST IN THE PRINT...SO...
WHICH MEANS THE DUST CAME AFTER THE FOOTPRINT.
IT'S A HUMAN FOOTPRINT IN THE DUST!
THERE'S SOMEONE ALIVE DOWN HERE!
WHAT?!
LET'S GO!
THEY LEAD THIS WAY!

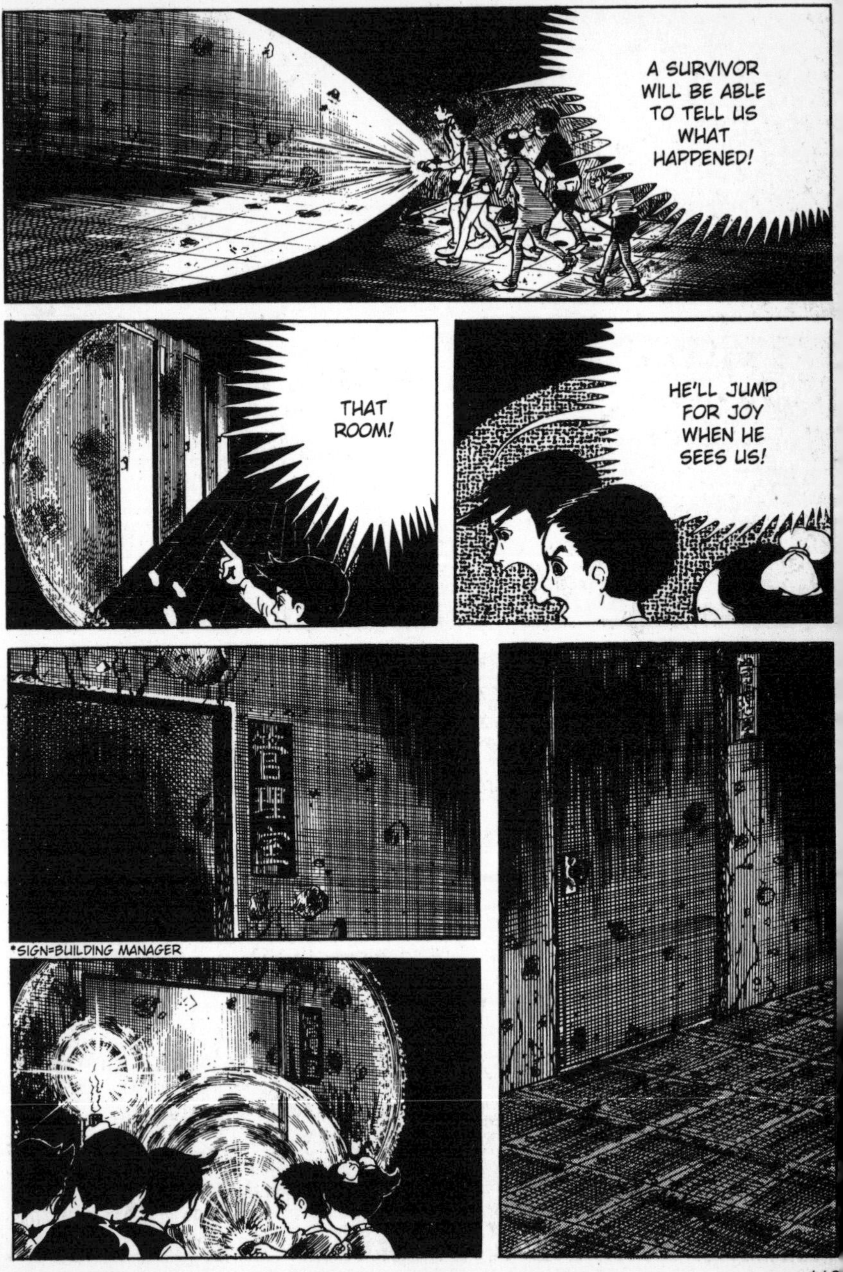
A SURVIVOR WILL BE ABLE TO TELL US WHAT HAPPENED!
HE'LL JUMP FOR JOY WHEN HE SEES US!
THAT ROOM!
管理室
*SIGN=BUILDING MANAGER

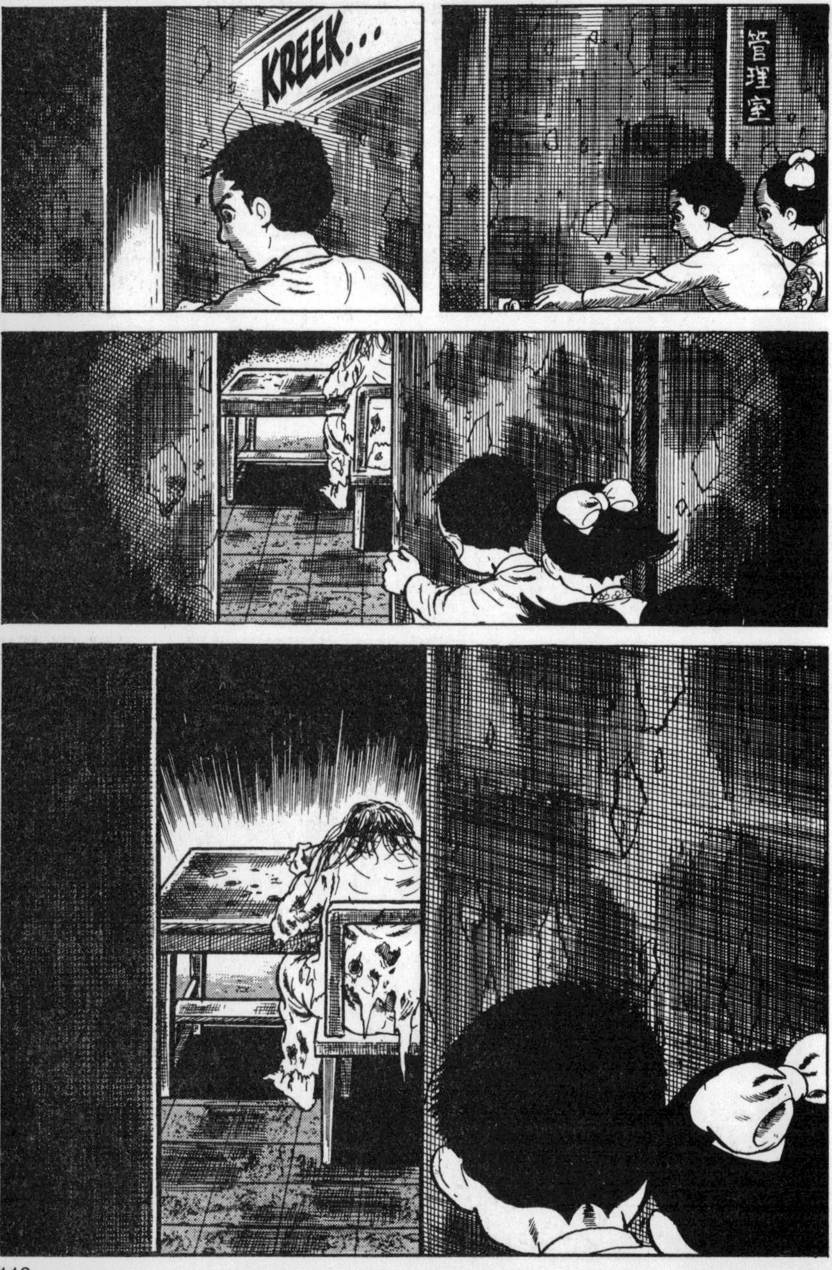

管理室
KREEK...

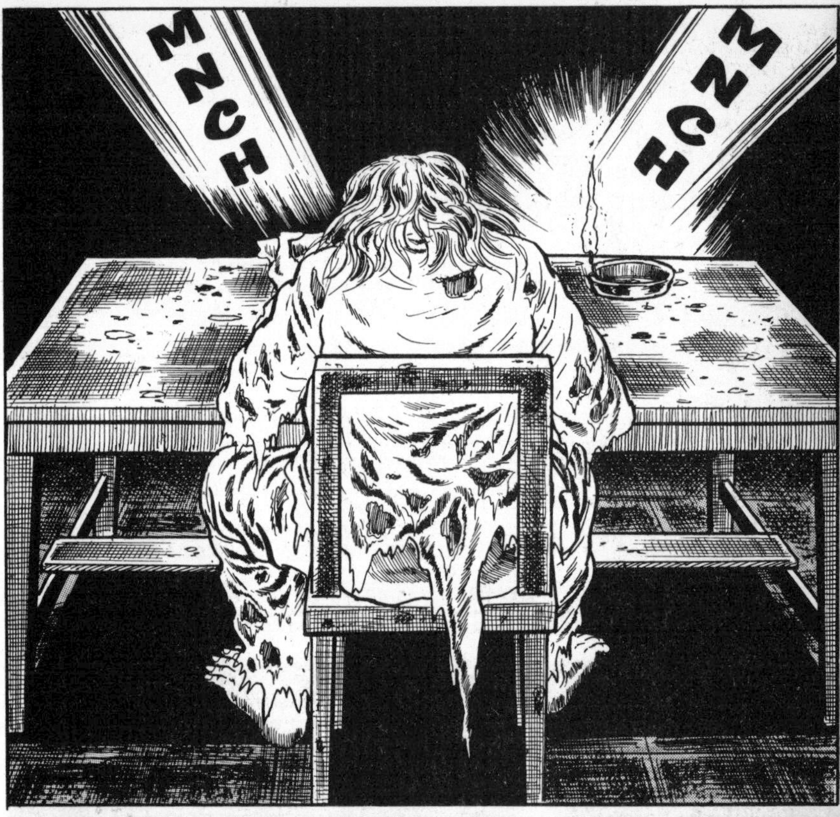
MNCH
MNCH

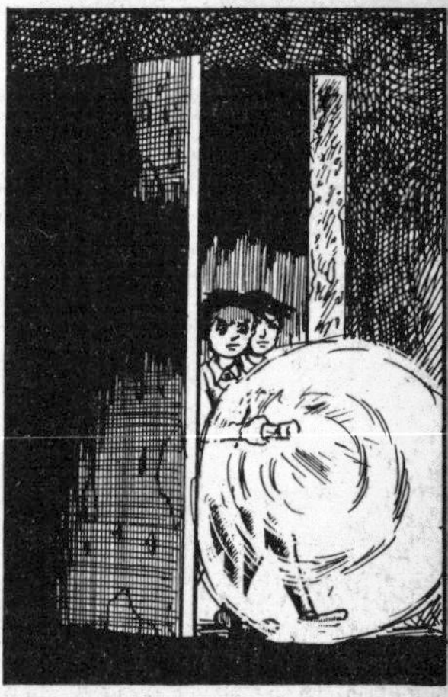

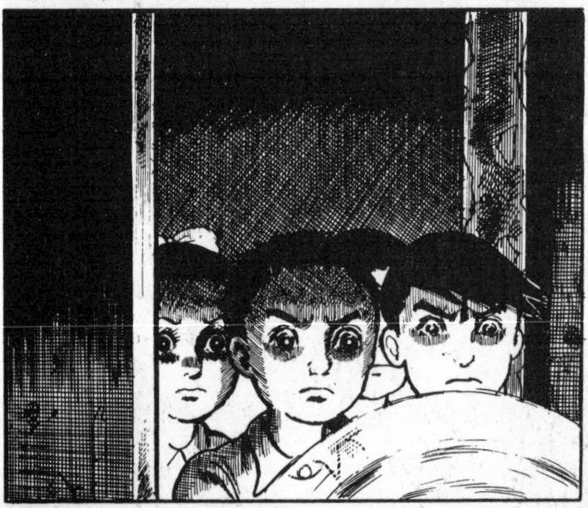

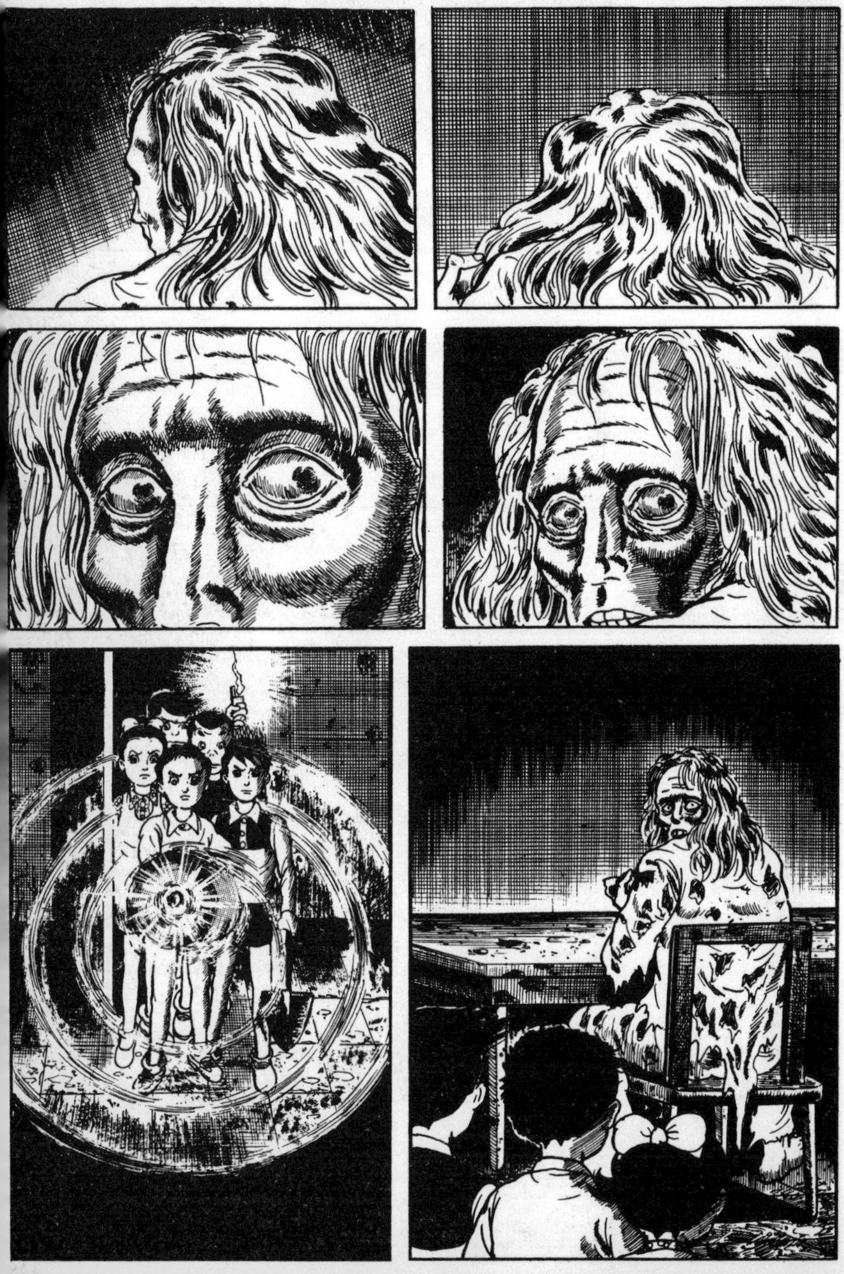

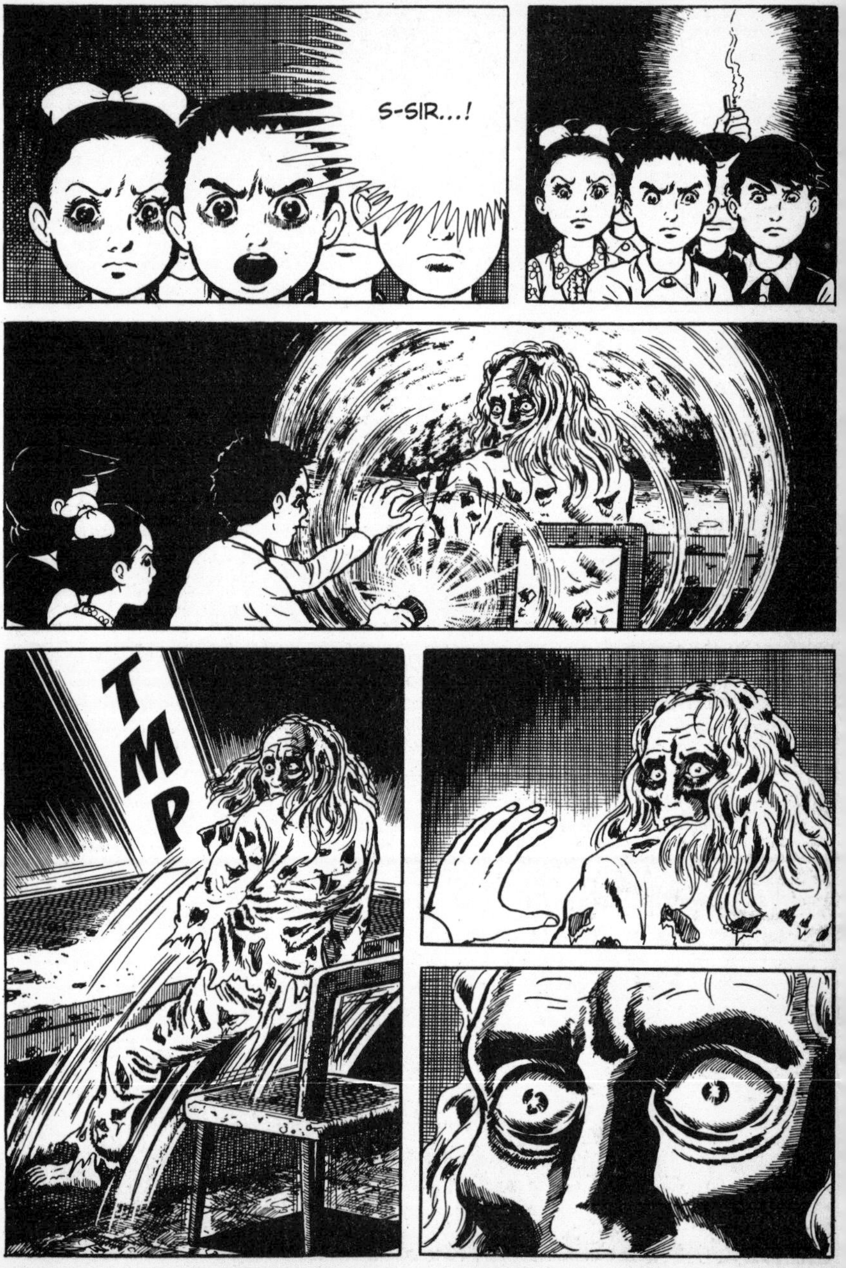
S-SIR...!
TMP

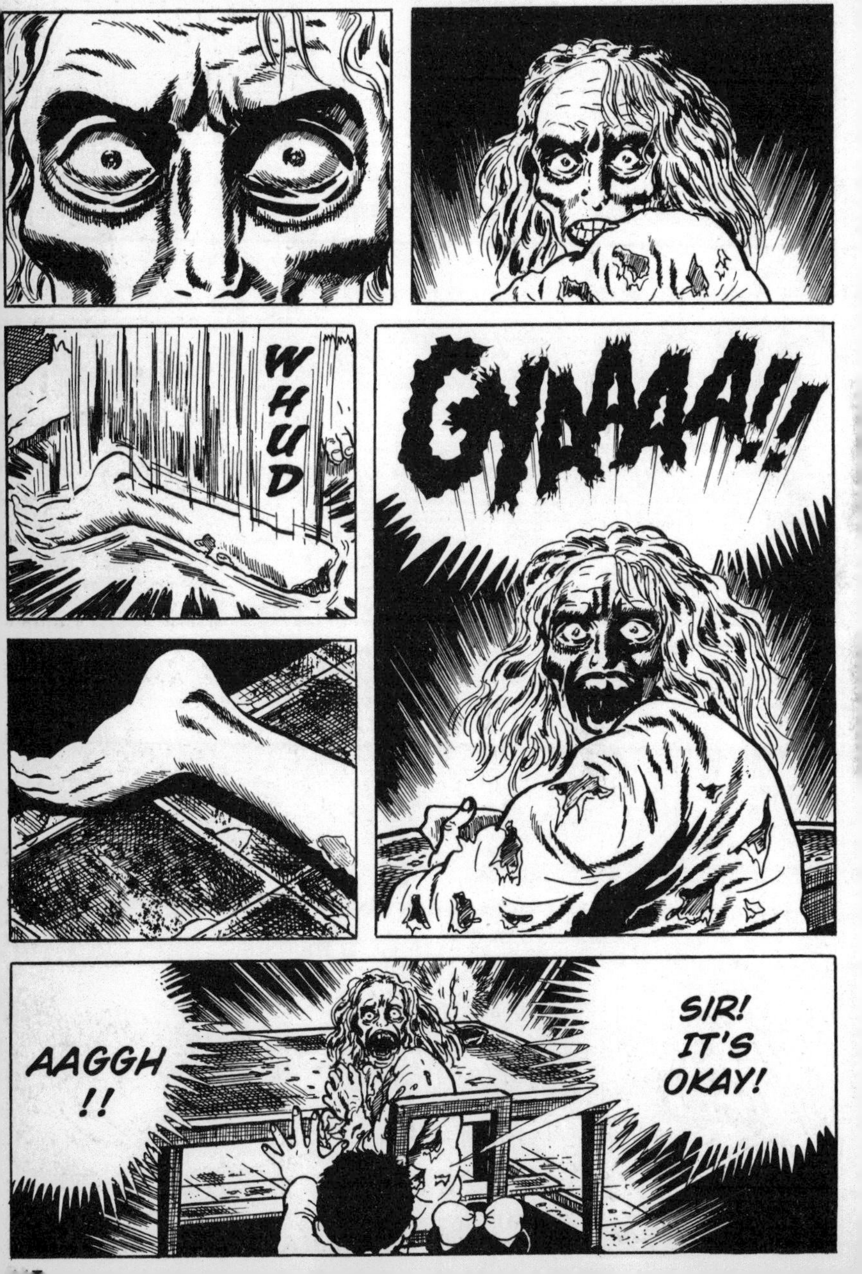
GYAAA!!
WHUD
SIR! IT'S OKAY!
AAGGH !!

MISTER!

AHH!

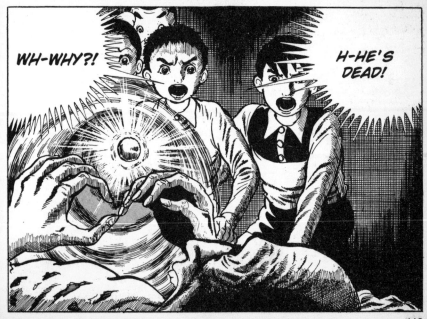

WH-WHY?!

H-HE'S DEAD!

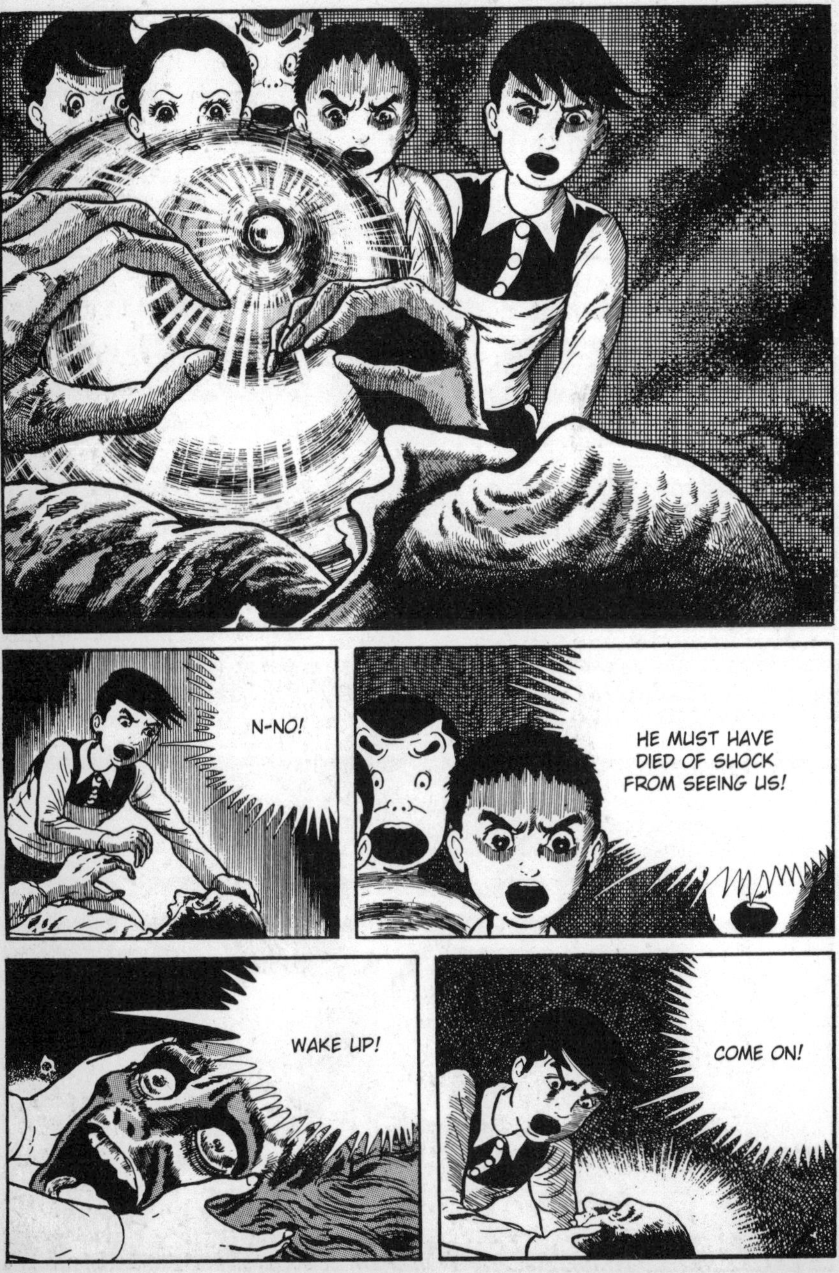
HE MUST HAVE DIED OF SHOCK FROM SEEING US!
N-NO!
COME ON!
WAKE UP!

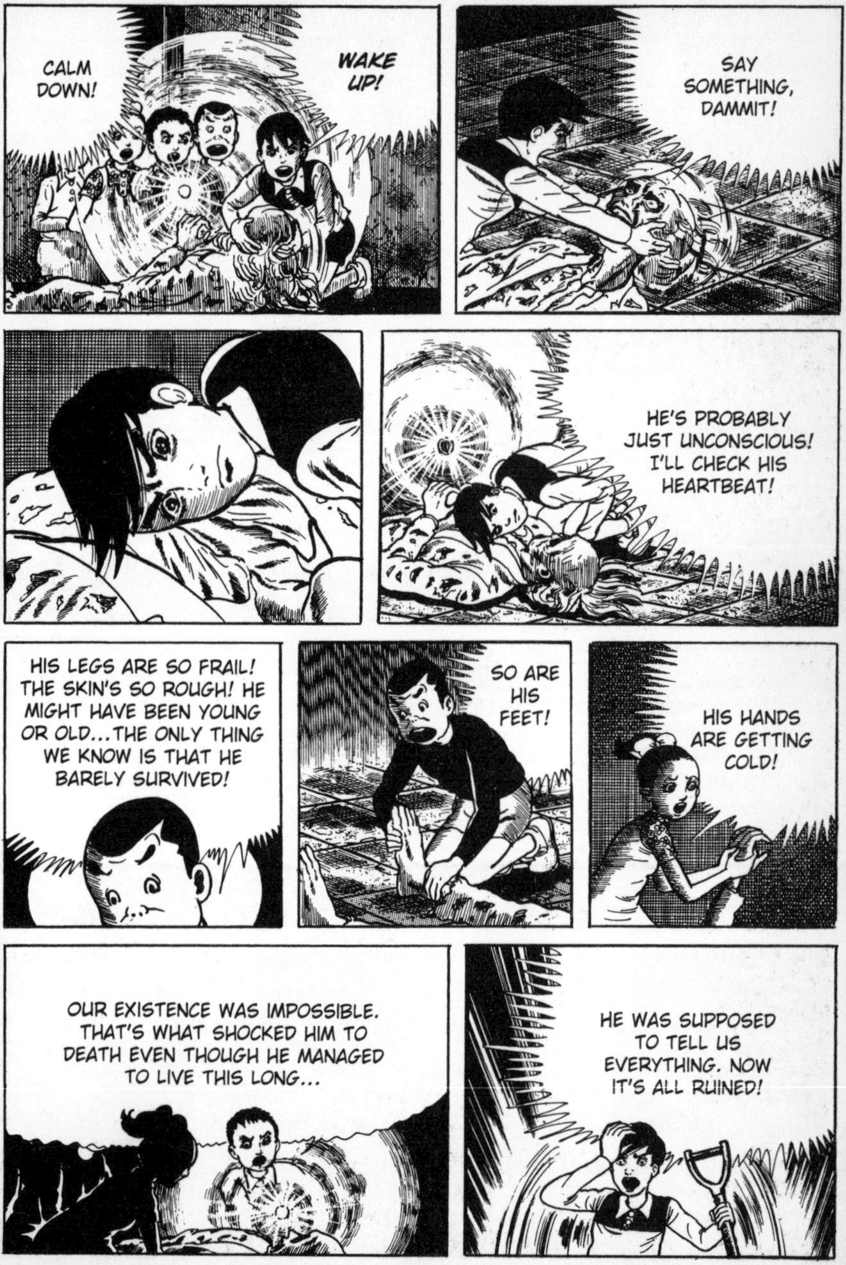
CALM DOWN!
WAKE UP!
SAY SOMETHING, DAMMIT!
HE'S PROBABLY JUST UNCONSCIOUS! I'LL CHECK HIS HEARTBEAT!
HIS LEGS ARE SO FRAIL! THE SKIN'S SO ROUGH! HE MIGHT HAVE BEEN YOUNG OR OLD...THE ONLY THING WE KNOW IS THAT HE BARELY SURVIVED!
SO ARE HIS FEET!
HIS HANDS ARE GETTING COLD!
OUR EXISTENCE WAS IMPOSSIBLE. THAT'S WHAT SHOCKED HIM TO DEATH EVEN THOUGH HE MANAGED TO LIVE THIS LONG...
HE WAS SUPPOSED TO TELL US EVERYTHING. NOW IT'S ALL RUINED!

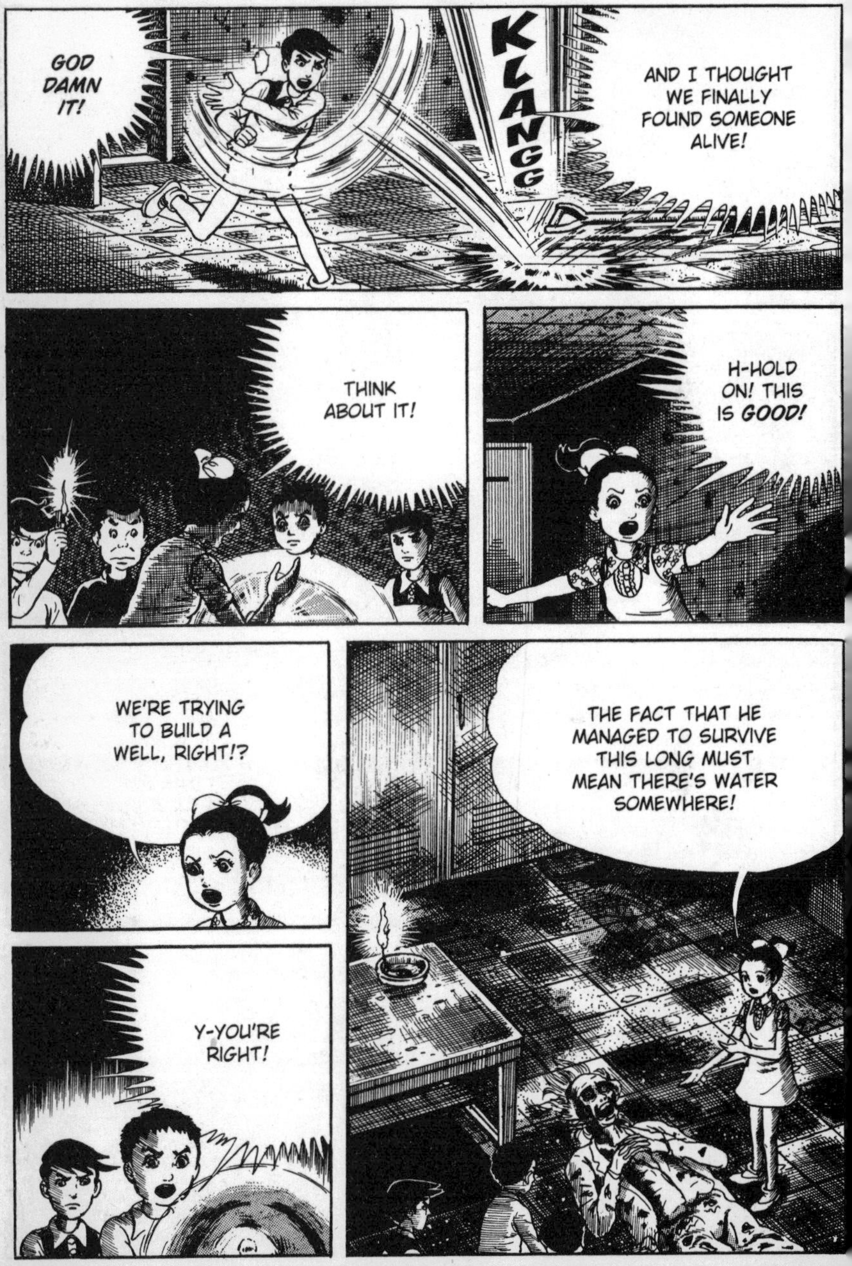
GOD DAMN IT!
KLANGG
AND I THOUGHT WE FINALLY FOUND SOMEONE ALIVE!
H-HOLD ON! THIS IS *GOOD!*
THINK ABOUT IT!
THE FACT THAT HE MANAGED TO SURVIVE THIS LONG MUST MEAN THERE'S WATER SOMEWHERE!
WE'RE TRYING TO BUILD A WELL, RIGHT!?
Y-YOU'RE RIGHT!

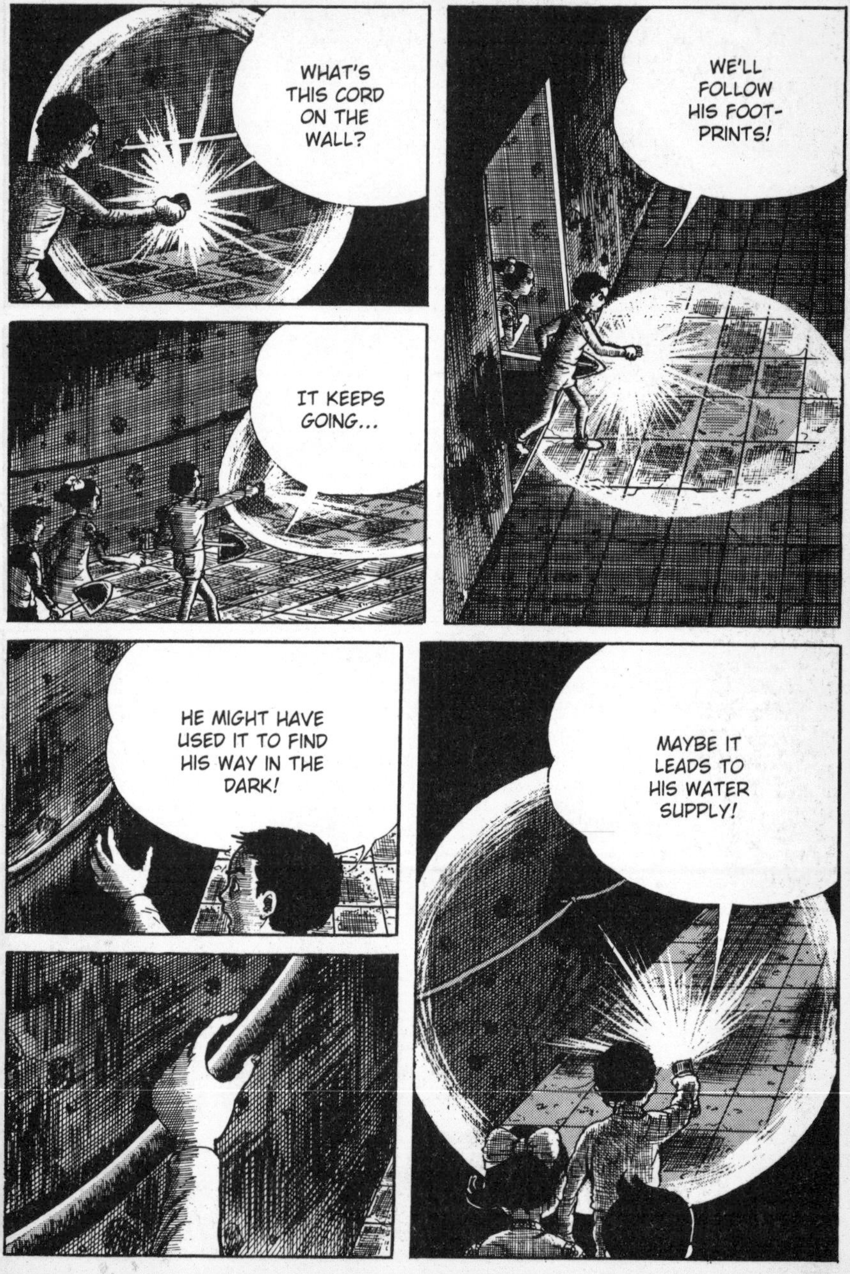
WHAT'S THIS CORD ON THE WALL?
IT KEEPS GOING...
WE'LL FOLLOW HIS FOOT-PRINTS!
HE MIGHT HAVE USED IT TO FIND HIS WAY IN THE DARK!
MAYBE IT LEADS TO HIS WATER SUPPLY!

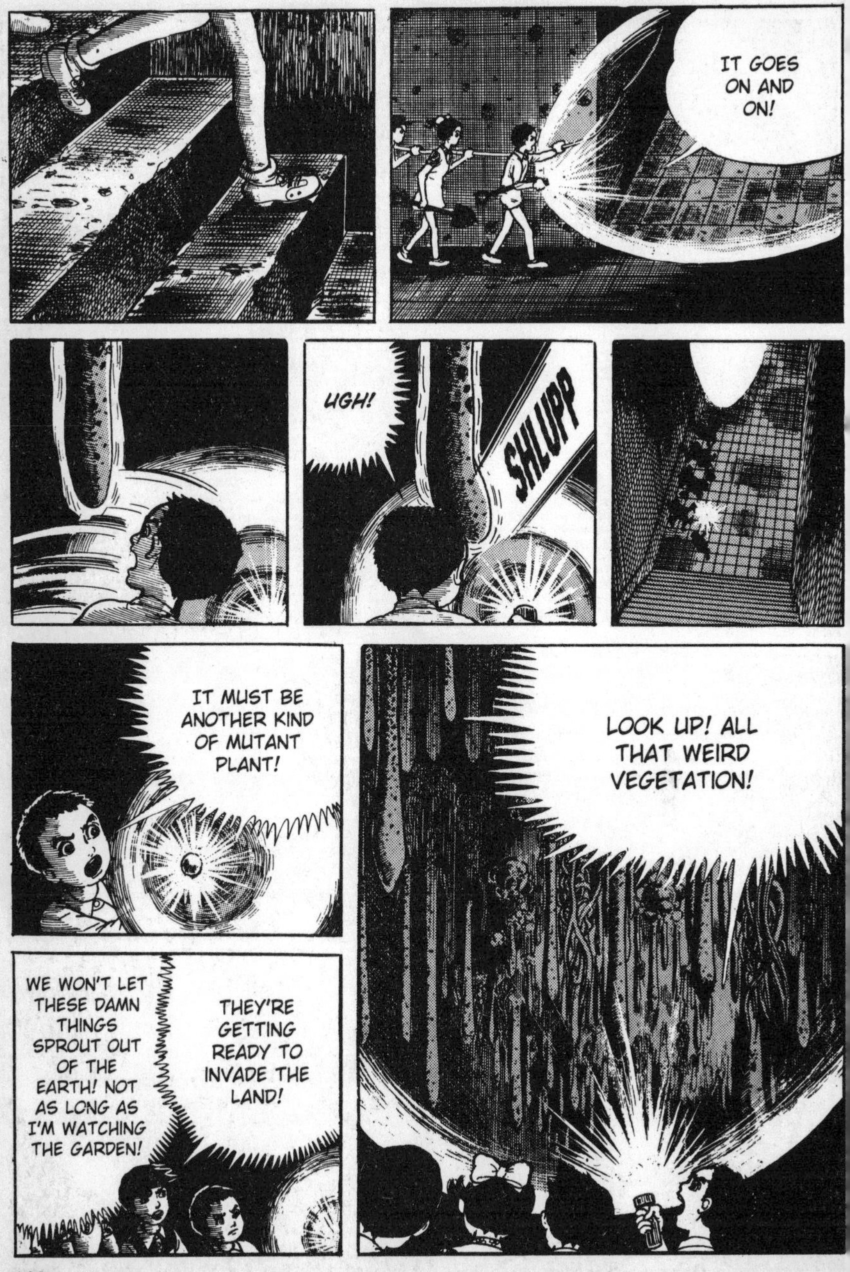
IT GOES ON AND ON!
UGH!
SHLUPP
IT MUST BE ANOTHER KIND OF MUTANT PLANT!
LOOK UP! ALL THAT WEIRD VEGETATION!
THEY'RE GETTING READY TO INVADE THE LAND!
WE WON'T LET THESE DAMN THINGS SPROUT OUT OF THE EARTH! NOT AS LONG AS I'M WATCHING THE GARDEN!

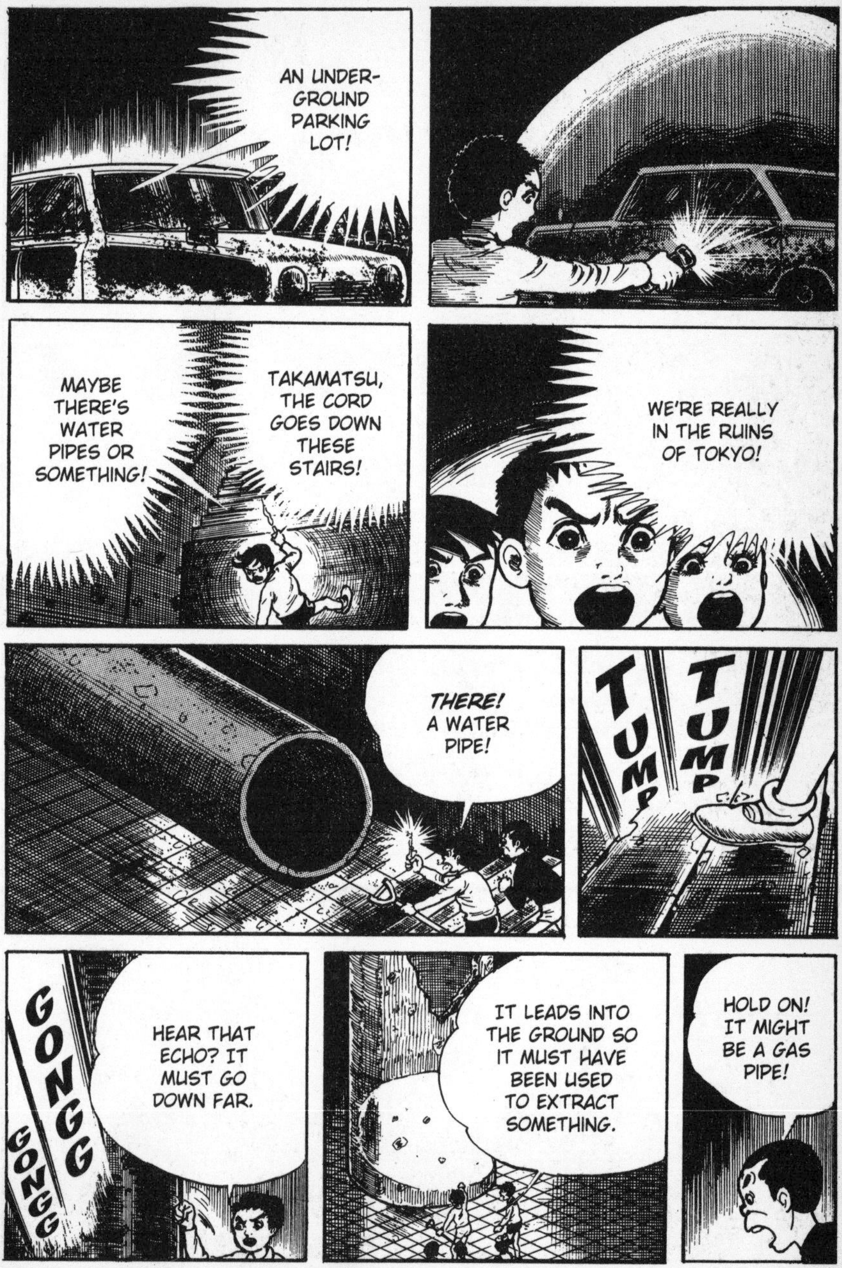
AN UNDER-GROUND PARKING LOT!
MAYBE THERE'S WATER PIPES OR SOMETHING!
TAKAMATSU, THE CORD GOES DOWN THESE STAIRS!
WE'RE REALLY IN THE RUINS OF TOKYO!
THERE! A WATER PIPE!
TUMP TUMP
GONGG GONGG
HEAR THAT ECHO? IT MUST GO DOWN FAR.
IT LEADS INTO THE GROUND SO IT MUST HAVE BEEN USED TO EXTRACT SOMETHING.
HOLD ON! IT MIGHT BE A GAS PIPE!

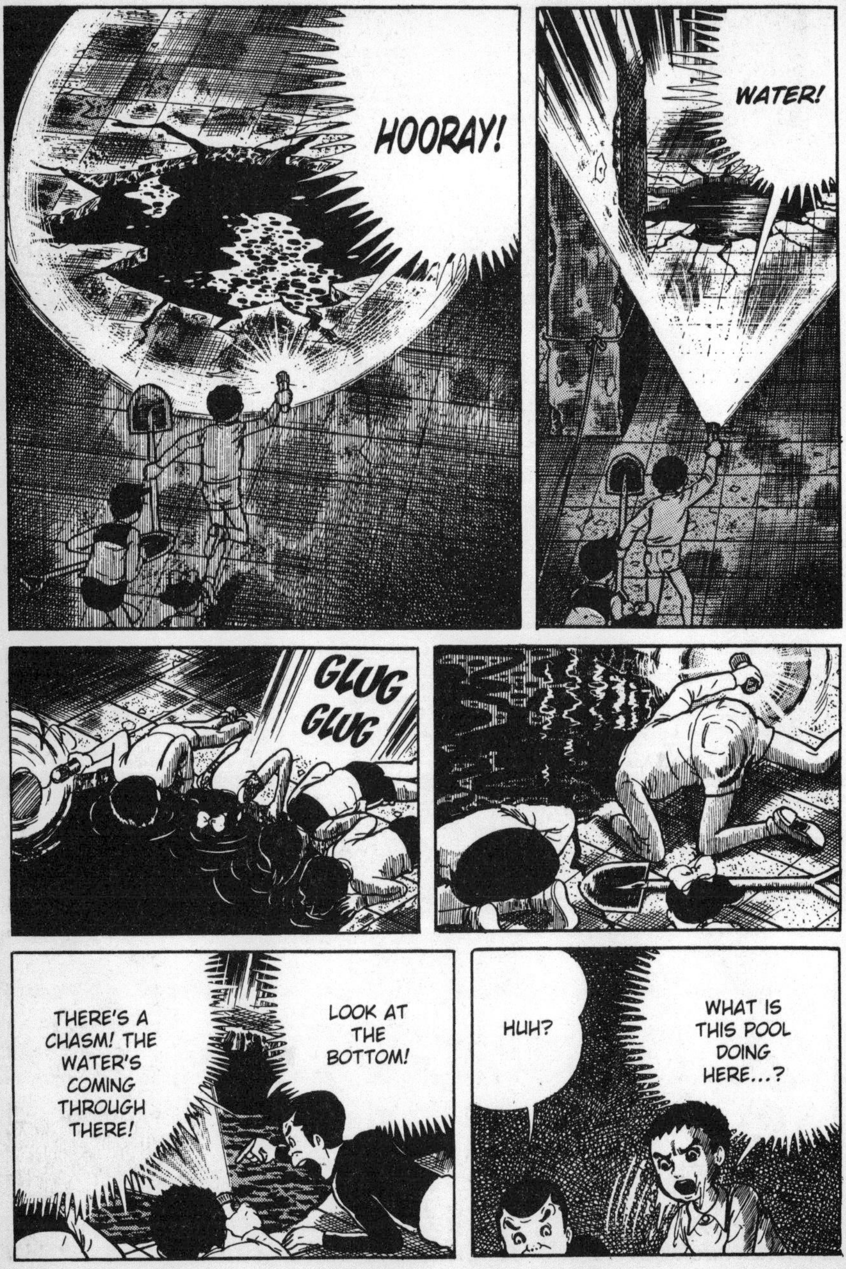
WATER!
HOORAY!
GLUG GLUG
WHAT IS THIS POOL DOING HERE...?
HUH?
LOOK AT THE BOTTOM!
THERE'S A CHASM! THE WATER'S COMING THROUGH THERE!

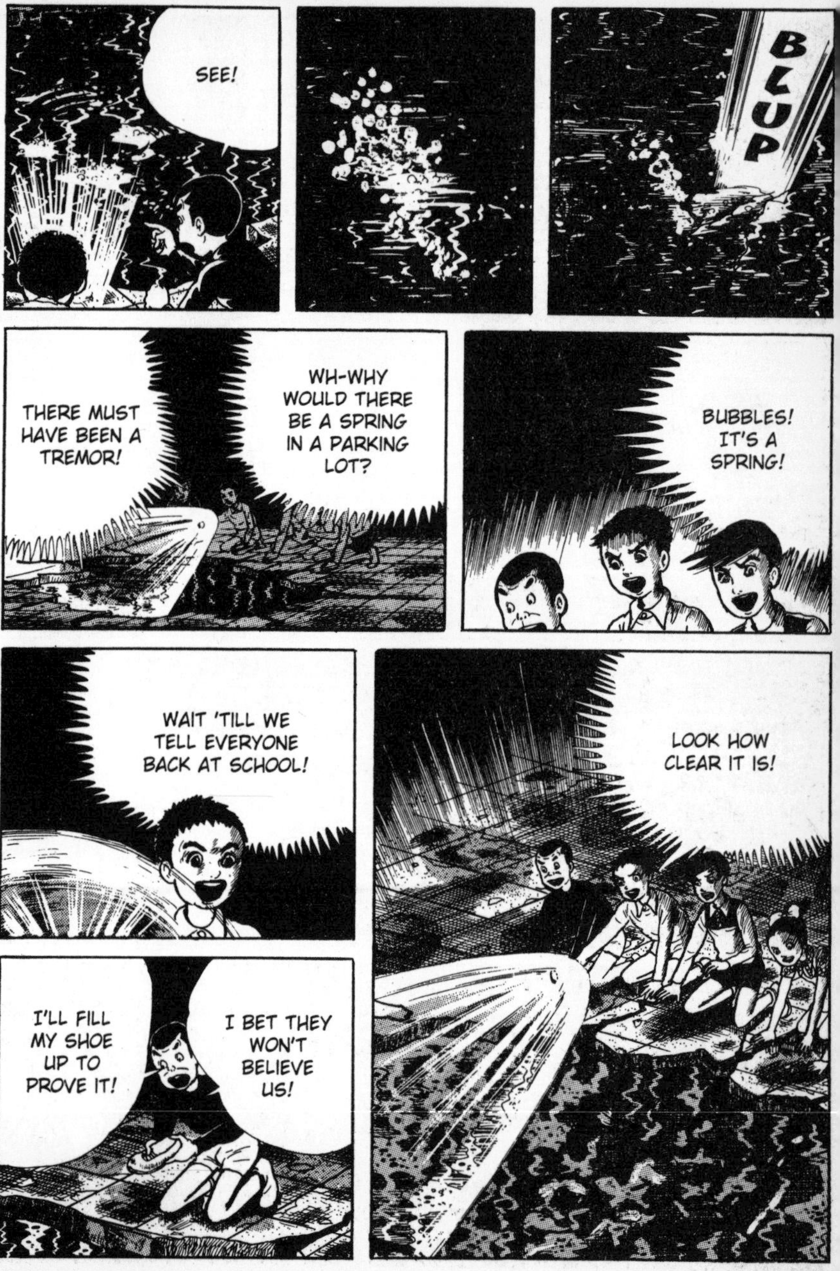
BLUP
SEE!
BUBBLES! IT'S A SPRING!
WH-WHY WOULD THERE BE A SPRING IN A PARKING LOT?
THERE MUST HAVE BEEN A TREMOR!
LOOK HOW CLEAR IT IS!
WAIT 'TILL WE TELL EVERYONE BACK AT SCHOOL!
I BET THEY WON'T BELIEVE US!
I'LL FILL MY SHOE UP TO PROVE IT!

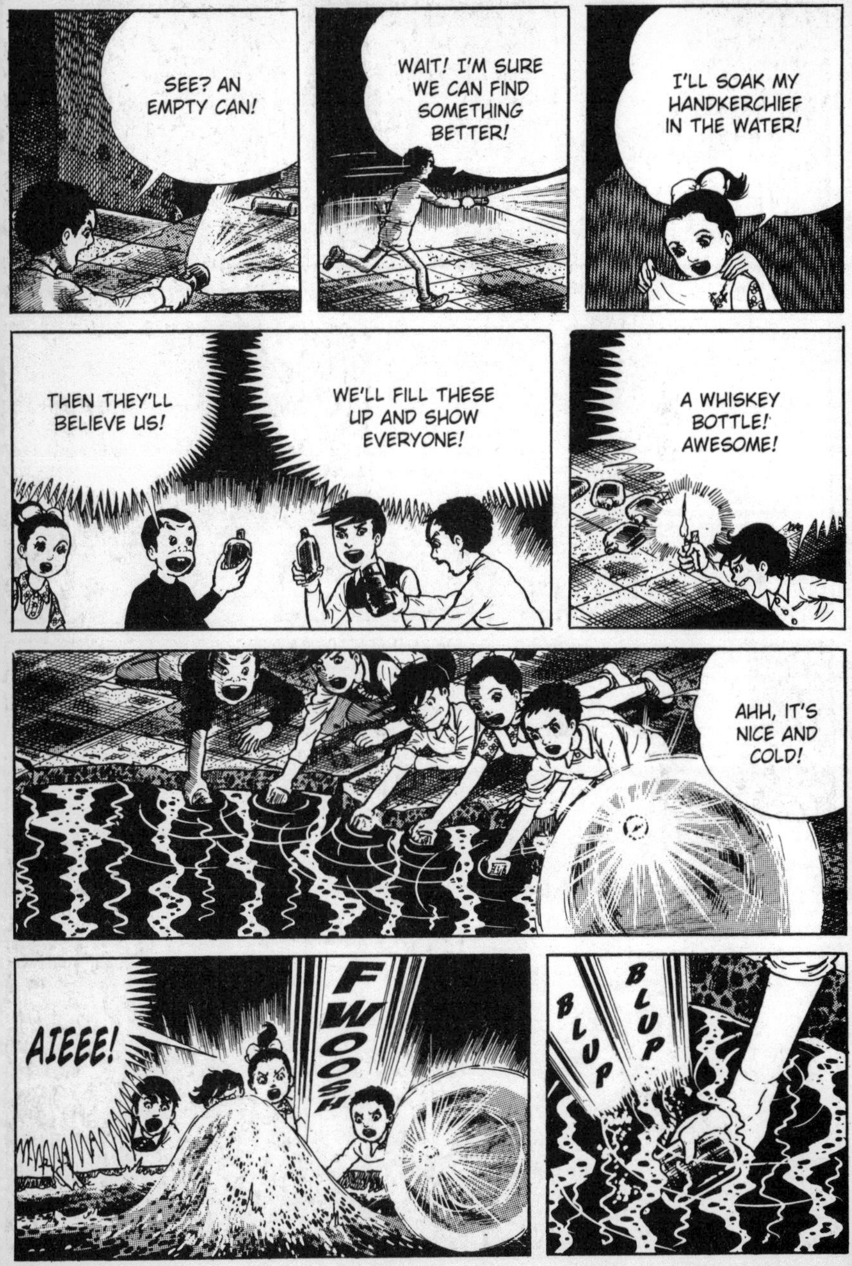
I'LL SOAK MY HANDKERCHIEF IN THE WATER!
WAIT! I'M SURE WE CAN FIND SOMETHING BETTER!
SEE? AN EMPTY CAN!
A WHISKEY BOTTLE! AWESOME!
WE'LL FILL THESE UP AND SHOW EVERYONE!
THEN THEY'LL BELIEVE US!
AHH, IT'S NICE AND COLD!
BLUP BLUP
BLUP
FWOOSH
AIEEE!

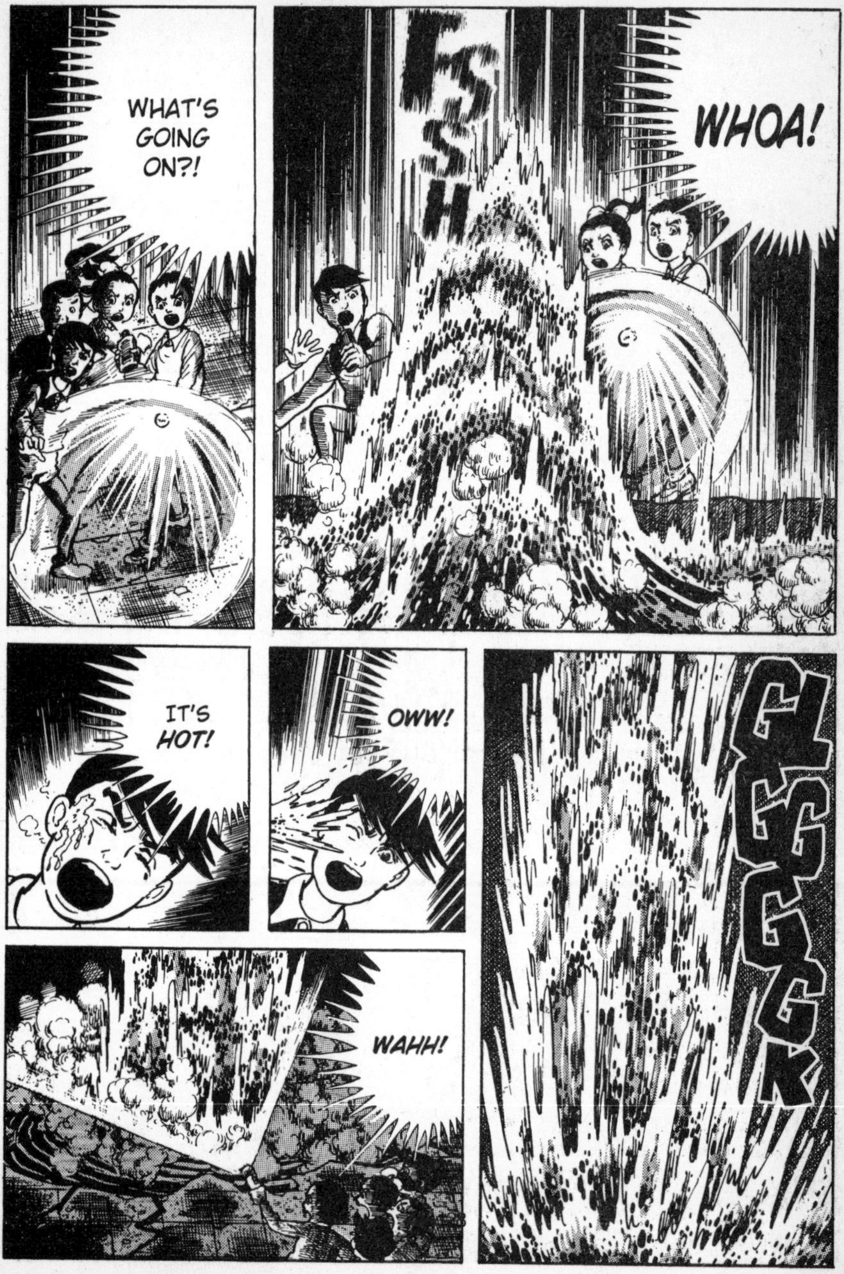
WHAT'S GOING ON?!
FSSH
WHOA!
IT'S HOT!
OWW!
WAHH!
GLGGK

KRAK

KABOOM

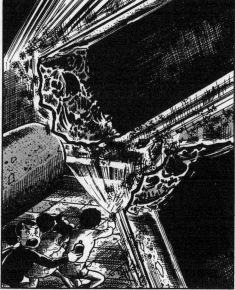

YAAGH!

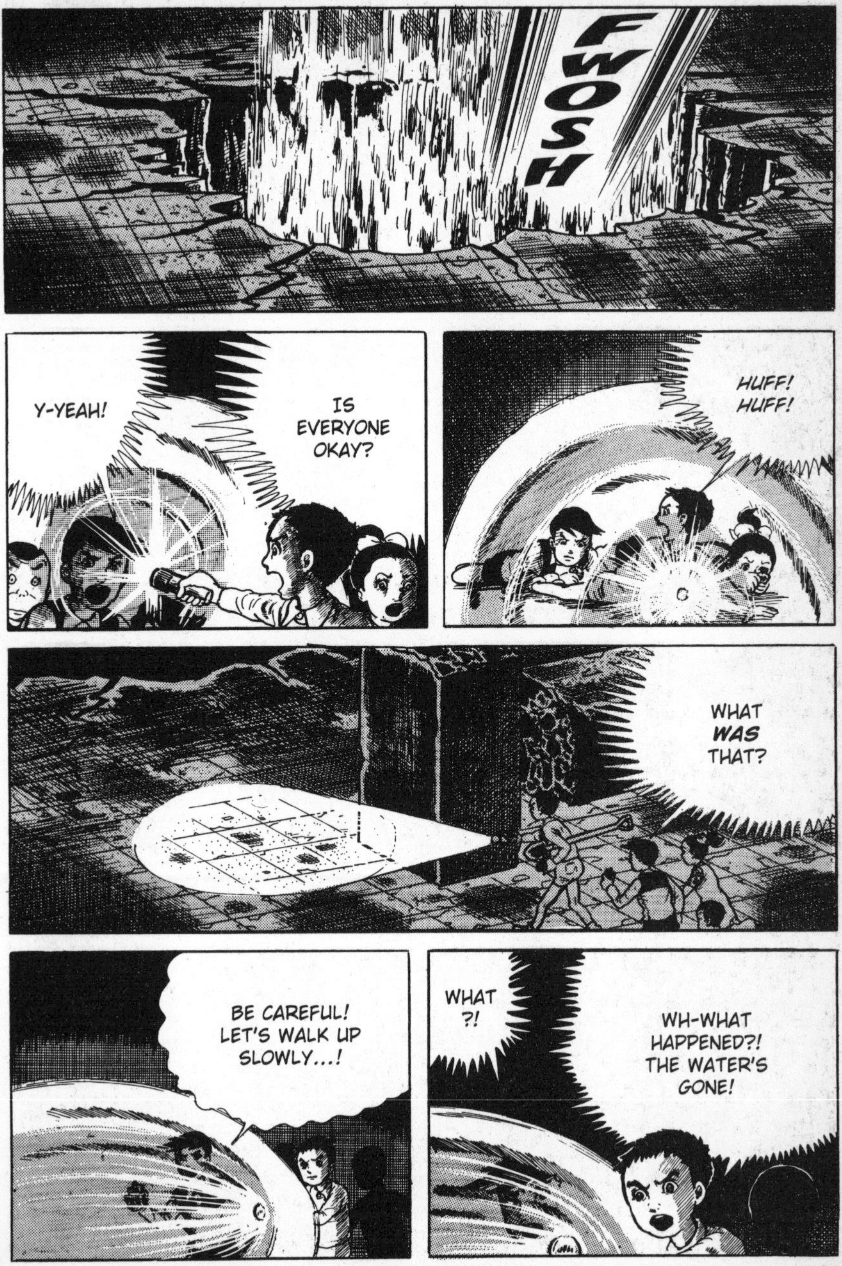
FWOSH
HUFF! HUFF!
IS EVERYONE OKAY?
Y-YEAH!
WHAT WAS THAT?
WHAT ?!
WH-WHAT HAPPENED?! THE WATER'S GONE!
BE CAREFUL! LET'S WALK UP SLOWLY...!

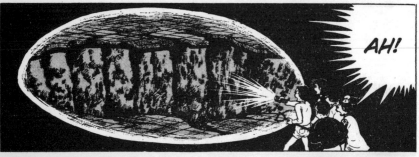

AH!

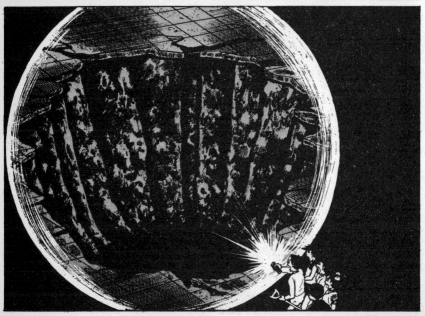

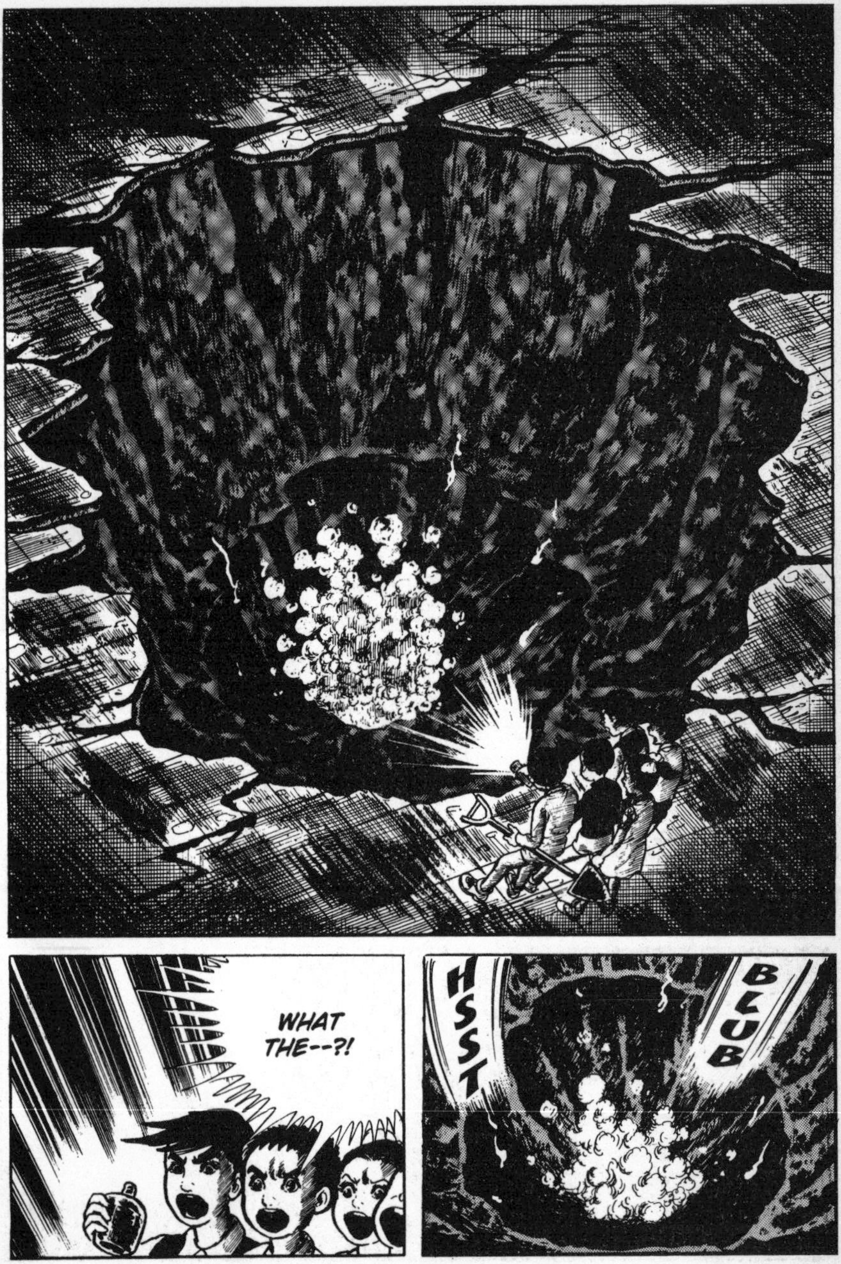
BLUB
HSST
WHAT THE--?!

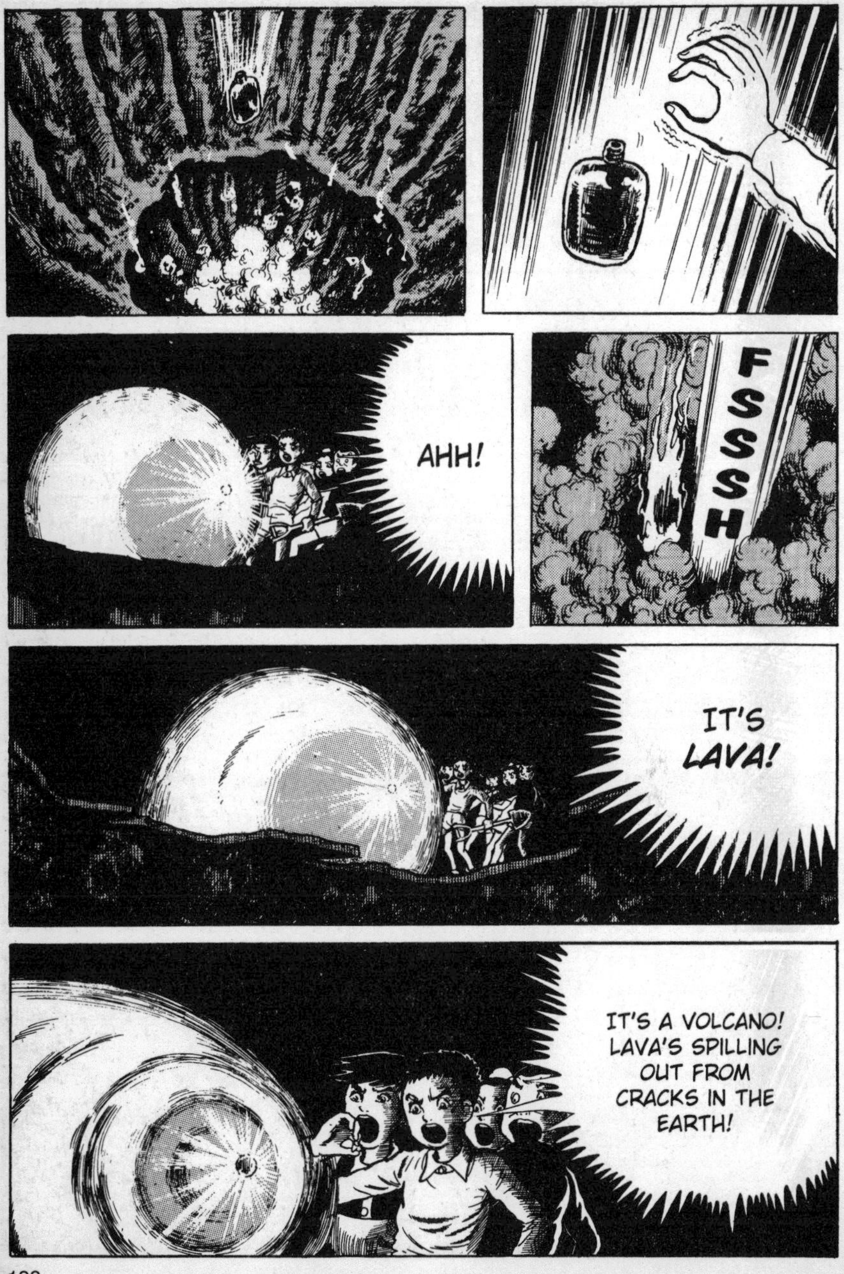
FSSSH
AHH!
IT'S LAVA!
IT'S A VOLCANO! LAVA'S SPILLING OUT FROM CRACKS IN THE EARTH!

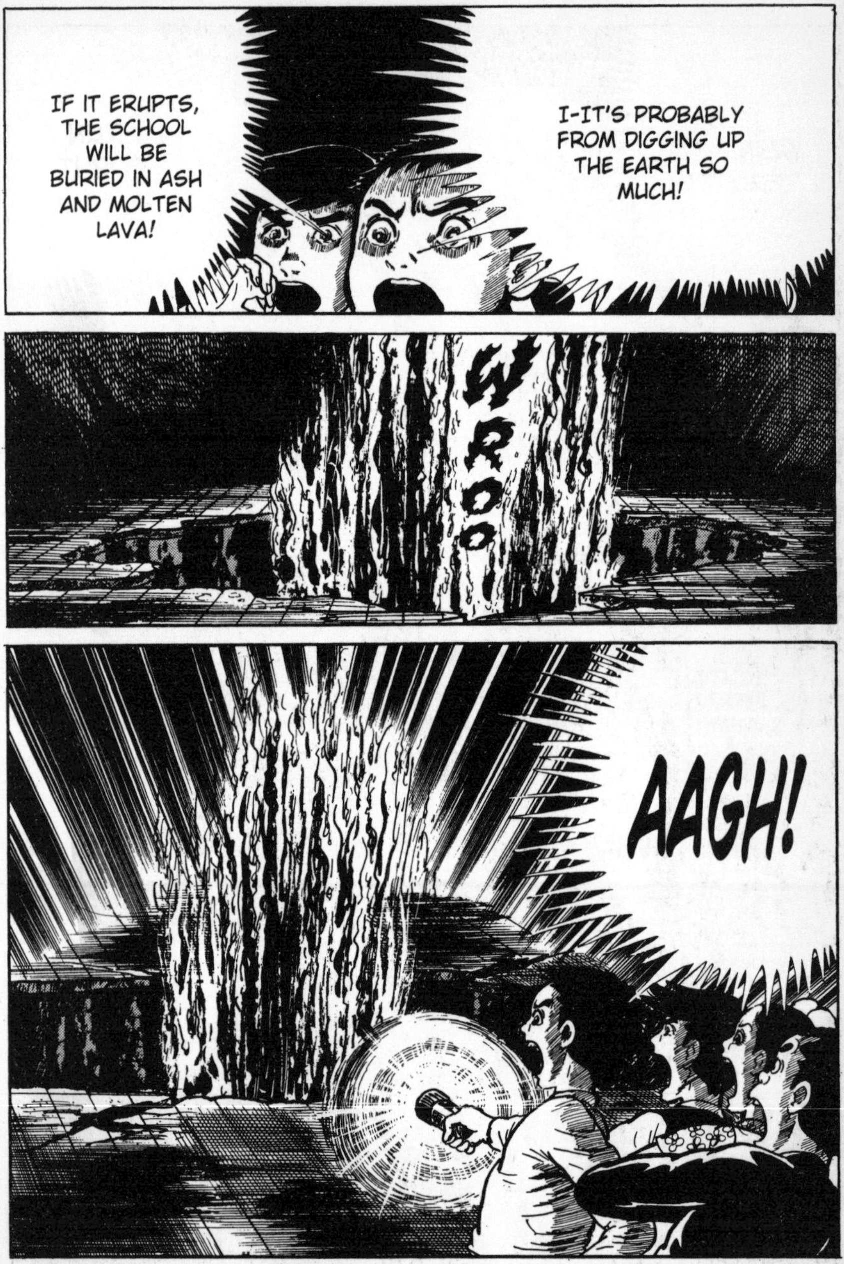
I-IT'S PROBABLY FROM DIGGING UP THE EARTH SO MUCH!
IF IT ERUPTS, THE SCHOOL WILL BE BURIED IN ASH AND MOLTEN LAVA!
WRROO
AAGH!

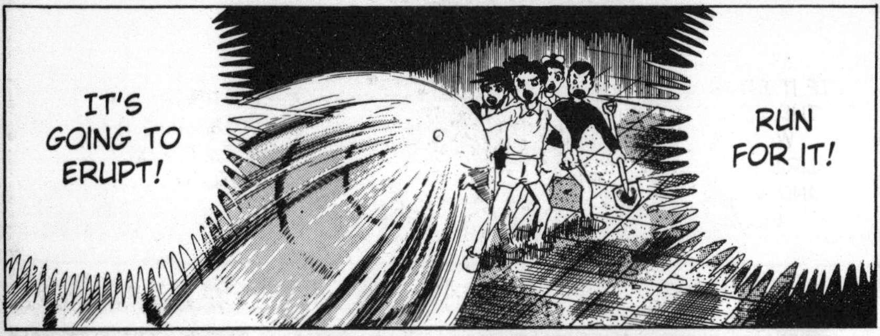
RUN FOR IT!
IT'S GOING TO ERUPT!
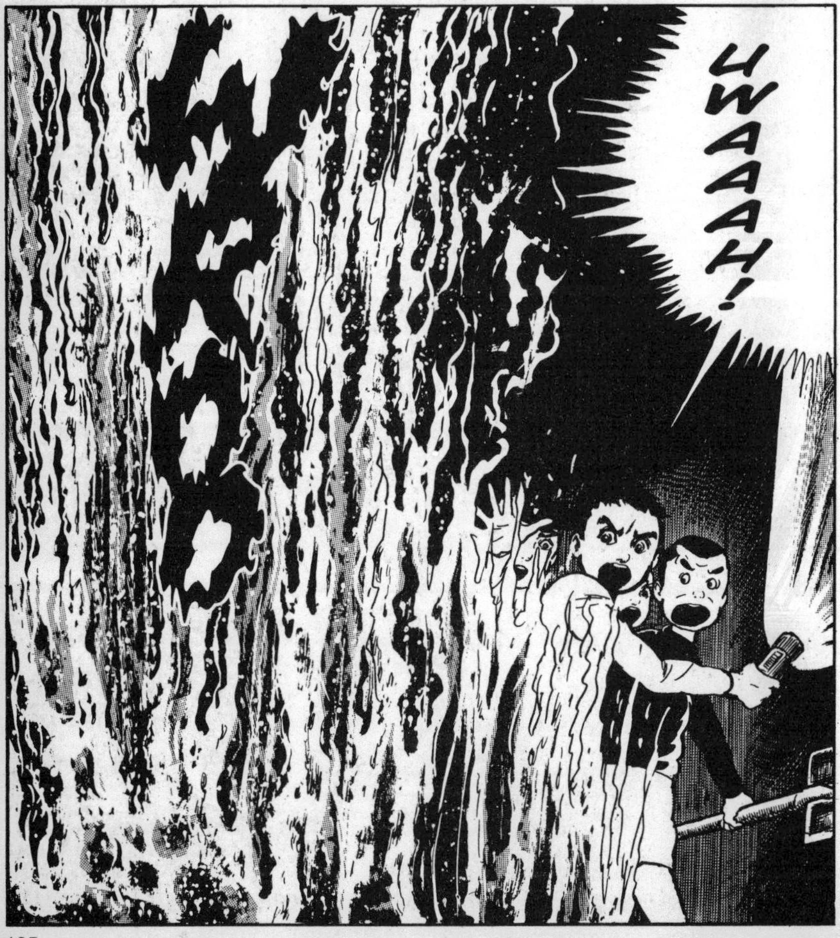
UWAAAAH!

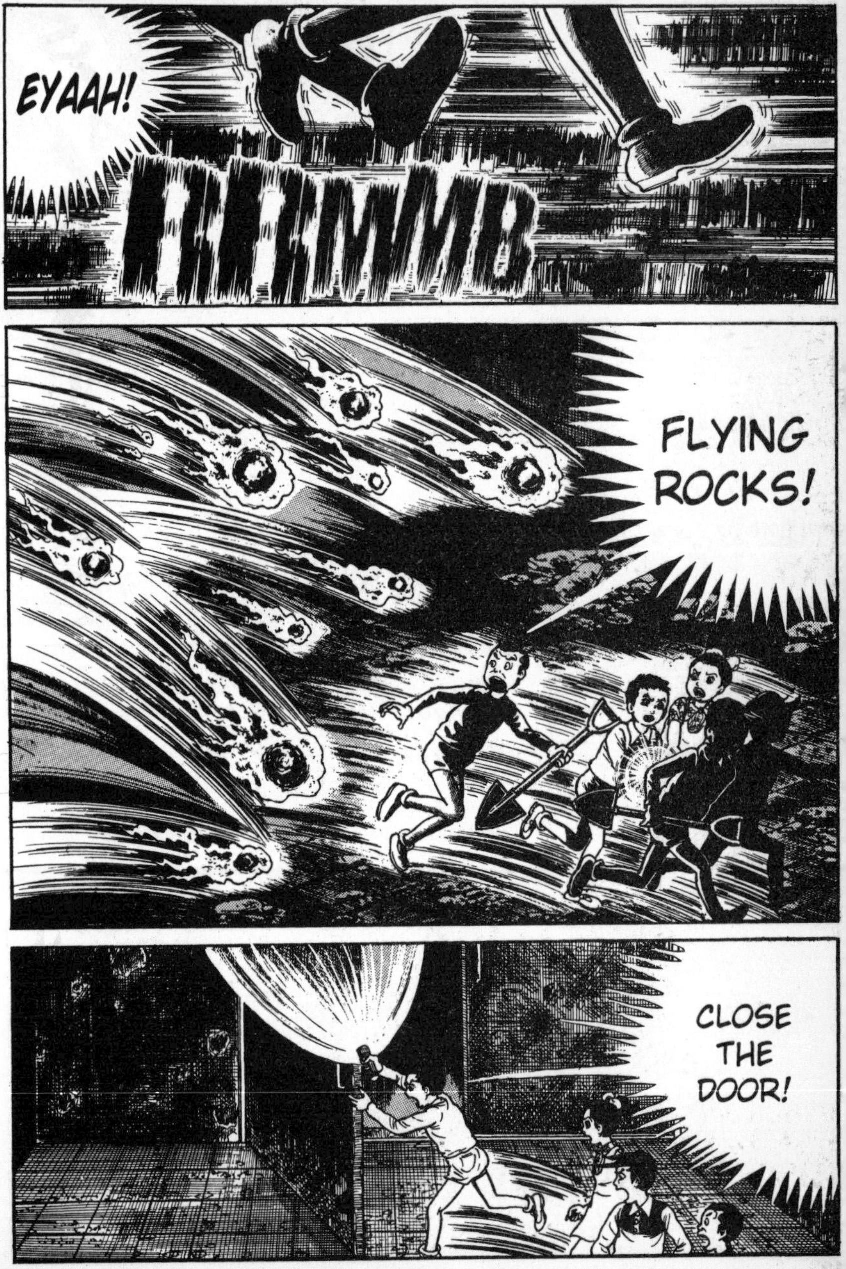
EYAAH!
FLYING ROCKS!
CLOSE THE DOOR!

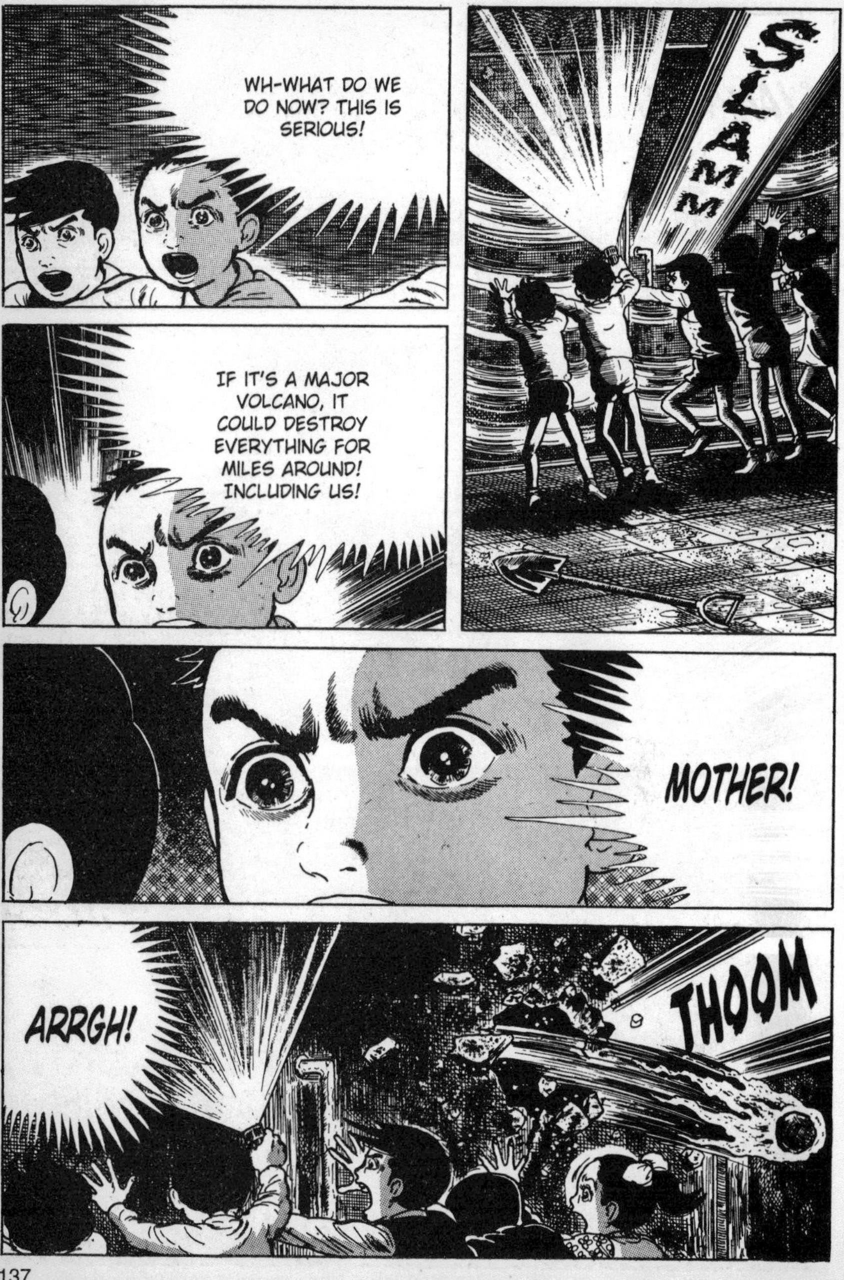
WH-WHAT DO WE DO NOW? THIS IS SERIOUS!
IF IT'S A MAJOR VOLCANO, IT COULD DESTROY EVERYTHING FOR MILES AROUND! INCLUDING US!
SLAMM
MOTHER!
ARRGH!
THOOM

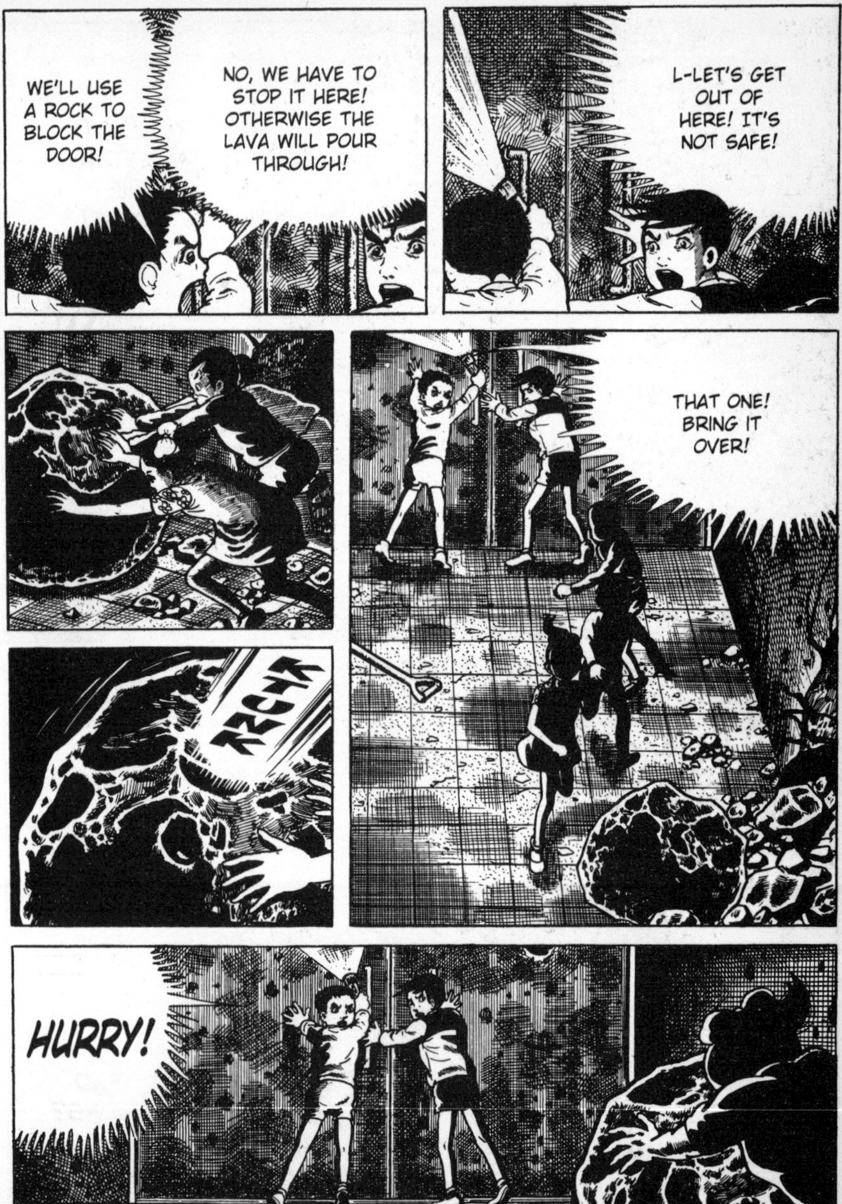
L-LET'S GET OUT OF HERE! IT'S NOT SAFE!
NO, WE HAVE TO STOP IT HERE! OTHERWISE THE LAVA WILL POUR THROUGH!
WE'LL USE A ROCK TO BLOCK THE DOOR!
THAT ONE! BRING IT OVER!
KLUNK
HURRY!

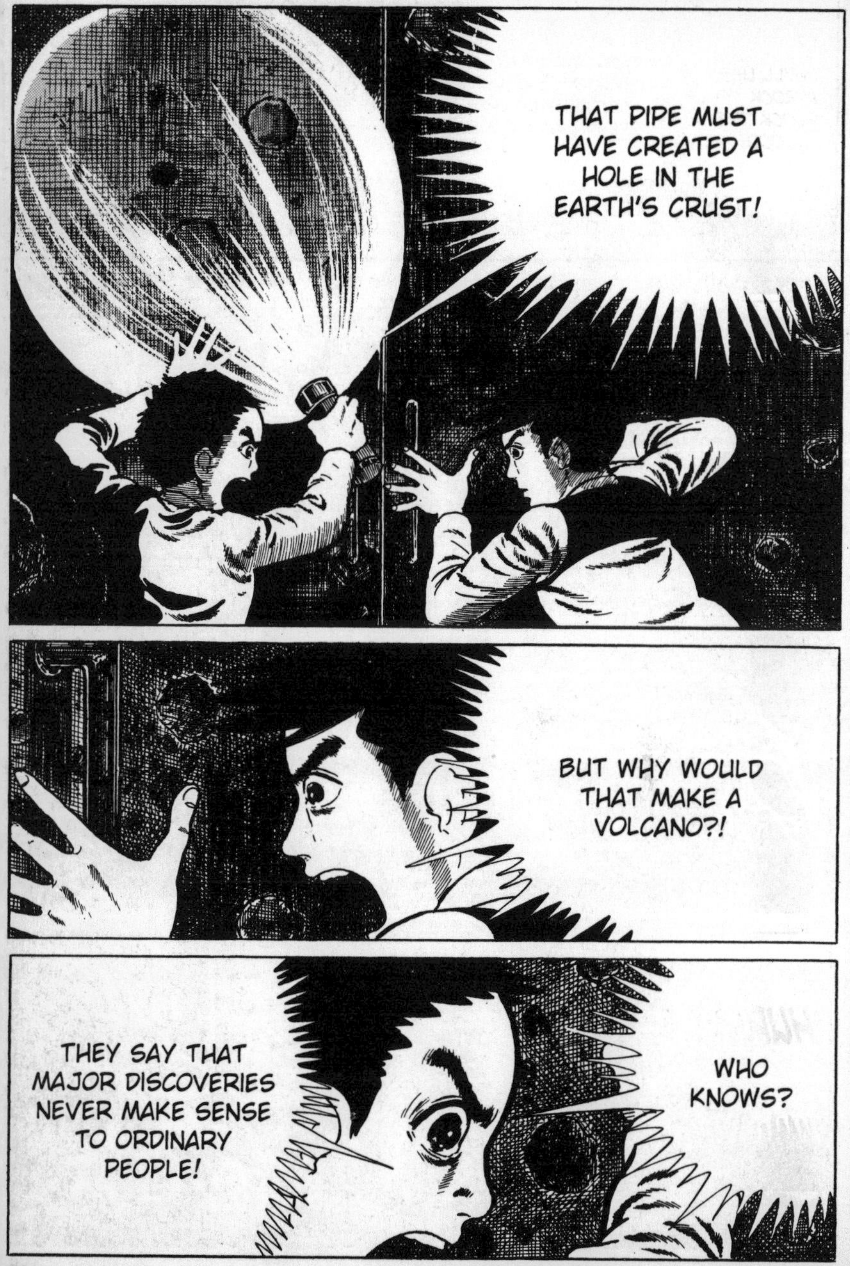
THAT PIPE MUST HAVE CREATED A HOLE IN THE EARTH'S CRUST!
BUT WHY WOULD THAT MAKE A VOLCANO?!
WHO KNOWS?
THEY SAY THAT MAJOR DISCOVERIES NEVER MAKE SENSE TO ORDINARY PEOPLE!

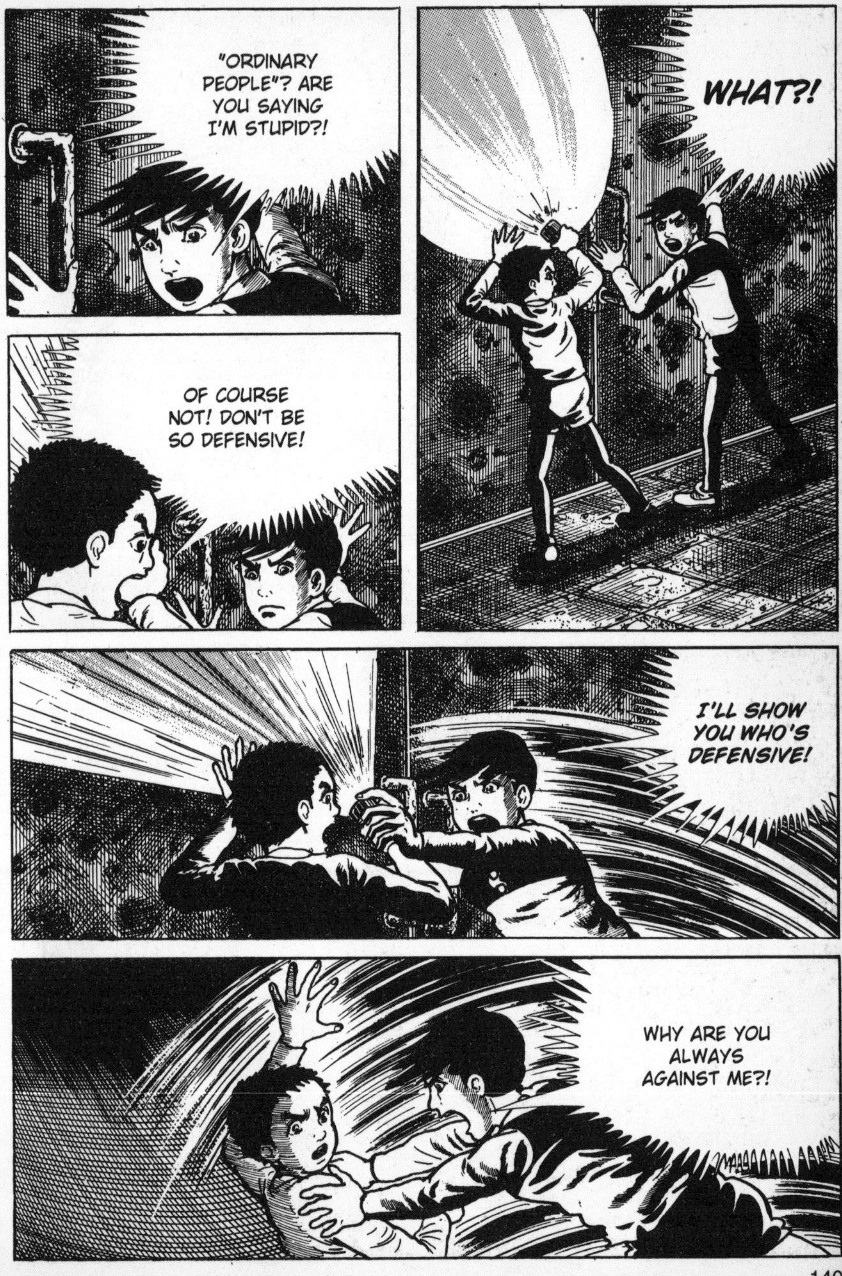
"ORDINARY PEOPLE"? ARE YOU SAYING I'M STUPID?!
OF COURSE NOT! DON'T BE SO DEFENSIVE!
WHAT?!
I'LL SHOW YOU WHO'S DEFENSIVE!
WHY ARE YOU ALWAYS AGAINST ME?!

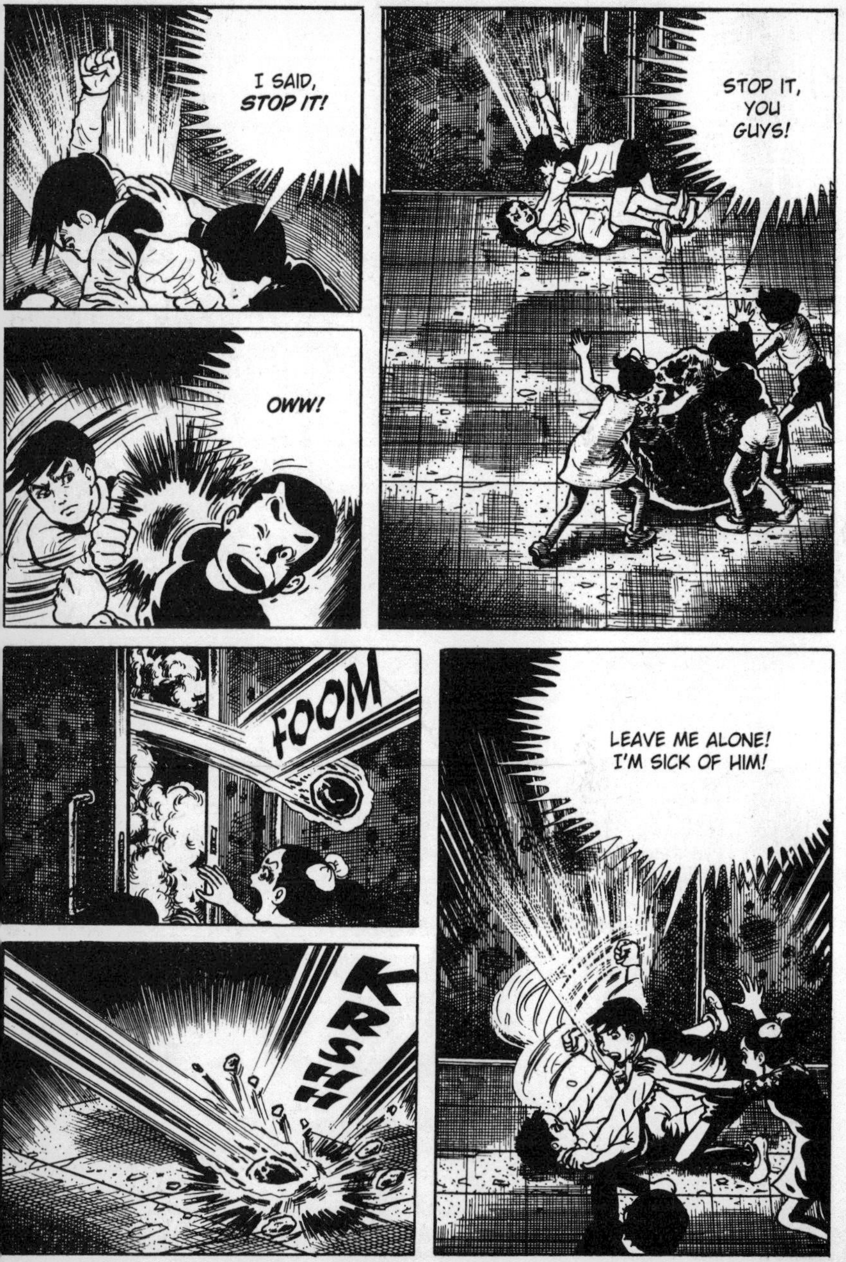
STOP IT, YOU GUYS!
I SAID, STOP IT!
OWW!
LEAVE ME ALONE! I'M SICK OF HIM!
FOOM
KRSHH

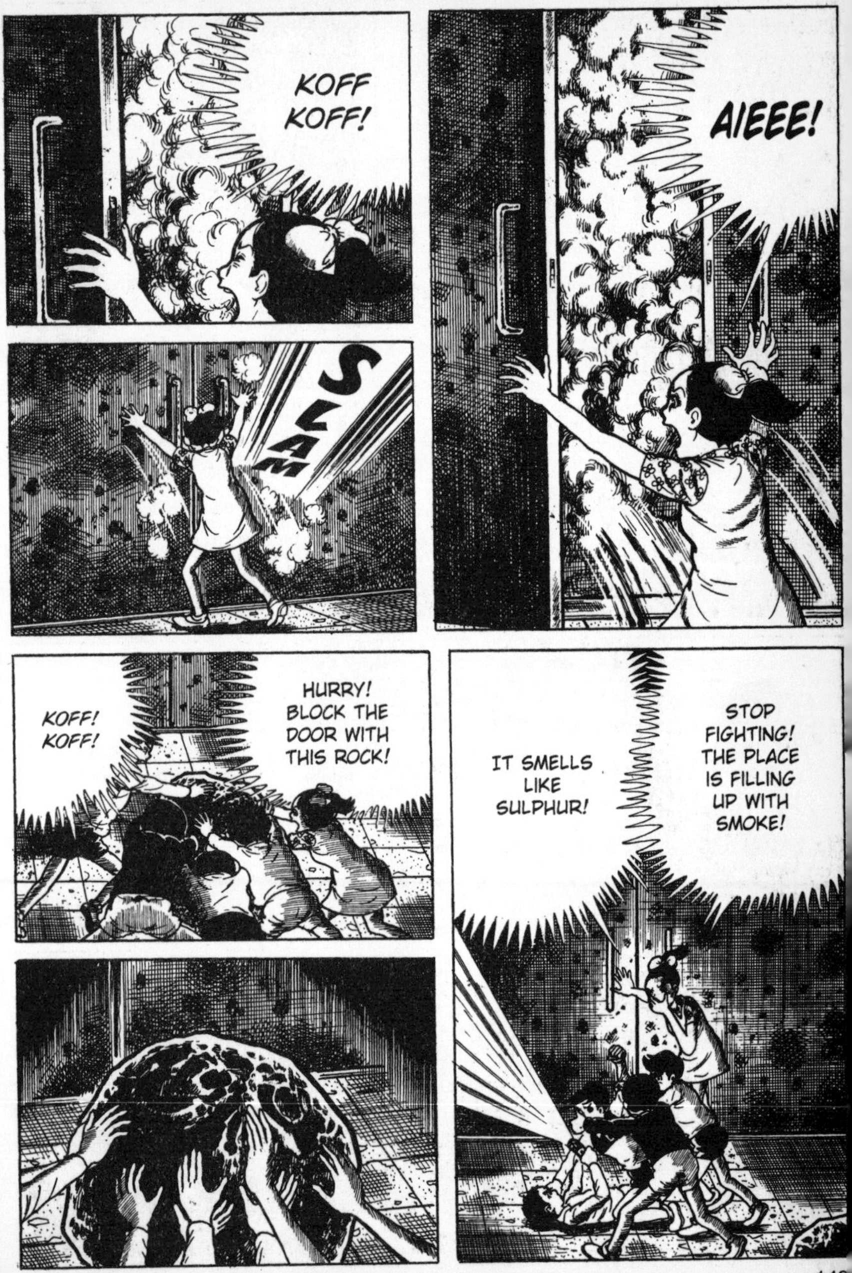
AIEEE!
KOFF KOFF!
SLAM
STOP FIGHTING! THE PLACE IS FILLING UP WITH SMOKE!
IT SMELLS LIKE SULPHUR!
HURRY! BLOCK THE DOOR WITH THIS ROCK!
KOFF! KOFF!

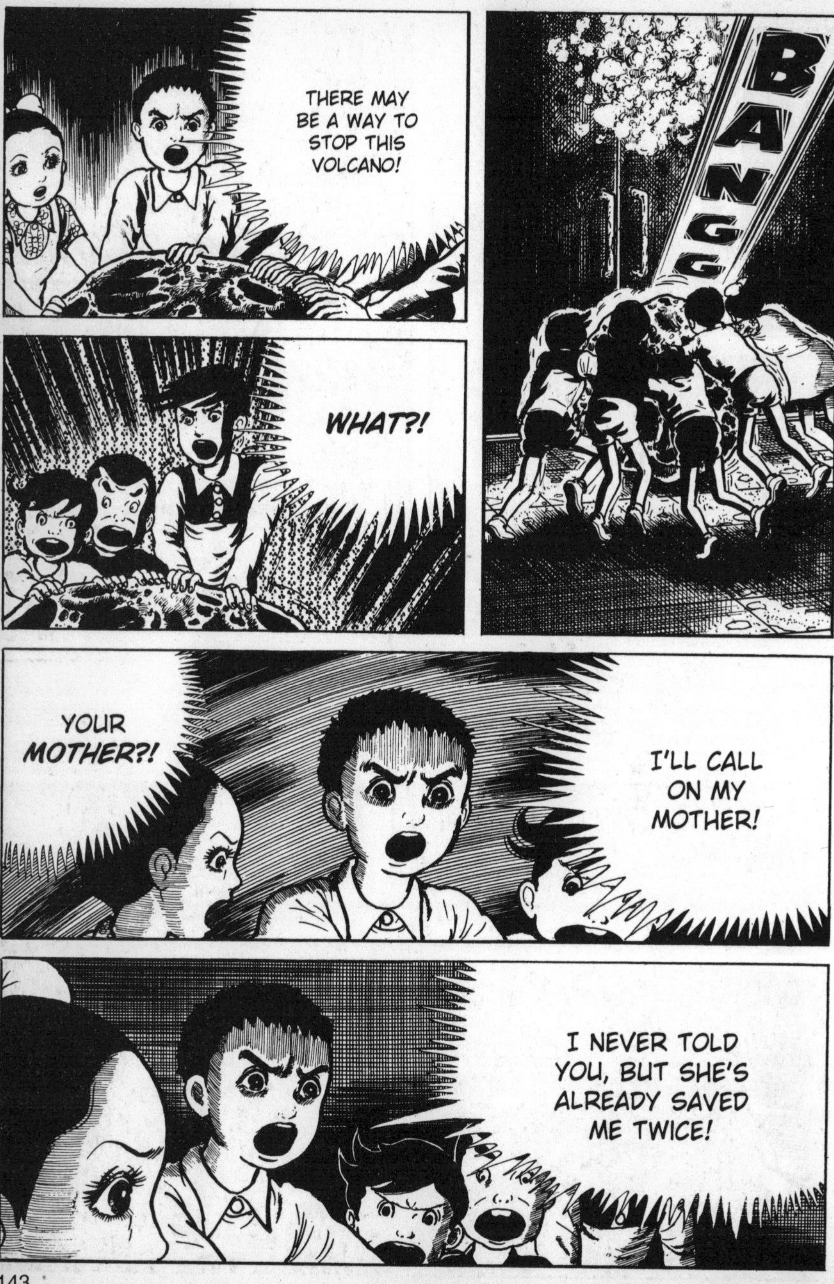
BANGG
THERE MAY BE A WAY TO STOP THIS VOLCANO!
WHAT?!
I'LL CALL ON MY MOTHER!
YOUR MOTHER?!
I NEVER TOLD YOU, BUT SHE'S ALREADY SAVED ME TWICE!

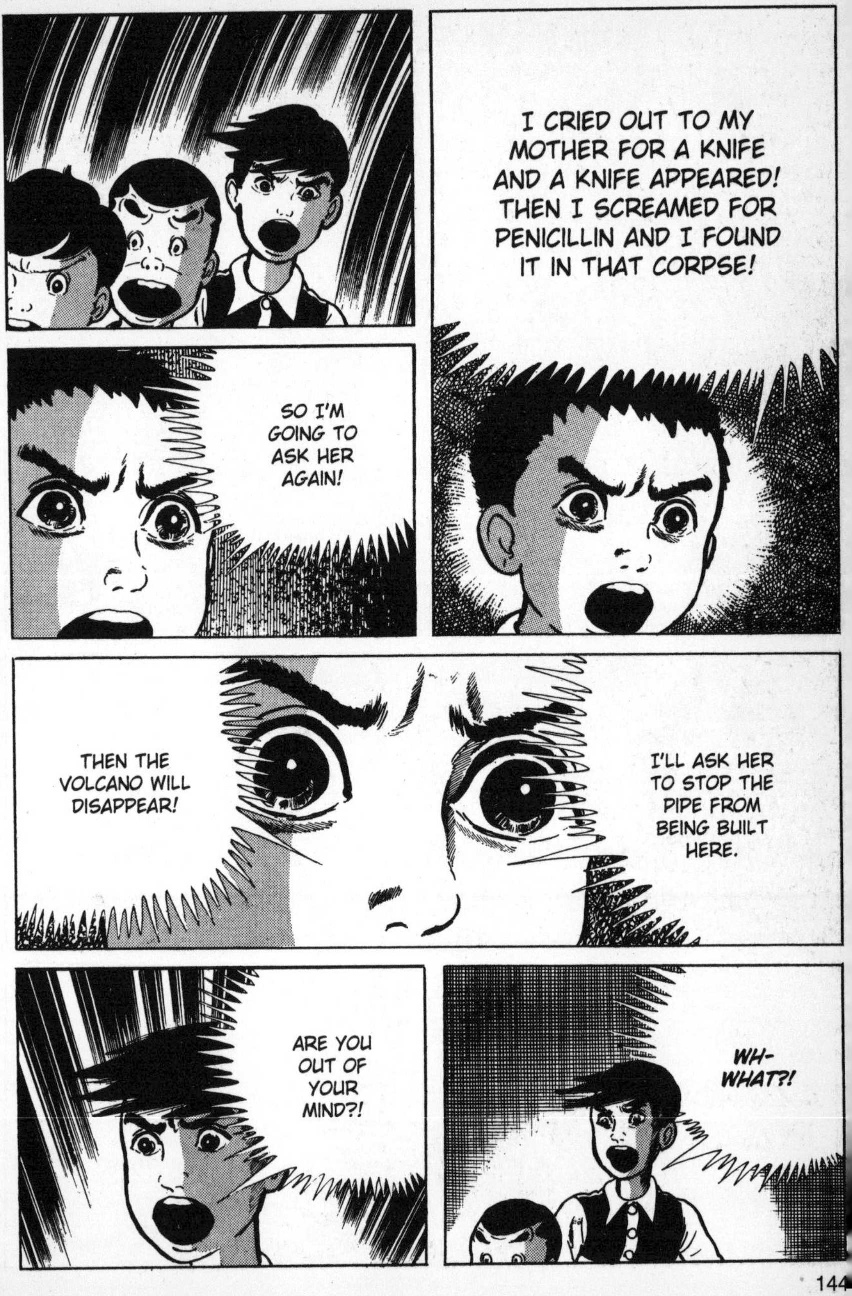
I CRIED OUT TO MY MOTHER FOR A KNIFE AND A KNIFE APPEARED! THEN I SCREAMED FOR PENICILLIN AND I FOUND IT IN THAT CORPSE!
SO I'M GOING TO ASK HER AGAIN!
I'LL ASK HER TO STOP THE PIPE FROM BEING BUILT HERE.
THEN THE VOLCANO WILL DISAPPEAR!
WH- WHAT?!
ARE YOU OUT OF YOUR MIND?!

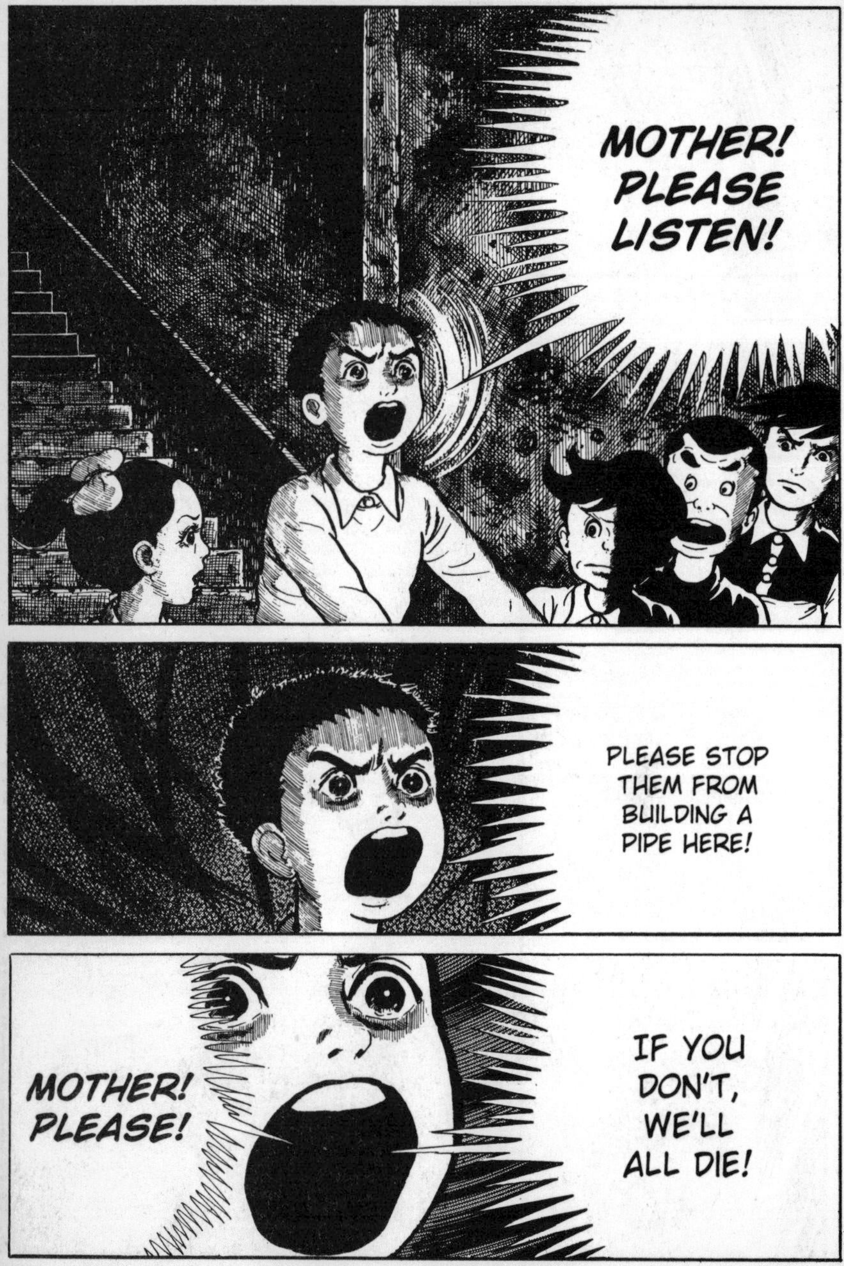
MOTHER! PLEASE LISTEN!
PLEASE STOP THEM FROM BUILDING A PIPE HERE!
IF YOU DON'T, WE'LL ALL DIE!
MOTHER! PLEASE!

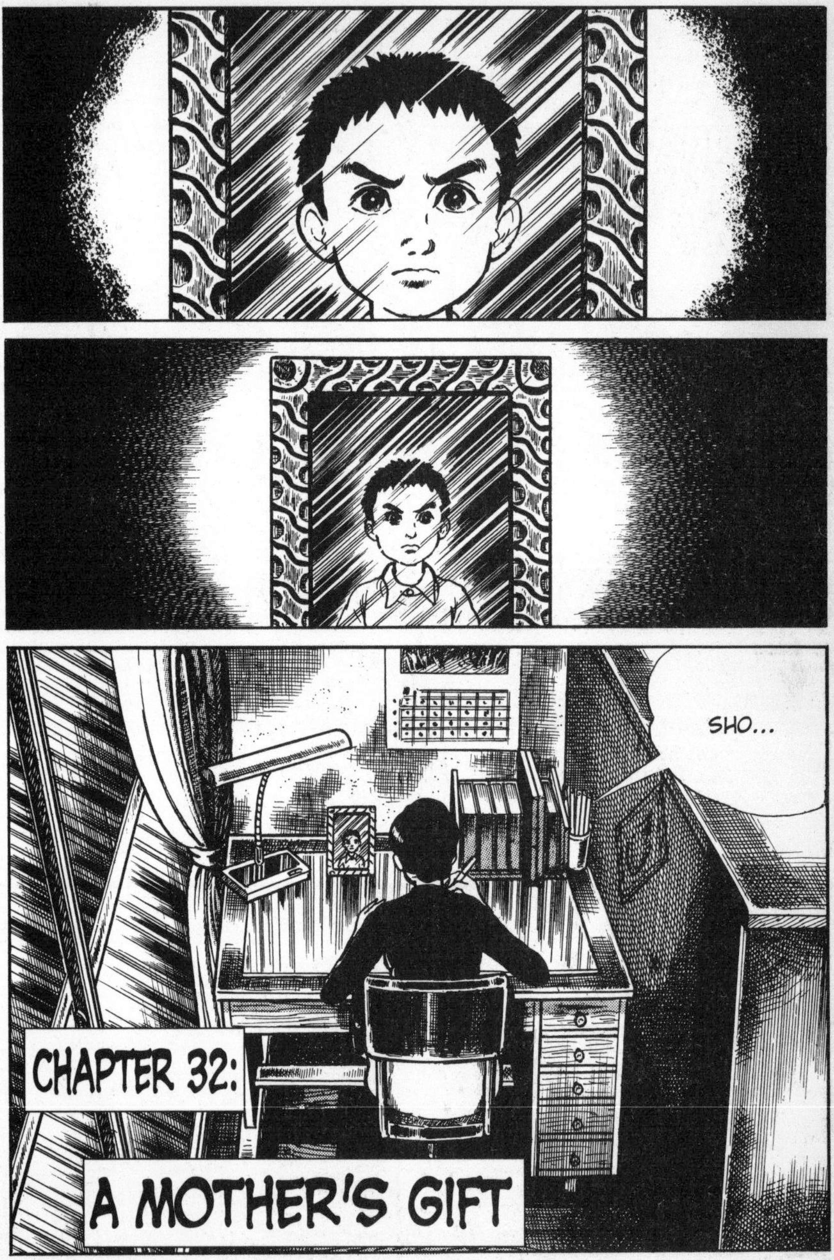
SHO...
CHAPTER 32:
A MOTHER'S GIFT

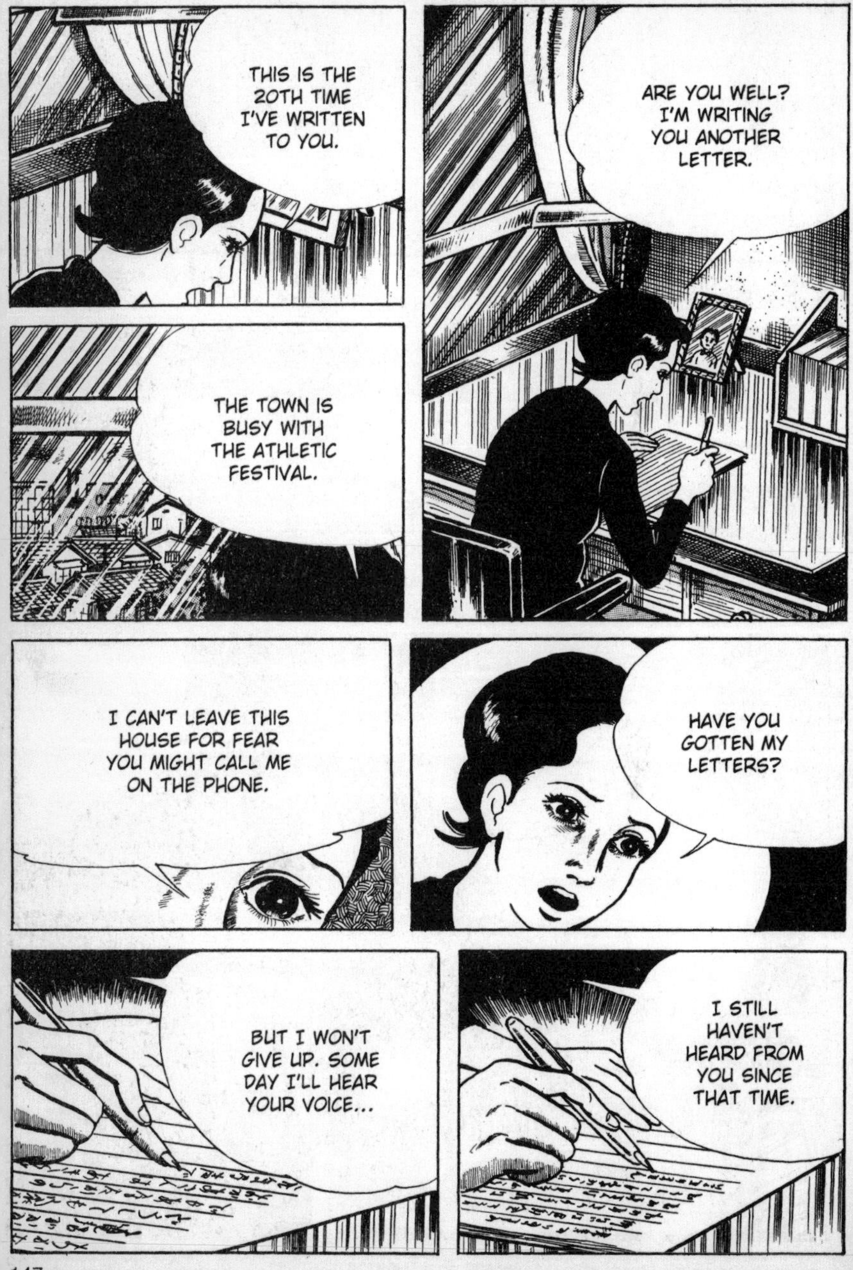
ARE YOU WELL? I'M WRITING YOU ANOTHER LETTER.
THIS IS THE 20TH TIME I'VE WRITTEN TO YOU.
THE TOWN IS BUSY WITH THE ATHLETIC FESTIVAL.
HAVE YOU GOTTEN MY LETTERS?
I CAN'T LEAVE THIS HOUSE FOR FEAR YOU MIGHT CALL ME ON THE PHONE.
I STILL HAVEN'T HEARD FROM YOU SINCE THAT TIME.
BUT I WON'T GIVE UP. SOME DAY I'LL HEAR YOUR VOICE...

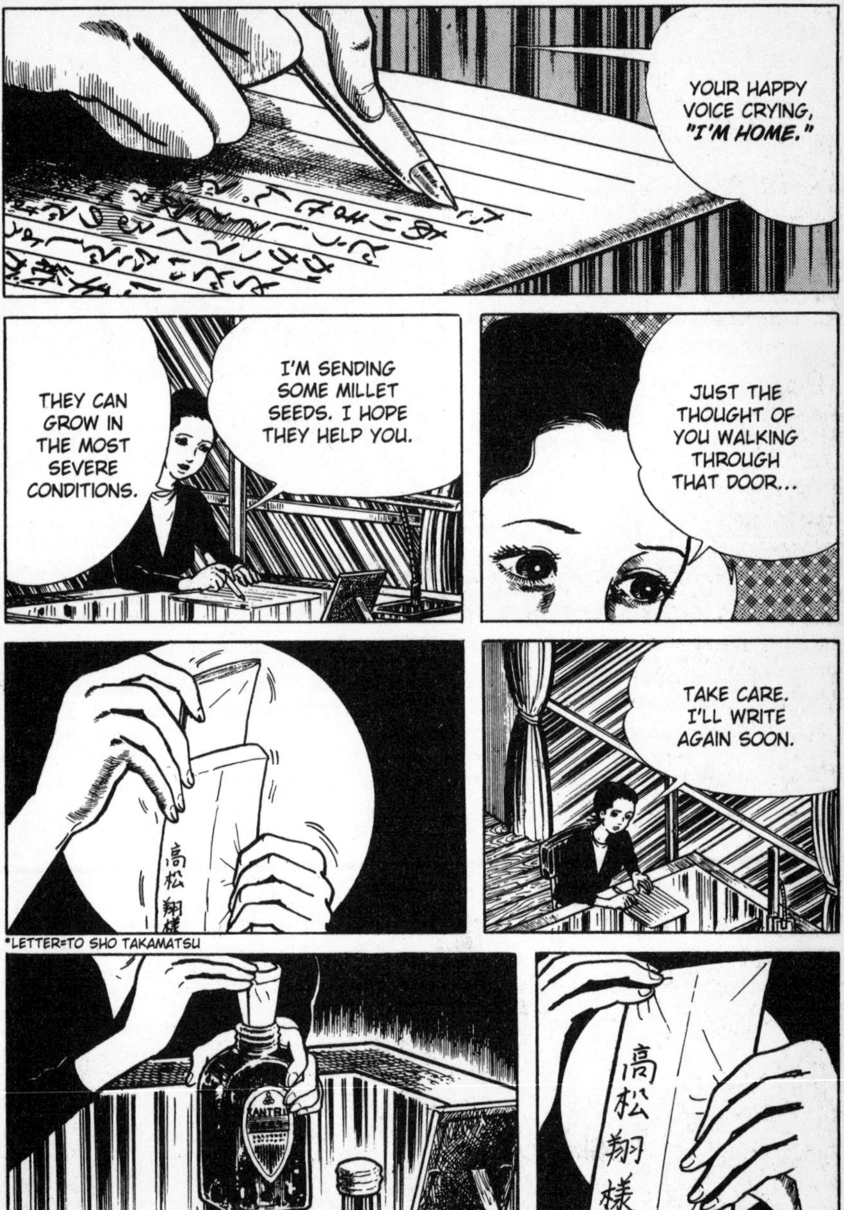
YOUR HAPPY VOICE CRYING, "I'M HOME."
JUST THE THOUGHT OF YOU WALKING THROUGH THAT DOOR...
I'M SENDING SOME MILLET SEEDS. I HOPE THEY HELP YOU.
THEY CAN GROW IN THE MOST SEVERE CONDITIONS.
TAKE CARE. I'LL WRITE AGAIN SOON.
高松翔様
高松翔様

*LETTER=TO SHO TAKAMATSU

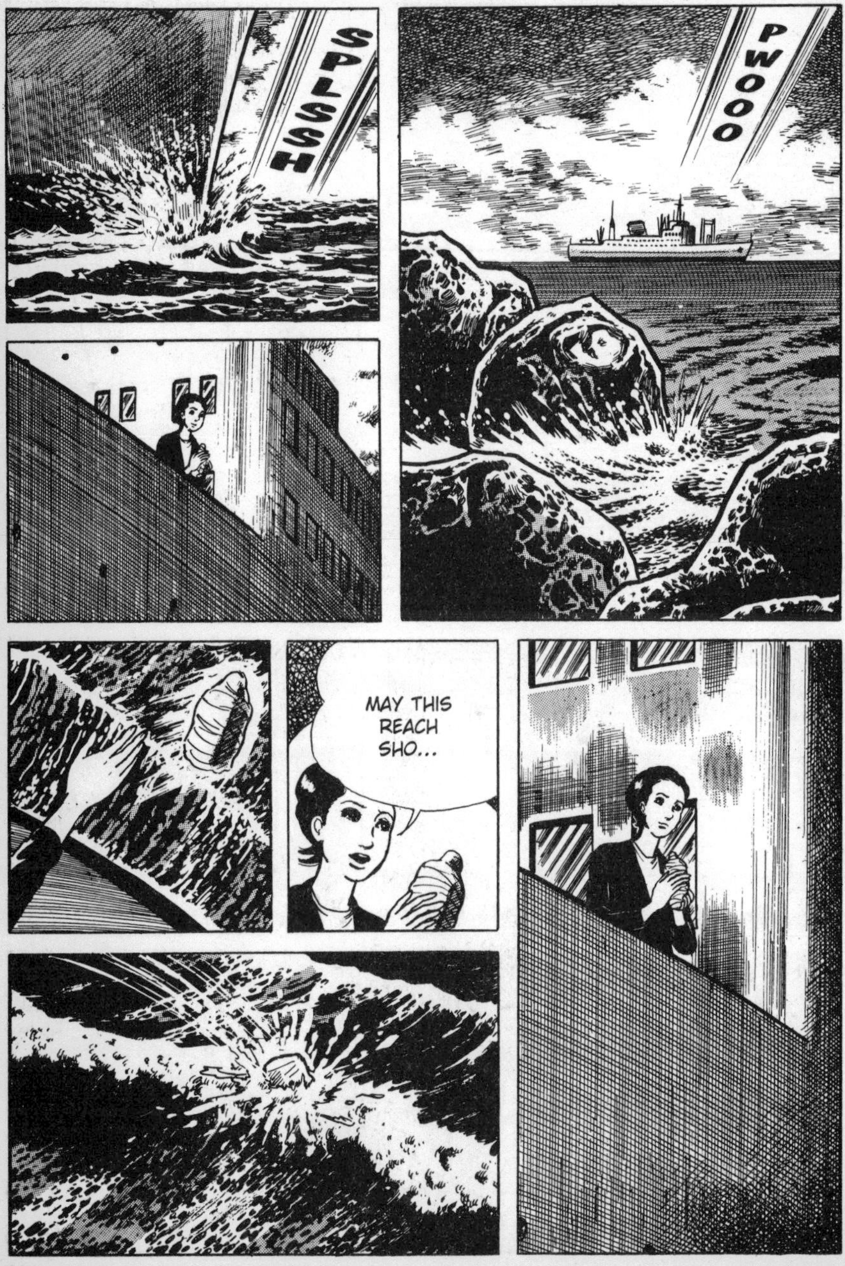
PWOOO
SPLSSH
MAY THIS REACH SHO...

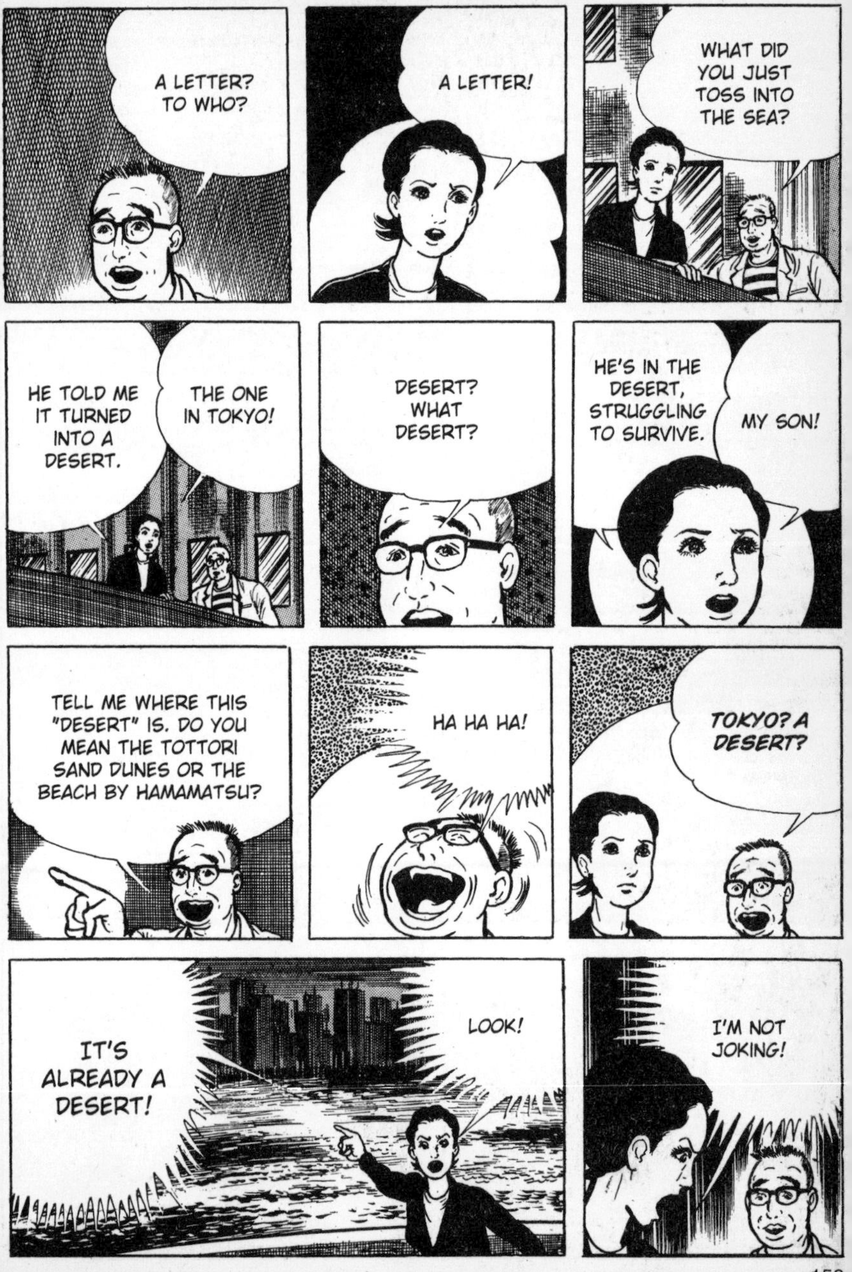
WHAT DID YOU JUST TOSS INTO THE SEA?
A LETTER!
A LETTER? TO WHO?
MY SON!
HE'S IN THE DESERT, STRUGGLING TO SURVIVE.
DESERT? WHAT DESERT?
THE ONE IN TOKYO!
HE TOLD ME IT TURNED INTO A DESERT.
TOKYO? A DESERT?
HA HA HA!
TELL ME WHERE THIS "DESERT" IS. DO YOU MEAN THE TOTTORI SAND DUNES OR THE BEACH BY HAMAMATSU?
I'M NOT JOKING!
LOOK!
IT'S ALREADY A DESERT!

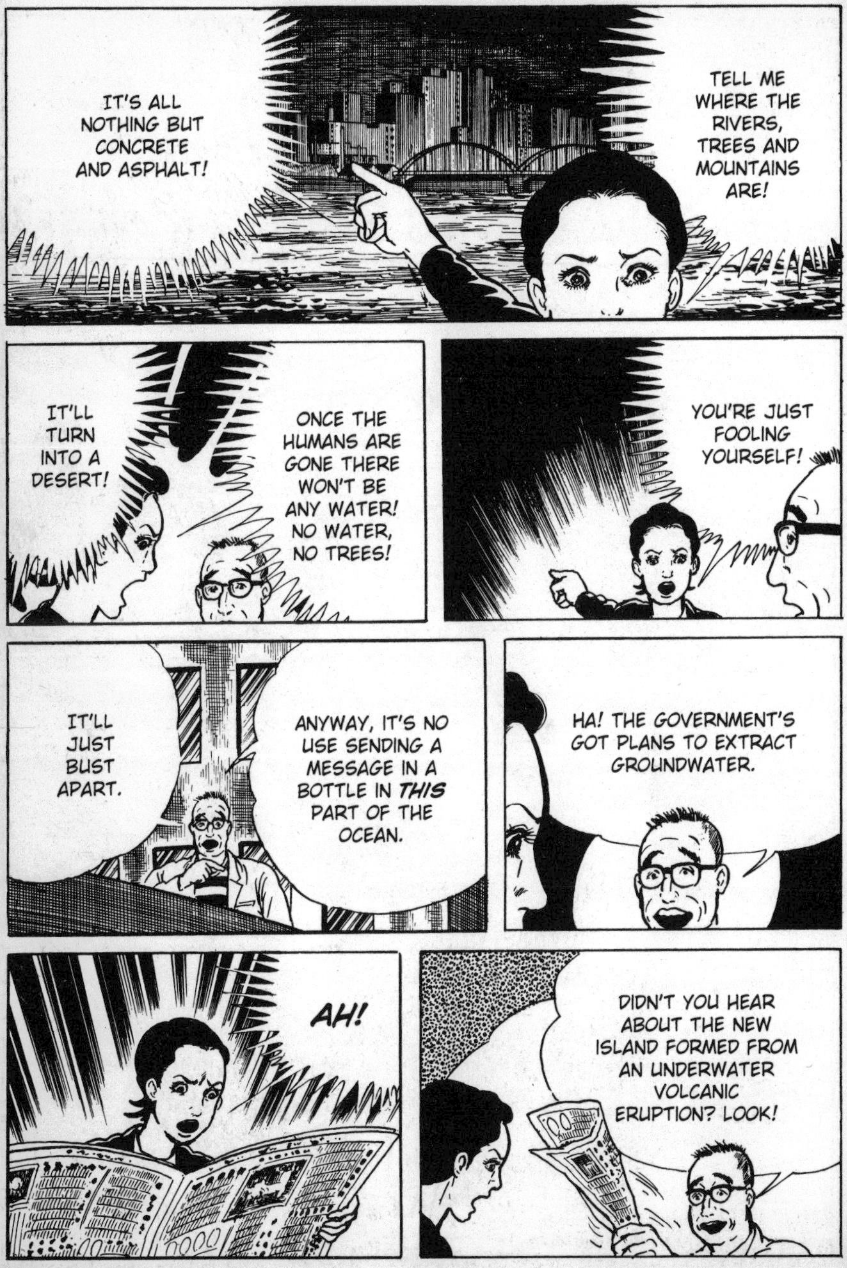
TELL ME WHERE THE RIVERS, TREES AND MOUNTAINS ARE!
IT'S ALL NOTHING BUT CONCRETE AND ASPHALT!
YOU'RE JUST FOOLING YOURSELF!
ONCE THE HUMANS ARE GONE THERE WON'T BE ANY WATER! NO WATER, NO TREES!
IT'LL TURN INTO A DESERT!
HA! THE GOVERNMENT'S GOT PLANS TO EXTRACT GROUNDWATER.
ANYWAY, IT'S NO USE SENDING A MESSAGE IN A BOTTLE IN *THIS* PART OF THE OCEAN.
IT'LL JUST BUST APART.
DIDN'T YOU HEAR ABOUT THE NEW ISLAND FORMED FROM AN UNDERWATER VOLCANIC ERUPTION? LOOK!
AH!

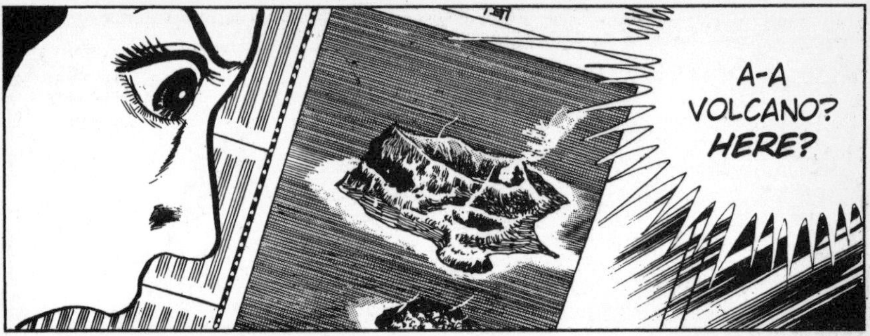
A-A VOLCANO? *HERE?*

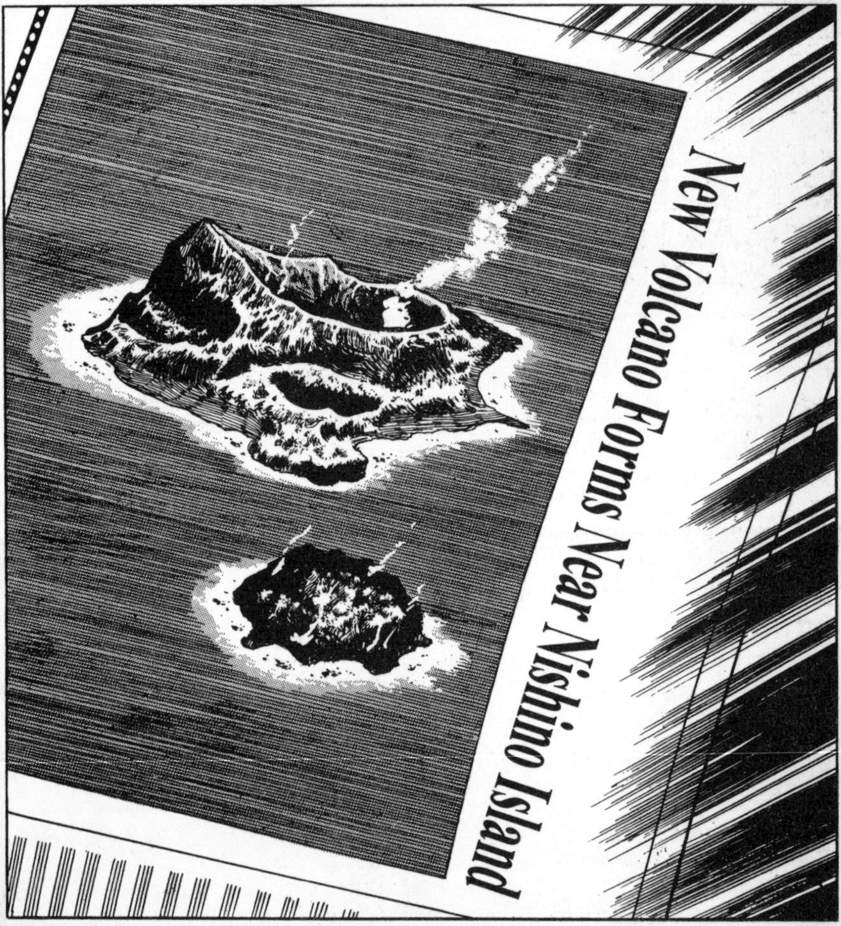
New Volcano Forms Near Nishino Island

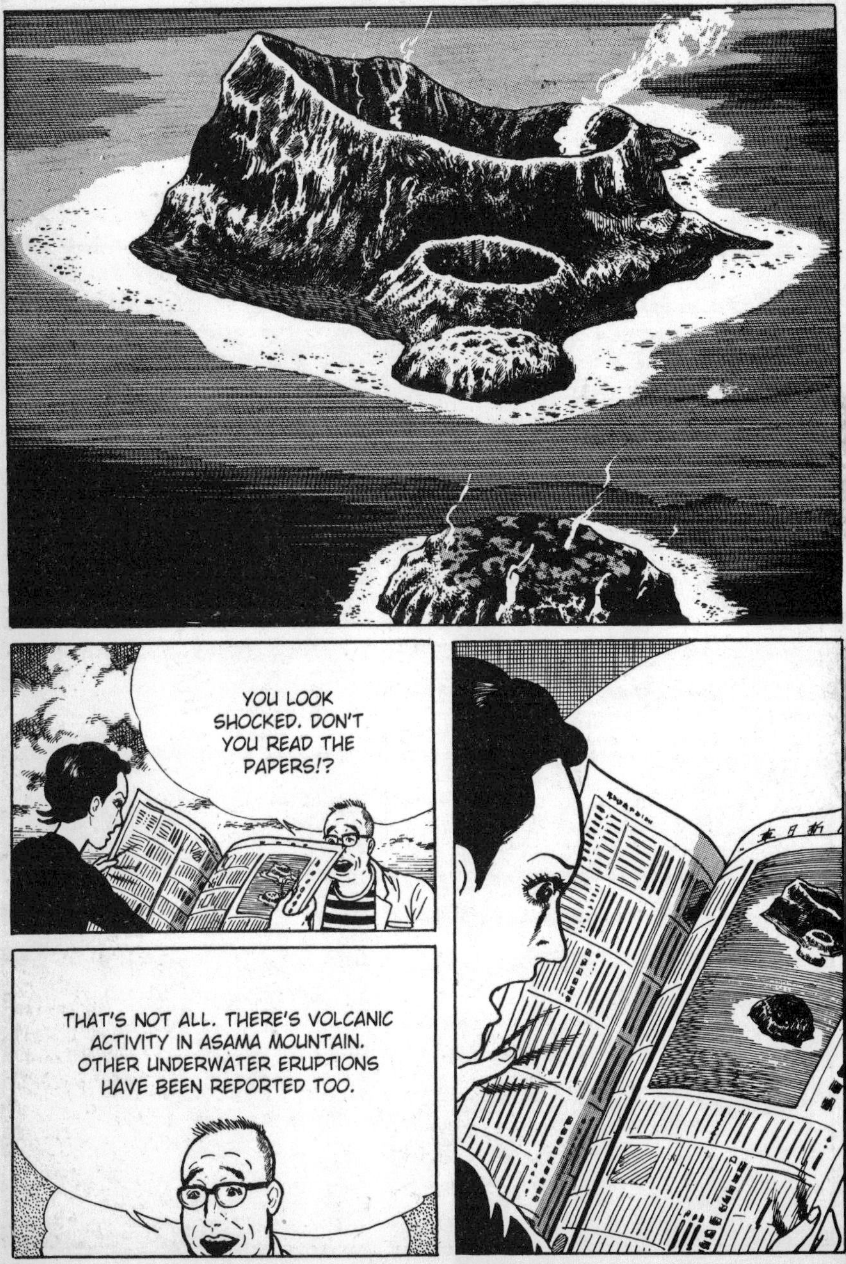
YOU LOOK SHOCKED. DON'T YOU READ THE PAPERS!?
THAT'S NOT ALL. THERE'S VOLCANIC ACTIVITY IN ASAMA MOUNTAIN. OTHER UNDERWATER ERUPTIONS HAVE BEEN REPORTED TOO.

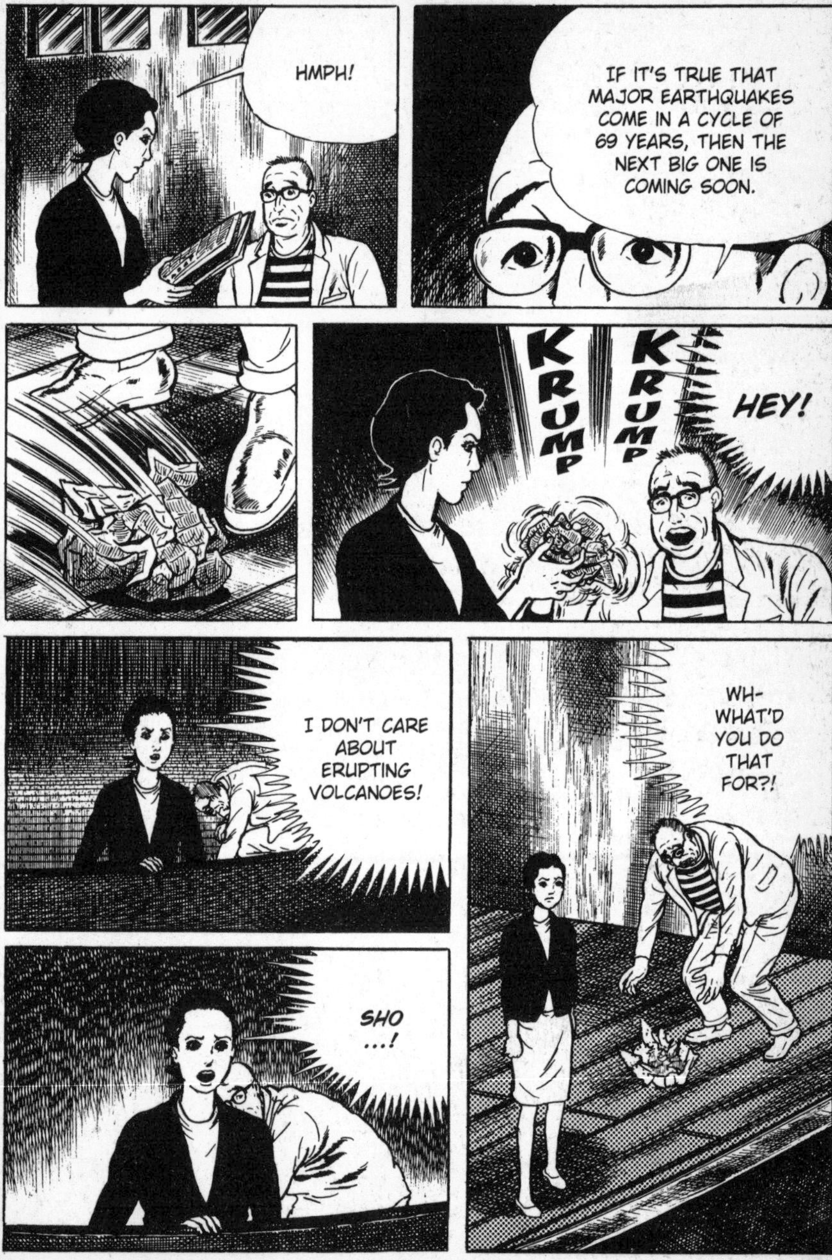
IF IT'S TRUE THAT MAJOR EARTHQUAKES COME IN A CYCLE OF 69 YEARS, THEN THE NEXT BIG ONE IS COMING SOON.
HMPH!
KRUMP
KRUMP
HEY!
WH- WHAT'D YOU DO THAT FOR?!
I DON'T CARE ABOUT ERUPTING VOLCANOES!
SHO ...!

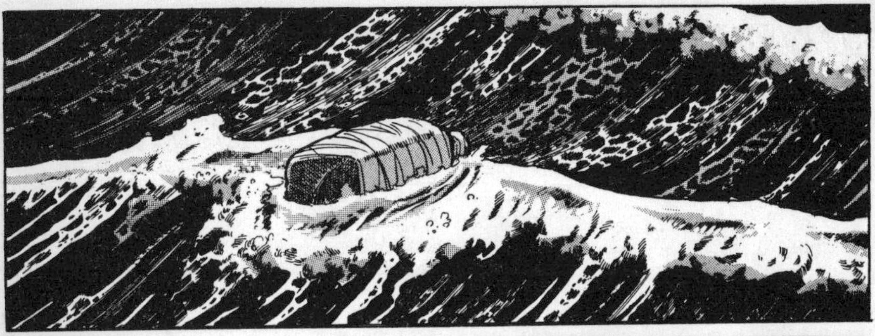
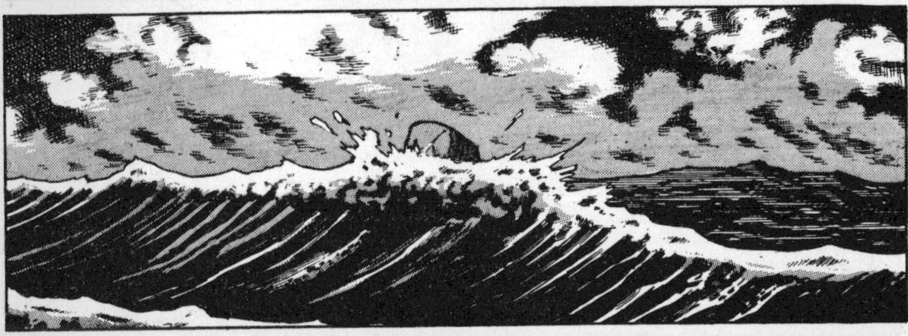
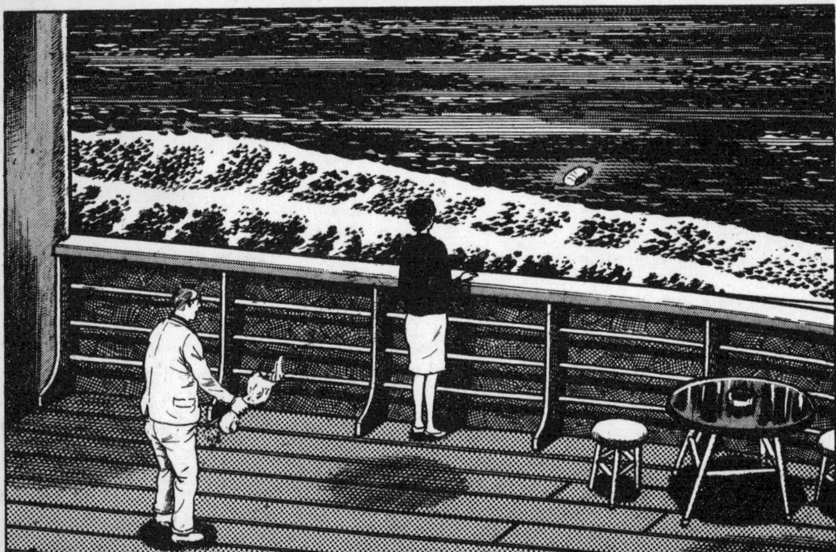

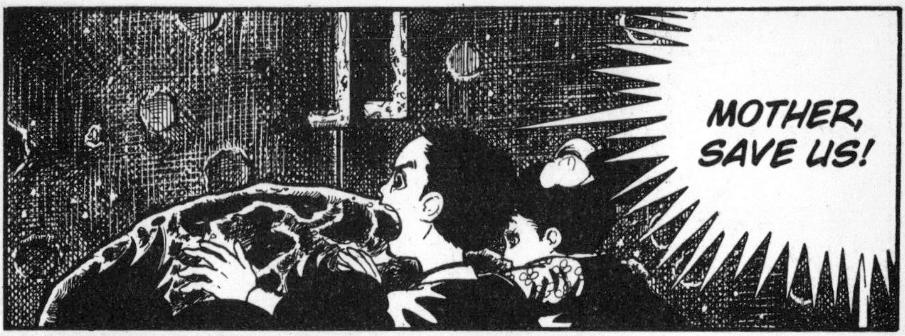
MOTHER, SAVE US!
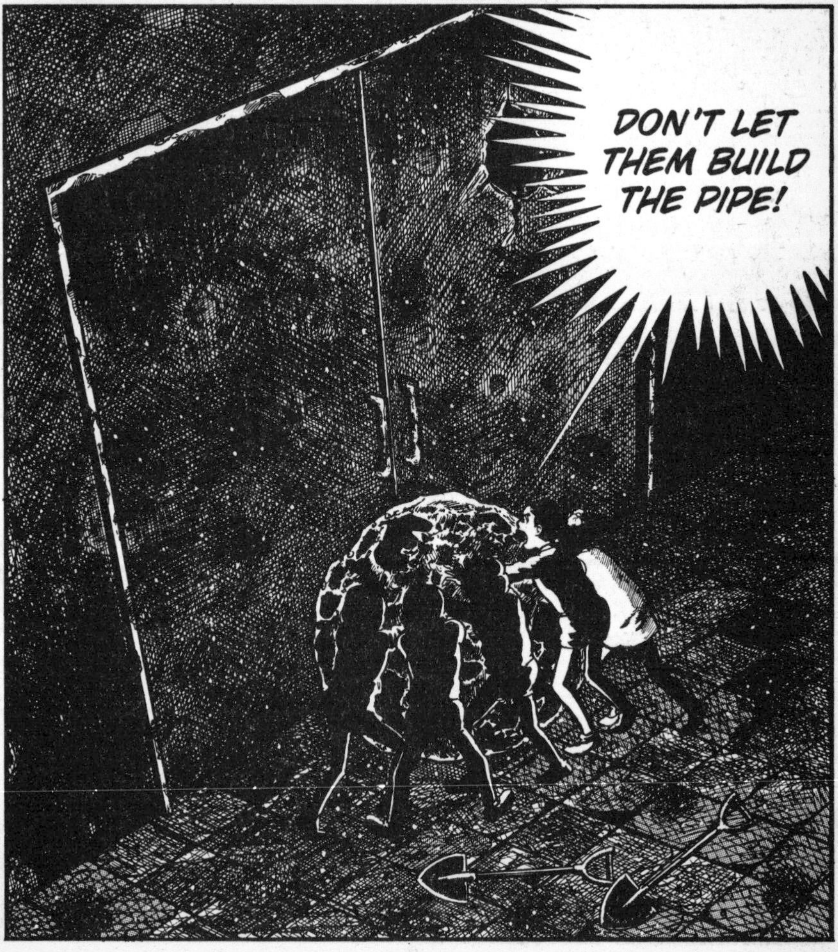
DON'T LET THEM BUILD THE PIPE!

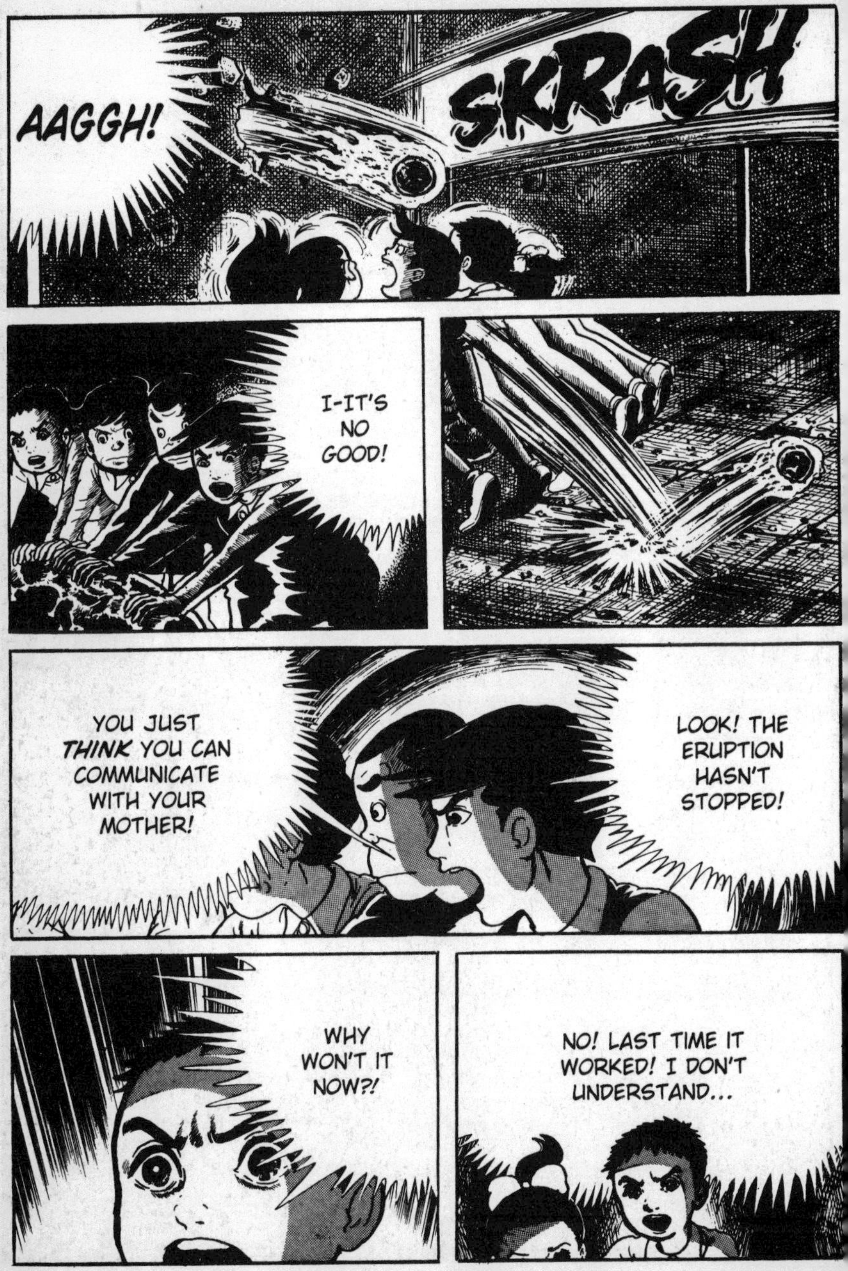
SKRASH
AAGGH!
I-IT'S NO GOOD!
LOOK! THE ERUPTION HASN'T STOPPED!
YOU JUST *THINK* YOU CAN COMMUNICATE WITH YOUR MOTHER!
NO! LAST TIME IT WORKED! I DON'T UNDERSTAND...
WHY WON'T IT NOW?!

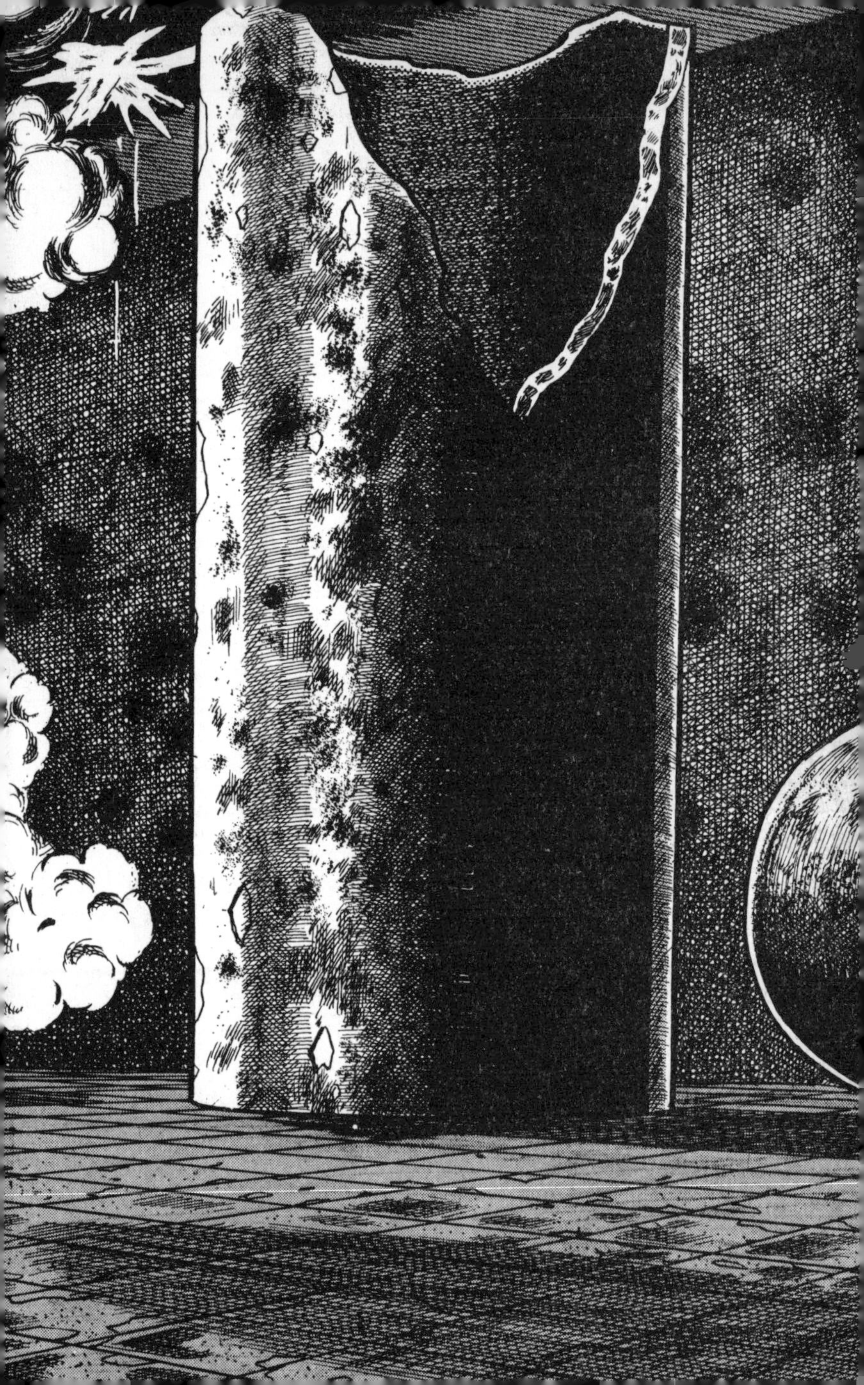

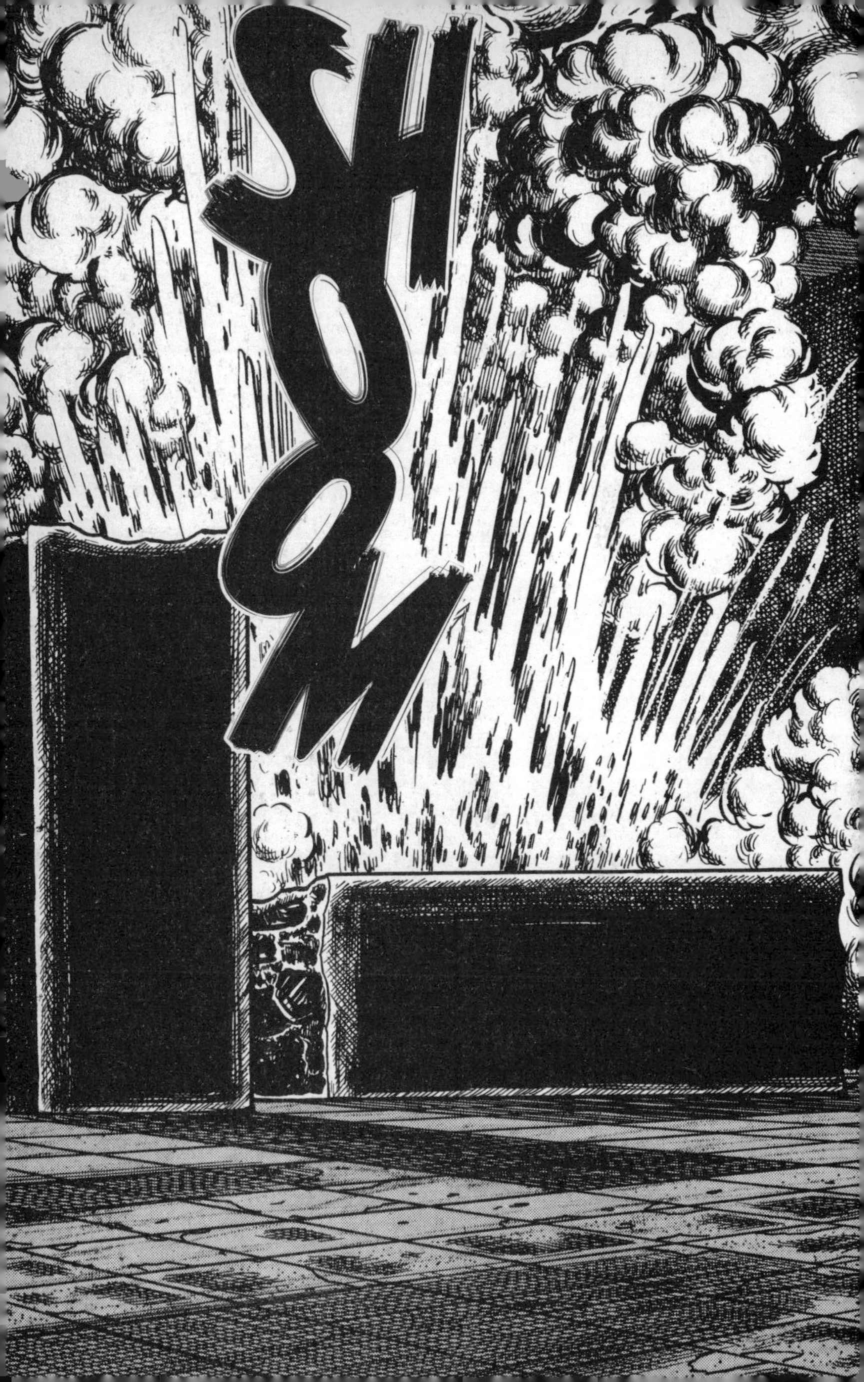
SHOOM

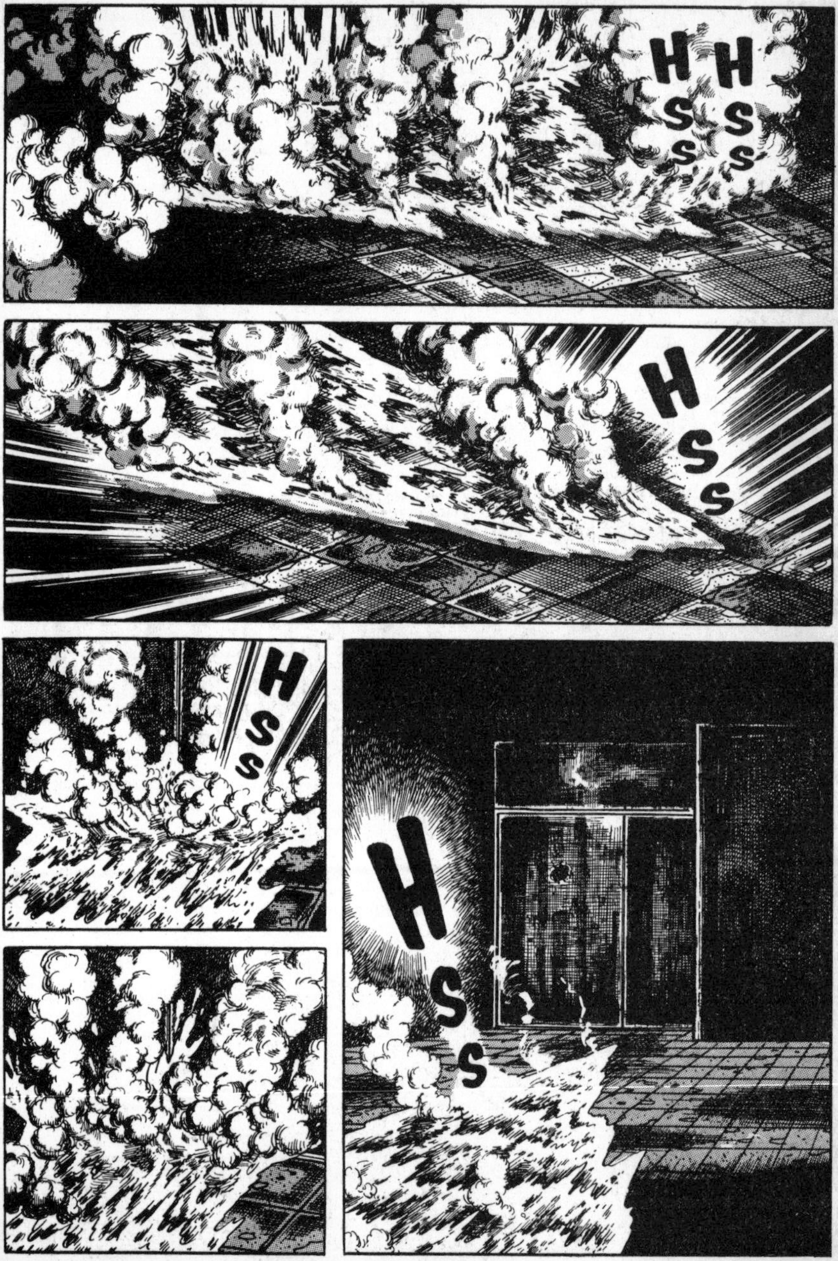
HSS
HSS
HSS
HSS
HSS

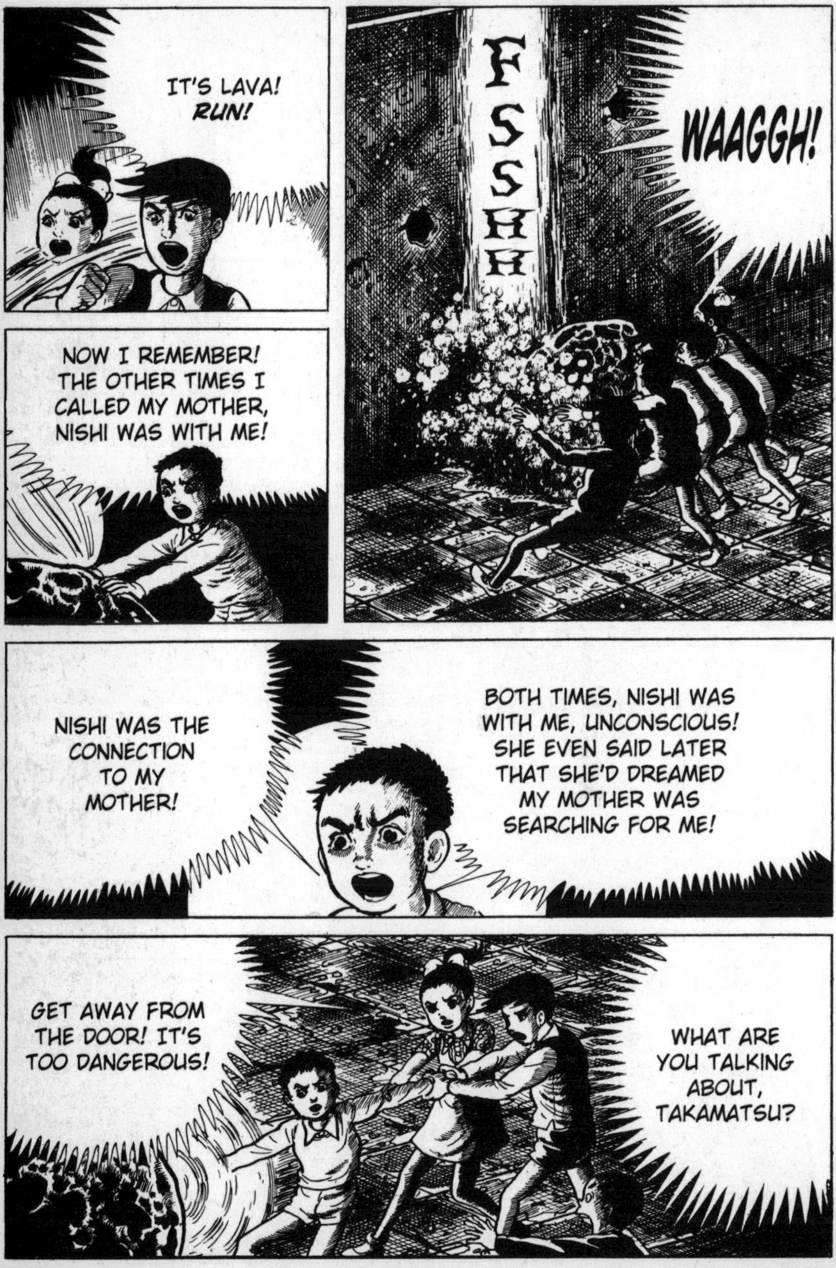
IT'S LAVA! RUN!
NOW I REMEMBER! THE OTHER TIMES I CALLED MY MOTHER, NISHI WAS WITH ME!
FSSHH
WAAGGH!
NISHI WAS THE CONNECTION TO MY MOTHER!
BOTH TIMES, NISHI WAS WITH ME, UNCONSCIOUS! SHE EVEN SAID LATER THAT SHE'D DREAMED MY MOTHER WAS SEARCHING FOR ME!
GET AWAY FROM THE DOOR! IT'S TOO DANGEROUS!
WHAT ARE YOU TALKING ABOUT, TAKAMATSU?

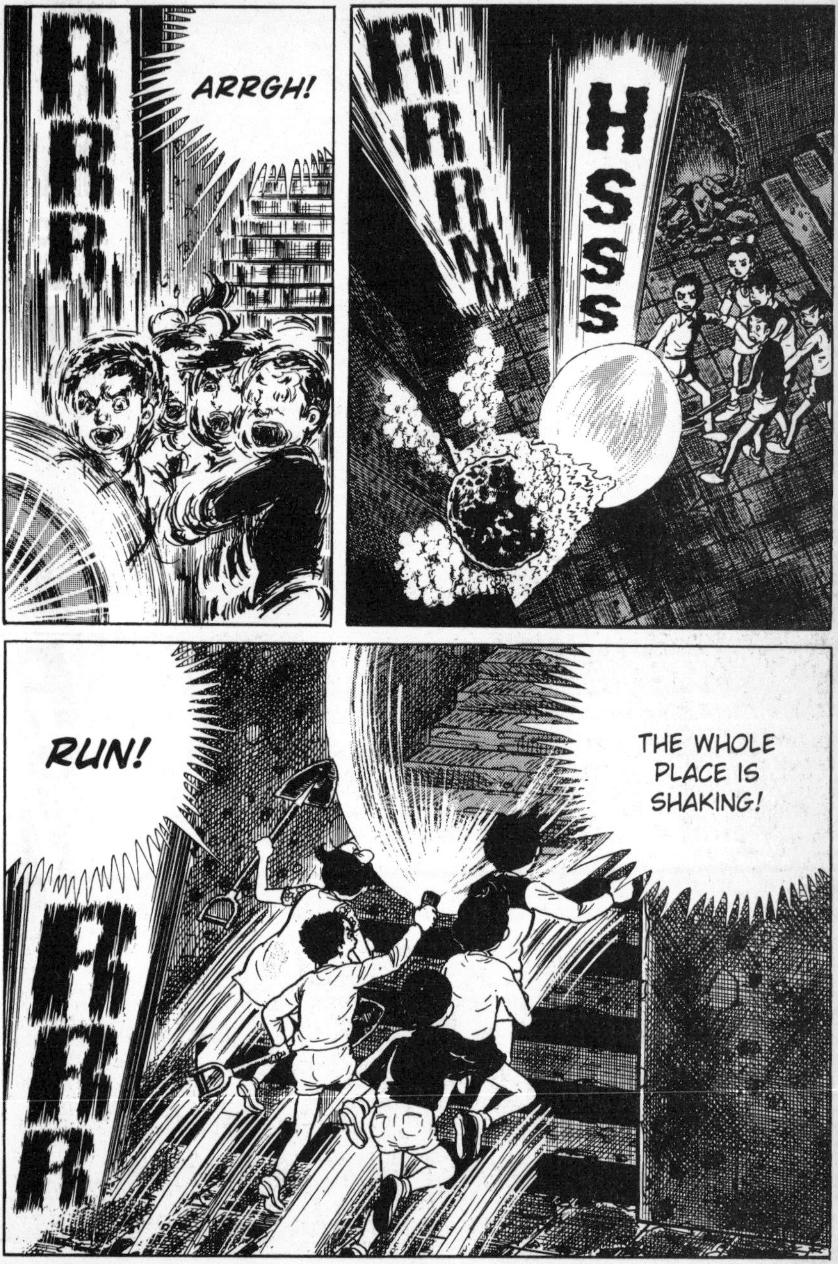
RRRM
HSSS
RRR
ARRGH!
THE WHOLE PLACE IS SHAKING!
RUN!
RRR

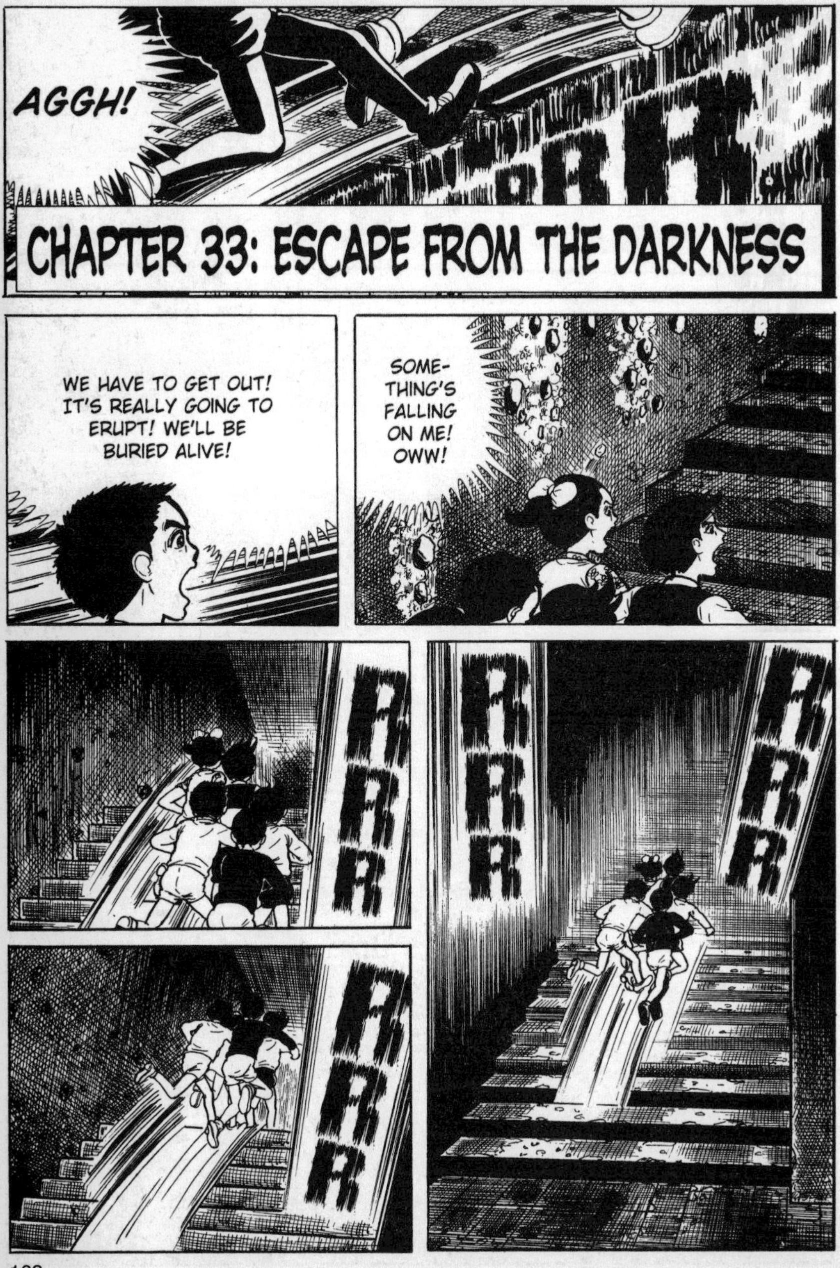
AGGH!
RRR
CHAPTER 33: ESCAPE FROM THE DARKNESS
SOME-THING'S FALLING ON ME! OWW!
WE HAVE TO GET OUT! IT'S REALLY GOING TO ERUPT! WE'LL BE BURIED ALIVE!
RRR
RRR
RRR
RRR

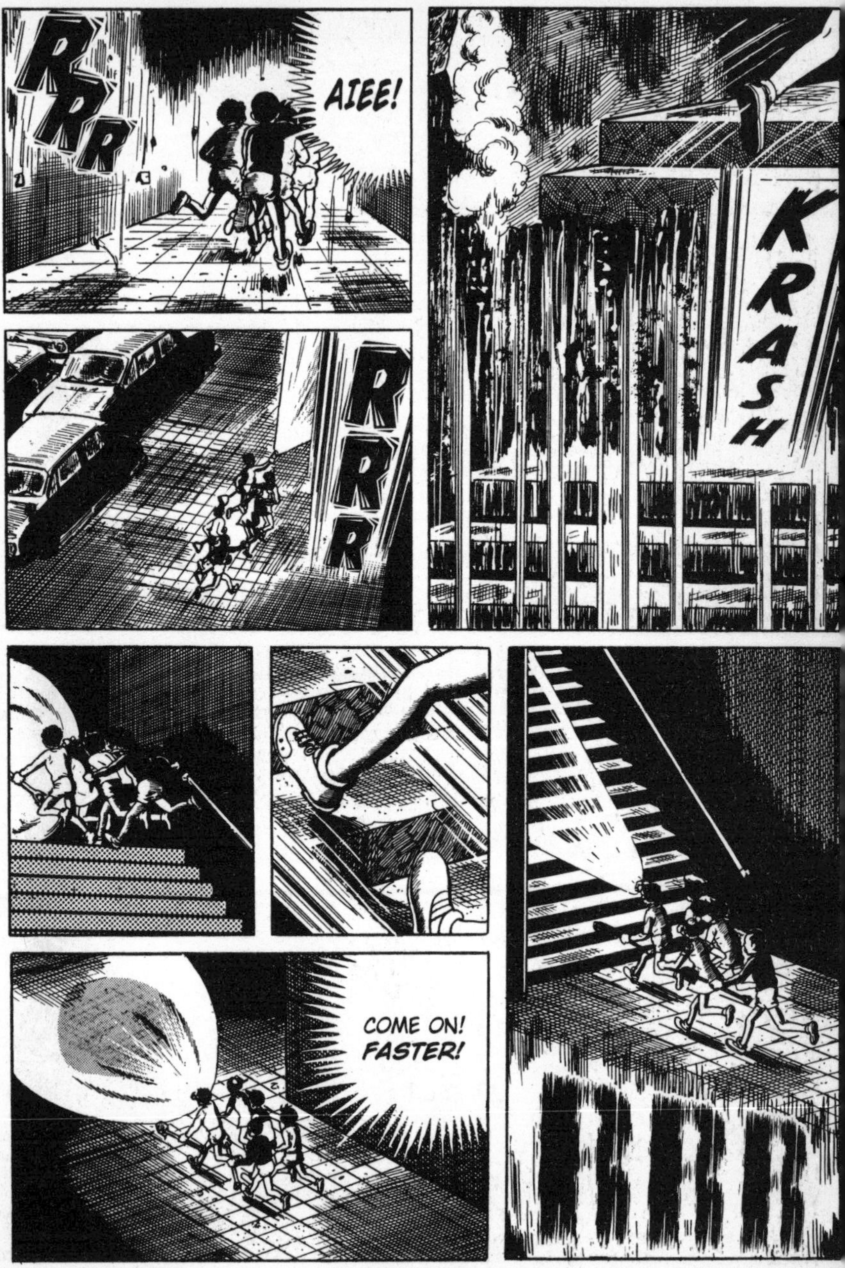
KRASH
AIEE!
RRR
RRR
COME ON! FASTER!

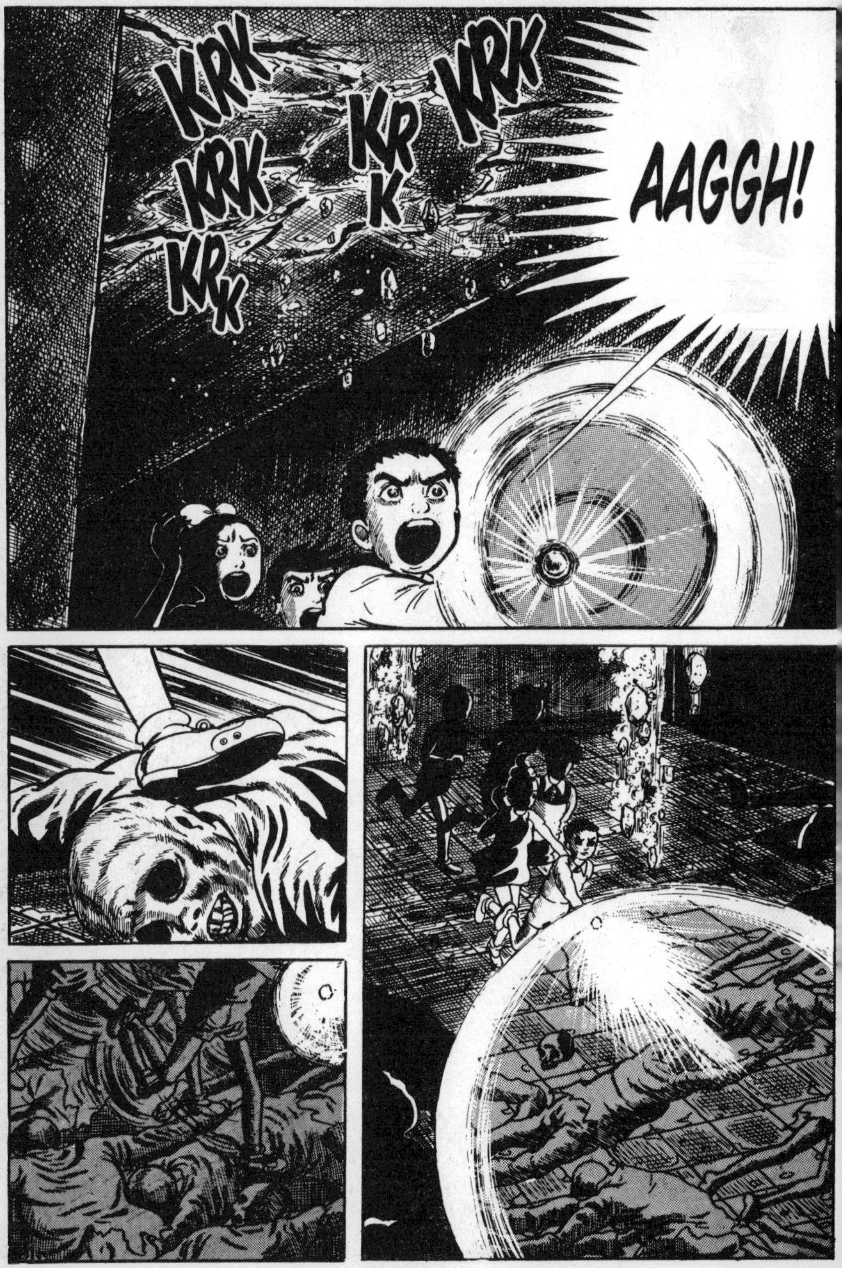
AAGGH!
KRK
KR
K
KRK
KRK
KRK

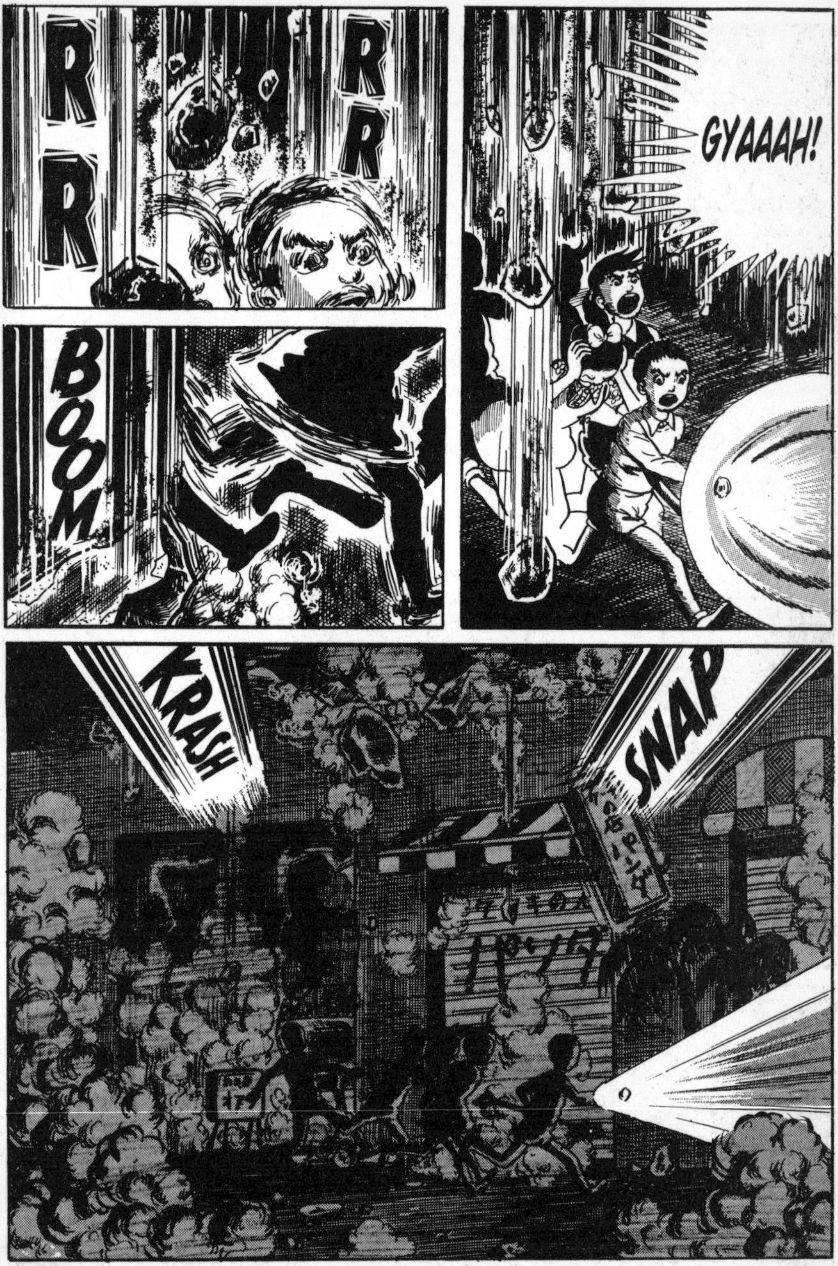
GYAAAH!
RRRR
BOOM
SNAP
KRASH

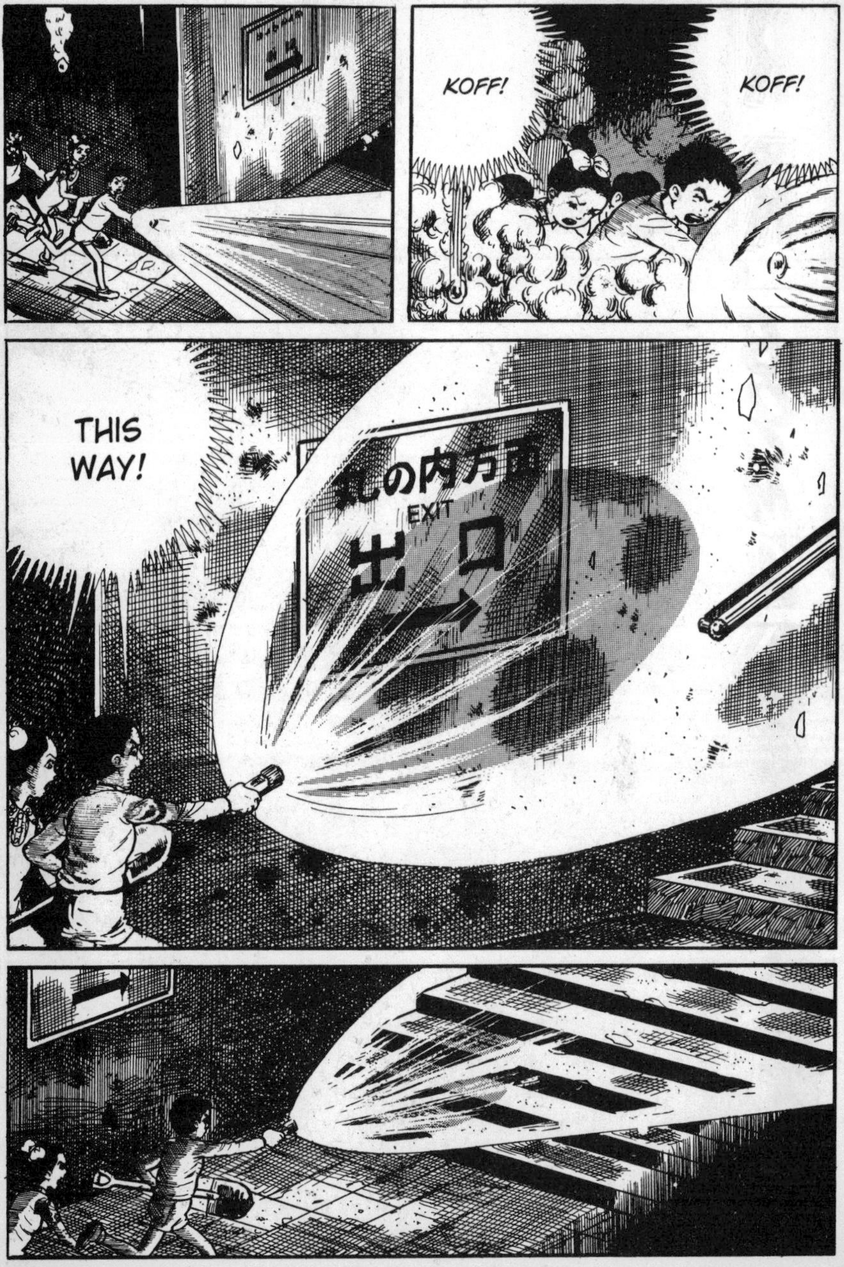
KOFF!
KOFF!
THIS WAY!
丸の内方面
EXIT
出口

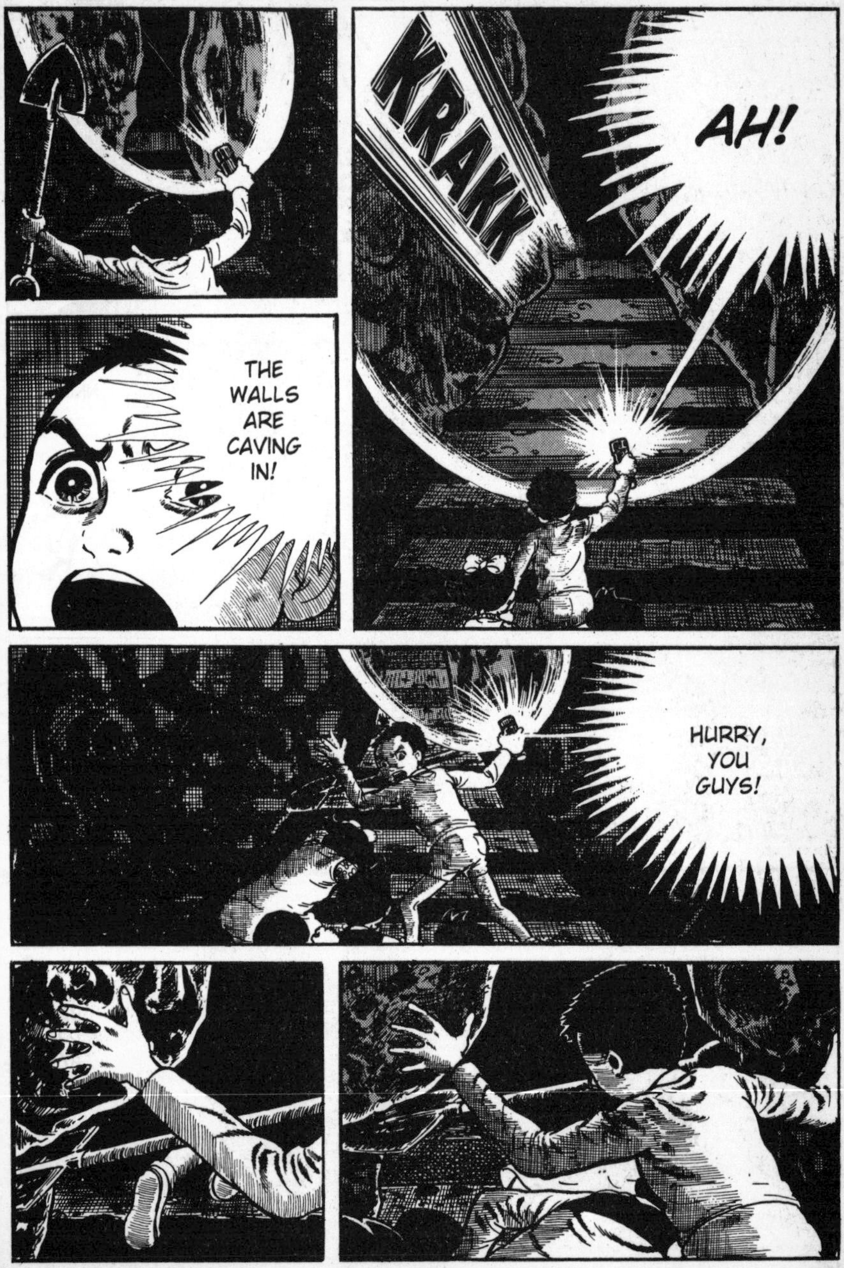
KRAKK
AH!
THE WALLS ARE CAVING IN!
HURRY, YOU GUYS!

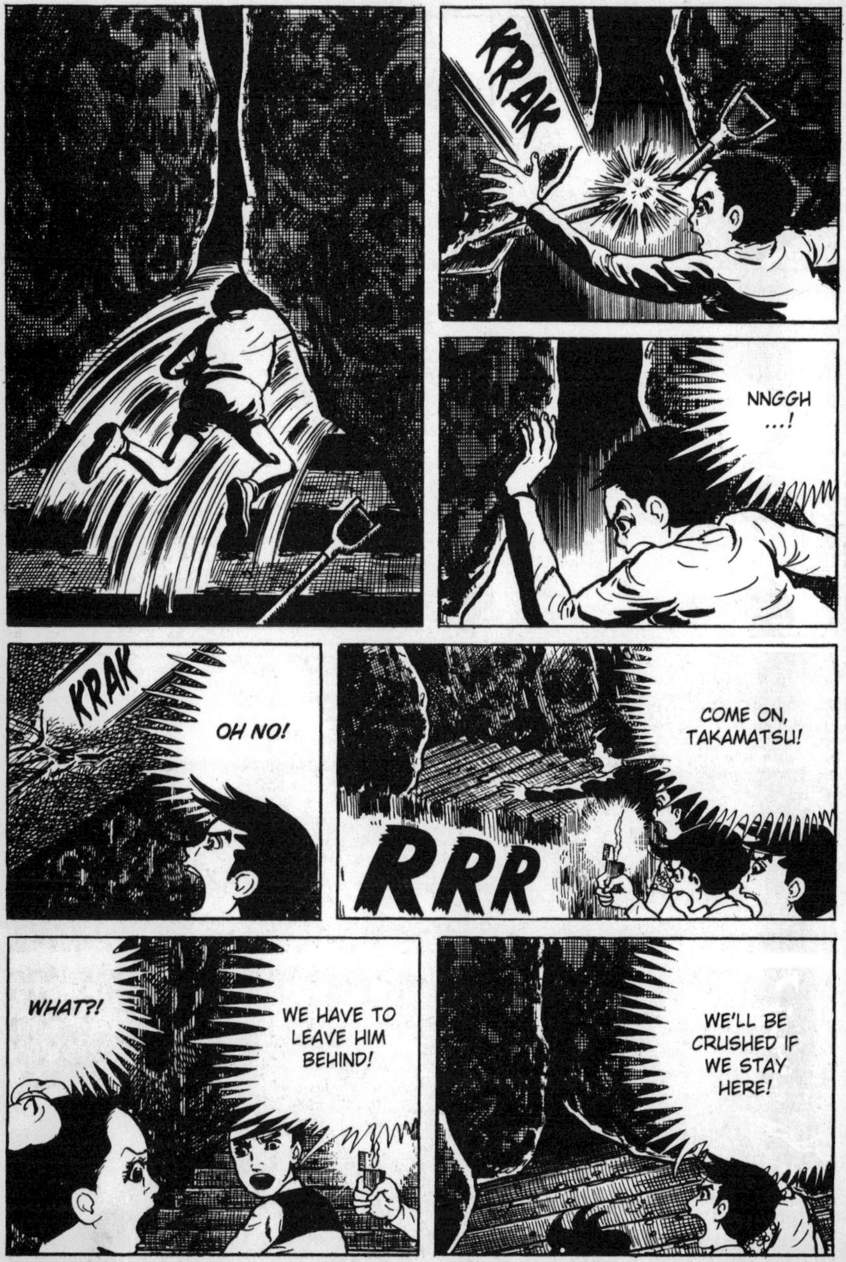
KRAK
NNGGH ...!
COME ON, TAKAMATSU!
RRR
KRAK
OH NO!
WE'LL BE CRUSHED IF WE STAY HERE!
WE HAVE TO LEAVE HIM BEHIND!
WHAT?!

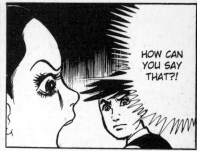

HOW CAN YOU SAY THAT?!

WH-WHY?! WE CAN SAVE HIM IF WE ALL TUG ON HIM!

FORGET IT, SAKIKO!

LOOK! HIS *HAND!*

IT'S HOPELESS. *LEAVE HIM!*

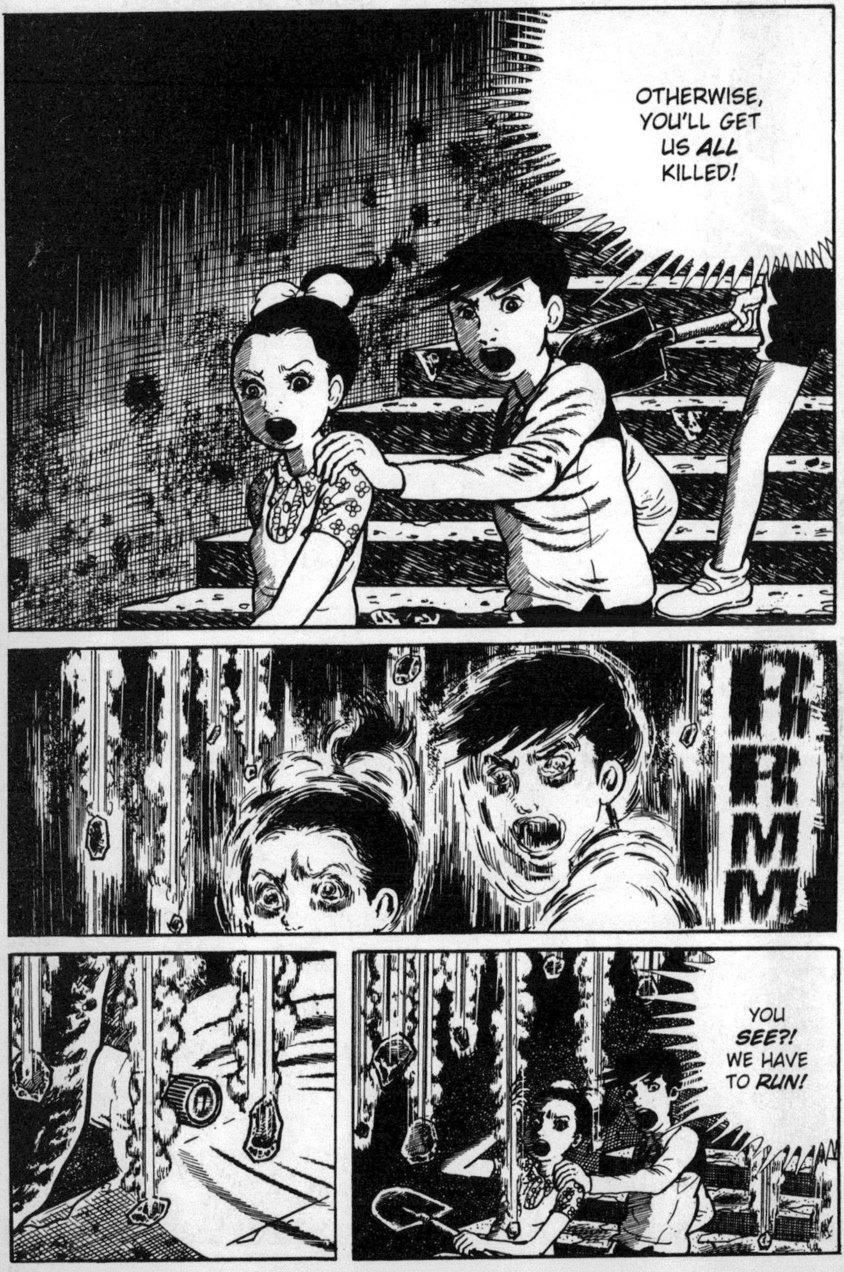
OTHERWISE, YOU'LL GET US *ALL* KILLED!
RRRMM
YOU *SEE?!* WE HAVE TO *RUN!*

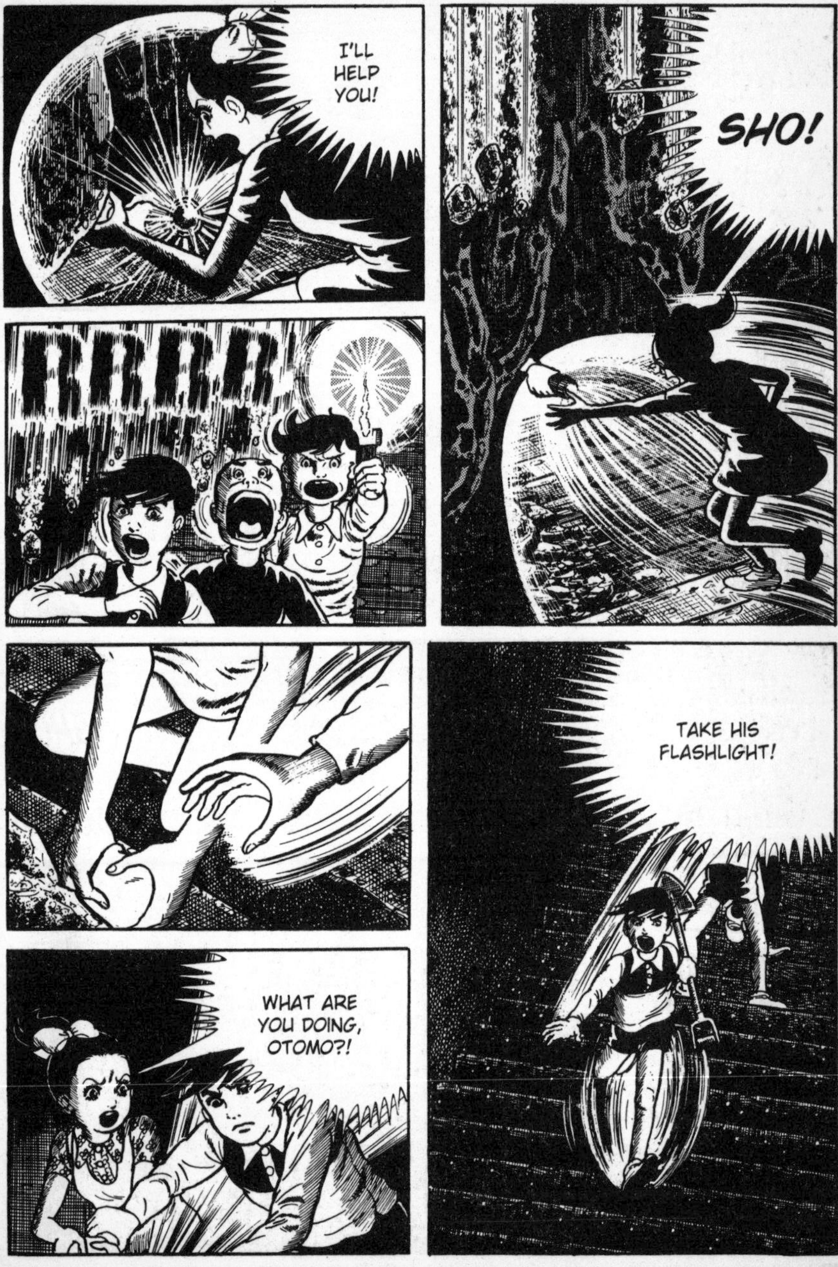
SHO!
I'LL HELP YOU!
BRRRR
TAKE HIS FLASHLIGHT!
WHAT ARE YOU DOING, OTOMO?!

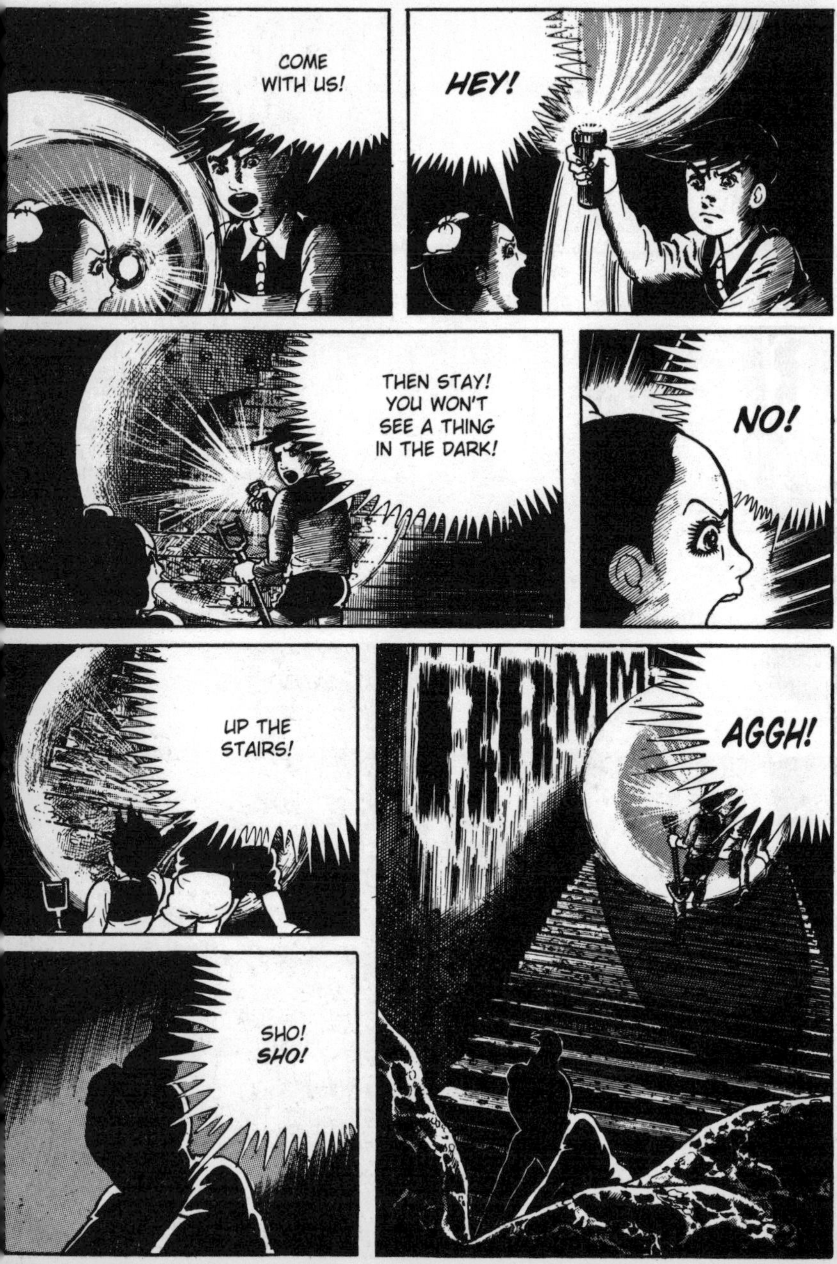
HEY!
COME WITH US!
NO!
THEN STAY! YOU WON'T SEE A THING IN THE DARK!
AGGH!
UP THE STAIRS!
SHO! SHO!

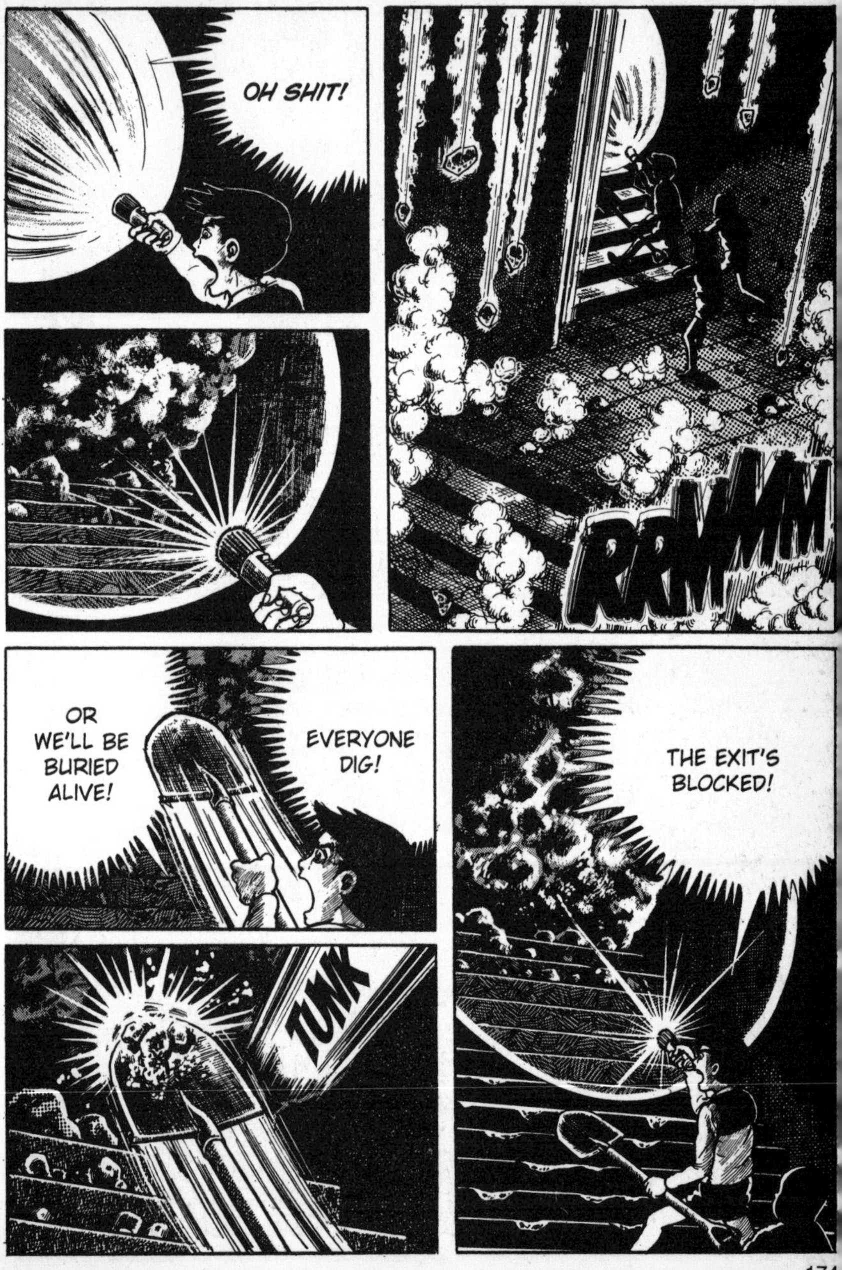
RRMMM
OH SHIT!
THE EXIT'S BLOCKED!
EVERYONE DIG!
OR WE'LL BE BURIED ALIVE!
TUNK

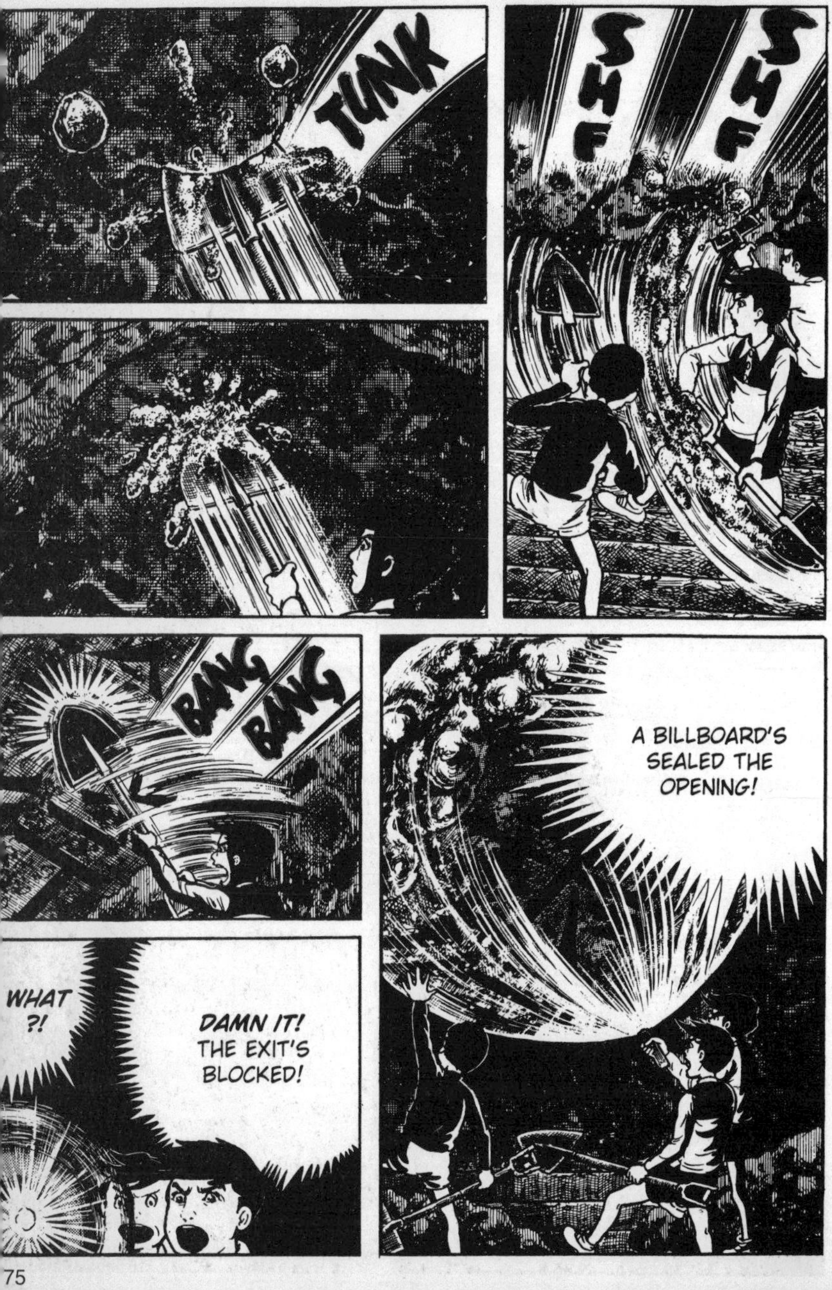
TUNK
SHF
SHF
BANG
BANG
WHAT ?!
DAMN IT! THE EXIT'S BLOCKED!
A BILLBOARD'S SEALED THE OPENING!

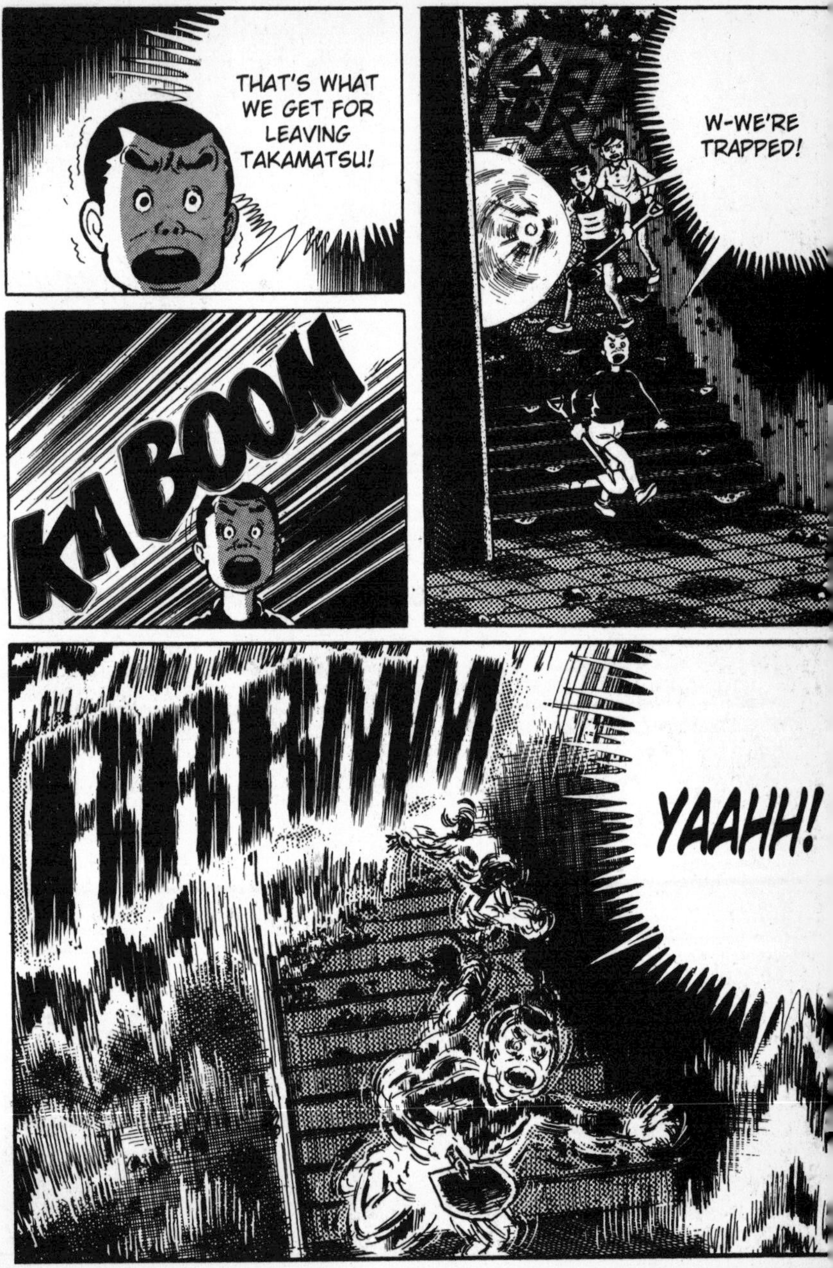
W-WE'RE TRAPPED!
THAT'S WHAT WE GET FOR LEAVING TAKAMATSU!
KABOOM
YAAHH!

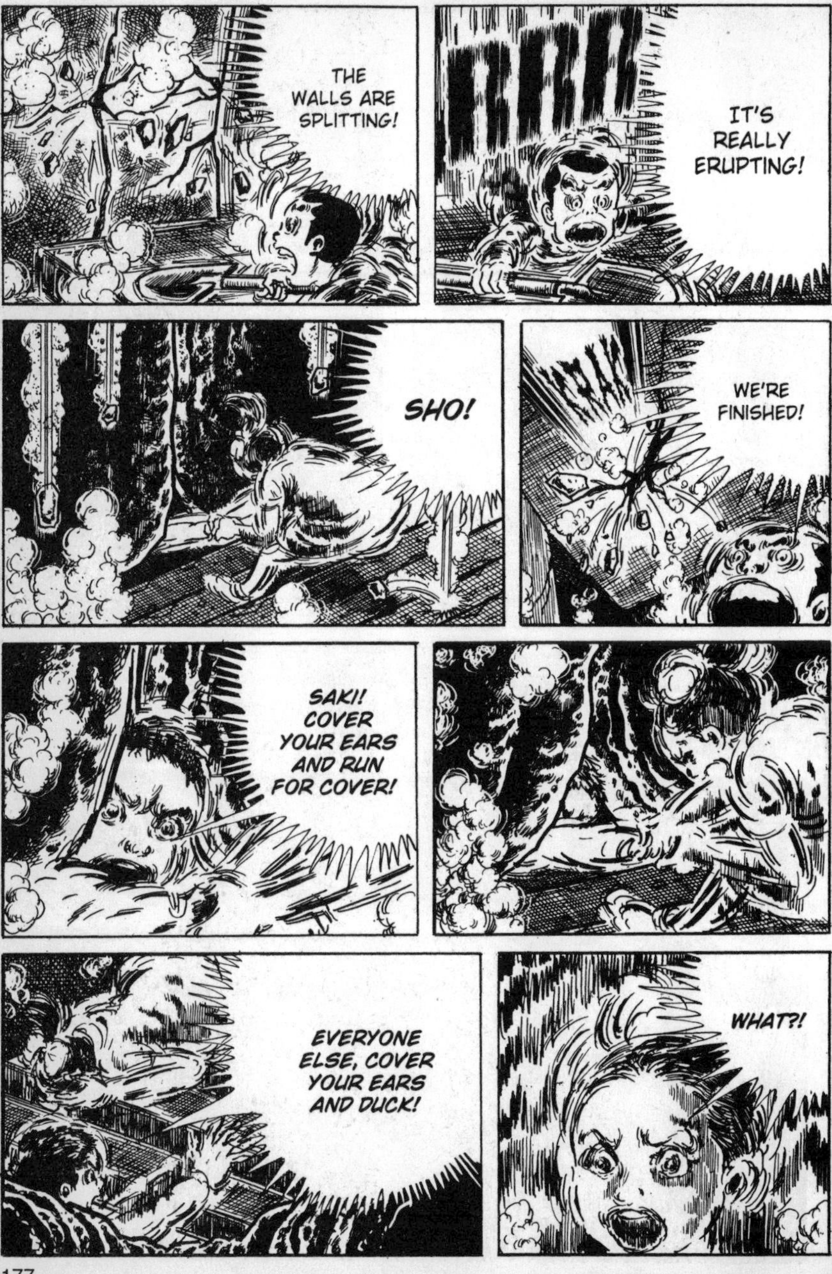
THE WALLS ARE SPLITTING!
IT'S REALLY ERUPTING!
SHO!
WE'RE FINISHED!
SAKI! COVER YOUR EARS AND RUN FOR COVER!
EVERYONE ELSE, COVER YOUR EARS AND DUCK!
WHAT?!

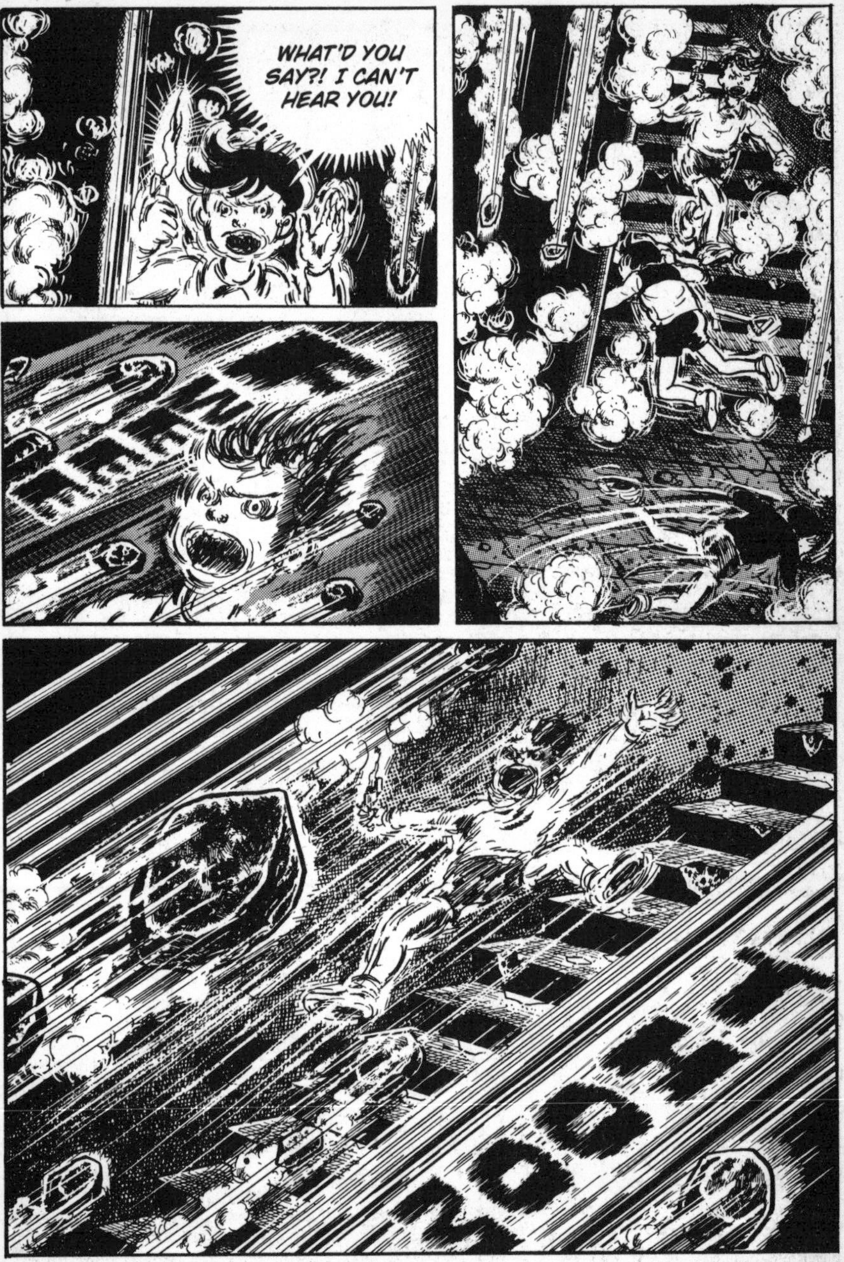
WHAT'D YOU SAY?! I CAN'T HEAR YOU!

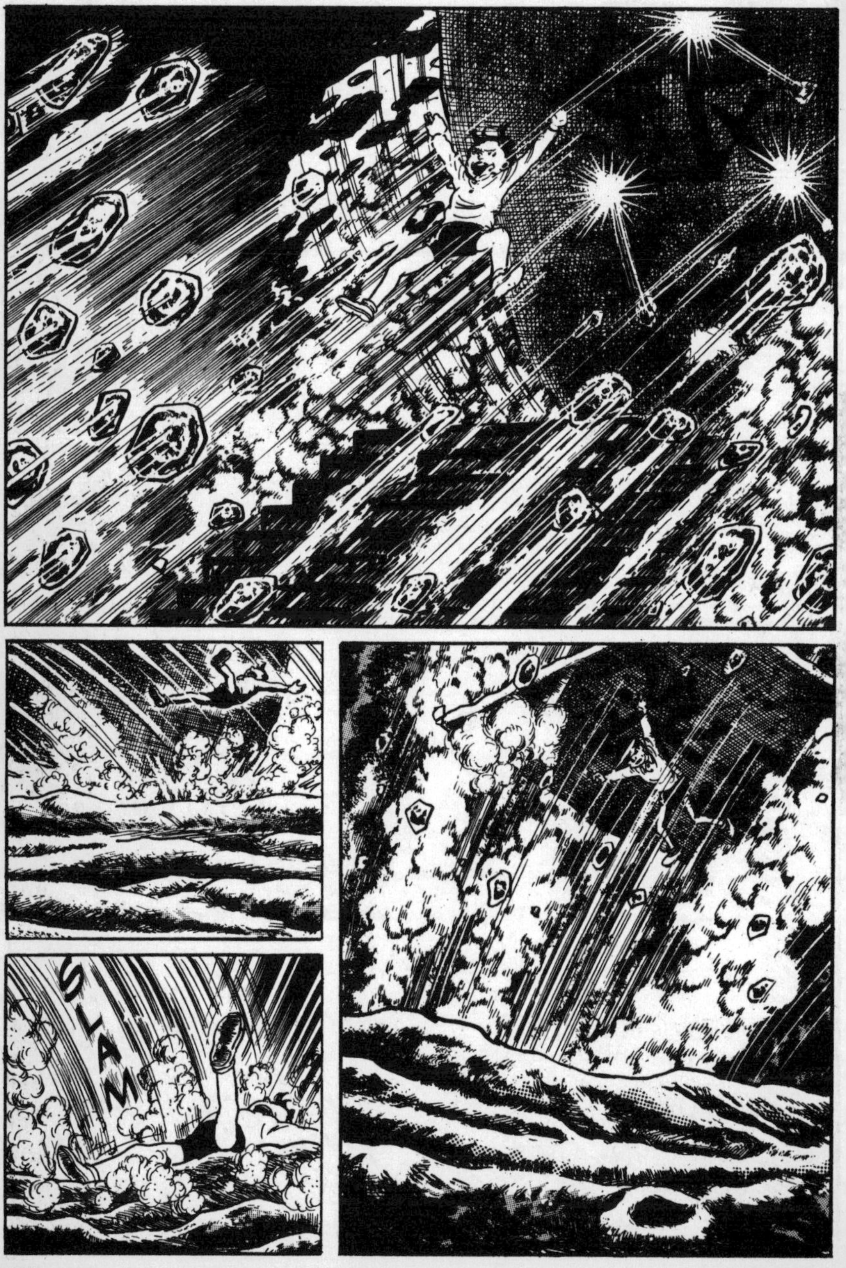
SLAM

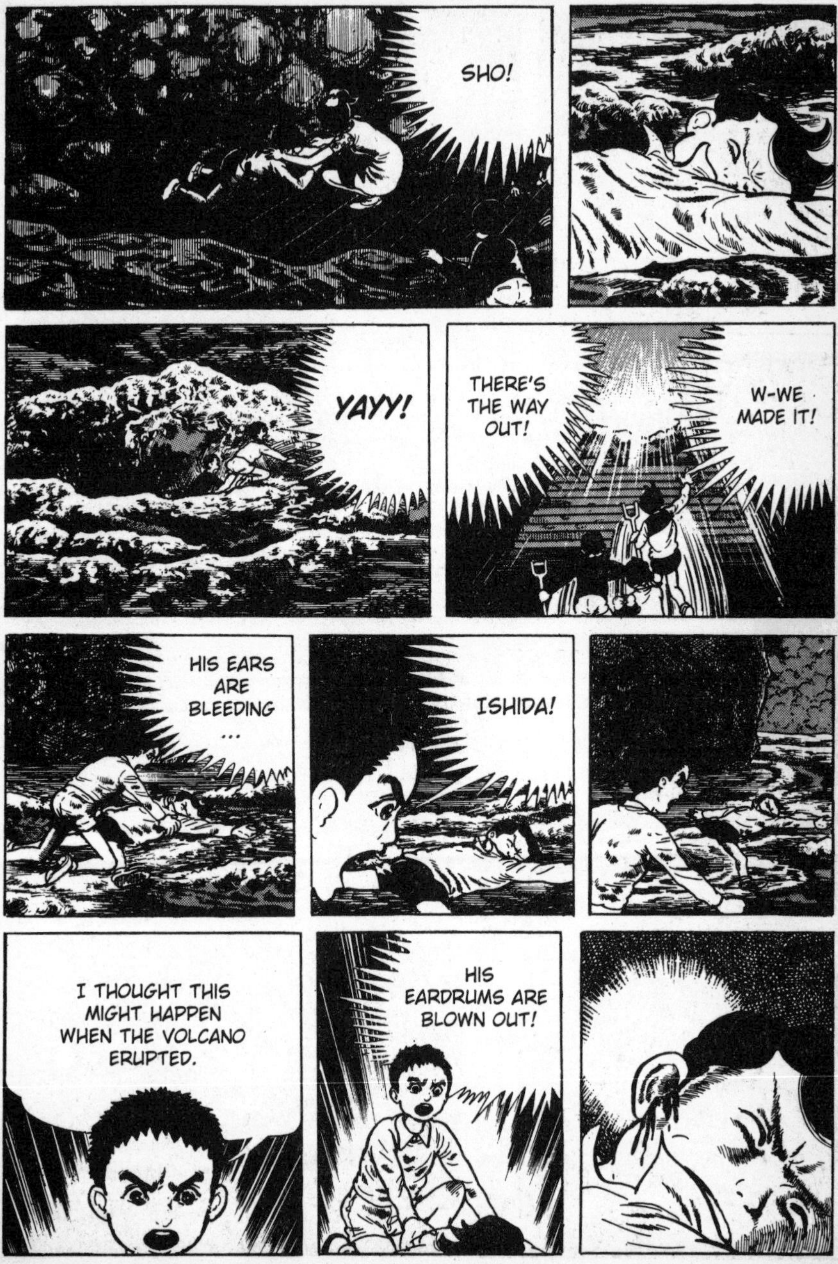
SHO!
THERE'S THE WAY OUT!
W-WE MADE IT!
YAYY!
ISHIDA!
HIS EARS ARE BLEEDING ...
HIS EARDRUMS ARE BLOWN OUT!
I THOUGHT THIS MIGHT HAPPEN WHEN THE VOLCANO ERUPTED.

THE SOUND ECHOED IN THE NARROW TUNNEL... I REMEMBERED MY EARS HURTING IN A TUNNEL THE FIRST TIME I RODE A BULLET TRAIN.

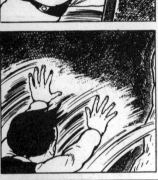

AAGGH!

WATCH OUT! THE STEEL WALL'S FALLING!

KYAAAH!

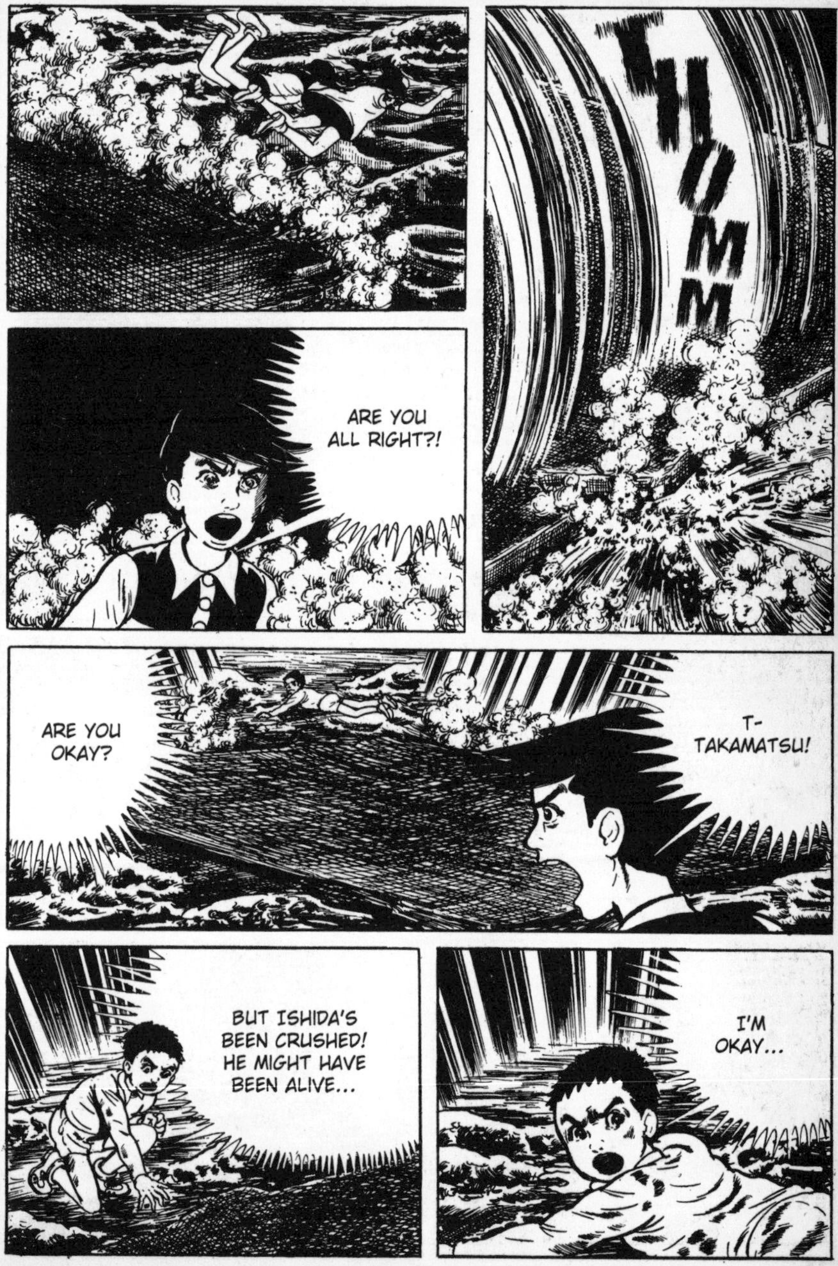
THOMM
ARE YOU ALL RIGHT?!
T- TAKAMATSU!
ARE YOU OKAY?
I'M OKAY...
BUT ISHIDA'S BEEN CRUSHED! HE MIGHT HAVE BEEN ALIVE...

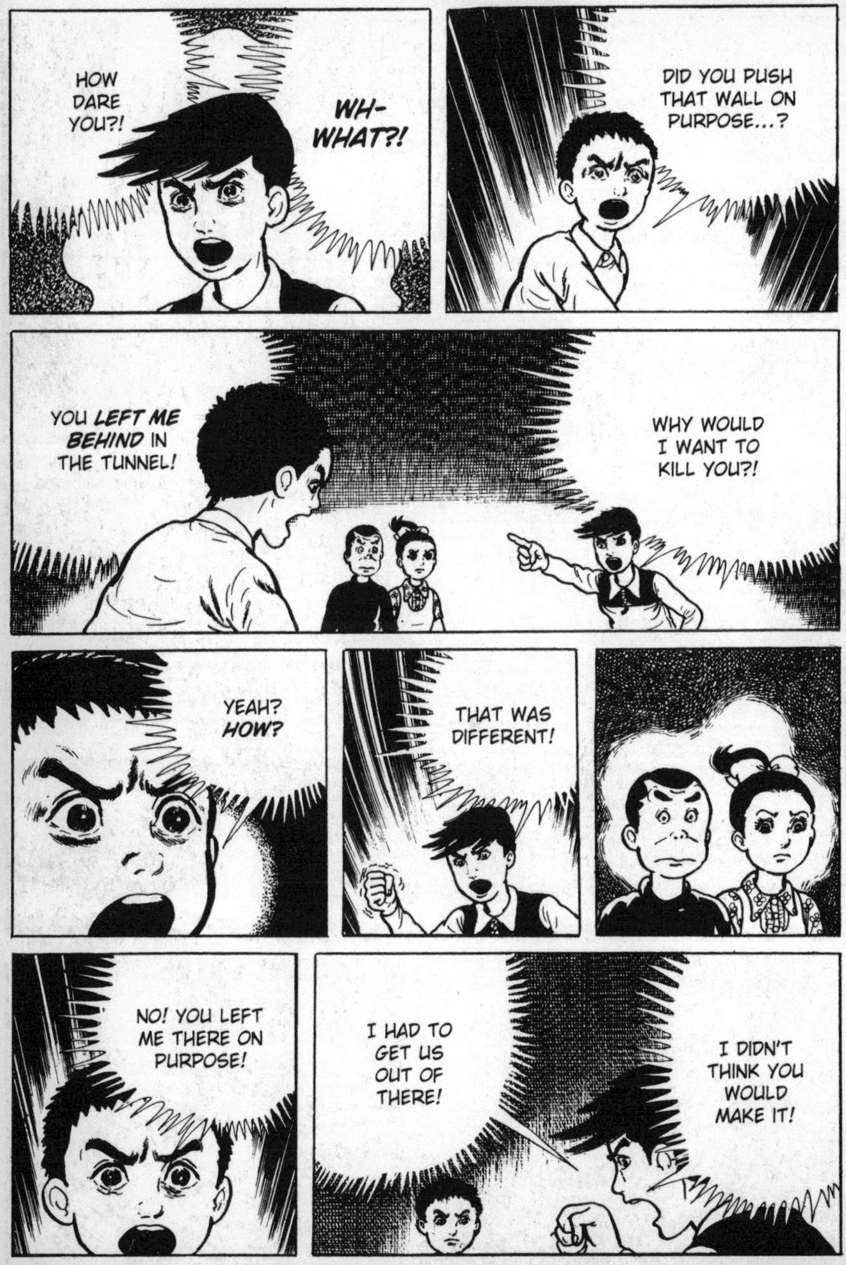
DID YOU PUSH THAT WALL ON PURPOSE...?
WH-WHAT?!
HOW DARE YOU?!
WHY WOULD I WANT TO KILL YOU?!
YOU LEFT ME BEHIND IN THE TUNNEL!
THAT WAS DIFFERENT!
YEAH? HOW?
I HAD TO GET US OUT OF THERE!
I DIDN'T THINK YOU WOULD MAKE IT!
NO! YOU LEFT ME THERE ON PURPOSE!

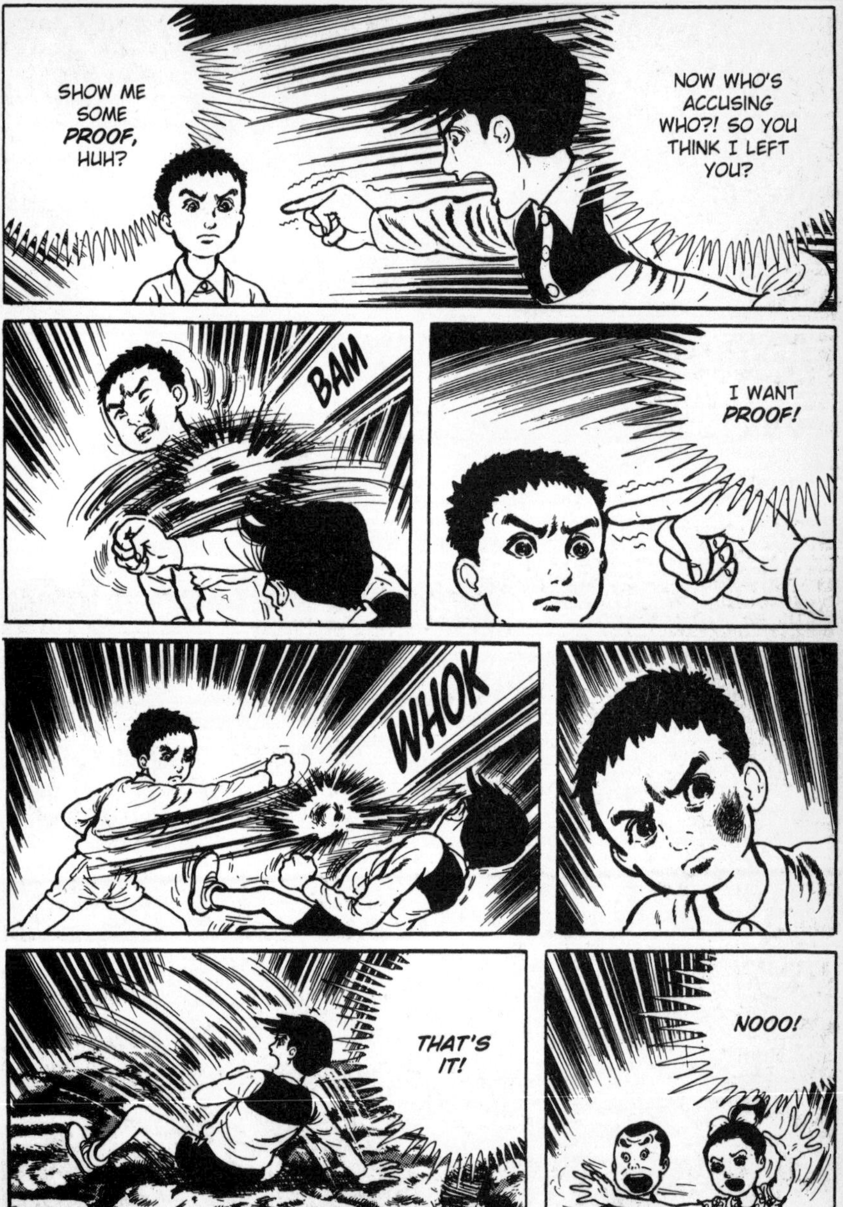
SHOW ME SOME *PROOF*, HUH?
NOW WHO'S ACCUSING WHO?! SO YOU THINK I LEFT YOU?
BAM
I WANT *PROOF!*
WHOK
THAT'S IT!
NOOO!

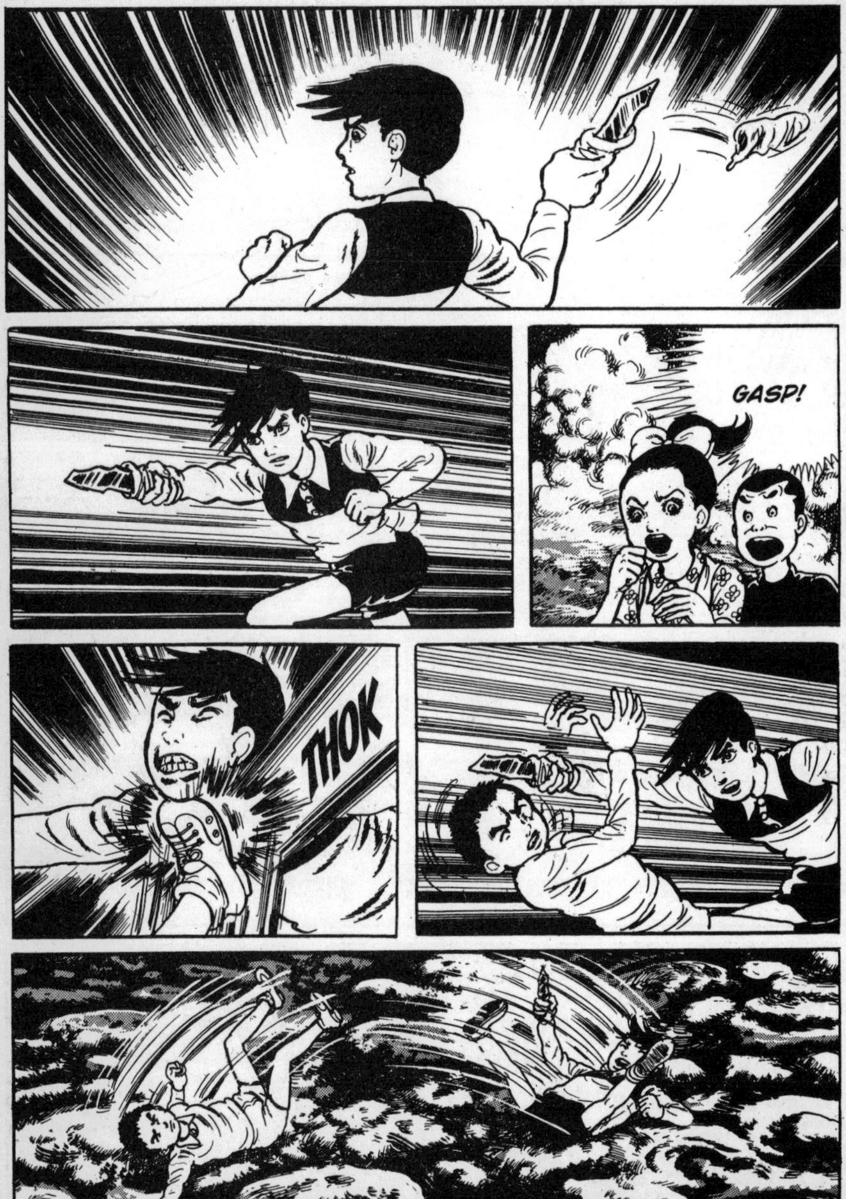
GASP!
THOK

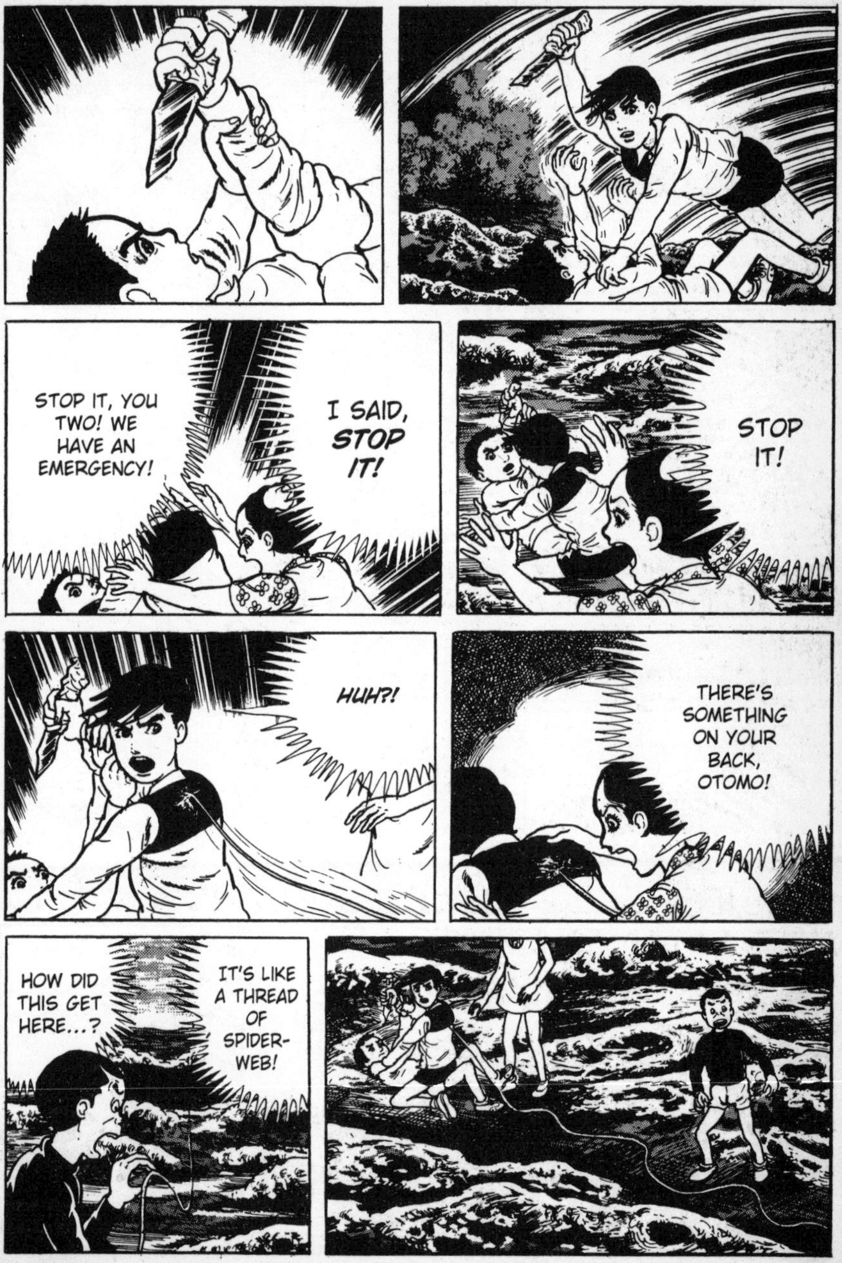
STOP IT, YOU TWO! WE HAVE AN EMERGENCY!
I SAID, STOP IT!
STOP IT!
HUH?!
THERE'S SOMETHING ON YOUR BACK, OTOMO!
HOW DID THIS GET HERE...?
IT'S LIKE A THREAD OF SPIDER-WEB!

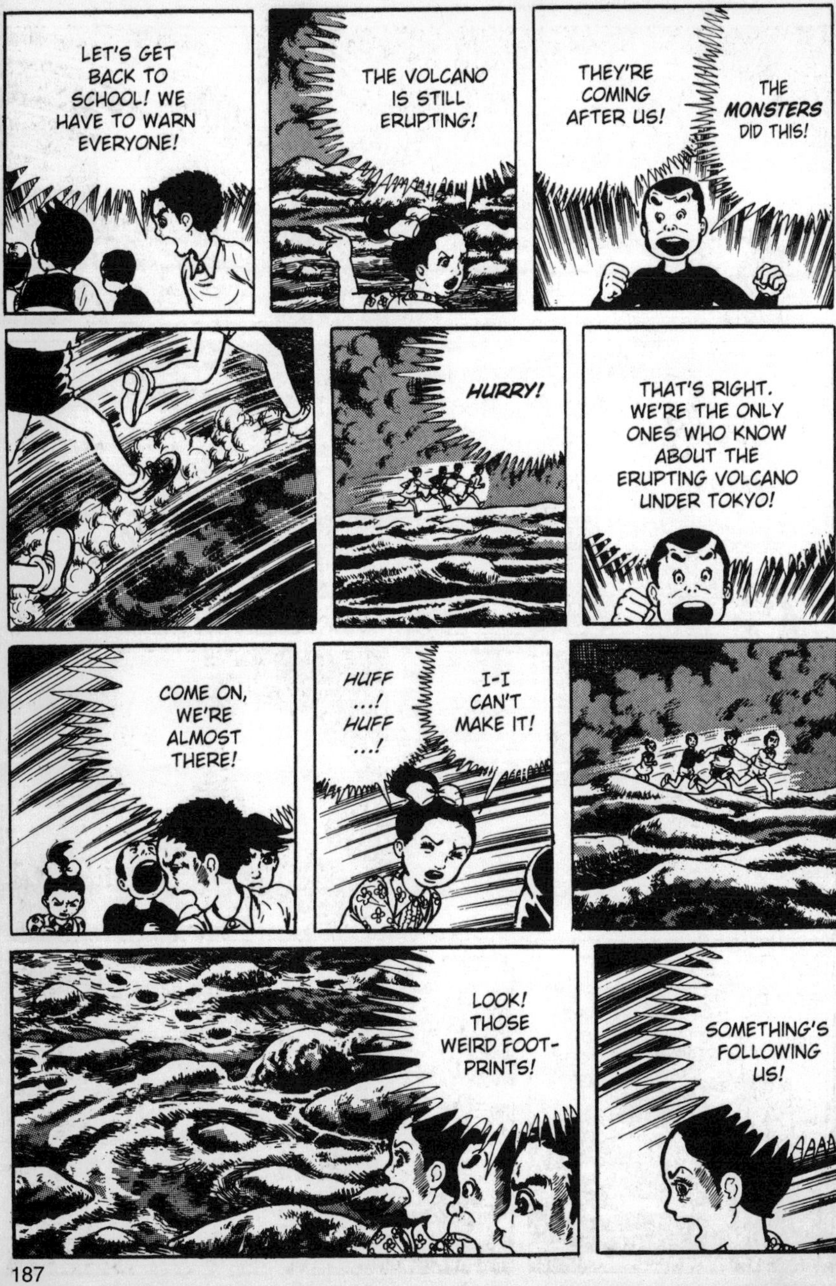
THE MONSTERS DID THIS!
THEY'RE COMING AFTER US!
THE VOLCANO IS STILL ERUPTING!
LET'S GET BACK TO SCHOOL! WE HAVE TO WARN EVERYONE!
THAT'S RIGHT. WE'RE THE ONLY ONES WHO KNOW ABOUT THE ERUPTING VOLCANO UNDER TOKYO!
HURRY!
I-I CAN'T MAKE IT!
HUFF ...! HUFF ...!
COME ON, WE'RE ALMOST THERE!
SOMETHING'S FOLLOWING US!
LOOK! THOSE WEIRD FOOT-PRINTS!

THEY WEREN'T FOOTPRINTS! THEY WERE EYEHOLES FOR THE MUTANTS!

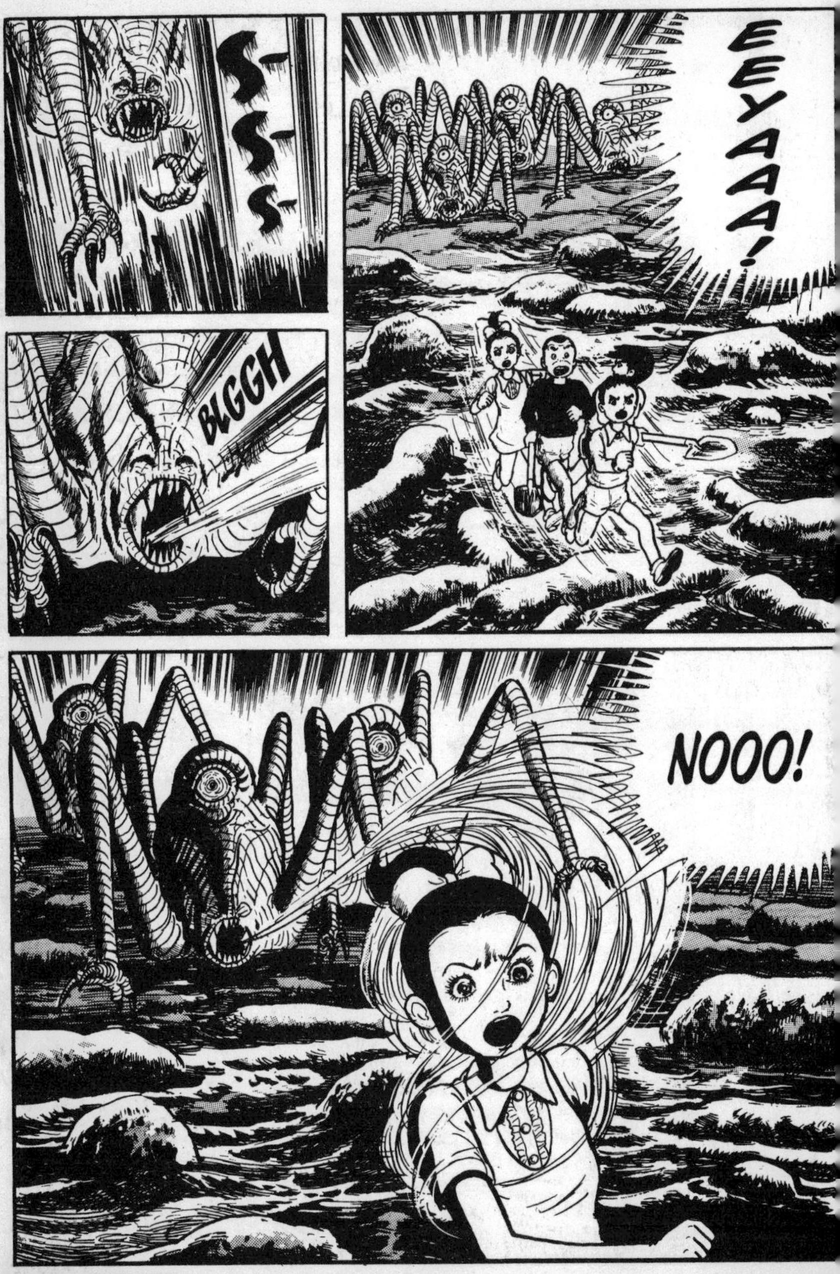
EEYAAAA!
S-S-S-
BLGGH
NOOO!

TO BE CONTINUED...

IN THE NEXT VOLUME...

Can Sho and his friends make it back to the school...and even there, will they be safe? As the polluted earth spews forth more and more horrifying mutants, panic reigns both inside and outside the school walls. Barricaded against the nightmares outside, the survivors must perform an emergency medical operation under the most primitive of conditions...
AVAILABLE DECEMBER 2007!

Where Violence Blossoms

Experience a whole new world of
disenchanted youth and back-to-
school boredom, where students
make the rules and popularity is
determined by who can survive
a fatal game of truth-or-dare.

A single volume manga from cult
favorite artist Taiyo Matsumoto,
creator of BLACK & WHITE and
NO. 5, also available from VIZ —
in stores now!

Only
$9.99!

LOVE

LET US ... NK!

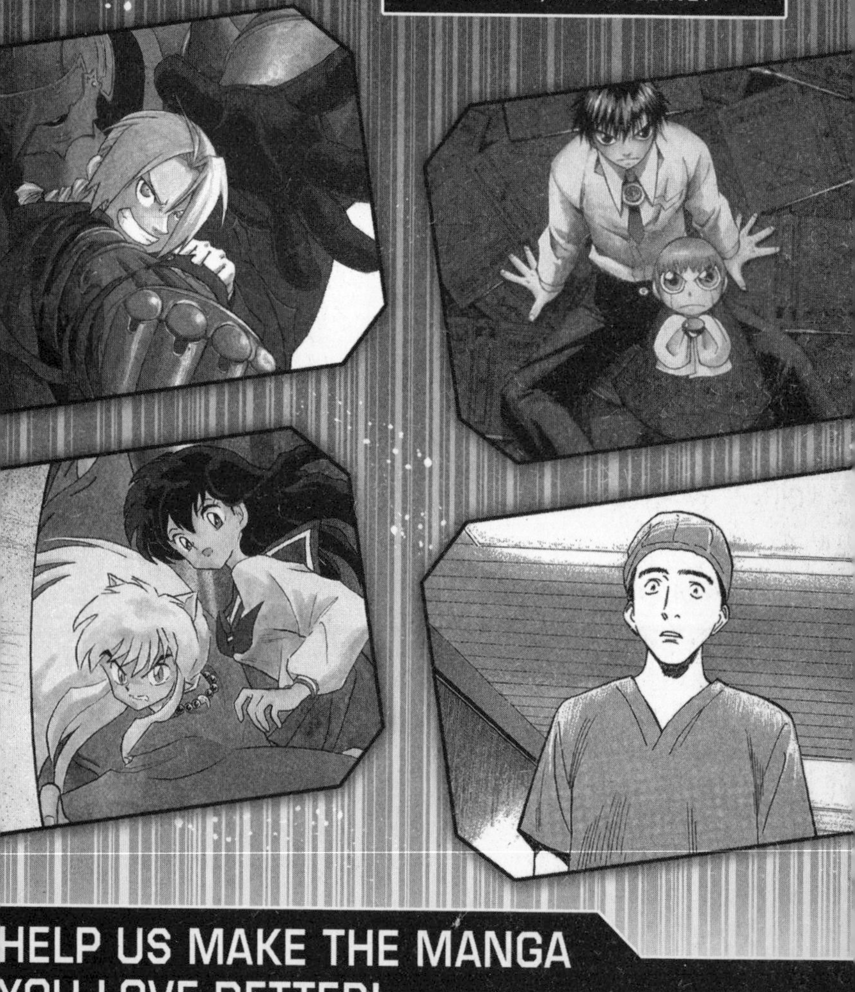